R. M. ADDINGTON
The Author

History
of
Scott
County
Virginia

Robert M. Addington

HERITAGE BOOKS
2009

HERITAGE BOOKS

AN IMPRINT OF HERITAGE BOOKS, INC.

Books, CDs, and more—Worldwide

For our listing of thousands of titles see our website
at
www.HeritageBooks.com

A Facsimile Reprint
Published 2009 by
HERITAGE BOOKS, INC.
Publishing Division
100 Railroad Ave. #104
Westminster, Maryland 21157

Originally published
Kingsport, Tennessee
1932

International Standard Book Numbers
Paperbound: 978-0-7884-2020-7
Clothbound: 978-0-7884-8224-3

To

THE GOOD WOMEN OF MY NATIVE COUNTY, BOTH
LIVING AND DEAD, WHOSE INDUSTRY, VIRTUE,
PATRIOTISM, AND CHRISTIAN CHARACTER
HAVE CONTRIBUTED SO MUCH TO THE
DEVELOPMENT OF THE HIGHER
AND BETTER THINGS OF LIFE

THIS BOOK IS RESPECTFULLY DEDICATED

TABLE OF CONTENTS

LIST OF ILLUSTRATIONS

ix

PREFACE

The year 1915 marked the one hundredth anniversary of the organization of county government in Scott. A number of leading citizens in various walks of life thought that this anniversary should be fittingly observed with appropriate ceremonies. The movement, when brought to the attention of the public, met with general approval. Supt. W. D. Smith arranged to have the school children of the county take large part in the celebration and, as an aid in interesting the school children in the coming celebration, I was asked to prepare a brief outline of the county history, which I did, calling it, "A Syllabus of Scott County History." It was distributed to the teachers of the county for use in their history classes.

Out of this event has grown this attempt to prepare a larger and more comprehensive history of my native county. If incentives were needed, they would be abundantly furnished in the fact that my ancestors have been living in this part of Virginia since 1785, most of this time within the limits of Scott County, and by long residence and intermarriage my people have become akin to the greater part of the population. Having taught school many years, a generation or two of my former pupils are now living in the county, so that in a very peculiar way Scott County people are my people.

Some years ago I undertook to gather data under the handicap of being unable to finance the cost of procuring material except in a limited way—just a little at a time. This caused delay, but I feel assured, however, that the work has lost nothing on account of it, for it has permitted a wider search for data. I have endeavored to make it as accurate as available material would warrant. How well I have succeeded, remains to be seen.

I make no claim to originality; I have gleaned wherever

I could find anything that pertained to Scott County history. Much of it has been taken from original sources, and much from the works of others. I have endeavored to assemble between the covers of this book as much of the available data as I could find. In case the matter has been quoted, effort has been made to give the author proper credit for the same.

I have given rather large place to Daniel Boone and the Kentucky Path, for which I make no apology. Boone not only carved out the most available route from the settlements on the Holston to Kentucky, but, historically speaking, he left the plainest trace for the historian of this section to follow, since almost his every movement was chronicled and the records preserved for posterity. There may have been other pioneers as deserving of mention as he, but none stand out in such bold, clear outline on the threshold of our county history as does he. An interesting chain of circumstances made it possible for him to render very important service to Fort Blackmore at a critical time in its history. These circumstances I have briefly sketched. Many miles of the Kentucky Path lay through Scott County territory, and some of the thousands who traveled that Path, growing tired of going west, turned aside and settled in Scott County territory. Thus a thin line of log cabins stretched all the way from the Blockhouse to Kane's Gap in Powell's Mountain on account of the Wilderness Road.

In the preparation of this work I have leaned heavily upon the Draper Manuscripts as a source of information. In fact, for much of the early history of this section, these papers are about the only available source, in so far as I know. These Manuscripts are now owned by the State Historical Society of Wisconsin, and I wish to express my appreciation of the uniform kindness and courtesy shown me by the officials of that Society in all of our business relations.

I am also greatly indebted to the Virginia State Library for courtesies extended to me. The Virginia state papers were a great source of information. Dr. H. R. McIlwaine, Dr. Earl G. Swem, and Mr. Morgan P. Robinson, the archivist, were very helpful to my sons who searched for material both in the State Library, and in the Library of William and Mary College.

In all matters of genealogy I have consulted my friend, Mr. I. C. Coley, whose knowledge of such matters is well known throughout the county. And sometimes, when I grew discouraged and thought the pressure of other duties too great to continue the work, one of Dr. John P. McConnell's encouraging letters would be received, and I would take heart and work with renewed energy.

Extensive use of the court records has been made, especially in the treatment of the period of the Civil War. Some of the records have been entirely rewritten, some written with only slight change in the text, and some quoted verbatim. In most cases they have only been edited.

The chapter on "Old Home Manufactures," etc., has been prepared for the purpose of preserving something of the old life which is already little known to the present generation and will be less known to future generations.

"The Old-Time School in Scott County" and "Scott County in the War with Germany" are reprints: the former was published as a bulletin of the State Teachers' College for Women, East Radford, Virginia, and the latter was published in Arthur Kyle Davis's book entitled *Virginia Communities in War Time.*

I have often had occasion to consult L. P. Summers' *History of Southwest Virginia and Washington County,* and his more recent book, *The Annals of Southwest Virginia.* Both books cover the territory of Scott County.

In sending forth this volume I realize that the best part of my county's history remains unwritten. I refer to the intangible spiritual values as they have been exemplified in the lives of the good men and good women of both the past and the present. These spiritual values constitute the best asset of any country, and yet they elude the historian when he tries to place them on paper, and so the rank and file with its great, common life go unchronicled.

In closing this confidential account of what has happened behind the scenes in the preparation of this work I should not omit to mention Capt. D. S. Hale, Maj. S. P. McConnell,

Ira P. Robinett, J. D. Carter, Sr., W. S. Cox, John Henry Johnson, Prof. Lee R. Dingus, Supt. W. D. Smith, and many others with whom I have either held conversation, or who have written me about some historical matter; nor, perhaps, should I fail to mention my own sons, Justin W., Gus N., Kermit R., and James R., who have made the completion of the enterprise possible.

R. M. ADDINGTON.

Gate City, Virginia.
July 1, 1932.

SOME IMPORTANT DATES IN SCOTT COUNTY HISTORY

1749–50—Dr. Thomas Walker and companions visit Cumberland Gap and adjacent regions.

1763—Treaty in which France gave up to England all claim to the mainland east of the Mississippi River.

1769—Daniel Boone passes through Big Moccasin Gap on his way to Kentucky.

1769—Uriah Stone, Casper Mansker, John Rains, and Abraham and Isaac Bledsoe pass through Big Moccasin Gap to Kentucky.

1769—Thomas McCulloch made the first settlement within the territory of Scott County near Fort Houston, on Big Moccasin Creek.

1770—The Long Hunters pass through Big Moccasin Gap on hunting expeditions.

1770—Peter Livingston settled on the North Fork of the Holston at the mouth of Livingston's Creek.

1771—Silas Enyart settled on Little Moccasin Creek.

1772—James Green settled near the mouth of Stony Creek.

1772—Patrick Porter settled on the west side of Fall Creek, near Osborne's Ford.

1773—James Boone, Henry Russell, and party were massacred by Indians in Powell's Valley.

1773—Daniel Boone takes his family to Castle's Woods and becomes a resident in the Valley of the Clinch.

1773—John Blackmore, Joseph Blackmore, John Blackmore, Jr., John Carter, and Andrew Davis settled at Fort Blackmore.

1773—William Nash settled in Rye Cove.

1773—Charles Kilgore settled on the east side of Fall Creek, near Osborne's Ford.

1773—Jonathan Wood settled on Big Moccasin Creek, near Fort Houston.

1774—Logan, the Mingo chieftain, captured two of Captain Blackmore's slaves at Fort Blackmore.

1

1774—Dale Carter was killed by Indians at Fort Blackmore.

1774—Daniel Boone and Michael Stoner were sent from Castle's Woods to warn surveying parties in Kentucky of the danger of Indian attack.

1774—Daniel Boone was placed in command of Fort Blackmore and other forts on the Clinch while the militiamen were absent on the Point Pleasant campaign in Dunmore's War.

1774—Patrick Porter was given permission to erect a mill on Fall Creek by the County Court of Fincastle.

1774—John Livingston settled at the mouth of Little Moccasin Creek, north side of Clinch Mountain.

1774—Samuel Livingston and Stephen Walling settled at the head of Little Moccasin Creek.

1775—Samuel Richey settled on south side of Clinch River (William Gray farm).

1775—Daniel Boone and companions cut a road through Big Moccasin Gap.

1776—A son of Jonathan Jennings and one of his slaves were killed at Fort Blackmore by Indians.

1776—Isaac Crisman and family were slain by Indians in the Rye Cove.

1776—The inhabitants of Martin's Station flee to Fort Blackmore for protection.

1776—Jacob Lewis and family were slain by Indians near the head of Stock Creek.

1776—The Rye Cove Fort evacuated by order of Colonel Bledsoe, the inmates going to Fort Blackmore.

1776—Samuel Stedham settled at the "Mint Spring" on Little Moccasin Creek.

1777—Benge and band of Indians visit Fort Blackmore. They Capture Polly Alley, and Jane Whitaker.

1777—Fannie Napper (nee Alley) and her five children were captured by Indians at Fort Blackmore.

1777—Col. Joseph Martin stationed in the Rye Cove to guard the frontier.

1779—Capt. John Blackmore and family, and Jonathan Jennings and family, leave Fort Blackmore in boats for Nashboro, Tennessee.

1781—Fort Blackmore attacked by Indians, four men captured, and a large number of horses taken away.

1782—Thomas Wallin settled at the mouth of Stock Creek.

1787—John Carter's wife and six children killed by Indians near Fort Blackmore.

1788—Indians capture two Carter boys in the Rye Cove.

1789—Joseph Johnson's house on "Flat," or "Mill" Creek was burned, his wife and one child killed, and his other children carried into captivity by Indians.

1790—Bishop Asberry, the great Methodist organizer, visited Fort Blackmore.

1790—Mrs. Henry Hamlin killed, and Champ Hamlin captured by Indians at Fort Blackmore.

1791—Benge attacks the house of Elisha Ferris, within the present limits of Gate City, and cruelly murders all but Nancy Ferris.

1793—Benge murdered Harper Ratcliff and his entire family, six in number, near Big Moccasin Gap.

1793—Benge attacked Ensign Moses Cockrell and his packhorse train on top of Powell's Mountain (Kane's Gap).

1794—Benge captured the Livingston family, and was killed by Vincent Hobbs and his company.

1814—An act forming Scott County from parts of Washington, Russell, and Lee counties, passed by the General Assembly of Virginia.

1815—The first court held in the dwelling of Benjamin T. Hollins at Big Moccasin Gap.

1815—The first county election was held, with just two voting places.

1815—The first Superior Court was held in May of this year.

1816—The first Court of Enquiry (Military) was held.

1817—A wooden courthouse was erected on the public square.

1829—Brick courthouse (the front part of present building) was received by the Court.

1870—The county was laid off into seven magisterial districts.

1870—In November of this year the first public free schools were opened in the county.

1887—The first passenger train reached Bratton's Switch, Gate City.

SCOTT COUNTY TERRITORY

Scott County territory was claimed by the French prior to the Treaty of 1763, in which France gave up all claim to the mainland east of the Mississippi River. At the close of the Revolution, France endeavored, by diplomacy in the Treaty of 1783, to regain the strip of territory between the English settlements on the Atlantic Coast and the Mississippi River, of which strip Scott County is part. France, however, was thwarted in her purpose by John Adams, who strongly insisted that the Mississippi River should be the western boundary of the United States. If France had been able to make good her claim in the treaty of 1783, the Mississippi Valley to the very headwaters of its eastern tributaries would have been French territory.

Scott has had a number of parent counties. It was part of Augusta County from 1745 to 1769; part of Botetourt County from 1769 to 1772; part of Fincastle County from 1772 to 1777; part of Washington County from 1777 to 1786; part of Washington and Russell counties from 1786 to 1792; part of Washington, Russell, and Lee counties from 1792 to 1814.

Scott County embraced a part of Wise County until 1856.

In 1814 a petition was presented to the General Assembly, asking that parts of the counties of Washington, Lee, and Russell be formed into a new county. This petition set forth the inconvenience to which its signers were subjected whenever they had need to attend the courts of their respective counties. In accordance with the wishes of the petitioners a bill was introduced in the General Assembly authorizing the formation of a new county. This bill was enacted into law November 24, 1814. It reads as follows:

An Act forming a new county out of part of the counties of Lee, Russell, and Washington, and for other purposes. (Passed November 24, 1814.)

4

Be it enacted by the General Assembly, that all that part of the counties of Lee, Russell, and Washington, contained within the following bounds, to-wit: Beginning at the head of Reedy Creek where the wagon road crosses the same in the County of Washington, thence down the Tennessee line to the South Fork of Clinch River, thence northward passing the Flag Pond to the top of Powell's Mountain in Lee County, and along it to the County of Russell, and with it to the Kentucky line, thence along Cumberland Mountain to the head of Guese's River, thence down it to Clinch River, thence to Kindrick's Gap, in Clinch Mountain, thence to the western end of Samuel Hensley's plantation, and thence to the beginning, shall form one distinct and new county, and be called and known by the name of Scott County.

2. A court for the said County of Scott shall be held by the Justices thereof on the second Tuesday in every month, after the same takes place, in like manner as is provided by law for the counties, and shall be by their Commissioners directed. And quarterly courts for the said county shall be holden in the months of March, June, August, and November in every year. And in order the more impartially and correctly to ascertain the most proper place for holding courts and erecting the public buildings for the said county, John McKinney, Reuben McCulley, and James Wallen, of the County of Lee; Jonathan Wood, Samuel Ritchie, and James Moss, of the County of Russell; and Andrew McHenry, Jacob Severs, and Abraham Fulkerson, of the County of Washington, shall be, and they are hereby appointed Commissioners, a majority of whom may act, for the purpose aforesaid, whose duty it shall be after having performed the services hereby required, to make report thereof to the Court of the said County of Scott; whereupon they shall proceed to erect the necessary public buildings at the place so fixed on by the said Commissioners or a majority of them, which when completed shall be the permanent place for holding courts for the said county. The said Commissioners shall be allowed each the sum of one and one quarter dollars per day, as a compensation for the duties hereby imposed on them, to be paid out of the levy to be collected in the said County of Scott.

3. The Justices to be named in the commission of the peace for the said County of Scott shall meet at Benjamin T. Hollins' at Big Moccasin Gap in the said county, upon the first day after the said county takes place, and after administering the

oaths of office to, and taken bond of, the Sheriff according to law, proceed to appoint and qualify a Clerk, and until the necessary public buildings are completed at the place pointed out by the Commissioners aforesaid, or a majority of them, to appoint such places within the said county for holding courts, as they may think proper: Provided, always, that the appointment of a Clerk and of a temporary place for holding courts shall not be made unless a majority of the Justices of the said county be present.

4. It shall be lawful for the Sheriffs of the counties of Lee, Russell, and Washington to collect and make distress for any public dues or officers' fees which shall remain unpaid by the inhabitants of the said County of Scott at the time it takes place, and shall be accountable for same in like manner as if this Act had not been made.

5. The Governor with the advice of Council shall appoint a person to be first Sheriff of the said County of Scott, who shall continue in office during the term and upon the same conditions as are by law appointed for other Sheriffs.

6. The Courts of the counties of Lee, Russell, and Washington have jurisdiction of all actions and suits depending before them at the time the said County of Scott takes place, and shall try and determine the same and award execution thereon.

7. The said County of Scott shall remain in the same judicial circuit with the counties of Lee, Russell, and Washington, and the courts thereof shall be holden on the eighth Monday after the first Monday of April and on the eighth Monday after the first Monday of September in each year, and be of the same brigade district in like manner as if this Act had not been made. In future elections of a Senator and Elector, and a Representative in Congress the said County of Scott shall be of the same district as the counties of Lee, Russell, and Washington.

This Act shall be in force from the passing thereof.

After the passage of the act it was discovered that a mistake had been made in naming the southern boundary of the county. The South Fork of Clinch had been named as the western limit, whereas it should have been the North Fork. This correction was by amendment passed December 17, 1814. By an act passed December 26, 1822, the boundary of the county was further changed. It was enacted "That the county line of Scott, which now runs a due north course from the head of Stock Creek, dividing Scott from Lee County, shall in future run from the head of said Stock Creek, around on the top of Powell's Mountain, to the Little Stone Gap; thence a due north course, so as to include within Lee County the residences of Beal Davis, William Wills, George Nethercut, and David Stedham."

By an act passed March 29, 1837, William Wilson, of Lee County, and Hezekiah P. Neil and Jacob Roller, of Scott County, were appointed Commissioners whose duties were to run and mark that part of the line between Scott and Lee which extended from the point in the Tennessee line where it crosses the North Fork of Clinch, thence northward by the Flag Pond to the top of Powell's Mountain, thence with the line dividing the counties of Lee and Scott, along the top of said mountain, to some convenient point north of the Gap, made by the passage of the North Fork of Clinch River through said mountain. The Commissioners were further directed to select a competent surveyor who was to run the line and make two correct plats of the course or courses and distances of said line. The plats were to be returned to the county courts of each county and therein to be recorded, and used as conclusive evidence in case controversies should arise respecting said boundary line. In pursuance with the provisions of this act, Thompson G. Martin was selected to survey and make plats of this line.

February 16, 1856, an act was passed forming Wise County from parts of Lee, Scott, and Russell counties. This act left the northern boundary lines of the county substantially as they are at present. The boundary lines have not been changed since the formation of Wise County.

For many years there was some dispute respecting the exact location of the boundary line between the two states. In 1779, while Tennessee was yet North Carolina territory, Thomas Walker and Daniel Smith as commissioners on the part of Virginia, and Richard Henderson and James Smith, on the part of North Carolina, surveyed the line in agreement until they reached the point where it crosses the North Fork of the Holston, north of the Great Island. Here the pilots gave it as their opinion that the line as it was then being surveyed would, if continued, place both Cumberland Gap and the settlements at Nashboro on the Virginia side of the line. When Henderson realized that there was a possibility of some of the lands in which he was interested being cut off to Virginia, he halted and said the line must be crooked. He urged that a test be made to see whether the surveyors had lost the true latitude of place. The test having been made, it was shown that no error had been committed by the surveyors; yet Henderson proceeded on a line two miles north but parallel to the line which Walker pursued.

Henderson turned back when he reached the Cumberland Mountain, while Dr. Walker continued his line to the Tennessee River. Thus between Walker's and Henderson's lines was a strip two miles wide and extending from the North Fork of Holston to the Tennessee River, which was claimed by both states. This condition of affairs existed until 1802, when commissioners were again appointed by the Legislature of both states. These commissioners agreed that a line midway between, and parallel to Walker's and Henderson's lines should be the boundary between the two states. In accordance with this agreement Brice Martin and Nat B. Markland surveyed and marked the line. It was believed that this location of the line would forever settle the controversy. But it did not. In 1856 the question again came up for adjustment. Both states again appointed commissioners to resurvey and mark the line of 1802. The report of these commissioners was rejected by the General Assembly of Virginia and the rejection, of course, reopened the whole subject of controversy. In 1869 Richard B. Cutts was directed by the United States Coast Survey to proceed to Bristol and during the eclipse of sun on August 7 make such observations as would determine the true latitude of the different lines surveyed. By these observations it was shown that none of the lines already surveyed were located on 36′ 30″ latitude.

The next important step in the controversy was the institution of a suit in the Supreme Court of the United States against the State of Tennessee, in which the court was asked to declare that the parallel of 36′ 30″ should be the boundary line between the two states. The Court decided, however, that the old compromise line of 1803 should be the boundary between the two states. A commission consisting of William C. Hodgkins, of Massachusetts, as chairman, James B. Taylor, of Virginia, as secretary, and Andrew H. Buchanan, of Tennessee, as treasurer, was then selected to locate the line in accordance with the Supreme Court's decision. The following is a list of cut limestone and other durable marks which locate the southern boundary of Scott County as well as the boundary between Virginia and Tennessee:

(38) On Boozy Creek road.

(39) On road to Hilton's, cut stone monument of 1858–59.

(40) On Timbertree road.

(41) Between two roads just east of Gate City road.

(42) In woods west of Gate City road, where there is a deflection of 8′ 30″ to the right or north from the general course on old Hickam place.

(43) In woods northeast of Bloomingdale, where this 8′ 30″ deflection from the general course of the line ends in going westward and line resumes its general course.

(44) On road to Bloomingdale.

(45) On Wall Gap road.

(46) On road up ravine.

(47) On Carter Valley road.

(48) On Gate City and Kingsport road, cut stone monument of 1858–59.

Coast and Geodetic Survey triangulation station, "Cloud," on bluff of North Holston River. Stone marked.

U. S.

X

C. S.

(49) On east bank of North Holston River.

(50) On road on west bank of North Holston River.

(51) At cross roads on Stanley Valley and cut stone monument of 1858–59.

(52) Stanley Valley road on hill at turn in road.

(53) On Cameron Post Office road.

(54) On Stanley Valley road south of barn of N. J. Bussell, cut stone monument of 1858–59.

(55) On Stanley Valley road, cut stone monument of 1858–59.

(56) On road which runs across Opossum Ridge.

(57) On Moore's Gap road.

(58) On Caney Valley road.

(59) On Little Poor Valley road, south of Mary Field house.

(60) On Poor Valley road, cut stone monument of 1858–59. On summit of Clinch Mountain, cairn of rocks erected a few feet south of the Coast and Geodetic Survey triangulation station, "Wildcat," which station is marked with

U. S.

X

C. S.

cut in sandstone rock.

(61) On Clinch Valley road.

(62) On road on east bank of Clinch River, above Church's Ford.

(63) On road at Jane Bagley's house. On summit of open hill east of Fisher Valley road the line crosses solid rock. Small hole drilled in it, with V cut in north side of hole and T south of it.

(64) On Fisher Valley road. On summit of a high ridge east of Robinette the line crosses solid rock. Small hole drilled in it, with T cut south of hole and V north of it.

(65) On road at Robinette. On side of ridge on east edge of woods line crosses rock. Small hole drilled in it, with V cut on north side of hole and T on south side of it. (Summers's *History of Southwest Virginia*.)

SOME COUNTY GEOGRAPHICAL NAMES

Most of the county's leading geographical features, such as its principal mountains and streams, had received their names before the coming of the first permanent settlers. In 1774, Capt. Daniel Smith made a map of the region now comprehended within the boundaries of Scott County. This map contains the following names: Clinch River, Guess's River, Rye Cove, Cove Creek, Stony Creek, Copper Creek, Copper Creek Ridge, Falling Creek, Hunters' (Osborne's) Ford, Sinking Creek, Castle's Run, Mockason Creek, Poor Valley, North Fork of Holston. Evidently, therefore, hunters and explorers had been here prior to 1774 and had applied these names often enough to somewhat fix them in the minds of the frontier people.

Holston—Stephen Holston discovered the river which bears his name some time prior to 1748. His cabin was located at the head spring of the Middle Fork of the Holston. Thus the river, sometimes called the Cherokee River, finally took the name of Holston.

Clinch River—Dr. Thomas Walker, in his Journal of 1749–1750, says that Clinch River took its name from one Clinch, a hunter who first found it. There is a somewhat fanciful story as to the origin of the name. This story relates that an Irishman who could not swim attempted the crossing of the river on a raft. Falling off the raft in mid-stream, he excitedly called to his companions, "Clinch me! Clinch me!" and that this circumstance led to the river's being called Clinch. There are other versions of this story. Clinch Mountain took its name from the river, no doubt.

Copper Creek and Copper Creek Ridge—In the survey of John Blackmore, Jr.'s, farm the ridge south of Clinch River was called, "Copper Creek Ridge." This survey was made in 1774. The author has been unable to find why the word "Copper" was used.

The Big Knob—A peak of Clinch Mountain, 3,217 feet high. It is situated five or six miles east of Gate City. A part of this highland is called Signal Pole Knob.

Hiltons—A small village situated on the Appalachia Division of the Southern Railway. It was named in honor of the Hilton family. One of the county's high schools is located there.

Clinchport—A town twelve miles west of Gate City, located at the confluence of Stock Creek and Clinch River. It was probably named in anticipation of the development of the Clinch as a navigable stream.

Big Poor Valley—A valley skirting the base of Clinch Mountain on the south side throughout the entire length of the county, and is named on account of the sterility of the soil.

Troublesome Creek—A small tributary of the Clinch, having its head near the Big Cut. Its significant name was given it by travelers over the Wilderness Road to Kentucky.

The Big Ridge—A close-in watershed of the Clinch Valley and so named on account of its size.

The Flag Pond—So named on account of the plants which once grew in a boggy sag, and mentioned in connection with the boundaries first given the County of Scott.

Pattonsville—A village situated at the base of Powell's Mountain and named for the Rev. Samuel Patton, a prominent minister and elder in the Methodist Church.

Stock Creek—Also once called Buckeye Creek, a northern tributary of the Clinch, which flows through the Natural Tunnel. Little Stock Creek, a tributary of Big Stock Creek, has part of its course underground.

Camp Rock—A sheltering cliff of rock, near the High Knob, about 4,000 feet above sea level, and so called because it furnished shelter to hunting parties in the early days.

Stony Creek—A northern tributary of the Clinch, which any one could have named on account of the rocky character of its bed.

Cove Creek—There are two Cove Creeks in the county, one a southern tributary of the North Fork of Holston, the other, a northern tributary of the Clinch, near the Rye Cove.

Sinking Creek—So called because, after a course of a few miles as a surface stream, it sinks beneath Powers' Hill, and also passes beneath Clinch River to become a northern tributary of this river. Perhaps no other stream in the world has the unique distinction of being on both sides of the stream into which it flows.

Falling Creek—A southern tributary of the Clinch, emptying into the same at Osborne's Ford. It is so named on account of the steep incline of its bed, and more particularly because of the falls in its lower course, at which Patrick Porter erected the first mill within the present limits of the county.

Livingston Creek—A southern tributary of the North Fork of Holston, named in honor of the Livingston family, who settled at its mouth very early.

Little Flat Lick—One of the well-known places on the Kentucky Path, near Duffield. "Licks" were rather numerous in the county. With the extinction of large wild game, the "lick" ceased to be important. Little Flat Lick and Double Lick

Branch are the only current names that carry the word
"lick" now.

The names of magisterial districts of the county were given
by the Commissioners who made the division of the county.
Mr. S. L. Cox, a member of this Commission, once told the
author that Maj. H. C. Wood, another member, did most of
the naming; that Powell District was named for Ambrose
Powell; that Taylor District was named in honor of the Taylor family; that Estillville District was named for the county
seat; that Fulkerson District was named in honor of James
and Abraham Fulkerson, influential early settlers of that section; that Johnson District was named in honor of the Johnson family; that Floyd was named in honor of Governor
Floyd; that the naming of his own district was left to him
(S. L. Cox); that in his search for a name he remembered his
lifelong friend, Tandy Flanary, who by some chance bore the
nickname "Dekalb," and that he named his own district Dekalb, in honor of his friend.

The Devil's Race Path Branch—Thomas W. Carter, in a
letter to Dr. Lyman C. Draper, explains the origin of the
name in these words: "About 1790, a man by the name of
James Paine made a settlement at the mouth of said branch
and another man by the name of Simon Dotson at the head.
Paine's house became the resort of bad men. Dotson made
whisky and sold to those men until it became dangerous for
travelers to pass through the gorge, and it received the name
of Devil's Race Path Branch." (Draper Manuscripts, 6 C
47.)

Moccasin Creek, it is said, was so named because early
explorers, on first coming to the creek, found many tracks
made in the soft mud of its banks by Indians who wore moccasins. Judge M. B. Wood, in his *History of the Wood Family in Virginia,* attributes the naming of the creek to Daniel
Boone and his companions, who came through Big Moccasin
Gap in 1769.

THE MURDER OF JAMES BOONE AND
HENRY RUSSELL

In the year 1773, an event occurred on the Southwest Virginia frontier which greatly influenced the early history of this section. It was a link in the chain of cause and effect which brought Daniel Boone into historical connection with Fort Blackmore and other settlements in the Valley of the Clinch. This event was ominously significant as indicating Indian hostility to further encroachment upon their territory by the whites.

In the summer of 1773, Daniel Boone, on his return from a trip to Kentucky, met Capt. William Russell, of Castlewood, somewhere in Clinch Valley, and at this meeting they seem to have agreed to unite in forming a strong party for the settlement of Kentucky. Boone had in the meantime enlisted the interest of his wife's people, the Bryans, in the enterprise. He also organized a party of five families in his own neighborhood on the Yadkin. These various groups were to assemble in Powell's Valley. On September 25, 1773, after a summer of active preparations, Boone and the North Carolina contingent started for the place of rendezvous in Powell's Valley. On reaching the neighborhood of Abingdon, Boone sent his son, James, 16 years of age, in company with John and Richard Mendenhall, of Guilford County, North Carolina, across country to Castlewood, to notify Captain Russell that the settlers were on their way, and also to obtain a supply of flour and farming tools. At Captain Russell's they were joined by Henry Russell, aged 17, son of Captain Russell, and by Isaac Crabtree and two of Russell's negro slaves Charles and Adam. Heavily laden with supplies, young Boone and Russell started down the Clinch by way of the Hunter's Ford and the Rye Cove to join the main body at the place of rendezvous in Powell's Valley.

The delay, occasioned by the detour to Captain Russell's, permitted the main body to reach the place of meeting in

Powell's Valley in advance of young Boone and his party, who missed their way and failing to come up with the main party before nightfall, went into camp about three miles in the rear. During the night wolves surrounded the camp and howled dismally, on which the Mendenhall brothers expressed fear and were twitted with cowardice by Isaac Crabtree, who jocularly told them that in Kentucky, the place to which they were going, they would hear wolves and buffaloes howling in the tree tops.

At daybreak the next morning, the party was attacked by Indians and all killed except Isaac Crabtree, and Adam and Charles, the two negroes. Young Russell was shot through the hips and thus rendered unable to escape. The Indians stabbed him with knives, and at each thrust he grabbed the knife blade with his hands. He was horribly mutilated. His hands were cut to pieces by the knife blades being drawn through them. His "corpse was mangled in inhuman manner and there was left in him a dart of arrows and a war club was left by him." (Draper. Manuscripts, 6 C 14.)

Crabtree made good his escape and was the first to return to the settlement. The negro, Adam, watched the butchery of his young master and others from a pile of driftwood. He became lost and wandered about several days before reaching the settlement. He was set free from slavery by the will of Madam Russell many years later. Charles was taken captive, and after traveling about forty miles two of his captors quarreled over possession of him and the leader of the party, to settle the quarrel, tomahawked and killed him.

Capt. William Russell and Capt. David Gass, who had arranged to join the Boone party, had lingered behind in Castlewood to complete some unfinished business. As they journeyed along the path taken by young Boone and his company they came suddenly upon the mutilated bodies. It appeared afterwards that the Indians had followed young Boone's party a considerable distance the day before.

This was not a battle, but a massacre. The attack was so sudden and unexpected that no resistance was made by young Boone and his companions. There is no record that they were armed.

The Cherokees were believed, at the time, to be guilty of

the massacre. In fact, Capt. John Stuart, British Indian
Agent among the Cherokees, urged them to give up the mur-
derers. As a result of his influence, one chief was put to
death and another escaped execution only by fleeing to the
Chickasaw Tribe. This band of Indians, however, was probably composed of both Cherokees and Shawnees, because some
of the books and farming tools carried by the James Boone
party were brought in and delivered to the whites by the
Northern Indians as a result of the treaty which followed Dunmore's War. (Draper Manuscripts.)

ISAAC CRABTREE, SURVIVOR OF THE
JAMES BOONE PARTY

Isaac Crabtree, an eyewitness to the massacre of James
Boone and his companions, and the sole white survivor of that
ill-fated party, was so incensed against the Indians that he
sought to kill every red man who crossed his path, without
regard to whether he was friend or enemy.

While in attendance upon a horse race in the Watauga
Settlement, Crabtree fired upon and killed one of three Indians
who were looking upon the races before the bystanders could
prevent the action. The other two Indians, one a squaw, were
saved from a like fate only with difficulty. The murdered
Indian was named Cherokee Billey and was said to be a kinsman of Oconastota, an influential Cherokee chieftain.

This act of Crabtree's threw the whole border into a panic
of fear lest the Cherokee's should go on the warpath to avenge
the death of their tribesman. Some of the leading settlers
hastened to assure the Indians of their disapproval of Crabtree's conduct. The Magistrates offered a reward of £50
for his arrest. This reward was supplemented by an additional one of £100 by Governor Dunmore of Virginia. Although many people knew of Crabtree's whereabouts, these
rewards did not lead to his arrest. In fact, frontier people,
having suffered so much from Indian attack and depredation,
had no very strong condemnation for the man whose offense
was no greater than that of having killed an Indian. For
the most part, their fear was that such conduct might provoke
the savages to war. It might be surmised that Crabtree, since

a reward hung over him, would desist from further hostile acts toward friendly and inoffensive Indians, but such was not the case. On hearing that a party of three Cherokees was hunting near Jacob Brown's on the Nola Chucky River, he hastened thither, it was thought, with intent to attack them. On his arrival, however, he found that instead of three the party consisted of thirty-seven. Acting on the principle that discretion is the better part of valor he returned to his father's at Big Lick, near Abingdon, Va. For a number of years, however, the county officers of Fincastle and Washington feared that some overt act of his and others like him would bring the horrors of savage warfare upon the thin line of settlers on the border. They sought, therefore, to furnish him an outlet for his warlike impulses by arranging that he go upon such military expeditions as were organized upon the border in his time.

THE KENTUCKY PATH

The path over which the early hunters and immigrants traveled from the "settlements on the Holston" to "the old settlements in Kentucky," and other points in the Central West, has been designated by several different names. These various names are: "The Kentucky Trace," "The Kentucky Trail," "The Great Road," (not great because it was paved with stone, like the Appian Way, but great because of the thousands of pioneers who traveled over it to conquer and take possession of the rich lands of Kentucky and the Central West), "the Kentucky Road" or "The Wilderness Road," "The Road to Caintuck," "The Kentucky Path." In Scott County, sections of it were called "The Blockhouse Road," "the Dug Road," "The Old Reedy Creek Road," and "the Road down Troublesome," and, many years later, the court records almost invariably designate it as the Main Western Road. It may be stated in this connection that the contemporary writers made use of the words, "Trace," "Path," or "Road," instead of "trail."

In the early days, those who sought to pass through the dense forests of the Appalachian Mountains endeavored to locate the "gaps," the "fords," and the "licks" of this vast and mountainous wilderness. They sought the "gaps" because they furnished the way of least resistance; they sought the "fords" because they furnished safety in crossing the swift flowing, and often turbulent streams; and they sought the "licks" because they furnished an abundance of wild game on the journey. Thus two great "gaps," Moccasin and Cumberland (to say nothing of many smaller ones), with convenient "licks" and "fords" made the "Kentucky Path" possible, even practicable.

It will never be known, perhaps, who was the first to travel over this route. No doubt it had been traveled, at least in part, by a number of white men prior to the time when Boone made his first journey to Kentucky. In fact, Boone himself first heard of Kentucky through others.

John Finley, whose acquaintance Boone had formed in Braddock's company against the French and Indians, had told him of Kentucky.

Boone's first trip into what is now Southwestern Virginia was made in the year 1767. On this trip, he gave the name, Indian River to the Holston; the name, Wolfe Creek, to the stream which flows through Abingdon, Va.; and the name, Buffalo Licks, to the site of Saltville, Va. Boone came into the valley of the Holston a number of times within the years 1767–68. In the year 1769, however, he made his first journey into the territory of Kentucky. Daniel Bryan, Boone's nephew and namesake, in 1843, wrote to Dr. Draper the following account of Boone's route through this section into Kentucky: "Boon agreed to go and took John Stewart as his companion, John Finley, Joseph Holden, James' Moone (Mooney) and Wm. Coole (Cooley) six in all.

"On the first day of May, 1769, started from Boons on the Head of the Yadkin they took their course westwardly crossing the blue or big mountain to the three forks of New River lower down called Kenhaway thence over Stone Mountain to a place called the Stares (stairs) thence over the Iron Mountain into Holston Valley then across the valley to Moccasin Gap in the Clinch Mountain, I Daniel Bryan have traveled this same rout they then continued their rout or course westwardly crossing Waldens Ridge Powels Mountain into Powels Valley then down the valley leaving Cumberland

Mount but a little to their right, so on to Cumberland Gap."
(Draper Manuscripts.) Daniel Bryan here traces Boone's
first trip over the entire distance of the Wilderness Road.
Prior to the time here mentioned, it seems, Boone had traversed the wilderness only as far as the valley of the Holston.
He had been pushing a little farther west into the wilderness
on each successive journey. Daniel Bryan further states that
Boone passed through Big Moccasin Gap, the first of the
great "gaps" that open from the Holston Valley to Kentucky
and the Central West.

In June, 1769, Uriah Stone, Casper Mansker, John Rains,
Abraham and Isaac Bledsoe, John Baker, and several others,
started from Reedy Creek of the New River, and, traveling
down the Holston River passed, as did Boone and his companions, through Big Moccasin Gap, into Powell's Valley, and
from thence on through Cumberland Gap into the territory of
Kentucky. Both parties, no doubt, traveled over practically
the same route. Furthermore, in the year 1770, the Long
Hunters took the same route, both in going to, and returning
from, the valleys of the Cumberland and the Ohio rivers
in which they hunted. In this way the most practical routes
through the mountains into Kentucky were gradually becoming known at the time Boone first made his way to the border
of the Bluegrass region. Boone was so much pleased with
what he saw on his first trip that he returned to his family
"with the determination," he says, "to bring them as soon
as possible to live in Kentucky, I esteemed a second paradise,
at the risk of my life and fortune." (Speeds Wilderness
Road.)

In 1773, Daniel Boone, accompanied by Benjamin Cutbirth,
went to Kentucky to hunt wild game and explore its fertile
lands. On their return from this trip, somewhere in the Clinch
Valley, they met Capt. William Russell of Castlewood and
told him of the rich lands they had seen, and of the abundance of wild game with which its forests and greenswards
teemed. Furthermore, Boone, it seems, disclosed to Russell
his intention of removing to Kentucky and settling there.
Arrangements were also made to procure supplies of flour,
seed corn, and farming implements, from Russell for the new
settlement when the same should be needed.

On returning to his home on the Yadkin, Boone, with as much dispatch as he could, gathered a party of immigrants and started back through the wilderness over the same trace by which he had returned from Kentucky a short time before. His immediate party consisted of his own and five other families. He was to be joined by a number of other immigrants in Powell's Valley. Boone and his immigrants, however, failed to reach their destination. The main party, after having traversed the wilderness at least as far as the neighborhood of Stickleyville, Lee County, Virginia, halted and went into camp to await the coming of the rear party. This rear party consisted of Boone's son, James, and others who had been sent by way of Captain Russell's, in Castlewood, for supplies. On leaving Captain Russell's, James Boone started down the Clinch River to rejoin his father's party, somewhere in Powell's Valley. He was accompanied by Henry Russell, Captain Russell's son, and by two or three white work people and some slaves. From Castlewood James Boone's party traveled over the route now known as "the old Fincastle Road," to the neighborhood of Stickleyville, where they went into camp, night coming on. They were attacked next morning by a band of Indians, and all but two were killed. Boone's party, on hearing of the murder of young Boone and Russell, were panic-stricken and turned back to the settlements, under Daniel Boone's protest, however. Some went to North Carolina, some to Castlewood, and some to the settlements on the Holston. But Boone, having sold his home on the Yadkin, went with his family to Castlewood, where he resided until a more favorable time in which to immigrate to the land of his choice.

While Boone and his family were sojourning in Castlewood, Dunmore's War broke out in August, 1774. Boone and Michael Stoner, both of whom were then residing in Castlewood, were sent by Captain Russell to warn the surveyors in Kentucky of the danger they were in on account of a threatened Indian outbreak. In the performance of this service, they made a circuitous route to the falls of the Ohio, and returned through Cumberland Gap by way of Fort Blackmore to Castlewood, having accomplished, on foot, a journey of eight hundred miles in sixty-one days. On his return home,

Boone gave his services to the people among whom he dwelt by helping to guard the exposed frontiers in the valley of the Clinch against the danger of Indian attack, during the continuation of hostilities. Dunmore's War culminated in the Battle of Point Pleasant, October 10, 1774. In this battle the northern Indians were defeated, and their power, in a large measure, was broken. This defeat of the Indians brought relief to the distressed frontiers in this portion of Virginia, and for a time made travel through the wilderness somewhat safer. It is alleged that Boone, availing himself of the comparative peace that now prevailed along the border, in the year 1775, stole away to Kentucky for a hunt, going thither over the trace which later became the old Fincastle Road. This trace may be regarded as the Clinch River division of the Kentucky Path. It entered the territory of Scott County at the western edge of Castlewood, and from there it followed the ridge which divides the valleys of Sinking Creek and Clinch River, to Powers Hill and Fall Creek. It crossed Clinch River at Hunter's Ford (now Osborne's Ford) and, passing down the river by way of Fort Blackmore, and through the Rye Cove, it united with the Holston Branch of the Kentucky Path somewhere in Stock Creek Valley. It probably passed over Tunnel Hill and united with the Holston branch at the base of the hill on the western side. Hunters, however, often turned aside from the path as here traced, and traveled down the narrow valley which skirts the base of Stone Mountain, hence the name Hunter's Valley. The "Kentucky Path" down Clinch is mentioned in a number of deeds.

The "path" and the old Fincastle Road had substantially the same location.

Boone's desire to establish a home in the fair and fertile lands of Kentucky was so strong that no ordinary difficulties could turn him aside from it. His desire was shared in by many others who dared make the journey through the wilderness at the peril of their own lives and the lives of their loved ones. Rich and poor, alike, heard the call of the near West at this time. Among the wealthy men who became interested in the settlement of Kentucky lands was Richard Henderson, of North Carolina. He conceived the plan of purchasing a vast tract of land in the Ohio River Valley and selling it again to settlers at a profit. The Cherokee Indians, however, asserted claim to the lands in which Henderson was interested. In fact, Donaldson's line, which was supposed to separate the colony of Virginia from the Cherokee lands, extended from six miles above the Great Island in the Holston to the mouth of Kanawha River. This line, thus located, cut off to the Cherokees, even the very approach to Henderson's lands from the Holston Settlements. These lands could not be reached without passing over land claimed by the Indians. Henderson, therefore, deeming it wise to take no risk of incurring their hostility, offered to buy the Cherokee claim, shadowy as it was, in order to secure a right of way to the region of his proposed colony. To do this a treaty with the Cherokees was necessary. The chiefs and leading men of the tribes must be called together for the purpose. Sycamore Shoals on the Watauga River was selected as the meeting place of the tribesmen, and the important task of securing their attendance upon this treaty was entrusted to Daniel Boone. Boone himself modestly says, in speaking of the Sycamore Shoals treaty, that he was asked "by a number of North Carolina gentlemen, that were about purchasing lands on the south side of the Kentucky River from the Cherokee Indians, to attend their treaty at Watauga, in March, 1775, to negotiate with them, and mention the boundaries of purchase. This I accepted, and at the request of the same gentlemen, undertook to mark out a road in the best passage from the settlement through the wilderness to Kentucky, with such assistance as I thought necessary to employ for such an important undertaking." More than twelve hundred Indians attended the meeting, and the principal chiefs of the Cherokee Nation, excepting Dragging Canoe, agreed to and signed the treaty.

When it became evident to Henderson that the Cherokees would sell him whatever claims they might have to the lands in which he was interested, he at once sent Daniel Boone, with a company of thirty men, to cut a road from the settlements on the Holston to central Kentucky. This road was a mere bridle path over which wagons were taken only as far as Martin's Cabin, in Powell's Valley.

Col. William Preston, in a letter to Governor Dunmore of Virginia, thus speaks of Henderson's treaty with the Cherokees, and Boone's road-making through the Wilderness.

"Fincastle March 10, 1775
"My Lord—Herewith your Lordship will receive two letters from Captain Russell and Colonel Henderson's proposals for settling the lands on the Ohio under the company's purchase. As one of the letters relates chiefly to that transaction, I shall only observe that between five hundred and a thousand Cherokees came in, and that the whole business was to be concluded this week, as the Indians had no objection to the Sale, that a great number of hands are employed in cutting a waggon road through Mockison and Cumberland Gaps to Kentucky which they expect to complete before planting time; and that at least five hundred people are preparing to go out this spring from Carolina besides great numbers from Virginia to settle there." (Thwaites and Kellog's Rev. on the Ohio.)

Boone's party of road-makers consisted of himself, his brother, Squire, Benjamin Cutbirth, Michael Stoner, Richard Callaway, William Bush, David Gass, Edmund Jennings, John Kennedy, John Vardeman, James Nall and others, about thirty in all. They cut and removed the underbrush and fallen timber from the "Trace" where the forest was dense, and blazed the trees along the Trace where the forest was open. They proceeded without encountering serious engineering difficulties until they reached the neighborhood of Big Moccasin Gap. Just here Little Pine Mountain is cut asunder by Big Moccasin Creek as is Clinch Mountain, also. The northern side of Little Pine Mountain is steep and could be crossed by pack horses, but something more was needed than the mere removal of underbrush to make it passable for wagons such as Henderson meant to send into the Wilderness. Whether Boone and his party graded this part of the Trace by digging is not known. They probably did not. But it is evident, however, that this part of the path was graded by digging not far from this time, a circumstance so unusual in those days that it was locally called the "Dug Road," a name which it still retains.

Boone and his party of ax and rifle-bearing road-makers succeeded in cutting the "Path" as far as the edge of the Blue Grass in Kentucky without unfavorable incident. Here,

however, they were attacked by Indians and two members of
the party killed.

After a delay of ten days, Henderson and his party began
the long and difficult journey over the first white man's road
through the Wilderness. The pack-horse train, being able to
travel more rapidly, reached Martin's Station much in advance of the wagons, for Henderson, it seems, had four wagons
making the trip; his own, Samuel Henderson's, W. Luttrel's,
and the fourth owner not named, which arrived April 4.
(Draper Manuscripts.)   A house having been built in which
to store the wagons, they were left at Martin's Station, and
their contents were transported the remainder of the way by
pack-horse train.

It is not possible, with the data at hand, to trace with absolute certainty, the location of the Kentucky Path at every
point throughout its length. Like other roads, both then and
now, it was subject to such alterations as suited either fancy
or convenience of those who traveled over it, and divergence
was, of course, always possible between the "gaps." Moccasin Gap was, no doubt, reached from the Holston Settlements by more than one way. In general, however, the following description of the Kentucky Path may be taken as
fairly accurate in so far as its passage through Scott County
is concerned. It passed from Shelby's Fort (now Bristol)
down Reedy Creek to the Blockhouse. Boone's original place
of rendezvous, however, was Fort Patrick Henry on the Long
Island of Holston. The modern town of Kingsport is situated
in the "forks" of the Holston. Boone's route, however, did
not usually take him as far west as the site of Kingsport. He
traveled down Reedy Creek to the neighborhood of Peltier,
and then turned north to the Tennessee-Virginia boundary
line, thence by way of the Blockhouse to the ford just above
Holston Bridge. From this ford he took a northwest course,
passing over Little Pine Mountain at a point where its eleva-
tion has been greatly reduced by Big Moccasin Creek. He
then passed through Big Moccasin Gap, the great eastern gateway of the Kentucky Path. Thence up Little Moccasin Valley to the low divide which separates Little Moccasin from
Troublesome Creek. The difficulty of traveling down the last-
named creek is still commemorated in the name it bears. At

or near the old Virginia & Southwestern depot at Speer's Ferry, the path turned aside from the narrow valley of Troublesome Creek, and passed along the south side of a limestone hill to the north of the late J. M. Horton's residence until it reached the narrow ravine at Horton's Chapel. Here it dropped down the ravine to the ford of the Clinch at Speer's Ferry. Persons yet living remember and point out the depression of the old Trace where it passed along the side of the limestone ridge from the old Virginia & Southwestern depot to Horton's Chapel. (See deeds, Michael Darter, George Graham, and George George.) After crossing Clinch River at Speer's Ferry, the Path passed up the west bank of the same to the "Ford of Stock Creek," the present site of Clinchport. From Clinchport it followed the meanders of Big Stock Creek up almost to the Natural Tunnel. Here it turned to the left around the Tunnel Hill by way of Horton's Summit, to the Little Flat Lick, near the new schoolhouse at Duffield. It may be stated in this connection that foot travelers and pack-horse trains often passed up the Devil's Race Path branch to the top of the Purchase Ridge, and then descended into the valley of the North Fork of Clinch, near the Little Flat Lick. Little Flat Lick, it seems, was one of the best known places on the Kentucky Path. Not one of the early travelers over the Path, who has left an account of his itinerary, has failed to mention Little Flat Lick. On the other hand, not one has deemed it worth while to make mention of the Great Natural Tunnel, which lay directly across his path traveling through Stock Creek Valley. From this may it not be inferred that a "lick" was of much greater interest to the mind of the hunter-traveler than any bit of natural scenery, however grand it might be?

From Little Flat Lick, there seems to have been, at least, two ways of reaching Powell's Valley. One of these, and this was probably the oldest, passed over Powell's Mountain, at or near Kane's Gap, and descended into Powell's Valley not far from the head of Wallen's Creek, where Scott's Fort was located. The other, and this, no doubt, was the route taken by wagons, passed from Little Flat Lick down the valley of the North Fork of Clinch, by way of Pattonsville, over Powell's Mountain to Stickleyville—very much as the present wagon road runs. William Brown, who traveled over the Kentucky Path in 1782, gives the distance from Little Flat Lick to the North Fork of Clinch as being one mile and the distance from the North Fork to Powell's Mountain one mile. These distances are approximately true only in the event that he crossed Powell's Mountain at, or near, the town of Duffield.

Furthermore, Thomas Speed, in his *Itinerary from Charlotte Courthouse to Kentucky,* in 1790, mentions Scott's Fort as one of the stopping places on the Kentucky Path. Scott's Station was located near the head of Wallen's Creek and the mention of it by Speed indicates that much, if not most, of the travel to Kentucky at that time crossed Powell's Mountain near Duffield.

The road marked out by Boone was but a trace—a mere bridle path. It was not suited to wagons or wheeled vehicles of any kind. In places it was barely passable for pack-horse trains; yet during the four years next following the time in which Boone marked it out, the travel over it was so great that it became the subject of legislative enactment. The Legislature of Virginia passed an Act providing that commissioners be appointed to explore the country on both sides of the mountains and select the best place for a road, and cause the same to be cleared and opened for travelers with pack horses. In accordance with the provisions of this Act, Evan Shelby and Richard Callaway were appointed commissioners. Shelby, for some reason, declined to serve and Capt. John Kinkead was appointed in his stead. Richard Callaway was a member of Boone's party of road-makers. John Kinkead, under date of December 1, 1781, presented a petition to the General Assembly of Virginia, "setting forth that agreeable to appointment of the county court of Washington, he, in conjunction with the other commissioner, proceeded to and effected the opening of a road through the Cumberland Mountains in Kentucky and praying to be paid for the service." (Summers, p. 280.)

The Act above mentioned further provided that a guard of fifty men be furnished for the protection of the commissioners and laborers while carrying out its other provisions. Notwithstanding legislative enactment, the Kentucky Path did

not become a wagon road until some years later. In the meantime, settlers were pouring into Kentucky along this Trace
in large and ever-increasing numbers. In 1790, the population of Kentucky was 13,000, and, in 1800, the population
was 220,000, and the greater part of this population had entered the region of Kentucky by way of the Wilderness Road.

Travel over this road was mainly on foot. In fact, it was
a better footpath than any other kind of road. A distance of
several hundred miles did not daunt the hardy pedestrian of
that day. Daniel Boone and Michael Stoner, in the summer
of 1774, walked eight hundred miles in sixty-one days and
stopped long enough at Harrodsburg for Boone to build a
house as a basis of a claim to land there.

Children, household and kitchen furniture, and such other
articles as the immigrant chose to take along, were carried
through the Wilderness on pack horses. Each pack horse was
equipped with a pack saddle, the framework of which was applied to the horse's back when the timbers were green and
allowed to season there under the pressure of a load in such
way as to be adjusted to the shape of the horse's back and
sides. Children were often placed in large baskets tied together, which were thrown across the horse's back, one child
serving to balance the other, and mutually keeping each other
from falling off. Much care had to be exercised to prevent
the baskets from being "rubbed off" by the saplings in the edge
of the path.

In 1795, the Legislature of Kentucky passed an Act to
convert the Kentucky Path on its side of the Cumberland
Mountains into a wagon road. Bids for this change were ad-
vertised for and Daniel Boone sought an opportunity to superintend the work as is shown by his letter to Isaac Shelby, who
was then Governor of Kentucky.

"Feburey the 11th 1796.
"Sir

After my best Respts to your Excelancy and famyly I wish
to inform you that I have sum intention of undertaking this
New Rode that is to be cut through the Wilderness and I
think myself intitled to the ofer of the bisiness as I first
marked out that Rode in March 1775 and never re'd anything

for my trubel and sepose I am no statesman I am a woodsman
and think myself as capable of making and cutting that Rode
as any other man Sir if you think with me I would thank you
to wright mee a line by the post the first opportunuty and he
will lodge it at Mr. John Miler son hinkston fork as I wish to
know where and when it is to be laat (let) so that I may
atend at the time"
    "I am Deer Sir you very omble Sarvent"
                                                    D. Boone"

    The records do not show that Boone was ever awarded the
contract to enlarge and improve his wilderness road. It is
very probable that someone else received the award.
    At the time when the travel to Kentucky was heaviest, there
was a very thin line of forts and ordinaries extending from
the Blockhouse on Holston to Boonesborough. How these
primitive log-house hotels managed to furnish food and shelter to the hundreds of emigrants who thronged the way is
difficult now to understand. No doubt they were often taxed
to their utmost capacity in furnishing entertainment for their
guests. Complaint that food supplies were almost exhausted
at Martin's Cabin were made to Colonel Henderson at one
time.
    William Brown, who traveled over the Kentucky Path in
1782, has preserved the following list of important places along
the way. I am quoting only those that were within the territory of Scott County or near to it.
    From Washington Courthouse to Head Reedy Creek

	Miles
Sullivan County, N. C.	20
To Block House	13
To North Fork of Holston	2
To Moccasin Gap	5
To Clinch River (Speer's Ferry)	11
Ford Stock Creek (Clinchport)	2
To Little Flat Lick (New Schoolhouse Duffield)	5
To North Fork Clinch	1
To Powell's Mountain	1
To Wallen's Ridge	5

William Brown in his *Observations and Occurrences* speaks as follows of that section of the Wilderness Road comprised within the limits of Scott County:

"Set out from Hanover, Monday 27, May, 1782; arrived at the Blockhouse about the first week in July. The road from Hanover to this place is generally very good; crossing the Blue Ridge is not bad; there is not more than a small hill with some winding to go over. Neither is the Allegheny Mountain by any means difficult at this gap. There are one or two high hills about New River and Fort Chiswell. The ford of New River is rather bad; therefore we thought it advisable to cross in a ferryboat. This is generally a good-watered road as far as the Blockhouse. We waited hereabouts near two weeks for company, and then set out for the Wilderness with twelve men and ten guns, this being Thursday 18, July. The road from this until you get over Wallen's Ridge generally is bad, some part very much so, particularly about Stock Creek and Stock Creek Ridge. It is a very mountainous country here about, but there is some fine land in the bottoms, near the water courses, in narrow slips. It will be but a thin settled country whenever it is settled. The fords of Holston and Clinch are both good in dry weather, but in a rainy season you are often obliged to raft over. From them along down Powell's Valley until you get to Cumberland Gap is pretty good." (Hulbert's *Boone's Wilderness Road,* pp. 126–127.)

The following is the list of the stopping places along the Wilderness Road as given by Thomas Speed in 1790.

From Washington Co. House to Blockhouse 35
To Farriss's (Old Kane Residence, Gate City) 5
To Clinch River 12
To Scott's Station (Head of Wallen's Creek) 12

The Virginia Daughters of the American Revolution have shown a commendable patriotic spirit in placing markers at various points along the Boone trace. The first marker on the Path, in Scott County, was placed on the walls, beside the main entrance of the Courthouse, at Gate City. It is a trail marker, and all the trail markers bear the legend:

"Daniel Boone
Trail
From North Carolina
Through Virginia
To Kentucky."

The next trail marker was placed on the walls of the school building at Clinchport, and the next one, on a monument erected for the purpose by the citizens of Duffield.

The tablet prepared for Fort Blackmore has been placed on the wall of the bank building there. A suitable monument should be erected where the old fort stood, and the tablet placed on it. The Fort Blackmore tablet bears the following inscription:

This Tablet Marks the Site of
Fort Blackmore
Here Boone and His Party Rested
From October, 1773, to March, 1775.

After 1795, the danger of Indian attack in this section of Virginia as well as elsewhere along the Appalachian frontier, grew less and less from year to year. In consequence of which, other routes were opened up to emigrants. From Northern Virginia and Pennsylvania, they could float down the Ohio and its upper tributaries without being greatly exposed to Indian attack. And as the travel to Kentucky over other routes increased, the travel over the Kentucky Path decreased until it eventually became local in character, it being confined to that travel which took place between western Virginia, eastern Tennessee, and Kentucky.

DANIEL BOONE IN CLINCH RIVER VALLEY

After the death of his son, James, Daniel Boone reluctantly turned back to the settlement in Castlewood. He was induced to accompany Captains Russell and Gass to their homes there in the hope, no doubt, that they would rejoin him in another attempt to occupy Kentucky at some future time. He must have spent the winter of 1773–74 in hunting to supply his family with meat and to obtain furs and pelts with which to purchase other necessary supplies. All along the Virginia frontier, during the fall and winter of 1773–74, there were many indications of impending trouble with the Indians, and the disaster which Boone and his party had recently suffered was to be taken as unmistakable evidence of savage hostility. Lord Dunmore, Governor of Virginia, addressed a circular letter to the commandants of the frontier counties in which he stated that "hopes of a pacification can be no longer entertained," and ordered them to muster the militia and defend the country, and to use their discretion in "providing extraordinary means for an extraordinary occasion." Efforts were made to place the frontier in a posture of defense by erecting and garrisoning forts, and by keeping out vigilant spies along the trails and streams of the wilderness.

Within the summer of 1774, many surveying parties were in the wilds of Kentucky, for the safety of whom much solicitude was felt. Captain Russell was authorized to employ two experienced woodsmen to go to Kentucky and notify the surveyors of the danger of Indian attack.

Captain Russell read Lord Dunmore's circular letter on muster day in Castlewood. The people made a quick response to its recommendations by voting to build two forts on the Clinch, the work to begin at once. Before Daniel Boone and Michael Stoner, who were both present at this muster, had left the assembly, they had agreed to search the great wilderness of Kentucky for surveying parties and warn them of the danger in which they were daily. Boone and Stoner received their instructions on Saturday, June 25; they kept the Sabbath, June 26, and on Monday morning, June 27, they plunged into the great forest wilds that lay between the Valley of the Clinch and the Ohio River, relying for food and safety upon Divine Providence, their own sagacious woodcraft, and well-tried rifles.

On August 26, after an absence of sixty-one days, Boone and Stoner returned to the Clinch Valley, having warned the widely scattered surveying parties, having traveled eight hundred miles, and having passed through many difficulties and dangers in their various wanderings.

On his return from Kentucky, Boone found that Captain

Russell, with most of the able-bodied men on the Clinch, had just started on the Point Pleasant campaign against the Indians. Boone immediately sent a messenger to overtake Captain Russell, with news of his return and with the request that he be permitted to join the expedition. Boone had actually started to join the troops already on the march to the Great Levels of Greenbrier, the place of rendezvous, when he was ordered back to the Clinch Valley to aid in defending it against Indian attack. Like the good soldier and citizen that he always was wherever he happened to be, Boone gave up his cherished ambition to join the army and turned back to help guard the weak and scattered Clinch Valley settlements from being either broken up or exterminated altogether.

At this time the inhabitants of Fincastle County were gathered in small forts and dared not venture out to attend to their plantations. The enemy approached the settlements in small parties and with so much caution that they eluded the vigilance of the best scouts. Some idea of the difficulties which confronted Boone when he undertook the defense of Castlewood and Fort Blackmore may be had from a recital of the events which crowded themselves into the days of September and October, 1774. The Fincastle Regiment, consisting of about two hundred and seventy-five rank and file, all of whom were first-class riflemen, had marched towards the mouth of the Kanawha under such leaders as Colonel Christian and Captains William Russell, William Campbell, Evan Shelby, John Floyd, Walter Crockett, William Herbert, and James Harrod, the latter with a company of twenty-two men who had fled from Kentucky. Thus weakened by the absence of the men in the army, a weakness of which the enemy seemed to know, the Clinch frontier was greatly exposed to danger.

September, 1774, was a month of unusual activity, alarm, and danger in the Clinch Valley. The depredations committed were not on a large scale, but were, nevertheless, sufficient to keep the people in a state of constant apprehension and alarm. The scouts were kept busy trying to find the inroads of the enemy.

On September 8, Samuel Lammey was taken prisoner on the North Fork of Holston, and at the same time the families of John and Archibald Buchanan narrowly escaped. Early in the morning of the same day, a party of twelve or fifteen Indians fired upon John Henry while he was standing in his own door and dangerously wounded him.   He fled to the woods, leaving his wife and three children, who were yet in bed, to be captured by the Indians.   Henry met John Hambleton, who concealed him in a thicket until Fort Christian could be alarmed and assistance brought.   Henry did not long survive his wounds.

When news of Henry's death reached the Rich Valley settlement, most of the people fled to Major Campbell's at Royal Oak, on the Middle Fork of Holston.   Great fear was entertained at this time for the safety of Fort Christian, as there were only eight men for its defense.   A scarcity of ammunition was everywhere keenly felt.

On Tuesday, September 13, three Indians attacked one of Captain Smith's men about one-half mile from Maiden Spring Station.   The soldier returned the fire and brought one of the Indians to the ground.   The soldier escaped without injury. A party of whites, hearing the report of guns, hastened to the spot and gave chase to the surviving Indians.   Much blood was found where the Indian fell and a large cave nearby into which he had crawled or been thrown.   No doubt was entertained as to the Indian's death.   "The pit is to be searched," writes Major Campbell, "by means of ropes, with lights, as our men are anxious to get his scalp."   Whoever could truly boast that he "had killed an Indian and got his hair" was regarded as a man of superior prowess and worthy the praise of a grateful people.

On the same evening Captain Smith's scouts discovered tracks of the enemy, which seemed to show that they had prisoners and stolen horses.   A party of twenty-one men was immediately dispatched in pursuit, but were unable to overtake the Indians.

During these times of danger, Boone was not idle.   Capt. Daniel Smith makes the following significant record: "September 22, Lieutenant Boone, fourteen men, four days, three pounds of beef per day."   The entry notes one of many scouting expeditions which Boone headed from time to time.   When active service was needed, Boone was ever ready to render it. He was soon to try conclusions with one of the most intelligent

and influential red men of whom history bears any record.
Sagacious woodcraft was to be pitted against sagacious woodcraft. No less personage than Logan, the Mingo Chieftain,
came into the Clinch Valley in search of scalps and prisoners.
On Friday, September 23, Logan's party appeared before
Fort Blackmore, on the Clinch, seventeen miles below Fort
Byrd, or Moore's Station, where Boone commanded. Finding some of John Blackmore's negroes outside the Fort, they
captured two of them and Logan himself gave chase to a third
one, whose capture was prevented by the timely aid of Capt.
John Blackmore. The captured negroes, after being paraded
to and fro for a quarter of an hour in full view of the fort,
were taken away, together with a large number of horses and
cattle. A painted war club was left at Blackmore's by Logan
as a token of defiance. From Fort Blackmore, Logan went,
it seems, to the neighborhood of King's Mill, now Kingsport,
Tennessee, where he murdered the Roberts family, except one
boy, whom he took captive. Here he left the letter written
in gunpowder ink, quoted elsewhere in this history. He also
left another painted war club here. On September 29, Logan
and his forest bloodhounds made their way to Moore's Station, of which Boone was in immediate command.

Just after sunset, three men from the fort visited a pigeon
trap, about three hundred yards distant, yet in plain view.
They were shot at by the Indians and John Duncan, one of
the three, was killed and scalped, and a war club left beside
his mangled body. On hearing the shots, Boone and his men
ran from the fort, but the crafty Logan and his tribesmen
made good their escape.

"Mr. Boone also informs," writes Major Campbell, "that
the Indians have been frequent about Blackmore's since the
negroes were taken, and Captain Looney, having only eleven
men, cannot venture to go in pursuit of them. Mr. Boone
has sent me the war club that was left; it is different from
that left at Blackmore's and Boone thinks it is the Cherokees
who are annoying us now."

Whether the Cherokees really did assist Logan and his
desperate band is not certainly known. He seems to have
solicited their aid. New outrages speedily followed those
already narrated. Two attacks, made almost at the same time

on places forty miles apart, probably indicate that Logan divided his force, sending one part against Capt. Evan Shelby's Fort at Bristol, Tennessee, and the other part against Blackmore's Fort at the mouth of Stony Creek. Logan seems to have led the force against Shelby's Fort in person. "On last Thursday evening," writes Major Campbell, under date of October 9, 1774, "the Indians took prisoner a negro wench, belonging to Captain Shelby, within three hundred yards of his house. After they took her some distance, they examined her, asking how many guns were in the fort and other questions relative to the strength of the place. They also asked her if the store was kept there now. After they had carried her off about a mile, they saw or heard a boy coming from the mill; they immediately tied the wench and went off to catch the boy; while they were gone, the wench luckily got loose and made her escape. She says they knocked her down twice when she refused to tell in what situation the fort was; and she says one was a large man, much whiter than the rest, and talked good English; it was the same kind of person Mr. Blackmore saw in pursuit of the negro he relieved. Some think Capt. John Logan is about yet; others, that it is Will Emery, the half-breed Cherokee, as he was mentioned in Shoat's deposition as being out, and he is known for some time past to be in the Shawanoese interest; he was interpreter when Donelson ran the line, and it was he who robbed Knox and Scaggs."

The attack on Blackmore's Fort was hardly more successful than that on Shelby's. Silently creeping along under the bank of the river, completely hidden from view by the fringe of dense underbrush that skirted the top of the bank, the Indians expected to make a sudden rush upon the fort and get possession of its entrance before the garrison was aware of their presence. Their plan would have succeeded, no doubt, had it not been for the timely warning of Dale Carter. Observing the approach of the enemy, he shouted, "Murder, murder," which warning enabled the men of the fort, who were sitting on logs some distance away, to reach the door of the palisade before the Indians. The enemy was with difficulty driven away.

Shortly after this second attack upon Fort Blackmore,

Captains Boone and Smith, with a force of thirty men, went to Blackmore's, and on the following morning set out in search of the enemy. Plenty of Indian and horse tracks were found close to the fort, but they were soon lost, and Boone and his party were never able to come up with the crafty enemy.

Captain Looney, the commandant of Fort Blackmore, was absent at his home near Kingsport at the time of Dale Carter's murder. This circumstance caused dissatisfaction with Looney. The settlers at Blackmore's wanted a military leader who lived closer by. Boone's services had been so acceptable to them that they petitioned Col. William Preston, the highest military officer in Fincastle County, that Boone be made captain, and that command of their fort be committed to him. This petition seems to have had its origin at Fort Blackmore. Furthermore, it seems to have been unanimously approved by the settlers in Castlewood, who were Mr. Boone's neighbors and the people best qualified to judge of his merits as an Indian fighter. The petition asked that he take charge of the lower forts on the Clinch, which were Blackmore's, Moore's Station, and Cowan's Fort. Colonel Preston, who had been furnished by Governor Dunmore with blank commissions for the purpose, at once acted favorably upon the petition by bestowing the title of captain, the highest military honor that had yet come to Boone.

Alarm after alarm followed each other in rapid succession, and there was no cessation of vigilance on the part of Boone and his scouts. Early in October, the Battle of Point Pleasant was fought, in which the men of the frontier gained a signal victory over their enemies, and the peace that followed brought much needed relief to the pent up settlers on the Clinch. The treaty which closed Dunmore's War provided that the Indians return all prisoners, horses, and other plunder taken from the whites; that they relinquish all lands and hunt no more south of the Ohio; that they molest no passengers on that river, but render them every assistance and protection possible; that they be governed, in their trade, by such regulations as should be dictated to them, and never more take up the hatchet against the English.

As a pledge for the fulfillment of the terms of this treaty, they gave six hostages, two of whom were to be chiefs, and the others to be either chiefs or their sons. The treaty was to be formally ratified at Pittsburgh the following spring, where all the Ohio Indians were to be present.

On November 20, 1774, the men under Boone's immediate command were discharged from service. With the close of the Point Pleasant campaign, Boone dropped back into the semi-civil, semi-military life peculiar to a border infested by savages. In the spring of 1775, he left the Valley of the Clinch for Kentucky, the land of his fondly cherished dreams, where for many years he took active part in the struggle for mastery then being waged between the white and red men.

One hundred and fifty years have elapsed since Boone dwelt on the Clinch, yet his name is still a household word there.

THE BLOCKHOUSE ON THE HOLSTON

"The Blockhouse on the Holston" was one of the most widely known places on the Wilderness Road. It stood in Carter's Valley on the outer edge of the Holston Settlements, about four miles southeast of Moccasin Gap. It seems to have been the only blockhouse within the limits of the county. The other forts in this immediate section, in so far as available data has revealed their character, seem to have consisted of log cabins and stockades.

The Blockhouse was built by John Anderson sometime prior to 1782. It had two rooms; that is to say, it had a lower and upper story. The walls of the upper story had the usual portholes and other openings peculiar to such buildings. During the period of greatest travel over the Wilderness Road, John Anderson, as proprietor of the Blockhouse, was host to hundreds of travelers on their way to Kentucky and elsewhere.

When danger of Indian attack had passed, John Anderson built nearby a larger two-story building with a "log kitchen," into which the family moved, and the famous old Blockhouse was converted into a "loom house." It was continued in this use until 1876, when it, together with the newer Anderson residence, was consumed by fire.

Dr. William A. Pusey, of Chicago, Illinois, author of *The Wilderness Road to Kentucky,* had a monument erected on, or near the site of the old Blockhouse. The inscription on this monument is as follows:

THIS TABLET MARKS THE SITE
OF
THE BLOCKHOUSE

The meeting point of the pioneer roads to Kentucky from Virginia and North Carolina, and the gathering place of pioneer travelers at the entrance to the Wilderness.

Erected by a descendant of William Brown, who recorded

MONUMENT MARKING SITE OF BLOCK HOUSE ERECTED BY
DR. WM. A. PUSEY OF CHICAGO

that, "We waited hereabouts near two weeks and then set out for the Wilderness, with 12 men and 10 guns, this being Thursday, 18th July." (1782)

In 1921, O. M. Smith and Geneva E., his wife, the present owners of the Blockhouse Farm, deeded to R. M. Addington, County Clerk, and his successors in office, seventy-five square feet of land to be held as a site for the Blockhouse Monument. The monument is built of Gate City marble, hewn out and put in place by Warwick D. Morison, Sr. (colored).

BIG MOCCASIN GAP IN HISTORY

It has been said that history has two eyes; with one it looks to see when an event happened; with the other it looks to see where the event happened. Certain it is that the history of any country is greatly influenced by its topography, and the history of Scott County is no exception to this generalization. The county's long, narrow, trough-like valleys, its ridges and mountain, its rivers and creeks, its gaps and fords have, each and all, in a very material way, influenced the historical happenings within its borders. But among the many beneficent things which kind nature has done for the county, no one act of hers has surpassed the cutting of Big Moccasin Gap through Clinch Mountain. By this gap, the two great valleys of the Clinch and the Holston Rivers are joined together as closely as the Siamese twins. In the very early days, the gap was an open gateway to Kentucky, and the near West. Even the Indians recognized the strategic importance of this rift in the mountain from a military point of view. The narrow pass, closely shut in by densely forested mountains, furnished an ideal place for attack by hidden enemies. Hence the pioneer traveler approached it with dread. Military companies expected attack while marching through its defiles. Under date of July 9, 1774, Col. Wm. Christian writes to Col. Wm. Preston, as follows: "Capt. Campbell marched on the lower settlement in Holston near the Island (Long Island of Kingsport, Tenn.) with odds of 40 men and will meet me tomorrow on Clinch (Castlewood, Va.), he goes through Moccasin Gap. I cross over by the head of

Moccison, the two (Gaps) may be 30 miles apart." (Thwaites and Kellogg's *Dunmore's War*, p. 76).

At the close of the Point Pleasant campaign, Col. Arthur Campbell ordered all of the militia on this section of the frontier discharged, except fifteen men at Fort Blackmore, and fifteen at Moccasin Gap.

In October, 1774, Lieut. John Cox was sent to range about Reedy Creek and Moccasin Gap until the flour which had been sent to King's Mill should arrive there. He then was to escort the pack-horse train loaded with flour through Moccasin Gap to Fort Blackmore (Thwaites and Kellogg's *Dunmore's War*, p. 229). Colonel Campbell further adds that he is "of late much put to it to get provisions carried out to Blackmores." (*Dunmore's War*, pp. 278–80.) Men were unwilling to conduct pack-horse trains through Moccasin Gap without military escort. Colonel Campbell, recognizing the strategic importance of this gap in defending the Holston Settlements against the Northern Indians, suggests that "a strong party be stationed within a mile or two of Moccasin Gap at which place and Blackmore's seems to be the most convenient to oppose the enemy especially a large party." (Draper Manuscripts.)

Benge, the half-breed Indian, made many predatory incursions into the neighborhood of Moccasin Gap. On August 26, 1791, he, with a small party of Indians, attacked the house of Elisha Ferris, about two miles from the Gap. Ferris lived where the old Kane dwelling now stands in the edge of Gate City, Va. Elisha Ferris was killed outright. His wife, daughter, Mrs. Livingston, Nancy Ferris, and a young child were carried into captivity. All but Nancy Ferris were cruelly murdered the first day of their captivity. An interval of almost two years then elapsed before Benge again made his appearance in the neighborhood of Moccasin Gap. This time he murdered Harper Ratcliff and his entire family, six in number.

On July 17, 1793, Benge made his third visit to the Holston Settlements near Moccasin Gap. This time he, with two companions, traversed the settlements, a distance of twenty miles or more, in order, it was thought, to spy out the location of negro property. While on this expedition, he fired upon a man named Williams and captured a negro wench, the property of Paul Livingston. Fortunately, the shot missed Williams, and the negress succeeded in making her escape after two days of captivity.

It is very probable that Benge approached the Holston Settlements by way of Moccasin Gap at the time he attacked the home of the Livingston's and that, fearing to return by the same route he had come, he crossed Clinch Mountain at what is now called the Hamilton Gap, near the present village of Hiltons, then the home of the Fulkersons.

In 1791, on the Russell County side of Moccasin Gap, Mrs. McDowell and Frances Pendleton were killed and scalped. (Ramsey's *History of Tennessee*, p. 557.)

At this gap was held the county's first court. Near it was located the county seat. Through it, in the spring of 1775, Daniel Boone and his companions carved the Wilderness Road to Kentucky. Through it, thousands of pioneer settlers sought homes in Kentucky and the great middle West. Through it most of the goods used in that part of Scott County lying north of Clinch Mountain, were hauled prior to the construction of the railway. Through it, the first railway to enter the county was built in 1886–7. Toward it, most of the leading highways of the county now converge. It is now the junction point of the Appalachia and Holston Valley divisions of the Southern Railway. A depot and store are located there. Just across the creek from the depot, on a small hillock, stands the monument erected by former Scott Countians to mark the site of the Benjamin T. Hollins house in which the first county court was held.

John Livingston was first owner of the land in Big Moccasin Gap. He assigned his holding to William Livingston. His grant consisted of 400 acres extending above and below the mouth of Little Moccasin Creek. The time of actual settlement was in 1774. In the same year Samuel Livingston settled at the head of Little Moccasin Creek.

If a watchman could have stood at Big Moccasin Gap through the years he would have seen, passing before him: the panther, the bear, and the buffalo; the Indian on hunting or warlike expeditions; then small groups of fur traders and long hunters, the vanguards of civilization, pushing their ways deep into the wilderness; then Daniel Boone and a few families on the way to settle Kentucky; later Boone and his road-makers cutting a path for the Henderson colonists, followed soon by the colonists themselves with four wagons, the first wagons to pass through the gap; then thousands of pioneers with their pack-horse trains on their way to the valley of the Ohio.

SLAVE QUARTERS (KANE ESTATE)

BIG MOCCASIN GAP

FORT BLACKMORE

Two traditional stories concerning the early settlements in Scott County have come down to us, the one transmitted through the Cox family, very early settlers here, and the other transmitted through the Porter and related families, who settled on Fall Creek, near Osborn's Ford.

The Cox tradition is substantially as follows: A young man by the name of David Cox is represented as having accompanied Daniel Boone on one of his hunting expeditions as far as the locality now known as Elizabethton, Tennessee. Here young Cox separated from Boone's party, and turning his course northward, passed through Big Moccasin Gap into what is now Scott County. In the course of his wanderings he came to the Clinch at the mouth of Stony Creek. Here on the south bank of the river were evidences of an early Indian village. The Indians selected this location, no doubt, because it possessed so many advantages. It was surrounded by dense forests that abounded in all the wild game ever known in this section. The Clinch River, a considerable stream at this point, was full of edible varieties of fish. The great fertility of the soil, the richness and variety of the furs, the superabundance of deer, bears, turkeys, and other wild game influenced young Cox to stay and hunt and trap for a while. He was not permitted, however, to enjoy this sport very long. The Indians came upon him, captured, and carried him away. He was held in captivity for a period of from two to four years. Upon his escape and return to his home in North Carolina he brought such glowing accounts of the Valley of the Clinch that a few families were induced to accompany him to that valley for the purpose of making a settlement at the mouth of Stony Creek. So in 1774, the Blackmores and two other families left the Yadkin River, on which they had lived, and settled on the Clinch at the mouth of Stony Creek. (Judge M. B. Wood in Draper Manuscripts, 4 C 27.)

The story of the Porter family is substantially as follows:

43

The first settlement in the county was made by Patrick Porter, Capt. John Montgomery, Porter's son-in-law, Raleigh Stallard, —— Hutchenson, and Samuel, Patrick Porter's oldest son. They settled on Clinch River "in the fall after Colonel Lewis fought the five tribes on the Ohio river." They came from Snoddy's Fort in Castlewood. Patrick Porter built a fort on what is now the Reuben Banner farm. The Porter tradition further states that the Blackmores came to this section from Fauquier County, Virginia. (Thomas W. Carter's Letters in the Draper Manuscripts.)

James Green settled in the neighborhood of Fort Blackmore in the year 1772. Capt. John Blackmore, Joseph Blackmore, John Blackmore, Jr., John Carter, and Andrew Davis settled at Fort Blackmore in the year 1773. These settlements were proven in court, and certified according to an Act of the General Assembly of Virginia, passed in 1779. The following is a copy of the certificate which the commissioners made to Capt. John Blackmore. Similar certificates were issued to the others mentioned above.

"We, the Commissioners for the District of Washington and Montgomery counties, do certify that John Blackmore is entitled to four hundred acres of land lying in Washington County at the mouth of Stony Creek on the north side of Clinch, being part of 518 acres of land surveyed for the said John the 25th of March, 1774, by virtue of an order of Council, dated the 16th of December, 1773, he having proved to the Court he was entitled to the same by actual settlement made in the year 1773. As witness our hands this 20th day of August, 1781.

JAS. CABELL,
HARRY INNESS,
N. CABELL,
Commissioners.

Test: JAMES REID, C. C. C."

Capt. William Russell, of Castle's Woods, in a letter to Col. William Preston, bearing date of July 13, 1774, states that only four families had collected in Fort Blackmore at that time. Three of these families, no doubt, were those of John Blackmore, Senior and Junior, and Joseph Blackmore. The name of the fourth family has not been ascertained, but there is a probability that it was that of James Green. The Blackmores owned most of the land adjacent to the fort. Captain John's farm, comprising 518 acres, was situated at the mouth of Stony Creek. It extended some distance up the creek in such way as to include the most desirable, level land. The lines widened as they approached the river and thus were made to include the delta at the mouth of the creek. They extended down the river to a point almost opposite the mouth of the Rocky Branch. The boundaries as shown in the records of the County Clerk's office of Montgomery County, Virginia, Plat Book "A," page 75, are as follows:

"Surveyed for John Blackmore 510 acres of land lying in Fincastle County on the North side of Clinch River on both sides of Stony Creek (agreeable to an order of Council of the 16 December, 1773) and part of the Loyal Company Grant and bounded as follows: Beginning at a lynn on the North side of the River, thence N. 40 W. 19 poles to a dogwood and white oak on the hillside N. 39 E. 77 to a hickory N. 47 E. 72 to a hickory N. 69 E. 75 to two hickories N. 32 E. 85 to a beech N. 61 W. 76 to a white oak N. 42 W. 115 to a sorrel tree on a flat N. 44 E. 50 to a hickory N. 5 W. 59 to a beech N. 39 W. 119 to a small maple N. 11 W. at 114 crossing Stony Creek in all 145 to a beech N. 57 W. 103 to a white oak N. 17 W. 54 to a dogwood N. 57 W. 113 to a white oak N. 53 E. at 59 a branch in all 71 to a white oak S. 57 E. 76 to a forked white oak S. 35 E. 130 to a white walnut by a branch S. 22 E. 62 to a white oak S. 43 E. 81 to two dogwoods S. 14 E. 151, crossing Stony Creek to a sweet gum on the bank thereof down the creek according to its meanders E. 24 poles in a direct line to a beech on "ye" East bank thereof, N. 72 E. 32 to a white oak S. 56 E. 10 poles to sorrel saplins on the river bank down the same according to its meanders to the beginning.

"25 March, 1774

DANIEL SMITH, Ast.
WM. PRESTON, S. F. C."

Young John Blackmore's land, a tract of 200 acres, was located south of the river, "between the river hills and Copper Creek Ridge." It later became a part of the Brickey farm and is now owned by Preston Brickey. "The old In-

dian Town Field" is a part of this land. Some very interesting Indian relics have been found on this land. The most
beautiful and interesting of these relics are two Indian pipes
now owned by Dr. John P. McConnell. Joseph Blackmore's
farm was situated on the north bank of the river, in the bend
thereof, below the fort. It probably joined Captain John's
estate on the east. In giving its boundaries, mention is made
of the fact that one of its corners was a "cluster of lynns on
the north bank of the river, a little below the mouth of the
Gut." Almost opposite to the old fort the river at low water
is divided into two channels. The southern channel is called
the "Gut" to this day. Reference to the "Gut" enables the
land of Joseph Blackmore to be definitely located. Thus, the
fort took its name from Capt. John Blackmore, its most
prominent citizen, and upon whose land it was located. In
fact, there is reason for thinking that it was his residence
until he emigrated to Nashboro, Tennessee, in 1779.

Fort Blackmore was located on an ancient flood plain on
the north bank of Clinch River, just opposite the mouth of
Rocky Branch, a southern tributary of the river. The exact
location is a rather more elevated portion of this plain, about
seventy-five paces from the river's edge at low water. From
the highest point the slope is by gentle undulation both
toward the river and toward the low range of hills north of
the fort. South of the fort, in the bank of the river and almost buried in its sands, is the spring, much changed, no
doubt, by the erosion of the floods of one hundred and forty-
four years. The door of the fort opened toward the spring,
thus affording a pleasant southern exposure. On the south
bank, across the river from the fort, two limestone cliffs arise
to great height almost from the water's edge. They are separated by the narrow channel of Rocky Branch. They were
used more than once by the Indians in their efforts to spy upon
the movements of the settlers. It was from the top of one
of them that Matthew Gray's unerring rifle sent the gobbling
Indian crashing down through the tree tops into the river
below.

On the north a series of hummocky river hills sloped down
to the rear of the fort. An extension of one of these hills
cuts the narrow flood plain almost to the bank of the river,

a short distance to the east of the fort. On the point of this extension, the burial ground of the old fort is located. Here the final resting places of the pioneers—some of whom were murdered by the Indians—are marked by a few rough, uncarved stones. Instead of a marble monument, suitably inscribed to these brave pioneers, there is now growing a giant elm, whose roots hold a large part of the burial ground within their embrace, and whose wide-spreading branches seem to be trying to bring their sacred dust within its friendly shade.

Unfortunately, no one has left us a complete description of the old fort itself. Although diligent search has been made for data on the subject, only brief, incidental references to it have been found here and there. All these references put together lead to the conclusion that in size, shape, and structure, Fort Blackmore conformed in all essential points very closely to the usual type of frontier fort. Capt. William Russell, in a letter to Colonel Preston, speaks of it as "the small fortification they have erected." It was built rectangular in shape, and consisted of cabins, stockades, and bastions. One or more sides of the fort were formed by rows of cabins, each separated from the other by log partitions. The cabin walls on the outside were ten or twelve feet high, the slope of the roofs being turned wholly to the inside. The clapboards of the roof were held in place by weights of wood or rock. The cabins sometimes had puncheon, but more often, dirt floors. Fort Blackmore had bastions built into its corners, instead of blockhouses, as was more often the case.

The fort was closed by a large folding gate, made of thick slabs and hung on the side nearest the spring. The gate was securely fastened at night or in time of danger by a strong bar or an ingeniously contrived wooden lock. Where there were no cabin walls, the space was filled with palisades of logs, deeply set into the ground and sharpened at the top. The palisades were held in place by strong horizontal stringers, fastened with wooden pegs near the top. The stockade, bastions, and cabin walls were furnished with portholes at proper heights and distances. The whole of the outside was made completely bullet-proof. The entire fort was built, no doubt, without the aid of a single nail or spike of iron. Even the roofs were held in place by weights.

A small stock pen, a kind of lean-to, of which the walls of the fort formed one side, was located on the north. Horses and cattle were kept within this enclosure at night, and from it horses were often stolen by the Indians, as many as six being taken in one night.

Captain Blackmore, in the selection of a site for the fort, was influenced, no doubt, by the proximity to water and the protection against the Indians which the river afforded.

The fort seems to have been located on the lands of Capt. John Blackmore. A part of it, however, may have been located on the farm now owned by Mr. James M. Cox.

No vestige of the old fort now remains, unless, perhaps, it be a few loose stones scattered about on the ground here and there—parts of the old chimneys and foundation stones. Mr. James M. Cox, who has lived many years within a very short distance, tells the author that ashes and bits of charcoal were often turned into view by the plowman as he cultivated the site.

For many years after the first settlement, the population of the fort was very transient in character. Hunters, explorers, adventurers, and homeseekers came and went, stopping at the fort only long enough to rest and refresh themselves. And when they had accomplished this purpose, they were then ready to pass on to other sections.

Life in the little fort was subject to much privation and suffering. Being for many years on the extreme frontier of Virginia, it was so exposed to Indian attack that often the few settlers within its walls dared not to venture forth to cultivate their small crops in the "clearings," unless accompanied by a strong guard. When a guard could not be had, they were compelled to remain much of the time within the stockade. In this way they were often reduced to narrow straits for food, for during the times of threatened famine most of the food, especially the much-needed flour, had to be transported on pack horses, under military escort, through Moccasin Gap from the older and less exposed settlements on the Holston. Maj. Arthur Campbell, in a letter to Colonel Preston, writes, "I have sent Michael Dougherty, with his party of seven men, to Reedy Creek to assist as guards in carrying out flour to Clinch." (Thwaites and Kellogg's

Dunmore's War, p. 251.) In another letter of the same date he says, "I have directed seven men from Capt. Crocket's company as low as King's Mill (near Kingsport), where Lieutenant Christian is stationed; which place I am obliged to make use of as a store house, from whence the flour is packed to Blackmore's, by way of Mockison Gap." (Thwaites and Kellogg's *Dunmore's War*, pp. 251–252.)

It was the habit of the early settlers on the Clinch to live on their farms and make improvements in the winter, and then on the approach of warm weather, when the Indians could go on the warpath, repair to the forts for safety during the summer. The old settlers dreaded the approach of warm weather, for it increased the danger of Indian foray. Sometimes, in the late autumn, several days of warm weather would occur, during which the Indians could take up again their tomahawks and go upon a short campaign for booty and scalps. These warm, smoky periods, being associated with the fear of Indian attack, led to their being called "Indian summer."

Early in the year 1774, the northwestern Indians began to show signs of hostility toward the whites. The tribesmen were alarmed at the attempts of the whites to settle the West, especially Kentucky, and thus encroach upon their hunting grounds. The territory within the present limits of Scott County seems never to have been the home of any considerable number of Indians. Like that of Kentucky, it was a kind of No Man's Land, possessed by no tribe of Indians, but hunted over and fought over by all. All these tribes were disposed to look upon the whites as intruders, a common enemy, whose extermination should be brought about by all the tribesmen. "The chief offense of the whites was that they trespassed upon uninhabited lands, which they forthwith proceeded to cultivate, instead of merely hunting over them." (Roosevelt's *Winning of the West, II,* p. 251.) The Indians sometimes had just cause of provocation against the whites, for the whites, incited by the many wrongs they had suffered, often killed their red enemies and occasionally even their red friends. An instance of the latter kind seems to have occurred at Yellow Creek on the Ohio, April 20, 1774. The consequences of this event were destined greatly to affect the lives and fortunes of the people then living on the frontier of Virginia, and more especially of those living at Fort Blackmore.

Upon the date last mentioned above, a party of Indians, consisting in part, at least, of very near relatives of an Indian chief commonly called Capt. John Logan, left Logan's camp and crossed the Ohio River to visit one Simon Greathouse, who made a business of selling rum to the savages. The whole party drank liquor until they became helplessly drunk, in which condition Greathouse and his companions killed the intoxicated Indians, nine persons in all. Upon hearing of the murder of his sister and other relatives, Chief Logan, who declared he had two souls, the one good, the other bad, now, in his desire to avenge the death of his kinsman, came under the dominion of his bad soul. Gathering a small band of warriors about him, he fell with terrible rage upon the unsuspecting settlers along the Clinch and Holston, killing and scalping as many as thirteen persons, six of whom were children. Of this levy of death, which Logan's vengeance laid upon the thin line of frontier settlements in Southwest Virginia at this time, old Fort Blackmore contributed its part, as we shall see later. Thus, by his conduct, the whole frontier of Western Virginia was thrown into a panic of fear. Capt. William Russell, of Castlewood, in a letter to Col. William Preston, dated May 7, 1774, states, "Upon my return from Williamsburg, finding the upper settlers on Clinch River had totally evacuated their plantations, I thought it my duty, agreeable to your instructions, to employ four men as runners in the service of the country, in hopes thereby to prevail on the remainder of the inhabitants to desist from so ruinous an undertaking. Accordingly, despatched them, giving them such instructions as I thought would most likely direct them to intercept the march of any parties of Indians that might be coming to annoy the inhabitants of either Holston or Clinch Rivers." (Thwaites and Kellogg's *Dunmore's War*, p. 20.) Furthermore, to the danger of attack upon Fort Blackmore and other forts on the Clinch and Holston by the Shawnees and Mingoes from the North was to be added the danger of Cherokee invasion from the South. Soon after the murder of James Boone and Henry Russell in Powell's Valley by a

Shawnee war party, Isaac Crabtree, who had been a member
of young Boone's and Russell's party, and who was the only
white survivor of it, attended a horse race on the Watauga
River. (Thwaites and Kellogg's *Dunmore's War*, p. 38.)
Three Indians, two men and a squaw, were in attendance
upon the race. Crabtree, without any provocation, attacked
the Indians, killing one of the men, called Cherokee Billy, a
relative of Chief Oconostota, and was with difficulty restrained
from murdering the other two. The behavior of the squaw
and the Indian fellow was such that a reprisal upon the
whites was expected at once, provided steps were not taken
to prevent it.

Crabtree's ruthless act, however, sent at least a part of the
Cherokee nation on the warpath to avenge the death of their
tribesman. With savage foes on almost every side, Fort
Blackmore seemed in imminent danger of being crushed.
During these days of apprehension and peril, Captain Campbell was sent to range down Clinch River a distance of twenty
miles, thus affording some protection to Fort Blackmore.
Although situated on Virginia's extreme western frontier, remote from strong forts and thickly settled communities, this
little band of stout-hearted settlers resolved to stand their
ground and defend their fort against all savage foes what-
soever. Capt. William Russell, in a letter dated July 13,
1774, thus expresses his solicitude for the safety of this devoted little band: "There are four families at John Blackmore's, near the mouth of Stony Creek, who will never be
able to stand it, without a command of men; therefore request you, if you think it can be done, to order them a supply
sufficient to enable them to continue the small fortification
they have erected." On July 12, just the day before the above
letter was written, Col. William Christian suggested that a
garrison of thirty men be ordered for the defense of "Blackmore's, back of Moccison Gap." Apprehensions for the
safety of the fort were still further increased by the scarcity
of flour and ammunition. At one time, Captain Russell wrote
that "one half the people could not raise five charges of
powder"; and at another, Col. Arthur Campbell wrote,
"Flour is badly wanted at Blackmore's." In fact, during the
summer and fall of the year 1774 the Indians were so fre-

quently seen about the fort and danger of attack seemed
so imminent that the little garrison may be regarded as having been almost in a state of siege during this time. The
men were kept so closely "forted in" that even the usual supply of wild meats, obtained by hunting, was very nearly
cut off.

It appears that the small garrison at Fort Blackmore was
first placed under command of Capt. James Thompson.
Captain Thompson, with his command, left the Clinch for
the Point Pleasant Campaign, on September 21. Capt. James
Looney was then left in immediate command of the fort, it
seems, during the remaining days of September. However,
Colonel Campbell, in a letter bearing date of October 6, gives
a list of the forts on the Clinch, in which he names Fort
Blackmore as then having a garrison of sixteen men, with
Sergeant Moore commanding. Daniel Boone was placed in
general command of the three lower forts on the Clinch, of
which number Fort Blackmore was one, during the absence
of the Fincastle men on the Point Pleasant Campaign.

In July, 1774, Capt. John Logan, the well-known Mingo
chieftain, captured a man named William Robinson on the
West Fork of the Monongahela River. He was taken to the
Indian towns and there he was condemned to die by torture
at the stake. Logan eloquently pleaded that the life of his
captive might be spared, but his savage associates were deaf
to his pleading. Logan, then, with his tomahawk, boldly cut
the cords which bound the captive and, in this way, rescued
him from death. Three days later Logan, furnishing Robinson with a piece of paper, and some gunpowder ink, ordered
him to write the following message to be left at some settler's
house upon whom his vengeance might fall:

"To Captain Cresap—What did you kill my people on
Yellow Creek for? The white people killed my kin at
Coneestoga a great while ago, & I thought nothing of that But
you killed my kin again on Yellow Creek and took my cousin
prisoner then I thought I must kill too; and I have been three
times to war since but the Indians is not Angry only myself.
    July 21st day (1774)
                                        Captain John Logan."

INDIAN MOUND, FORT BLACKMORE

SITE OF FORT BLACKMORE IN CANE FIELD JUST BEYOND MAN

Robinson had difficulty in making the statements of this letter strong enough to suit Logan's burning desire for revenge. It was written three times before its phraseology was emphatic enough to be accepted by the angry chieftain. Taking this letter along, he and a band of Mingoes and Shawnees departed from New-Comer's-Town, on the Muskingum River, for the frontier settlements on the Clinch and Holston. On his way hither, however, he seems to have turned aside in order to visit the Cherokees, and, if possible, to induce them to go on the warpath with him. But Oconastota and the Little Carpenter, two influential chiefs of the Cherokee tribe, strongly opposed a war with the whites at that time. They tried to restrain their blood-thirsty young warriors from becoming members of Logan's band. It is probable, however, that a few of the more hot-headed young Cherokee braves may have secretly joined the expedition, despite the advice of their chiefs. Disappointed, no doubt, at the refusal of the Cherokee chiefs to assist him in wreaking his revenge upon his white foes, Logan and his forest bloodhounds turned their footsteps toward the Clinch, and arrived at Fort Blackmore, on Friday, September 23. Stealthily approaching the fort, they found some of Capt. John Blackmore's negroes on the outside, two of whom they managed to capture, and Logan himself was in close pursuit of a third one when the timely aid of John Blackmore prevented the negro's capture. The Indians then forced one of their negro captives to march back and forth, in full view of the fort, "near a quarter of an hour." No doubt, relying upon a superior number, they hoped to provoke the defenders of the fort until they would sally forth to rescue the slaves, and thus expose themselves to an ambuscade. But Captain Looney, who was then in command of the fort, had only eleven men, "and some of them indifferent." Rescue of the negroes and pursuit of the taunting savages, therefore, was fraught with too much danger to be attempted by such a small force. Before taking their departure from the neighborhood, however, Logan and his dusky warriors wantonly shot down a large number of horses and cattle, thus inflicting a very heavy property loss upon Captain Blackmore and his neighbors. An Indian war club was left behind, as a threat and a challenge. With baffled rage, Logan and his blood-thirsty band, it would seem, hastened away from Fort Blackmore, through Moccasin Gap, to the neighborhood of King's Mill, on Reedy Creek, near the present site of Kingsport. Here they attacked the home of John Roberts. Roberts, his wife, and children were all brutally killed and scalped, except the eldest child, James, a boy of ten years of age, who was carried into captivity. This bloody event occurred Saturday, September 24, the day following the attack upon Fort Blackmore. Desiring that the whites should know that he had murdered the Roberts family in revenge for the murder of his own kinsmen, Logan left at the Roberts home the letter written in gunpowder ink, which he had dictated to Robinson. This letter, no doubt, and not the war club, would have been left at Fort Blackmore had Logan been able to satiate his thirst for blood there by shooting down its people instead of horses and cattle.

Logan's connection with the events just described is shown by Col. William Christian's letter to Col. William Preston, bearing date of Nov. 8, 1774. In it he says: "Last Friday was two weeks (Oct. 21) Logan a famous chief went home with a little boy, a son of Roberts on Holston & two of Blackmores negroes. He said he had taken them on the Frontiers next the Cherokee Country & had killed I think either 5 or 7 people. The boy and negroes will be soon in." (Thwaites and Kellogg's *Dunmore's War*, p. 305.)

Captain Russell, writing on the same subject from Point Pleasant, to Colonel Preston, says, "When I took water at Hochocking to come down, two white men and a captive negro of Blackmores, with a horse for each man, set out to come down by land. They might have been here two Days past; but at present there is not the least Acct. of them, I much fear the Indians have killed them, or as the Governor has a parcel of prisoner taken at Hill Town, of the Mingoes; I fear they will try to get as many of our people, to redeem theirs reather than give Hostages, especially if they intend to be troublesome hereafter." (Thwaites and Kellogg's, *Dunmore's War*, p. 309.)

On September 29, five days after the murder of the Roberts family, Logan, who had not yet "fully glutted his vengeance," completed his bloody triangle by secretly lying in wait for whomsoever might venture outside the walls of Moore's Fort which Boone commanded. Between sunset and dark, three men, who went to visit a pigeon trap about three hundred yards distant from the fort, were fired upon by Logan's warriors. John Duncan was shot dead, but the other two men reached the fort unhurt. On hearing the report of the gun, Daniel Boone and a party of men ran at once to the place where Duncan lay. But before they could reach the spot the Indians had scalped Duncan, and leaving a war club beside his mangled body, had run off into the woods. Night prevented Boone and his men from following the enemy then. Early the next morning, however, Boone prepared to go immediately in search of them but was unable to find them.

T. W. Carter's mother, who was Patrick Porter's youngest daughter, Catherine, may have been an inmate of Moore's Fort at the time Duncan was murdered. She often told her children the story of finding Indian war clubs at the spring near the fort. The story is substantially as follows: Catherine, upon going to the spring for water, found a number of Indian war clubs all beautifully painted and with a letter lying on top of them. Setting down her water vessel, she gathered the war clubs into her apron, and with the letter in her hand, she ran for the fort at the same time calling as loud as she could. Frightened by her noise, the men ran from the fort to meet her, her father and brother, Samuel, leading the way. On examining the contents of her apron her father remarked: "Well, Kate, you have had a powerful fight with the Indians and took their war clubs from them." One of the war clubs, supposed to be the property of the Mingo Chieftain Logan, was kept many years by Mrs. Carter. T. W. Carter, her son, says he has seen both the letter and the club. (T. W. Carter's Letters in Draper Manuscripts.)

News of the attacks upon Fort Blackmore, the Roberts family, and Moore's Fort, spread rapidly and widely. The settlers were alarmed. Many of the more exposed fled from their homes to less exposed settlements for safety. Col. Arthur Campbell, in writing of the attack on Blackmore's to Colonel Preston, says, "It was very unfortunate that Capt. Thompson had left Blackmores only two days before the damage was done as he had his full complement of men:

When the enemy came there was only 12, and some of them indifferent." (Thwaites and Kellogg's *Dunmore's War*.) Four days later, Colonel Campbell again writes, "It is certain We want Men badly as it is now impossible to get a man to leave this River (Holston) to go to Clinch as they look upon themselves in equal danger. Blackmores and the Head of Clinch is extremely thin, so that it is out of Capt. Looneys or Capt. Smiths power to pursue the Enemy if there was but a dozen of them. The Middle Stations on Clinch (Castle's Woods) is pretty strong of the Inhabitants and of late they are so close Garrisoned that they are afraid to mind their crops; And now employ themselves in small ranging parties. Mr. Boone is very diligent at Castles Woods and keeps up in good Orders. I have reason to believe they have lately been remiss at Blackmores, and the Spys there did not do their duty." In a postscript to this letter he adds, "I luckily procured one pound & half of Powder before the militia went out, which I divided to such as had none, 8 loads apiece, which they went very cheerfully out on. If you could possibly spare me one or two pounds I would divide it in the same sparing manner, in case of another alarm. Please hurry ye Flour out as there is great need of it." (Thwaites and Kellogg's *Dunmore's War*, pp. 217–219.) In a letter to Colonel Preston, dated October 1, Colonel Campbell says, "Mr. Boone informs me that the Indians has been frequently about Blackmores, since the negroes was taken; and Capt. Looney has so few men that he can not venture to go on pursuit of them, having only eleven Men. Mr. Boone has sent me the War Club that was left (at Moore's Fort) it is different from that left at Blackmores; Mr. Boone thinks it is the Cherokees that is now annoying us." (Thwaites and Kellogg's *Dunmore's War*, p. 220.)

On Oct. 5, 1774, Lieut. John Cox, with twenty-four men, was sent to range down Reedy Creek, and about Moccasin Gap, until the wagons loaded with flour for Fort Blackmore should arrive there. He was ordered then to escort the packhorse trains which were to carry the flour across to Fort Blackmore.

About the same time, Samuel Shannon came up "with 21 head of cattle several of them very indifferent." These cattle were being taken to the forts on the Clinch. Shannon refused to go through Moccasin Gap without a guard; so Lieutenant Cox furnished safe conduct, it seems, for both flour and cattle to their destination on the Clinch.

After the murder of John Duncan in Castlewood, Logan's movements during the next five or six days can not be definitely traced. He must have remained on the border during these days, searching for further opportunities to satiate his thirst for revenge. During this interval of time his party may have been increased by the accession of some Cherokee warriors to it. At any rate, he seems to have made a division of his forces; one part, he led against Capt. Evan Shelby's settlement on the present site of Bristol, Tenn.; the other, he sent to strike yet another blow against Fort Blackmore, on the Clinch. These two places, although forty miles apart, were both attacked on the same day. Both the former attack upon Fort Blackmore, and also the attack upon the Roberts family were led by Logan in person. But, in this incursion, Logan himself led the attack against Captian Shelby's settlement, and entrusted the leadership of the attack against Fort Blackmore to one of his followers. In a letter of October 9, Maj. Arthur Campbell thus reports the raid upon Shelby's Fort: "On last Thursday evening, ye 6th instant, the Indians took a negro wench prisoner, belonging to Capt. Shelby, within three hundred yards of his house. After they took her some distance, they examined her, asking how many guns were in the fort, and other questions relative to the strength of the place. They asked her if the store was kept there now. After they had carried her off about a mile, they saw or heard a boy coming from mill; they immediately tied the wench, and went off to catch the boy; while they were gone the wench luckily got loose and made her escape. She says they knocked her down twice when she refused to tell in what situation the fort was; and she says one was a large man much whiter than the rest, and talked good English; it was the same kind of a person Mr. Blackmore saw in pursuit of the negro he relieved."

In the foray against Shelby's Fort, Logan failed in securing the substantial result which usually attended his bloody enterprises; nor was the other part of his plan executed with much more success. Secretly approaching Fort Blackmore, the Indians came within about seventy-five yards of the gate before they were discovered. Most of the men at the time were sitting upon some logs which lay a short distance from the gate. Evidently seeing this, the Indians decided to make a bold push to enter the fort before the men could recover from their surprise. So, creeping along under the bank of the river, completely hidden from view by the bank and a fringe of trees and underbrush, they were just ready to rush into the fort when Dale Carter, who happened to be about fifty-five steps from the fort, saw them and began to halloo, "Murder, murder!" Upon hearing Carter's cry of alarm, the men ran toward the fort with all possible speed. They succeeded in reaching the gate before the Indians. Thus frustrated in their designs of cutting the men off from the fort, the Indians next turned their attention to Carter. One Indian shot at him but missed him; another shot him through the thigh, inflicting a wound, which though not mortal, rendered him too lame to escape into the fort. One Indian, more bold than the rest, soon ran up to Carter, and killing him with his tomahawk, scalped him. In the meantime, a Mr. Anderson and John Carter, who, with their guns, were either outside the fort, or, on hearing the firing, quickly ran to the outside, endeavored to prevent Carter's being scalped. Anderson shot at the Indian who was in the act of scalping Carter, while John Carter shot at another Indian who was near by. It is not known whether either of these shots took effect; they caused the Indians, however, to scamper off about one hundred yards, from which point they began firing at Anderson and his companion. Fortunately both men were unhurt by this fusillade, although some of the shots hit the stockade only a few inches from Anderson's head. By this time some of the men who had been on the logs hastily climbed into the bastion of the fort nearest the enemy, and opened a well-directed fire upon them. This drove the enemy into the woods where the little garrison dared not follow them. For a few moments the excitement was great in the little fort. Although Dale Carter's halloo of murder, sadly prophetic of his own fate, had cost him his own life, yet, no doubt, his timely warning averted the destruction of the fort.

News of Carter's murder spread rapidly throughout the frontier settlements. By the twelfth of October, it had reached Arthur Campbell, of Royal Oak, near Marion. Runners were sent to various forts to give warning and ask aid. No one knew against what settlements the next attack would be made. At the time of this attack, there were only sixteen men in the fort, and Captain Looney, who had been stationed there for its defense, happened to be absent on a visit to his family. His family were rather close neighbors, it seems, to the Roberts family, so recently murdered, which fact made him solicitous for their safety. Lieut. John Cox, and his company from the upper Holston, though on the way, as a guard for the flour, had not yet arrived. The nearest fort, then, from which aid could be had, was Moore's in Castlewood, seventeen miles distant. This fort was under the direct command of Daniel Boone. As soon, therefore, as the news of Carter's murder reached Castlewood, Boone and Capt. Daniel Smith, with a party of thirty men, started for Blackmore's. The night after their arrival there the Indians stole six out of seven of their horses, from a small lean-to, of which the stockading of the fort formed a part. The Indians had generously left them one horse, on which to carry their army baggage. The next morning early, Boone and Smith, with twenty-six choice men, all greatly anxious to proceed, went in search of the enemy. They found many Indian and horse tracks close in about the fort, but they were unable to follow them far enough into the wilderness to come up with the wily enemy. Captain Smith, writing from Castlewood, thus reported the results of their fruitless search to his superior officer, Colonel Preston: "I am this far on my return from the lower settlements (Fort Blackmore) to the head of the river (Clinch). Mr. Boon can inform you of the bad success we've had after the inhuman savages, the murders they've committed, and the mortification we've suffered of putting horses into a pen adjoining the fort for the Indians to take away and whose trace we could by no means discover. I shall be as expeditious as possible in getting to the head of the River (Clinch) lest they should invade those parts that are particularly under my care.

"Whilst I was in the lower settlement (Fort Blackmore)

I was shown a paper signed by many of the inhabitants representing their situation to be dangerous because they've been so irregularly supply'd with the number of men alloted to the district; and also requesting you to appoint Mr. Boone to be a Captain, and take charge of these lower forts, that he may be at liberty to act without orders from Holston captains who by their frequent absence·leave the inhabitants sometimes in disorder. Instead of signing this paper I chose to speak my sentiments to you concerning Mr. Boon and the paper which I suppose he will show you. As to the paper I believe it contains the sense of the majority of the inhabitants in this settlement. Mr. Boon is an excellent woodsman. If that only would qualify him for the Office no man would be more proper. I do not know of any objection that could be made to his character which would make you think him an improper person for that office. There may be possibly some impropriety in it because of Captain Russell when he returns, but of this you are much the best judge." (Thwaites and Kellogg's *Dunmore's War*, pp. 248–249.) Maj. Arthur Campbell, in writing to Colonel Preston concerning the people's petition that Boone be made a captain, says, "I wish Mr. Boones application or rather ye people for him may not have a similar tendency. I think it is men, and not particular Officers, they are most in need of. This much I am informed that it was not proposed by Mr. Boon for to petition you as they do; but it arose from a notion that a distant Officer would not be so particularly interested for their safety as he who lives among them. And some disgust at Capt. Looney for being away at home the time of the late alarm which he pleads in excuse that he wanted to see to the safety of his own Family, when Roberts was Killed in his Neighborhood." (Thwaites and Kellogg's *Dunmore's War*, p. 250.) Thus according to Captain Smith's and Major Campbell's letters, the petition to have Daniel Boone appointed captain, and placed in command of the three lower forts on the Clinch, seems to have originated at Fort Blackmore during the Indian alarms there. Fort Blackmore was "the lower settlement" from which Captain Smith was just returning, and, in which he had been shown "a paper signed by many of the inhabitants representing their situation to be dangerous, etc." Daniel

Boone was well known in the little fort. He often stopped there in passing up and down the Clinch Valley. He had hurried to the aid of the fort, both when Captain Blackmore's negroes were captured, and also when Dale Carter was killed. The services which he rendered in these times of peril inspired great confidence in him, not only at Fort Blackmore, but also throughout the valley of the Clinch. In fact, one of his biographers has very fittingly styled him, "The hero of Clinch Valley." (Reuben G. Thwaites' *Life of Daniel Boone*.) Furthermore, there were perhaps some grounds for complaint as to the fort's small allotment of men. As early as July 12, Col. William Christian had stated in a letter to Colonel Preston that a garrison of thirty men was to be ordered "At Blackmores Back of Moccison Gap." As a matter of fact, the garrison, up to the time of Carter's death, had never numbered more than sixteen men. Since their exposed position made theirs a buffer settlement, in times of danger it was an easy matter, no doubt, for them to think they were being neglected by the less exposed settlements farther east. It may be added, too, in this connection, that the "disgust at Capt. Looney for being away at home the time of the late alarm," would naturally be much stronger at Fort Blackmore than anywhere else, since he was stationed there.

After what has now been said, it is not at all improbable that the movement to have a well-merited honor bestowed upon the great hunter and Indian fighter, should have had its origin at Fort Blackmore. Prior to this time, Boone had never, it seems, ranked higher than lieutenant. It need scarcely be added that Colonel Preston, who had been furnished with blank commissions for the purpose by Governor Dunmore, at once responded to the people's petition by commissioning him captain. He was immediately assigned to the command of Blackmore's, Moore's and Cowan's forts.

On Sunday, October 9, three days after Dale Carter's murder, Mr. Anderson reported that he saw an Indian behind a blacksmith's shop just outside the fort, "at break of day."

The distressed condition of the frontier at the time of which we write, can be best shown by the following letters, written by men who were in position to realize fully the gravity of the situation.

(Maj. Arthur Campbell to Col. William Preston.) (Draper Manuscripts 3 QQ 112.)

"Royal Oak, Oct. 4th, 1774.

"Dear Sir—Since I closed my Letter Yesterday, Capt. Thompson came here; and give me a particular account of the situation of the People in the lower Settlement; he was much put to it to get Men to go out of the inhabitants, however with 9 Men he ventured thro' Mockison Gap, and somewhere between the Northfork and Clinch Mountain he came upon fresh tracks but could not make them out any distance.

"Upon the late alarm I ordered out Sergt. Commands to range along the back side the Settlement on Holston so that there is now a second Chain of rangers from the Great Island up. I also Ordered 4 men to Mr. Bledsoe 4 to Mr. Shelby and 4 to Mr. Cummins for particular protection.

"Upon consulting with Capt. Thompson it was agreed that I should make application to you for his having the Command of these upon Duty in this side Clinch mountain, and that he would endavour to have a party of 20 always with himself to range, besides it was necessary that some officer on Duty should be among the lower inhabitants at this time to encourage them and regulate matters.

"Since I wrote the above I received yours by Mr. Montgomery and am glad to receive Orders anticipating my application for a third Capt. on Duty, and I make no doubt you will approve my appointment of Capt. Thompson, especially as I find it is the best way he can do anything at his other business which it rendered very difficult for him to perform on account of confusion among the Inhabitants. I make no doubt but your last supply of Ammunition will encourage the Inhabitants, much as, I think every man have ½ doz shoots apiece having directed the Powder to be divided by Gun-Measures.

I am Sir your Obedient Servt.

Arthur Campbell."

(George Adams to Col. William Preston.) (Draper Manuscripts 3 QQ 113.)

"Holston River October ye 4th, 1774.

"Sir—I need not relate ye Distressed Circumstances of those Parts to you I imagine you have Such acount too Frequent Ye Mockinson people is Left home some time ago and some of them is Now at my hous where there is a few of us Gathered and hopes to tary here untill we heare how Circumstances promis with our Army at ye same time if it is in your Power and you Will be so Kind as to alow them a few men the time they are gathering theire Crops they then can Suport there familys and if not they canot suport theire famileys here they must unavoidably Remove theire Fameleys from Those Parts they have Large Crops it is a Pity so much Grain Should be Lost I would beg ye favour of you to Write if you Can aford them aney asistance as ye vermin is now Distroying theire Grain very fast I Could Equally Beg for Maney other places But I dout yt Every Place Canot be Suplyed with men.

"Amunition is very scarce with us Which is ye ocasion of abundanc of Feare from Sir your Humble Servt. With Esteeme

Gore. Adams

To Colon. Wm. Preston, this."

(Capt. Daniel Smith to Col. William Preston.) (Draper Manuscripts 3 QQ 114.)

"Dr. Sir—The late Invasions of Indians hath so much alarm'd the Inhabitants of this River (Clinch) that without more men come to their Assistance from other parts some of the more timorous among us will remove to a place of Safety, and when once the example is set I fear it will be followed by many. By what I can learn the terror is as great on Holston, so that we've no room to hope for Assistance from that quarter. Kingkeid is an intelligent man and can give you an account of the Situation of the Clinch inhabitants; To him I refer you for the same. I am just going to the Assistance of the Castles Woods men with what force could be spared from this upper district. I am Dr. Sir Yours most respectfully

Dan Smith

Elk Garden 4th Oct. 1774."

(Maj. Arthur Campbell to Col. William Preston.) (Draper Manuscripts 3 QQ 114.)

"Dear Sir—John Cox is just arrived here with 24 men I shall send him down the River, to range about Reedy Creek and Mockison Gap until the flour you mentioned arrives and then he may serve as an Escort to the provisions over to Blackmores; Mr. Cummins will wait upon you, and he can inform

you his Sentiments of the situation. I wish you could do something for him I have done all I can.
    I am Dear Sir your most Obedient Servt.
                                            Arthur Campbell
Oct. 5, 1774"

    (Maj. Arthur Campbell to Col. William Preston.) (Draper
Manuscripts 3 QQ 115.)
                                      "Royal Oak Oct. 6, 1774
    "Sir—The Evening after Mr. Cummins left this, I received
your letter of ye 1st. Inst. sent out by Paddy Brown; who
tho't proper to carry the letter past, and it was returned me
this day open. I wish it was in my power to humour every
Inhabitant, consistant with Justice to the Service; but there
is many of them so unreasonably selfish I despair of succeeding
in every case.
    "Paddy Brown is an old Weaver Body, that lives with one
of the Doughertys he came here one day and applied for to
get in for a spy, I very flatly refused him; he then went off
in dudgeon.
    "Upon the alarm of Lammey being taken, Vances & Fowlers
Wives with several other Families convened at Mr. Harrisons
which lyes upon the Main path to Clinch, in Rich Valley,
opposit to the Town-House, upon the request of several inhabitants in both side. I ordered Six Men to be Stationed
there for ten Days; two of which was always to be out ranging.
Heny. & Joso Dougherty moved their Families to this side the
mountain, disagreeing with ye. Majority of ye. Inhabitants,
as to the place to build a fort. Mr. John Campbells Wife has
been in this side the mountain this two months past, and himself has acted as Ensign to Capt. Smith, on Clynch ever since
that Gent. was ordered on Duty, Archibald & John Buchanans
Families, and Adnw. Lammeys came here who has continued
in this side yet; Capt. Wilson went immediately with 15 men,
and ranged near a Week in the Neighborhood where Lammey
was taken, and he left four of his best Woodsmen with the
Neighbours for several days longer. I also ordered two of the
most trusty persons I could get, for to act as Spys along
Clynch Mountain for 10 days which they performed I am
satisfyed faithfully; besides the Six Men, at Harrisons, I ordered Mrs. Vance & Fowlers Wife 3 Men a Week particularly,
to assist about saving their fodder, which they got removed
with safety.

"All the men stationed in this side Clynch, I give particular directions that they should if possible, be Young Men; and be ready to march to other places if called upon; Indeed when I first ordered these men I had a scheme in it, to send such good hands as could be best Spared out of them over to fill up Capt. Looneys and Smiths Companys on Clynch when the fears of the people in this side was a little abated. It has fell out extremely unlucky that both them Gentlemens ranging Stations was very thin when ye. Indians came. Capt. Smith having to wait until he was reinforced from this side before he could pursue. And at Blackmores the other Day the Indians coursed one of the Negroes they took near a quarter of an hour, several times in view of the Fort.

"In short the most of the People in this Country seem to have a private plan of their own, for their own particular defence.

"The people in the Wolf-Hill Settlement, will have the Indians to come up the Valley & North fork, opposite to them, and then make a Right-Angle to their habitations, they people on ye. South Fork will have the Enemy, to steal slyly up the Iron Mountain, and make one Grand attack on the Head of Holston and Sweep the River down before them; the Head of New River will have it, that the Cherokees will fetch a Compass, round Wattago Settlement, and come down New River, on a particular Search for their scalps. The Rich-Valley and North fork people will have Sandy the dangerous pass. for proof of which they quote former and recent instances; Stalnaker & Henry's Family being carried out the same road. You may thus see what a task one would have to remove every ones fears; I wish I could be instrumental in defending from real ones, imaginary dangers would give me less anxiety.

"I am Sir your Most Obedient

Arthur Campbell."

(Maj. Arthur Campbell to Col. William Preston.) (Draper Manuscripts 3 QQ 116.)

"Thursday Evening Octr. 6, 1774.

"Sir—Samuel Shannon came here today with 21 head of cattle several of them indifferent. I have detained him until the Beginning of next week as he says he wont go further without a guard; by which time I expect the flour Waggons will be up, and I can send both together to Mockison Gap, you will see by Capt. Smiths Letter that there is near cattle enough for his Fort. One of Snodgrasses says he seen an Indian a little below Capt. Thompsons the day before Yesterday. I rather think if he seen anything it was some of Donelsons and Masons party in disguise as I hear they have threatened the Sheriff. The Boy that was scalped is dead, he was an extraordinary example of patience and resolution to his last, frequently lamenting 'he was not able to fight enough for to save his mammy.' (This was the Roberts boy mentioned above.) I divided the last of the 8 lb. powder that came by Vance to Lieut. Cox Men yesterday. They had shoots apiece and with perswasions I got them to go down the River, they said they would turn home if they did not get more next Week. I hope Branders powder will be up by that time.

"I am sir your Most Hbl. Servt.

Arthur Campbell"

On the back of this letter the following list of forts was written:

Men Miles

	Men	Miles	
Blackmores	16		Sergt Moor
Moores	20	20	—— Boone
Russells	20	4	Poage Sergt
Glade Hollow	15	12	John Dunken Sergt.
Elk Garden	18	14	John Kinkead Sergt.
Maiden Springs	5	23	Joseph Craven Do.
Whittons, Big Crab Orchd.	3	12	Ensign Campbell

"To Colo. William Preston pr. fvr. of Mr. Hen. Thompson."

"It is remarkable," writes Major Campbell to Colonel Preston in a letter dated October 12, "that Capt. Shelby's wench was taken the same day, and about the same time of the day, that this affair happened on Clinch. So many attacks in so short a time, give the inhabitants very alarming apprehensions. Want of ammunition and scarcity of provisions are again become the general cry. Since I began this, I am mortified with the sight of a family flying by. If ammunition does not come soon, I will have no argument that will have any force to detain them; and if our army is not able to keep a garrison at the Falls (Louisville, Ky.) the ensuing winter, I expect we shall be troubled with similar visits the greater part of the coming season."

Since the name of Daniel Boone has been brought into connection with Scott County history in the foregoing recital of events, it seems appropriate at this point in our story, to relate how it came about that he lived, for more than a year, in Castlewood and was thus enabled to help shape the history of one of our first settlements, almost at its very beginning.

On September 25, 1773, Daniel Boone and his family, in company with a number of other families left his home on the Yadkin River, for Kentucky. On his way to Powell's Valley, where he was to await the coming of a rear party, he sent his eldest son, James, a boy seventeen years of age, in company with some men leading pack horses, to Captain Russell's in Castlewood, for flour and farming tools. Sometime prior in the year 1773, Boone, it seems, had met Captain Russell on the Clinch, at which time a very warm friendship had sprung up between the two men. Dr. Thwaites in his *Life of Boone* says, "They were returning laden, in company with Russell's son, Henry, a year older than James, two of Russell's negro slaves, and two or three white work-people, when, missing their path, they went into camp for the night only three miles from Boone's quarters. At daybreak they were attacked by a Shawnee war party, and all killed except a white laborer named Isaac Crabtree and a negro. This pathetic tragedy created such consternation among the movers that, despite Boone's entreaties to go forward, all of them returned to Virginia and Carolina." Boone, having sold his farm on the Yadkin, had no home to which to return. He, therefore, accepted the invitation of Capt. David Gass, a member of the party, to accompany him home to Castlewood, and there reside in a vacant cabin on his farm. Boone was probably further induced to take this step by the hope of later being joined by Captains Gass and Russell, in another attempt to settle Kentucky.

Boone reached Castlewood in the early autumn, too late, however, to grow any crop. Winter was approaching, and preparations had to be made to meet it. His chief supply of food during this period must have been furnished by his stock of cattle and his trusty rifle. Dr. Lyman C. Draper in his manuscript life of Boone, has this to say of Boone's first winter in Castlewood: "How the winter of 1773–74 passed away with Boone, we must leave the reader to judge. Hunting, however, must have been his chief occupation for the supply of his family with meat, and the procurement of other necessaries by the sale or barter of pelts and furs. He used to relate this hunting adventure, which occurred at that period and in the Clinch region, with the parties to which he was well acquainted. One Green and a brother-in-law, who resided near Blackmore's, on Clinch about fifteen miles below Capt. Gass' place, where Boone was sojourning, went out some considerable distance among the mountains to hunt. They selected a good hunting range, erected a cabin, and laid up in store some jerked bear meat. One day when Green was alone, his companion being absent on the chase, a large bear made his appearance near camp, upon which Green shot and wounded the animal, which at the moment chanced to be in a sort of sink-hole at the base of a hill. Taking a circuit to get above and ahead of the bear, there being a slight snow upon the ground covered with sleet, Green's feet slipped from under him, and in spite of all his efforts to stop himself he partly slid and partly rolled down the declivity till he found himself in the sink-hole, when the wounded bear, enraged by his pain, flew at poor Green, tore and mangled his body in a shocking manner, totally destroying one of his eyes. When the bear had sufficiently gratified his revenge by gnawing his unresisting victim as long as he wished, he sullenly departed, leaving the unfortunate hunter in a helpless and deplorable condition, all exposed, with his clothing torn in tatters to the severities of the season.

"His comrade, at length returning, found and took him to camp. After a while, thinking it impossible for Green to recover, his companion went out on a pretense of hunting for fresh meat, and unfeelingly abandoned poor Green to his fate, reporting in the settlements that he had been killed by a bear. His little fire soon died away from his inability to provide fuel. Digging, with his knife, a hole or nest beside him in the ground-floor of his cabin, he managed to reach some wild turkey feathers which had been saved, and with them lined the excavation and made himself quite a comfortable bed; and with the knife fastened to the end of a stick, he cut down, from time to time, bits of dried bear meat hanging over head, and upon this he sparingly subsisted. Recovering slowly, he could at length manage to get about. When spring opened, a party of whom Boone is believed to have been one, went from Blackmore's Settlement to bury Green's remains with the brute of a brother-in-law for a guide; and, to their utter astonishment, they met Green plodding his way towards home, and learned from him the sad story of his sufferings and desertion. The party were so indignant that they could scarcely refrain from laying violent hands on a wretch guilty of so much inhumanity to a helpless companion. Green, though disfigured, lived many years." (Draper Manuscripts.)

The cabin in which Boone lived was situated within two miles of Moore's Fort (sometimes called Fort Byrd), and a "little off South of Clinch River." It was to Moore's Fort that Boone and his family repaired when there was danger of Indian attack.

Many surveying parties spent the summer of 1774, surveying lands in Kentucky. Soon after the departure of these parties for Kentucky, the Indians began to show so many signs of hostility, that their friends, back in the settlements, felt a deep solicitude for their safety. Measures were at once taken to warn them of impending danger. Colonel Preston directed Captain Russell to send two reliable woodmen to proceed at once to Kentucky and apprise the surveyors "of the eminent Danger they are Daily in." In a letter to Colonel Preston, Captain Russell thus announces his selection of the men to go upon this important and dangerous mission. "I am Sensible, good Sir, of your Uncommon concern for the Security of Capt. Floyd and the Gentlemen with him, and I sincerely Sympathize with You, lest they should fall a Prey to such Inhuman, blood-thirsty devils, as I have so lately suffered by; but may God of his Infinite Mercy, Shield him and Company, from the present impending Danger, and could we (thro' Providence) be a means of preserving such Valuable Members by sending out Scouts, such a procedure wood Undoubtedly be of the most lasting, and secret Satisfaction to us; and the Country in general. I have Engaged to start Immediately, on the occasion, two of the best Hands I could

think of Danl. Boone and Michl. Stoner; who have Engaged
to search the country, as low as the falls, and to return by
way of Gasper's Lick, on the Cumberland, and thro' Cumberland Gap; so that by the assiduity of these Men, if it
is not too late, I hope the Gentlemen will be apprised of the
eminent Danger they are Daily in.   The Report prevailing
among You, of the Family being kill'd on Copper Creek is
altogether groundless, as is that of three Cherokees on the
Head of Clinch." (Thwaites and Kellogg's *Dunmore's War,*
pp. 50–51.)

Boone received instruction for this journey at a muster held
in Castlewood, on Saturday, June 25, 1774.   The next day
being Sunday, he observed it; and, on Monday morning, the
27th, he and Stoner started on their long and perilous journey
through the wilderness.   Having accomplished their mission,
Boone and Stoner returned to the Clinch on August 26, 1774,
after an absence of sixty-one days, during which time they
had traveled eight hundred miles.   Captain Russell had already started upon the Point Pleasant campaign when Boone
returned to Castlewood.   Boone wanted to go, too, so he hur-
riedly sent a messenger to overtake Captain Russell with the
news of his return, and, at the same time, expressing the hope
that he might be permitted to join the expedition.   Capt.
William Russell thus speaks of Boone's return: "Mr. Jno.
Green and three others of Mr. Taylor's company have arrived on Clinch, but did not see them, as they only came to
Blackmores the night before we started; and this day an
express from Mr. Boone overtook me to inform me of his
return and desire to go on the expedition." (Thwaites and
Kellogg's *Dunmore's War,* p. 172.)

Two days after Boone's return from Kentucky Maj. Arthur
Campbell writes, "Capt. Floyd seems very uneasy at the way
Drake has used him, as he now plainly discovers that he was
expecting to be appointed to a separate command.   For this
reason, and to relieve Floyd's anxiety, I wrote pressingly to
Mr. Boone to raise men with all expedition to join Capt.
Floyd; and I did not doubt but you would do everything
in your power to encourage him.   And what induced me particularly to apply to Mr. Boone was seeing his Journal last
night, and a letter to Capt. Russell, wherein he professes a

great desire to go on the expedition, and I am well informed he is a very popular officer where he is known. So I hope Capt. Floyd will still succeed, as I have good reason to believe Mr. Boone will get all in Capt. Looney's company that intended to go with Bledsoe, and perhaps you can assist a little out of Waggoner's recruits, as I have heard to-day he is likely to get some men. I have been informed that Mr. Boone tracked a small party of Indians from Cumberland Gap to near the settlements (Fort Blackmore). Upon this intelligence, I wrote pressingly to Capt. Thompson to have a constant lookout and to urge the spies strictly to do their duty."

Captain Floyd himself writes of Boone as follows: "You will hear of Mr. Boone's return, and desire of going out. If Mr. Drake gets a berth down there, and does not immediately return to me and assist according to your instructions, pray let Boone join me and try. Capt. Bledsoe says Boone has more interest (influence) than any other man now disengaged; and you know what Boone has done for me by your kind directions, for which reason I love the man. But yet do as you think proper in everything respecting me." (Thwaites and Kellogg's *Dunmore's War*, p. 168.)

Boone had started to the Great Levels of Greenbriar, the place of rendezvous for the troops on their way to the mouth of the Kanawha, when he was met with orders to return to the Clinch Valley and defend it against the Indians during the absence of the Fincastle militia, on the Ohio. Disappointed, no doubt, in not being permitted to join his friends in the campaign on the Ohio, he turned back to the Clinch, where he so valiantly and efficiently performed the duties thus enjoined upon him as to win the praise of the settlers all along the frontier. How they showed their appreciation of his services has been spoken of in another place.

The discharge of Boone's military duties required that he go from fort to fort, wherever there was need for his services. His is said to have been a most familiar figure along the Clinch, as, "dressed in deerskin colored black, and his hair plaited and clubbed up," he visited, in an official capacity, the various forts under his command.

During the month of October, following the murder of Dale

Carter, at Fort Blackmore, Boone and his well-trained rifle-men were often called upon to track and run down the lurking foe. Sometimes they came up with the enemy, fighting brief but desperate skirmishes. Sometimes the wily enemy, on reaching the forest, seemed to vanish without leaving a track. But Boone, although now forty years of age, seems to have been the most active commander at this time in the valley of the Clinch.

The victory of the southwest Virginia men over the Indians at Point Pleasant, October 10, 1774, practically closed the war on the frontier, so far as the Shawnee and Mingo tribes were concerned. The Cherokees, also, showed a disposition to live on terms of peace with the whites by putting to death those of their nation who had been implicated in the murder of James Boone, Henry Russell, and their companions.

The Shawnees were so humbled by their defeat at Point Pleasant that they threw themselves upon the mercy of Gov-ernor Dunmore, asking him to name the terms of peace, and, at the same time, signifying that whatever terms he might propose would be complied with. They promised to return all prisoners, together with stolen horses, and such other plunder as they had taken from the whites. They, further-more, agreed to give up all lands, and hunt no more south of the Ohio; to permit travelers to pass on that river unmolested, even rendering them such assistance and protection as they could; to trade according to regulations dictated to them by the whites; and, to bury the tomahawk forever so far as the Virginians were concerned.

As a guaranty that the terms of this peace agreement would be faithfully kept, the Indians were required to give six of their number as hostages, two of whom were to be chiefs and the remaining four to be either chiefs or the sons of chiefs. Chief Logan was not present at this peace con-ference. When Governor Dunmore noticed his absence, he at once directed his interpreter, Col. John Gibson, to invite Logan to the council chamber. He refused to come by saying that he was a warrior, and not a peace-maker, and, at the same time, he delivered the following speech: "I appeal to any white man to say if ever he entered Logan's cabin hungry and he gave him not meat; if ever he came cold and naked and he clothed him not? During the course of the last long and bloody war, Logan remained idle in his camp, an advocate for peace. Such was my love for the whites that my countrymen pointed as I passed and said, 'Logan is the friend of the white man.' I had even thought to have lived with you, but for the injuries of one man. Colonel Cresap, the last spring, in cold blood and unprovoked, murdered all the relations of Logan not even sparing my women and children. There runs not a drop of my blood in the veins of any living creature. This called on me for revenge. I have sought it. I have killed many. I have fully glutted my vengeance. For my country I rejoice at the beams of peace; but do not harbor a thought that mine is the joy of fear. Logan never felt fear. He will not turn on his heel to save his life. Who is there to mourn for Logan? Not one." (Taylor's *Historic Sullivan*, p. 45.)

Twelve Mingoes refused to accede to these peace terms; they were taken, therefore, to Fort Pitt and put into prison. The Shawnee hostages were taken to Williamsburg, Va. This treaty was ratified by the Ohio Indians, at Pittsburg, the following year.

In the meantime, as a protection to the Virginia frontier, especially along the Clinch, the following forts were built and garrisoned along the upper Ohio: Fort Blair, at the mouth of the Great Kanawha, one hundred men; Fort Fincastle, at Wheeling, twenty-five men; and, Fort Dunmore, at Pittsburg, seventy-five men. Except the forces required to garrison the forts mentioned next above, the troops under Dunmore and Lewis were discharged and permitted to return to their respective homes. During the winter, the Indians complied with the terms of the peace agreement by bringing in, and delivering up their prisoners and plunder. By their ready compliance, the Indians showed such a disposition for peace that Governor Dunmore at once ordered these forts evacuated and the men discharged. Major Campbell, under date of November 21, writes thus to Colonel Preston, "Upon the first intelligence of peace being concluded, I wrote to the officers on duty to discharge the whole of the militia except fifteen at Blackmores and the like number at Mockinson Gap. Upon receiving your letter of the 13th and Col. Christian's of the 11th inst. I directed them to be discharged also."

Dr. Draper, in his manuscript, *Life of Boone*, summarizes the results of Dunmore's War in these words: "Thus ended the war, which cost the people of Virginia about one hundred thousand pounds, many valuable lives, and an incalculable amount of individual suffering and privation along the exposed frontiers. Boone was most actively engaged during the whole contest, and had, in all situations, and under all circumstances, proved himself equal to the trust reposed in him. With this consciousness of having done his duty, he rejoiced, like Logan, "at the beams of peace"; when the hardy settler could once again retire from the pent-up fort, and in safety re-occupy his isolated cabin-home, and the fearless hunter could once more roam the bewitching forests with the wild freedom he loved so well. And among Boone's manuscript papers, we find evidence that he soon plunged deep into the wilderness, for in January ensuing he was encamped on Kentucky river, probably silently enjoying one of his highly prized hunts." (Draper Manuscripts 3 B 151–56.)

Boone, upon returning from this hunt in Kentucky, next left Castlewood, it seems, to attend a great council, which was held at Sycamore Shoals, between the Transylvania Company, and more than a thousand Cherokee Indians whom Boone had caused to assemble for this purpose. During this council, Richard Henderson, the chief promoter of the company, purchased from the Cherokees whatever title they may have had to all the lands lying between the Kentucky and Cumberland rivers, including a path to these lands from the east, through Moccasin Gap and Powell's Valley. When it was seen that the issue of this treaty would be favorable to the Transylvania Company, Boone, in company with about thirty men, was sent on ahead to mark a trace through the wilderness to these lands on the Kentucky River. Over this trace, Henderson and his colony were to pass later. Boone seems to have spent most of the summer of 1775 in Kentucky; and sometime within the first week of September, his wife and family arrived there, having, no doubt, passed down the Clinch, by Fort Blackmore, through Rye Cove, to the Kentucky Trace at some point in Stock Creek Valley. Thus,

with the immigration of his family to Kentucky, Boone passed
out of the history of Fort Blackmore and the valley of the
Clinch, only to become a leading figure in laying the foundation of a great commonwealth. Many stories of him are yet
repeated at the firesides of the great-great-grandchildren of
those who knew him. I have been unable to find any record
of events which occurred at Fort Blackmore within the year
1775. This dearth of records, however, may be taken to indicate that it was a year of comparative peace and quietude to
the inmates of the little fort. No doubt they ventured forth
to work upon their clearings and grow a crop of grain, a
thing which they had dared not do during the turmoil and
danger of the previous year. Although the happenings in the
neighborhood of the fort during 1775 do not seem to have
been preserved for us, yet at this time events, destined greatly
to affect the fortunes of the settlers at the mouth of Stony
Creek, were shaping themselves elsewhere in the country.
The Revolution was impending. Loud mutterings of discon-
tent with George III's government were beginning to be heard,
even among his subjects along the valley of the Clinch. The
Battles of Lexington, Concord, and Bunker Hill had been
heard from, and the spirit of the militia who opposed the
King's troops was understood and approved by the people in
the valley of the Clinch. Capt. William Russell, of Castlewood, in a letter to Col. William Fleming, written from Fort
Blair, June 12, 1775, thus comments upon current events:

"I had some days before the receipt of yours been favored
with the shocking account of three battles being fought near
the city of Boston, between the British Troops, and American; though I must acknowledge my great joy, in our victories
obtained over the enemies' tyrannic pride.
"The unheard of acts of barbarity, committed by the British Troops, will doubtless stir up every lover of his country to
be zealous and forward in its defence, to support our liberty;
though, I doubt not, but many sycophants to Britain's interest,
will now appear patriots; as long as our arms prove victorious;
but, should ever our present success change, and in so small
a manner be sullied, you'll find traitors enough prick up their
ears, and in a prophetic language, display their pre-suggested
knowledge of events.

"The Corn Stalk left me, last Thursday; and in the space
of four days conversation, I discovered that it is the intention
of the Pick tribe of Indians to be troublesome to our new
settlements whenever they can; and he further assured me,
that the Mingoes behave in a very unbecoming manner, frequently upbraiding the Shawnees, in cowardly making the
peace; and called them Big Knife People; that the Corn Stalk
can't well account for their intentions. If this be true, and
a rupture between England and America has really commenced, we shall certainly receive trouble at the hands of
those people in a short time, as they got news of the battles
in the Shawnee towns, eight, or ten days before the Corn Stalk
came here." (Thwaites and Kellogg's *Rev. Upper Ohio*, pp.
13, 14, 15.)

Captain Russell's prophecy as to trouble with the Indians
was not long in being fulfilled; for very early in the Revolutionary struggle, the British Ministry adopted the policy of
enlisting the Indians in the service of the British government.
British agents infested every Indian tribe on the western frontier. These agents were so successful in bribing and stirring
up the tribesmen against the settlers in the valleys of the Holston and the Clinch that, by the early spring of 1776, the
Cherokees, Choctaws, Creeks, and Chickasaws were ready to
go on the warpath in behalf of their British allies. Of these
tribes, the Cherokees were the nearest, most numerous, and
therefore, the most dangerous enemies of the settlers within
the present limits of Scott County at that time. The following affidavit, made by Jarret Williams, an Indian trader, before Anthony Bledsoe, a magistrate of Washington County, in
July, 1776, very clearly shows the causes for apprehension
which the settlers of this section had.

Williams "deposeth and saith; that he left the Cherokee
nation on Monday night, the 8th inst. (July.)
"That the part of the nation called the Over-Hills were then
preparing to go to war against the frontiers of Virginia, having
purchased to the amount of 1,000 skins or thereabouts, for
mocksons. They were also bearing flour for a march, and
making other warlike preparations. Their number, from cal-
culation made by the Raven Warrior, amounts to about six
hundred warriors, and, according to the deponent's idea, he

thinks we may expect a general attack any hour. They propose to take away negroes and horses, and to kill all kinds of sheep, cattle &c.; also to destroy all corn, burn houses, &c. And he also heard that the Valley towns were, a part of them, set off; but that they had sent a runner to stop them till all were ready to start. He further relates that Alexander Cameron informed them that he had concluded to send Captain Nathaniel Guest, William Faulin, Isaac Williams and the deponent with the Indians, till they came near to Nolichucky, then the Indians were to stop and Guest and the other whites above mentioned were to go to see if there were any King's men among the inhabitants and if they found any they were to take them off to the Indians or have a white signal in their hands or otherwise to distinguish them. When this was done they were to fall on the inhabitants and kill and drive all they possibly could.

"That on Saturday, the 6th inst. in the night, he heard two prisoners were brought in about midnight, but the deponent saw only one. That the within Williams saw only one scalp brought by a party of Indians, with a prisoner; but, from accounts, they had five scalps. He also sayd he heard the prisoner examined by Cameron, thought he gave a very imperfect account, being very much cast down. He further sayd that the Cherokees had received the war-belt from the Shawnese, Mingo, Taawah, and Deleware nations, to strike the white people. That fifteen of the said nations were in the Cherokee towns, and that few of the Cherokees went in company with the Shawnese &c. That they all intended to strike the settlers in Kentucky; and that the Cherokees gave the Shawnese four scalps of white men, which they carried with them. The said Shawnese and Mingoes informed the Cherokees that they were at peace with every other nation; that the French were to supply them with ammunition, and that they wanted the Cherokees to join them to strike the white people on the frontiers, which the Cherokees have agreed to.

"And the deponent further saith that, before he left the nation, a number of the Cherokees of the Lower Towns were gone to fall on the frontiers of South Carolina and Georgia; and further saith not.

Jarrett Williams"

The foregoing deposition reveals the conditions which made it necessary for the frontiersmen on the Clinch to fight the savage allies of Great Britain here on the border in defense of their own homes and loved ones, instead of joining Washington's army in the struggle with the enemy along the Atlantic Coast. It may be said in this connection that the pioneers who fought against the Indian allies of Britain, here in Southwest Virginia, during the period of the Revolution, as truly fought for liberty as did their compatriots at Saratoga and Yorktown.

The settlers along the Holston and the Clinch, realizing that a long and bloody war was threatening, proceeded at once to put their frontier settlements into an attitude of defense.

Isaac Crisman built a fort in the Rye Cove, a few miles west of Fort Blackmore. Old Fort Patrick Henry at Long Island was repaired and strengthened. A fort was erected at Amos Eaton's, seven miles east of Long Island. Such supplies of food and ammunition as could be had were obtained and stored away against the day of need. But preparations and precautions could not avert the impending stroke. Isaac Crisman, the builder of the Rye Cove Fort, and two members of his family were attacked and killed by the Indians. Sometime in June, 1776, two men were killed at Fort Blackmore; and in September of the same year, a son of Jonathan Jennings, and one of his negro slaves, were murdered at Fort Blackmore. But in this connection, Capt. John Redd, who was living in Powell's Valley, in 1776, and who in that year fled to Fort Blackmore for safety, has related the conditions that prevailed in this section at that time.

He said that "Capt. Penn's Company was discharged, and Gen. Martin returned home about the first of December. On arriving at home, Gen. Martin gave notice that he wished to raise a company to go out and settle Powell's Valley. The company was soon raised, and on the 25th of December we set out. The company was composed of 16 or 18 men, with all necessary implements to settle. Early in January, 1775, we arrived in the Valley, and halted in a large old Indian field where a few years before, Gen. Martin attempted to make a settlement.

"Of Gen. Martin's first trip to Powell's Valley, I know nothing except such facts as I obtained from the Gen. and his brother, Brice. In his first trip to Powell's Valley, he was accompanied by only 5 or 6 men. The day after he arrived in the valley, a large company of Indians, who were on a hunting expedition, came to his camp. The Indians appeared to be very friendly and delighted at seeing their white brethren. Most of them had very inferior guns, and seemed to be pleased with the appearance of the guns of Martin's men. The Indians seemed to be very talkative but unfortunately none of the whites could speak the Indian language nor the Indians, the language of the whites. Gen. Martin, perceiving that the Indians took a great fancy to his guns, gave his men orders not to let the Indians take any of them out of their hands. The Indians soon gave signs to Martin and his men that they wished to exchange their guns with the whites. Their offers, in every instance, were sternly rejected. Martin set his gun down, and the moment he turned his eye from it, a very large Indian picked it up, and put his gun in the place of it, and walked off a few yards to his companions. As soon as Martin discovered that his gun was gone, he picked up the old one laying in the place of his, and walked to where the Indians were. Seeing the Indian with it in his hand, he threw the old gun at the feet of the Indian, laid hold of his own. The Indian refused to give it up, and a scuffle ensued. Martin threw the Indian down, and wrenched the gun from his reluctant grasp. The Indians who were standing by and witnessed the scuffle between their companion and Martin, raised a great laugh and yell at the scuffle. The Indian from whom the gun had been taken, was very much enraged, and soon went off with his companions. On leaving, the Indian said a great deal in a very excitable tone. Martin, not understanding his language, took all he said to be threats of revenge. After the affair of the gun, Martin and his men held a counsel and concluded that they had better return home for they knew not to what extent the Indians might carry their revenge. Accordingly next morning they set out for home.

"We immediately set to work and built several strong cabins and stockaded them, which made it a good fort for defence. We then fenced in with brush and rails a large portion of the old field in which we made a large crop of corn. The valley abounded in almost every species of games, and the time we had to spare from cultivating our corn was employed in killing game. We soon had a large supply of meat.

"About the first of April Col. Richard Henderson, with something like forty men who were on their way to Kentucky

to make the first permanent settlement, stopped at the fort
6 or 8 days to supply themselves with meat; as for bread
we had none for ourselves. As soon as they were supplied
themselves, they set out on their journey.

"During the year (1775) we were not uninterrupted by
Indians. During the fall, William Priest, with 8 or 10 men
came out and built a fort a few miles above Martin's. About
the same time William Mumps, with a small party of men,
built a fort at the Sinking Spring, 20 miles from Martin's
where Lee Courthouse now is; at the forts the settlers cut
down, and killed the timber on a good deal of land, and, in the
spring they were surrounded by fences, made of brush and
rails, and planted in corn. During the past fall, several small
parties past on their way to Kentucky, many of whom were
murdered by the Indians. This produced a very great excitement with the settlers in the valley.   In May, 1776, Gen.
Martin returned home, promising to return in four weeks.
The four weeks expired, and we had heard nothing from Gen.
Martin. The settlers at Priest and Mump's fort had all left,
and some of our men. Days rolled on, and we could hear
nothing from Martin nor the settlement. We became alarmed
at our situation. We knew that something of great moment
had taken place or Martin would either have returned or sent
a messenger out to let us know why he did not come at the
appointed time. As our number had decreased to about ten,
and we could not hear from Martin, we held a counsel, determined to remain 3 days longer, and, if we could hear
nothing from the settlement, in that time, to start for home.
The day we held our counsel, William Parks, one of our number, insisted upon our going some 8 miles below the fort, and
put up a few poles in the shape of a house, kill some trees, dig
some holes in the ground, and plant his corn, so as to secure
a corn right, and return the third morning time enough to
start with us, if we should (leave) for the settlement. We
very reluctantly gave our consent. On the same evening,
Parks, his nephew, Thomas, and his negro man set out to secure his corn right. The 3d morning after Parks left, the
day he promised to return, to our great surprise young Parks
came, and informed us that his uncle had left the evening
before to kill some meat. Shortly after his leaving he heard
him shout, and had heard nothing from him since. I and 2
others set out with young Parks, and, on arriving at his cabin,
he showed us the way his uncle went. We found his track,

and followed it with great care. After going about one mile, we came to where some Indians had been lying among some lime stone rocks, on the Kentucky Trace about fifty yards from where the Indians had been, we saw old Parks lying dead on his face. On examining him, we found he was shot through the heart. From his tracks, he must have run some thirty yards from where he was shot. He was scalped, and a war club left sunk in his brain. We skinned some tough bark, with it lashed the body of old Parks to a pole, and two of us, with an end of the pole on our shoulders, carried him to his cabin, and buried him. The same evening returned to the fort. On arriving there, we found an express sent out by Gen. Martin, informing us that the Indians had declared war, and were doing a great deal of mischief. The morning after the arrival of the express, we broke up, and came to Blackmore's Fort on Clinch River. At this fort, we found the greater part of the men who had left Mump's and Priest's forts. We soon raised a company of some 20 men returned, and thinned our corn; after this I came home.

"Capt. Martin was ordered to the Rye Cove Fort about 50 miles off, on the North Fork of Clinch; the balance of the army were discharged. Capt. Martin set out immediately for the fort. At this place a man by the name of Isaac Crisman had built a fort some time before and while we were gone to the Indian towns, Crisman and 2 of his family were murdered by the Indians. I did not accompany Capt. Martin on this expedition for I was appointed Sergeant Major by Col. Campbell, and remained at Long Island while Capt. Martin was on his way to the Rye Cove. He had to pass through a very dangerous gap called Little Mockison Gap. At this place the trail went through a very narrow, deep gorge in the mountain; at the place the Indians had killed a great many whites. As Capt. Martin passed through the gap, he had his men in very fine order, and drawn out in single file. Just as the head of the column emerged from this narrow place, the whole company was fired upon by the Indians from the top of the ridge. They were in a column as long as Capt. Martins. As soon as the Indians fired, they ran off. They did not kill any of Martin's men, but wounded one by the name of Bunch; he had five balls shot through the flesh. Capt. Martin, finding that the Indians had all fled, marched on his way to Rye Cove unmolested. Capt. Martin remained here until the first of May, at which time his company was ordered back to Long

Island, and he remained here until July, 1777, when the treaty was finally concluded as soon as peace was concluded, the army was disbanded." (John Redd's *Narrative*.)

In June, 1776, George Rogers Clark was a guest at Mump's Fort, in Powell's Valley. Fear of Indian attack had caused him to travel the entire distance from Kentucky, avoiding the usual trail. He had only one companion on this journey, a man by the name of Rice. On the morning following Clark's arrival at Mump's Fort he set out for the settlement, accompanied by Rice and Captain Redd. It is very probable that they stopped at Fort Blackmore on their way east.

Captain Redd, in his *Narrative*, gives an account of the murder of Jacob Lewis and his family near the head of Stock Creek, and of the murder of Ambrose Fletcher's wife and children at Fort Blackmore. I here quote his account of these murders in full.

"You requested me to give you all the particulars of white killing Indians, or Indians killing whites between the peace of '64 & the spring of '74. I know nothing so as to give an account accurately. I will relate one or two murders, committed by Indians in '76. In the spring of '75, a man by the name of Jacob Lewis came out to Martin's Station in Powell's Valley with a wife and 7 children. Some of the men knew him to be a man of bad character, and he was ordered not to settle near the Station. Lewis took his family & came in the direction of the settlement, about 35 miles, and built him a small cabin, near the head of Stock Creek, and there lived entirely on the game he killed. In June, '76, when on my way to the settlement, I passed by his house, and advised him to move to the settlement that the Indians had declared war. He said he was in no danger; that Indians would never find him. In July following, as I returned to the Holston, I learned that Lewis & wife, and 7 children were killed, and scalped by the Indians.

"In '76, when the Cherokee Indians declared war, most of the extreme settlers broke up, and most of them came to the settlement. A man by the name of Ambrose Fletcher, who settled in Martin's Station, took refuge in Blackmore Fort. He had a wife & 2 children. After he remained in fort 3 or 4 days, it became so crowded that he built a cabin some 30 or

40 yards back of the fort, (and) shortly after moved in his cabin. He went out one morning, at a short distance, to get his horse, and on his return, found his wife and children murdered & scalped by the Indians." (John Redd's *Narrative.*)

It is to be seen from the foregoing quotation that Fort Blackmore was a place of refuge for the more exposed and weaker settlements between it and Cumberland Gap, during the Cherokee uprising in 1776.

In 1777, Fort Blackmore was approached by a party of Indians under the leadership of Benge, a Cherokee by birth, who had resided so long among the Northern Indians as to be regarded one of them. (Haywood, 275.) Benge, it seems, was accompanied on this expedition by a renegade white man, named Hargus, who, having once lived in the neighborhood of Fort Blackmore, no doubt, acted as a guide for Benge and his red warriors. In fact, being a fugitive from justice, the expedition may have been inspired by Hargus himself. This story of Benge and his gang, with more or less variation as to details, but with little change as to a small group of essential facts, has been repeated at the firesides of the people of Scott County for a period of nearly one hundred and fifty years. It is our most popular and best known traditional story. As commonly told, its unvarying parts are: (1) an Indian in a tree, gobbling in imitation of a turkey; (2) he is approached from behind, and shot through the head by Matthew Gray; (3) Gray has a thrilling race for his life back to the fort. The story is based entirely upon tradition; there are no references to the things of which it relates to be found in written or printed documents, contemporary with it. It was first published in the *Life of Wilburn Waters* by Charles B. Coale, of Abingdon, Va. I quote the story in full from Coale's *Life of Wilburn Waters.*

"During the spring of 1777, a party of Indians, under the lead of the half-breed Benge and a savage white man by the name of Hargus, crossed the range of hills north of Clinch at High Knob, and made their way to Bluegrass Fort (Fort Blackmore) on Stony Creek, which was not far from what is now known as Osborn's Ford, in Scott County. [Formerly the name Blue Grass was applied to a section just above the fort site where the young men of the neighborhood met for horse racing, etc. The name is no longer used and few remember it. (Milo Taylor.)] The white man, Hargus, had been living in the neighborhood, but had absconded to the Indians to evade punishment for crime, and became an inhuman persecutor of his race.

"The Indians, having cautiously and stealthily approached the river down Stoney Creek, and fearing they might be discovered, crossed some distance below and came up in the rear of a high cliff south of, and opposite the fort, concealing their main body in the bushes at the base. In order to command a view of the fort, they sent one of their number to the summit of the cliff to spy out the condition of the fort and to act as a decoy. He ascended in the night, and climbed a tall cedar with thick foliage at the top, on the very verge of the precipice, and just at the break of day he began to gobble like a wild turkey. This imitation was so well executed it would have been successful but for the warnings of an old Indian fighter present by the name of Matthew Gray. Hearing what they supposed to be a turkey, and desiring him for breakfast, some of the younger members of the company proposed to go up the cliff and shoot him, but Gray told them if they wanted to keep their scalps on their heads they had better let that turkey alone, and if they would follow his directions he would give them an Indian for breakfast.

"Having promised to obey his instructions, he took several of them with him to a branch which he knew to be in full view of the Indians, and told them to wash and dabble in the stream to divert the attention of the enemy for half an hour, while he went to look for the turkey, which still continued to gobble at short intervals. Gray, having borrowed an extra rifle from David Cox, crouched below the bank of the stream and in this manner followed its course to where it emptied into the river, half a mile below at a place known as Shallow Shoals. Here he took to the timber, eluding the vigilance of the Indians by getting in their rear. He then crept cautiously up the ridge, guided by the gobbling of the Indian in the top of the cedar on the cliff. Getting within about seventy-five yards of the tree, and waiting until his turkeyship had finished an extra big gobble, he drew a bead upon him and put a ball in his head. With a yell and spring the Indian went crashing through the tree-tops and over the precipice, a mangled mass of flesh and bones. Then commenced a race for life. Gray had played a desperate game, and nothing but his fleetness and his knowledge of savage craft could save him. He knew that the Indians in ambush would go to their companion on hearing the report of the rifle, and that they were not more than two hundred yards away. He did his best running and dodging, but they were so close upon him that he would have been captured or killed, had not the men of the fort rushed out to his rescue.

"The Indians, finding that they had been discovered, and that they were not strong enough to attack or besiege the fort, started in the direction of Castlewood. The persons at Bluegrass (Fort Blackmore) knowing that the settlement at Castle's Wood was not aware that the Indians were in the vicinity, determined to warn them, but the difficulty was how this was to be done, and who would be bold enough to undertake it, as the Indians were between the two forts. When a volunteer for the perilous expedition was called for Matthew Gray, who but an hour before had made such a narrow escape, boldly offered his services, and, getting the fastest horse and two rifles, started out through the almost unbroken forest. Moving cautiously along the trail, he came near Ivy Spring about two miles from the fort, when he saw signs which satisfied him that the Indians had halted at the spring. There was no way to flank them, and he must make a perilous dash or fail in his mission of mercy. Being an old Indian fighter, he knew that they seldom put out pickets. The trail making a short curve near the spring, he at once formed the plan of riding quietly up to the curve and then, with a shot and a yell, to dash through them. This he did, and before they had sufficiently recovered from their surprise to give him a parting volley, he was out of reach. He arrived at the settlement in safety, and thus in all probability saved the lives of all the settlers. The Indians, however, captured two women on the way—Polly Alley at Osborn's Ford, as they went up the river, and Jane Whitaker near Castlewood.

"Finding the fort at Castle's Woods fully prepared for their reception the band had to abandon their murderous purpose and pass on with their captives, without permitting themselves to be seen. Reaching Guess' Station, they remained part of the night; finding it well prepared for defence, they continued their journey to the "Breaks," where the Russell and Pound forks of Big Sandy pass through the Cumberland Mountain.

"After this they traveled every day, resting at night, until they reached the Ohio at the mouth of Sandy. Crossing the river on a raft of logs with their prisoners, who suffered more than can be described or conceived on the long march, they reached their destination at Sandusky. The two young women were closely confined for some time after their arrival though they were eventually stripped and painted and allowed the liberty of the village, closely watched for a month or more, but seeing they made no attempt at escape the Indians abated their vigilance. Observing this the girls determined to make an effort at escape. Having been permitted to wander about at pleasure from time to time and punctually returning at night, the Indians were thrown off their guard. Having wandered one day farther from the village than usual, and being in a dense forest, they started out on the long journey toward their home. After traveling all night, they found themselves only about eight miles from the village, and finding a hollow log, they crept into it, with the determination of remaining concealed during the day. They had been in it but a few minutes before Hargus and two or three Indians came along in pursuit and sat down upon it, and the girls heard them form their plans for the next day's search. Returning late in the afternoon, having lost the trail, the Indians sat down upon the same log to rest, and again the occupants beneath them heard their plans for pursuit. These were, that a party should pass down each of two rivers which had their sources near their village and emptied into the Ohio. They became very much enraged at having been baffled by two inexperienced girls, and threatened their victims with all sorts of tortures should they be recaptured. Hargus, more furious than the Indians themselves, striking his tomahawk into the log to emphasize his threats, and finding it return a hollow sound, declared the girls might be in it, as they had been traced thus far, where the trail was lost and sent one of the savages to the end of the log to see. The savage went and looked, but seeing that a spider had stretched its web across the aperture, he made no further examination. This web, which probably had not been there an hour, saved them from recapture, and it may be from a cruel death.

"After the Indians left, the girls, having heard their plans, left the log and resumed their weary journey, taking a leading ridge, which ran at right angles with the Ohio and led them to it not far from opposite the mouth of Sandy. They could hear the yells of the Indians in pursuit each day and night until they reached the river, when, from a high promontory, they had the satisfaction of seeing their pursuers give up the chase and turn back towards their village. They had nothing to eat for three long days and nights but a partially devoured squirrel from which they had frightened a hawk and on the night of the third day after the Indians had relinquished the pursuit, they ventured to the river, where they were fortunate enough the next day to see a flat-boat with white men in it descending the stream, who, on being hailed, took them aboard, set them across at the mouth of Sandy, and furnished them with a sufficiency of bread and dried venison to last them two weeks and blanket each, in which time they expected to make their way back to one of the settlements on Clinch. They took their course up Sandy on the same trail they had gone down some months before, but in one of the rapid and dangerous crossings of that stream, they lost all of their provisions as well as blankets. This, though a great calamity, did not discourage them, but pushing on, with blessing of kindred, friends and home in view, they found their way through Pound Gap and reached Guess' Station about the middle of September, having been on the journey about a month, after encountering hardships and dangers under which many of the sterner sex of the present day would give way." (*Life of Wilburn Waters*, pp. 171–76.)

In August, 1776, the Virginia Council ordered Col. William Christian with his army to invade the country of the Cherokees "for the purpose of severely chastising that cruel and perfidious nation." Jonathan Jennings, a resident of Fort Blackmore at the time, served as private in this expedition. It is very probable that other residents of the fort took part in this expedition, yet their names cannot certainly be recognized in the list of those who participated in it.

At the close of his campaign against the Cherokees, Colonel Christian ordered Capt. Joseph Martin to proceed to the Rye Cove with eighty men. Captain Martin remained in the Rye Cove until the first of May, 1777, when he was ordered back to the Long Island, where he remained until the treaty of peace was concluded between the Indians and the whites on July 1.

The first election under the new State Constitution was

held in the summer of 1776. In this election Arthur Campbell and William Russell were chosen as members of the House of Delegates for Fincastle County, and Col. William Christian was chosen as Senator for Fincastle and Botetourt counties. The citizens of Fort Blackmore, no doubt, were ardent supporters of these candidates, all of whom they knew, and one of whom, Russell, was a neighbor.

In the year 1779, Capt. John Blackmore, the man for whom Fort Blackmore was named, with his family emigrated to Nashboro (now Nashville), Tennessee. He was accompanied by his son, John Blackmore, Jr., and his family, together with Jonathan Jennings and his family. Their voyage was a very remarkable one, the entire journey, from Fort Blackmore by way of Muscle Shoals to the mouth of the Tennessee River and thence up the Ohio and Cumberland to Nashboro, having been made in flat-bottomed boats. Sailing unknown rivers, dropping over dangerous shoals and falls, and passing through villages of savage and hostile Indians, these stout-hearted emigrants accomplished a journey that now seems almost impossible. Added to the difficulty and dangers of their long and perilous journey was the bitter cold of the winter of 1779–80.

The exact date of Captain Blackmore's departure from the settlement at the mouth of Stony Creek is not known, but Col. John Donaldson, who with a fleet of about thirty flat-bottomed boats made the voyage from Kingsport to Nashboro at the same time, made the following entry in the journal of the voyage. "Sunday, 5th. (March, 1780.) Cast off and got under way before sunrise; 12 o'clock passed the mouth of Clinch; at 12 o'clock M. came up with the Clinch River Company, whom we joined, and camped, the evening proving rainy."

Further on in the journal he states: "And here we must regret the unfortunate death of young Mr. Payne, on board Captain Blackmore's boat, who was mortally wounded by reason of the boat running too near the northern shore opposite the town, where some of the enemy lay concealed."

He makes the following entries concerning Jonathan Jennings and his family.

"Jennings' boat is missing. We have now passed through the Whirl. The river widens, with a placid and gentle current, and all the company appear to be in safety except the family of Jonathan Jennings, whose boat ran on a large rock projecting out from the northern shore and partly immersed in water immediately at the Whirl, where we were compelled to leave them, perhaps to be slaughtered by their merciless enemies. Continued to sail on that day and floated throughout the following night.

"Friday, 10th. This morning about 4 o'clock we were surprised by the cries of 'Help poor Jennings' at some distance in the rear. He had discovered us by our fires and came up in the most wretched condition. He states that as soon as the Indians discovered his situation they turned their whole attention to him and kept up a most galling fire at his boat. He ordered his wife, a son nearly grown, a young man who accompanied them, and his negro man and woman to throw all his goods into the river in order to lighten his boat for the purpose of getting her off, himself returning the Indians' fire as well as he could, being a good soldier and an excellent marksman. But before they had accomplished their object, his son, the young man, and the negro jumped out of the boat and left them. He thinks the young man and the negro were wounded before they left the boat. Mrs. Jennings, however, and the negro woman succeeded in unloading the boat, but chiefly by the exertions of Mrs. Jennings, who got out of the boat and shoved her off, but was near falling a victim to her own intrepidity on account of the boat starting so suddenly as soon as loosened from the rock. Upon examination, he appears to have made a wonderful escape, for his boat is pierced in numberless places with bullets. Their clothes were very much cut with bullets, especially Mrs. Jennings'." (Donaldson's Journal, quoted in *Taylor's Historic Sullivan*, p. 75 et seq.)

Jonathan Jennings had not resided at the Nashboro settlement very long before he was attacked and killed by a party of Delaware Indians at the point of the first island in the Cumberland River, above Nashville, Tennessee. Both Jonathan Jennings and Capt. John Blackmore are mentioned as having been given land for distinguished services against the Indians. (Haywood, p. 219.) Their descendants still reside in Middle Tennessee. The Fincastle County Court on

July 6, 1773, fined Jonathan Jennings forty shillings for speaking of the court with contempt and saying that they were selfish and partial. (Summers, p. 135.)

In the early days salt was a scarce and highly prized article. Prior to the discovery of salt at Saltville, the chief supply on the border was brought in wagons from Eastern Virginia. It was usually brought to Black's Fort (now Abingdon), Washington County, and from that point distributed to the various settlements. The coming of the salt wagon was an important event on the frontier. In 1781, the salt wagon came to Washington County and from the supply which it brought Fort Blackmore no doubt received its quota.

During the spring of 1781, "the Northward Indians," coming in small parties up Sandy River, gave the settlers on the Clinch much trouble and alarm. These small parties were often able to enter the settlements unawares, capturing or wounding or killing whomsoever they might meet. The settlements on the Clinch were guarded by a company of rangers in Powell's Valley at this time, but the militia, not having received their pay for former services, were complaining. This condition made it difficult to get men to patrol the long line of frontier from the Sandy River to Cumberland Gap. The southern frontier was also threatened with invasion by the Creek and Cherokee Indians and Tories under the leadership of the British Indian Agent. It needed to be also patrolled. "The sudden condemnation of the Continental money, and the neglect or refusal of the government to pay the militia for their various services last year, together with the time and attention necessarily spent to have our landed claims adjusted," were assigned as reasons for military unpreparedness on the border. (Virginia State Papers.)

Bishop Asbury, in his journal, makes the following entries concerning his visit to Fort Blackmore:

"1790. Wednesday, April 28. We have had cold weather and severe frosts for two nights past. We had a dreary ride down to the ford of Clinch, through a solitary plain; many attended at L——s. We rode down to Blackmore's Station, here the people have been forted on the north side of Clinch. Poor Blackmore had had a son and daughter killed by the Indians. They are of opinion here that the Cherokees were the authors of this mischief; I also received an account of two families having been killed, and of one female that was taken prisoner, and afterwards retaken by the neighbors and brought back. "Friday, 30. Crossed Clinch about two miles below the fort. In passing along I saw the precipice from which Blackmore's unhappy son leaped into the river after receiving the stroke of the tomahawk in his head; I suppose, by the measure of my eye, it must be between fifty and sixty feet descent; his companion was shot dead upon the spot; this happened on the 6th of April, 1789. We came on a dreary road over rocks, ridges, hills, stones, and streams, along a blind, tortuous path, to Mockeson Gap, and Creek; thence to Smith's Ferry across the north branch of Holstein. Here I found some lies had been told on me; feeling myself innocent, I was not moved."

November 9, 1792, Senator John Preston, in making recommendations to the Governor and Privy Council concerning the defense of the Southwest Territory, suggests that a sergeant, corporal, and twelve privates be placed at Fort Blackmore.

Andrew Lewis, speaking of the capture of the Livingstons, in a letter to the Governor, bearing date of April 17, 1794, states that Blackmore Station, by which the enemy must have passed, was left unguarded for the following reasons: The inhabitants there lived in stations so near as to be in a situation, in some measure, to defend themselves. The troops that had been garrisoned at that place had been ordered to protect Lee County, with instructions to return to Fort Blackmore on the arrival of Captain Hawkins' company in Lee. Benge and his party, finding the inhabitants of Blackmore's Station on their guard, passed on until he found people living, as they thought, in perfect security.

A PEACEABLE INDIAN INVASION

An authentic tradition relates the following story concerning the last appearance of Indians in the vicinity of the Stony Creek Settlement.

About the year 1817 the people in the neighborhood of Fort Blackmore were startled by the appearance of a band of Indians under the leadership of a chief whose name was never learned. These Indians, crossing Stone Mountain at the High Knob, had entered the settlement, it seems, by coming down Stony Creek. The excitement of such a visit can well be imagined. Many people were then living who remembered the forays of Benge and his gang. The route, too, by which these late arrivals had come was the one over which many hostile bands before them had traveled in their efforts to surprise the settlers at the fort. Why had they come now? Was their mission one of peace or war? Every man who saw them instinctively thought of his loved ones and his rifle. But while the people were thus perplexed as to whether the motives of their redskin visitors were friendly or hostile, the Indians, without delay, marched Indian file, the chief in the lead, to the mound located on the farm of the late Emory Cox.

On reaching the mound, a rather elaborate ceremony of a memorial character, it is supposed, was begun. This ceremony consisted mainly of gestures, the chief leading. Approaching the mound, the chief circled about it, making gestures in the direction of the four cardinal points of the compass. He then ascended the mound to its summit, still continuing to gesticulate, slowly and solemnly, toward the four cardinal points. His followers imitated the movements of their chief. When the ceremony was finished, the Indians again formed themselves into Indian file and marched toward the west. They were never heard of afterward. (W. S. Cox.)

HENRY HAMLIN

Henry Hamlin was living in the Rye Cove, May 15, 1788. In a letter to Governor Randolph, bearing this date, Alexander Barnett, County Lieutenant of Russell, complains that Henry Hamlin induced the Rangers, who had been sent out under the command of Ensign Blackmore to protect the settlers in the Cove, to return from their expedition, by telling them that the people wanted men stationed at the forts for their protection instead of Rangers. The records and the traditions preserved by the descendants of Henry Hamlin state that he was born March 25, 1740; that on coming to Southwest Virginia he married a Miss Dickenson; that four sons, Francis, Charles, Champ, and John, were born to this marriage; that

Mrs. Henry Hamlin was killed at Fort Blackmore by the Indians, August 17, 1790; that at the same time Champ, then a boy ten years of age, was captured and carried west, but eventually was transported into Canada, where he was ransomed by a French trader and taken to Quebec, from which place he was sent by boat to Norfolk, and that from Norfolk he made his way back to his home near Fort Blackmore; that two of the boys, Charles and John, were saved from the Indians by a negro slave, a giant in stature and weighing three hundred and fifty pounds; that for this act the slave was given his freedom and a small farm some six miles south of Jonesville; that Henry Hamlin died at Fort Blackmore, August, 1815. (J. S. Hamlin's Letter, May 19, 1918.)

Mrs. Fannie Napper, whose maiden name was Alley, and her five children were killed and scalped near Fort Blackmore in 1777. (Sam Alley in Draper Manuscripts.)

In 1789 one of the Blackmores' homes was attacked by Indians. (Draper Manuscripts.)

In January, 1781, a body of Indians, supposed to be Cherokees, attacked Fort Blackmore, capturing four men and taking away a large number of horses. In consequence of this depredation it was strongly urged upon Governor Jefferson that strong garrisons be stationed in Powell's Valley and on the banks of the Tennessee River. This or similar action was represented to the Governor as being "absolutely necessary for the preservation of the southwestern frontier and keeping up the communication with Kentucky." (Virginia State Papers, Vol. I.)

There are a number of variant spellings of the name Blackmore. Captain John, Sr., and John, Jr., in signing the Nashboro Compact, May 13, 1780, spelled the name Blackemore. John, Jr., in making an assignment of his land to Samuel Haddox, spelled his surname Blackeymore. In the court records of the time the name is found spelled Blackmore, Blackemore, Blackamore, and Blackeymore.

THE RYE COVE

Capt. Daniel Smith, in a letter from Castlewood to Col. William Preston, under date of March 22, 1774, writes, "This

day I leave this neighborhood to go towards the Rye Coves."
This is the earliest mention of Rye Cove of which I can find
any record. How the name originated or when it was first
applied to the section so designated are questions which available data do not answer. The words "cove" and "lick" were
often employed by the early settlers as geographical names.
The adjectives used with these words usually had reference
to some fitting condition or circumstance.

Captain Smith, assistant surveyor of Fincastle County, went
"towards the Rye Coves" at this time for the purpose of
making land surveys for some of the first settlers within the
present limits of Scott County. Of the entire number, the
following names with dates of survey may be given: Joseph
Blackmore, March 24; Capt. John Blackmore and Isaac
Crisman, March 25; John, Thomas, and Dale Carter, March
26; and John Blackmore, Jr., March 29, 1774. Isaac
Crisman became a citizen of the Rye Cove. His land, consisting of two hundred and twenty-five acres, was situated
on Cove Creek, probably five or six miles from its mouth.
Sometime prior to 1776, Crisman built a stockaded fort west of
Cove Creek and about a mile distant from it. The stockade
enclosed one-half acre of land, and was considered unusually
large for that day. Nearby were several excellent springs.
Sometime within the year 1776, a band of Indians attacked
Crisman's Fort, killing Crisman himself and two members of
his family. Whereupon Capt. Joseph Martin and a company of men were then ordered to the Rye Cove to protect
it from Indian invasion. Captain Martin remained in the
Rye Cove until the first of May, at which time he was
ordered back to Long Island. Isaac Crisman served as a
private in the Glade Hollow Fort during the Point Pleasant
Campaign. (See Captain Redd's *Narrative,* and Thwaites
and Kellogg's *Dunmore's War.*)

The following pension statement of Charles Bickley relates
his service under Capt. William Russell in the Rye Cove:

"Charles Bickley entered the service of the United States in
the month of September or October, 1775, within the limits
of Russell County, Virginia, under Capt. William Russell,
Lieut. William Bowen, and Ensign James Knox, and was ren-

dezvoused and stationed at the Rye Cove, in the County of Scott, in the State aforesaid, where he remained in service guarding and defending that fort until the 23d day of January, 1776, when he was discharged and returned home.

"That in the ensuing summer of 1776, exact date not remembered, he was engaged hoeing corn in the County of Russell, when an alarm that Indians were in the neighborhood was raised. The people assembled at the fort and the company of militia from Reed Creek, in Wythe County, under the command of Capt. John Montgomery, Lieut. Michael Dougherty, and Ensign John Simpson, were on their march to the Rye Cove Fort, preparatory to an expected expedition against the Cherokee Indians, when he, Charles Bickley, enrolled as a private, and marched under said officers to Rye Cove, where they remained a short time. Colonel Bledsoe, then in command of the forces on the frontier, ordered the evacuation of Rye Cove Fort and marched to Blakemore's Fort, on Clinch River, where a junction was formed with the forces then in the fort. While at Fort Blackmore they were informed through Capt. Daniel Smith that the Indians were upon the waters of Moccasin Creek. Bledsoe's and Smith's companies were united and went in pursuit of the Indians, following their trail to within a short distance of Houston's Fort upon Big Moccasin Creek. They were unable to find the Indians. No attack had been made upon the fort. Samuel Cowan, already in the fort, proposed to return horseback to his family in Castle's Wood, under the protest of the soldiers, who admonished him of the danger of such an undertaking. He persisted and had not gone far when the report of gunfire was heard. When found, he had been shot and scalped, and died soon after being carried into the fort. The Indians fled and the company returned to Fort Blackmore. They marched from Fort Blackmore into Tennessee, where they were joined by Colonel Christy (Christian) and Major E. Shelby." (Pension Statement of Charles Bickley in Clerk's Office of Russell County.)

On the return of Colonel Christian's army, at the close of the Cherokee Campaign, it was disbanded, except a few companies scattered here and there on the frontier. One of these companies, in command of Capt. Joseph Martin, was stationed in the Rye Cove during the winter and spring of 1777. They were stationed at Crisman's Fort. While here, Martin's company was attacked by Indians under the leadership of a son of Nancy Ward's, known among the whites by the name of Little Fellow. In this engagement, Captain Martin and Little Fellow were accidently brought into personal contact with each other. The personal conflict was without casualty on either side, but they thus learned to respect each other and were friends ever after.

During Captain Martin's sojourn in the Rye Cove, messengers were sent from Kentucky to announce that the settlement there had been attacked by Indians, and to ask aid. Just beyond the Rye Cove, these messengers were fired on from ambush and one of them killed, but not before he had wounded his enemy. The wounded Indian was traced to a cave by his blood; General Martin entered and killed him, although the Indian was armed with a gun and had the advantage of darkness. (Week's *War of the Revolution in the West*, pp. 428–474.)

John C. Monroe, who volunteered in Montgomery County to guard the frontier on the Clinch, was stationed for a time at Fort Blackmore, while the Revolutionary struggle was in progress. He spent a month on the Clinch, though not all of this time at Fort Blackmore. (Pension Statement, McAlister's *Virginia Militia in the Revolution*.)

James Kincaid entered the Revolutionary service at Castlewood, Virginia. The settlers of Powell's Valley had been driven from their homes in such haste by the Indians that they were unable to bring their personal property to Fort Blackmore or the Rye Cove for safety. Many of them, therefore hid their "plunder" until such time as it could be brought away in safety. Capt. John Duncan and his company were ordered out to guard the people of Powell's Valley and outlying settlements while they were bringing their goods into the settlements. James Kincaid was a member of Captain Duncan's company and spent one year in such service. This service, he says, was rendered in the same year in which Capt. Joseph Martin was stationed in the Rye Cove to guard the frontier there. While campaigning in Powell's Valley, one of Kincaid's comrades in arms, a man by the name of Bunnill, became very sick, and they brought him to the Rye

Cove for treatment. (Pension Statement, McAlister's *Virginia Militia in the Revolution*.)

In Hanson's Journal, under date of August 9, 1774, the following entry is found: "We kept that river (Guess's) in sight till we came to Clinch River in the afternoon, to Mr. Blackburn's, near the Rye Cove, where we found them forted in, prepared for war with the Shawnees." (Thwaites and Kellogg's *Dunmore's War*, p. 133.)

At a meeting of the field officers of Montgomery and Washington counties, held July 6, 1782, it was decided that Rye Cove should have a garrison of twenty men and two scouts. (Virginia State Papers, Vol. 3.)

December 31, 1787, Arthur Campbell, Andrew Cowan, Samuel Edmiston, Daniel Boone, and Thomas Carter jointly recommend to Governor Randolph that a detachment of men be stationed at Rye Cove and other places along the border, in case it is found that war with the Indians is unavoidable the ensuing spring. (Virginia State Papers, Vol. 4.)

The following is a letter written by John Anderson to Arthur Campbell in regard to Indian depredations committed in the Rye Cove settlement:

"Blockhouse, May ye 17th, 1789.

"Dear Sir: I wrote to you a few days ago, wherein I informed you respecting Mr. Wallen's being driven from home. Wallen lived at the mouth of Stock Creek (now Clinchport). I seen a certain Mr. Joseph Johnson a few hours since, who informed me that on the 15th instant he had his family, which consisted of his wife and eleven children, all killed and taken except two. He found his wife and youngest child about three quarters of a mile from his house. He lived on Clinch, where the path crossed the same between here and Rye Cove. They burnt his house, and he found the bones of one of his children in the ashes. The others he allows they took prisoners. I am fully persuaded from the many and late hostilities committed in that quarter that the inhabitants will move off if they do not get some assistance shortly. I am surprised to think we guarded our frontiers in the time of the late war, when we were attacked on both sides, and now can get no help. I am doubtful the Government has false representatives or else none at all. You may depend the people of

our situation in this quarter are much alarmed by the many
and late acts committed. Please write me the first opportunity.

              I am yours affectionately,

                                  JOHN ANDERSON.
Col. Arthur Campbell."

Alexander Barnett, County Lieutenant of Russell, after reporting to Col. Arthur Campbell the Indian depredation on
Joseph Johnson's family, goes on to state: "Attempts have
been made by voluntary enlistment to raise the number of
fifty men in our county, but to no purpose, it appears they
can not be got. I request you in behalf of our county to furnish us with the number of fifty men and their proper proportion of officers, to be continued on duty until the 1st of
September, or longer, if needed, and provisions to supply until
that time. Present necessity requires part for the Rye Cove
and the remainder in Powell's Valley." (Virginia State Papers, Vol. 4.)

Under date of August 1, 1789, Col. Arthur Campbell informs Governor Randolph that "hostile detachments had been
sent out by McGillivary to Kentucky and the settlements on
Clinch." That about two weeks ago a skirmish had taken
place in Powell's Valley with a small party of Indians who
were stealing horses. That in this skirmish one white man
was badly wounded. The settlements on the Clinch referred
to above, were Rye Cove and Fort Blackmore. (Virginia
State Papers, Vol. 4.)

August 29, 1787, Alexander Barnett informs the Governor
that on July 9, last, the Indians had again attacked the frontier, this time killing the wife of John Carter and six of his
children, at the same time plundering and setting fire to his
house, thus reducing the bodies of his wife and children to
ashes. (Virginia State Papers, Vol. 4.)

John Carter, it seems, was a brother of Dale Carter, who
was murdered when Chief Logan's band of Indians attacked
Fort Blackmore in 1774. Some years after Dale Carter's
murder, John Carter settled on Clinch River, where Joseph
Salling now lives, four miles below Fort Blackmore. He had
married Joseph Blackmore's daughter and had seven chil-

dren. In a short time after moving to his farm, having planted his crop and completed such other preparations as were necessary to move back to the fort, he went out one morning to listen for his horses and cattle which had bells on, intending to collect them up prior to moving to Fort Blackmore on the next day. This was locust year, and he went out early in order to collect his stock before the locusts began their noises. He had proceeded about sixty yards from his house when he heard his wife cry out, "Oh, John." On turning, he saw eight or nine Indians entering his house, and at the same time they fired at him. Realizing his perilous situation, he thought it best to make his escape and go for assistance, rather than fight and only exasperate the savages in an unequal contest. Hastening to the fort, he collected a company and returned to his home, which he found in flames. With some poles, his companions succeeded in pulling out of the burning coals the charred remains of his wife and six children, which they buried. When they had done this, they heard a plaintive groaning a little distance from the house, in the weeds and grass. They went to the place from whence the sounds came and found his little daughter, about ten years of age, with an awful gash across her abdomen and her entrail falling out. They carried her to the river and washed her, but she died before they had finished. (Judge Wood and Peter Honnycut in Draper Manuscripts, 4 C 27.) As soon as Mr. Barnett heard of the murder of Carter's family, he ordered out a party of Rangers to hunt down the Indians, but it was all to no purpose. They had made good their retreat. (Virginia State Papers, Vol. 4.)

On April 20, 1788, Indians came into the Rye Cove settlement at Carter's Fort and captured two boys, the sons of Thomas Carter, and a negro slave boy, the property of the two Carter boys' father. Thomas Carter at that time represented Russell County in the Legislature. The Indians did not kill anyone on this raid.

On learning of the capture of the Carter boys, Mr. Barnett ordered out men of three companies, under the command of Ensign Blackmore, and sent them to range in search of the Indians near the Rye Cove. On reaching the Rye Cove, Ensign Blackmore and his men were turned back by Henry

Hamlin, who told them that the people there wanted men stationed among them as a garrison instead of Rangers. As a protection for this settlement, Mr. Barnett then suggested to Governor Randolph that three small stations of ten men each be maintained, one near Rye Cove and two in Powell's Valley.

One of the Carter boys was restored to his father through the kindness of Governor Simcoe of South Carolina. William Fatham, in a letter to the Governor of Virginia, dated July 30, 1793, states the following facts concerning the capture of the Carter boys:

"Just before I left Holston a few weeks ago, I saw old Mr. Carter (brother to the member from Russell of that name), who told me his son had lately returned safe through the bounty and benevolence of Governor Simcoe, with whom, I think, the negro boy is left, the Governor not being at liberty, in his own opinion, to deliver up the boy without more substantial proof of the property; this, however, he need not hesitate about, as the story is well known on the Clinch, where I suppose the negro's attachments are, and where (as you know) they are treated as the white children of the family." (Virginia State Papers, Vol. 6.)

As the Carter children were restored to their parents through the friendly offices of Governor Simcoe of South Carolina, William Fatham, in the same letter quoted above, asks that an effort be made through Governor Simcoe to restore the children of Joseph Johnson to their grief-stricken parent. In order to facilitate the work of restoring the children, he furnished the Governor with the following facts concerning them:

"Joseph Johnson, living now upon Flat Creek, had his wife and three children killed on May 15, 1789, and five others taken by the Indians on the road leading to the Flour Ford, near the Rye Cove on the Clinch. 1, Isabel, now. 21 years old; 2, Matthew, now 15; 3, Elizabeth, now 13 years; 4, Rebecca, now 10; and 5, Joseph, now 8 years old. Isabel was carried by the Cherokees near to the Guyandot Nation, where she was sold and brought back to the Cherokee nation, and was there purchased and sent to her father. Elizabeth is now in the possession of the Otter Lifter (a warrior of that name near John Meton's, a trader on Cheakonskie in the Cherokees). The other three are said to be in the Guyandot nation, together with Mary Ann and Elizabeth Carter, and a negro boy called Cooper, who were taken from the neighborhood." (Virginia State Papers, Vol. 6.)

I have been unable to find any record as to whether these children were ever restored to their parents and friends. It is very probable some, if not all, of them were, because their location seemed to be definitely known, and many influences could be brought to bear on the Indians to induce them to restore the children.

Senator John Preston's recommendation to the Governor and Privy Council concerning the defense of the Southwest Territory, November 9, 1792, advises that a captain, sergeant, corporal, and twenty-four privates be stationed "at Carter's in Rye Cove." It will now be noticed that Carter's Fort is regarded as being a much more exposed position than Fort Blackmore, because the garrison of the former is made twice as strong as the latter.

In the year 1791, Simon Cockrell urges the addition of ten more men to the Rye Cove garrison. (Virginia State Papers, Vol. 4.)

The conditions prevailing in the region of the Cove are shown by the following letter of Andrew Lewis to the Governor of Virginia, bearing date of April 9, 1793:

"Sir: I am sorry that the distressed situation of the frontiers compels me to send to you by express. On Sunday week, Ensign Moses Cockrell and two men were passing from this into Powell's Valley with several horses loaded. On the top of Powell's Mountain (about nine miles from the Cove) they were fired on by twelve Indians. The two men were shot dead on the spot, himself pursued to the foot of the mountain, two of the horses killed, all the loads lost. The enemy being in the rear of him, obliged him to run to the valley. No person passing from there, had no information here for several days. Captain Neel raised some men, and is in pursuit of them. I am in hopes that if my ensign gets intelligence in time, as he is stationed in the lower end of the valley, will meet with them on their return. Same day fourteen persons were killed on the Kentucky Road near the Hazel Patch. About twenty days past several people were killed on the Kentucky Road and several wounded. Sent a sergeant and seven men to Rye Cove. Appointed two scouts to the Rye Cove." (Virginia State Papers, Vol. 6.)

Charles B. Coale, in his *Life of Wilburn Waters*, says that the leader of the Indians who attacked Ensign Cockrell and his men on the top of Powell's Mountain was the notorious Benge, though on what authority he so states, I do not know. (*Wilburn Waters*, pp. 153–154.)

Carter's Fort, in the Rye Cove, was built in 1784 by Thomas Carter and Joseph Carter. It was located on the farm now owned by Floyd Richmond, six miles west of Fort Blackmore, on the Boone and Porter's Road down the Clinch. Norris Carter lived in Fort Blackmore until danger from the Indians was over. He then moved to his farm, where John Carter's family was killed, and lived there until his death in 1816. It is reported that Thomas and Joseph Carter retreated to Fort Houston on Big Moccasin for safety when their fort was threatened by Indians. The first settlement and fortifications were so weak that they were abandoned. Norris Carter returned to Fort Blackmore, and Thomas and Joseph went to Black's Fort. Later the Carter brothers returned to the Rye Cove and made a permanent settlement. They greatly strengthened their fort on their return. At that time Carter's settlement was the farthest west in the Clinch Valley. George Rogers Clark once visited Rye Cove as paymaster in Col. Andrew Lewis' command. Dale Carter, father of T. W. Carter, was a soldier under Lewis.

William Stewart and David Neeley were two Revolutionary veterans who lived in the Rye Cove. They both drew pensions on account of their services.

Two of the Kentucky Traces passed near this fort, one from Big Moccasin Gap and the other one from Castlewood. The one from Castlewood passed down the southern side of the ridge between Sinking Creek Valley and Clinch River by way of Powers' Hill to Hunter's Ford (later called Osborne's Ford.) From Hunter's Ford, the trace passed down the valley to Fort Blackmore, thence to the Rye Cove. The trace from Big Moccasin Gap crossed Moccasin Ridge somewhere near the old Red Hill meeting house to Copper Creek, near the mouth of Flour Branch, thence up Flour Branch and by the way of the "Set Rock" on the farm of the late James H. Quillen to the top of Copper Ridge, near the former home of Mark Kidd. From the top of Copper Ridge it passed to the Flour Ford of Clinch River, now called Craft's Ferry, thence up Flat Creek, now called Mill Creek, to its headwaters, and thence by Carter's Fort to Cove Creek, thence up Cove Creek to Maple Gap, and from Maple Gap to Big Stone Gap, etc.

Rye Cove served as a buffer settlement for Fort Blackmore during the later years of the Revolutionary War. Its settlers seem to have abandoned it during the earlier years of the Revolution, going to Fort Blackmore and other forts less exposed to Indian attack. (Redd's *Narrative*.)

The two Carter boys, Morgan and Elijah, are said to have been sons of Thomas Carter, the builder of Carter's Fort. (Coley's *Genealogy of the Carters in Scott County*.)

PORTER'S FORT

April 1, 1774, 214 acres of land were surveyed for Patrick Porter, on the west side of Falling Creek, now called Fall Creek, and, on the following day 256 acres for Charles Kilgore on the east side of the same creek. The Porter survey is now owned, in part at least, by Sheridan and Emory Banner, and the Kilgore survey by the Blackwell heirs and others.

Patrick Porter actually settled on his survey in the year 1772, and sometime within the year 1775, Porter built on his survey a fort, which was called Porter's Fort. The six original settlers at Porter's Fort were: Patrick Porter; Raleigh Stallard; Capt. John Montgomery, Porter's son-in-law; Samuel, a son of Patrick Porter; and a man named Hutchinson, whose Christian name is not given and Charles Kilgore. These men all came, it seems, from Snoddy's Fort in Castlewood to settle at Porter's Fort.

March 2, 1774, the County Court of Fincastle gave Patrick Porter permission to erect a mill on Falling Creek. In accordance with the orders of the Court, Porter built a mill at the falls of Fall Creek, on the site where Nash's mill stood many years later. The court order is as follows: On motion of Patrick Porter Leave is given him to Build a Mill on Falling Creek the Waters of the Clinch. (Summers' *Annals of Southwest Virginia,* p. 599.)

This, so far as any reliable records show, was the first mill built within the present limits of Scott County. Prior to the erection of this mill, flour and meal could be obtained only by mashing the grain with a kind of mortar and pestle arrangement or in a "slow John." This mill, therefore, was patronized by the settlers of a large section of country, a no less distinguished personage than Daniel Boone himself is represented as being among its patrons. Another authentic tradition relating to this mill is that the first Masonic Lodge ever organized in this section held regular meetings in its loft. (T. W. Carter in Draper Manuscripts.)

Patrick Porter, Colonel Snoddy, William and John Cowan were born in Ireland. They were brothers-in-law, having married four sisters prior to their immigration to America, about the middle of the eighteenth century. They first settled in Surry County, N. C., then later they came to Castlewood. Porter and Snoddy were Freemasons and desired to enjoy the rights and benefits of the order in their new home. Procuring a charter from Dublin, Ireland, they proceeded at once to organize a lodge whose stated communications were held in the loft of Porter's mill as stated above. Colonel Snoddy was the Worshipful Master of the lodge until his removal to Kentucky, then Patrick Porter became the Worshipful Master. This charter, it is said, was written on vellum, and was in the possession of Thos. W. Carter, a grandson of Patrick Porter, in Rye Cove, until the Civil War, when by some chance mice destroyed it.

Tradition relates that during the siege of Boonesborough, in March, 1778, a runner was sent to Porter's Fort, imploring aid. The courier arrived at the fort late in the evening, and, as soon as his message had been made known, twenty-three young men volunteered to go to the aid of the besieged, under the command of Samuel Porter, who previously had been with Boone in Kentucky. The fort was soon all astir with warlike preparations. The volunteers began to rub up their guns and make arrangements for the campaign. Some of the women were put to molding bullets while others were set to cooking rations.

Early the next morning, the brave band of volunteers set out and after five days of almost incessant marching reached Boonesborough without accident. These militiamen, it seems, arrived a week too late to take part in raising the siege of Boonesborough. Although Blackfish and his dusky warriors had been driven from the beleaguered fort when they reached it, yet opportunity was offered them to participate in a number of minor raids against the Shawnees upon their own soil.

It is said that among Porter's company was a young man named Stuffly Cooper, who had a long steel-barreled gun, called yager (pronounced *yawger*). The yagers are represented as having had much longer range than ordinary rifles of that time. While on this Kentucky campaign, Cooper was furnished an opportunity to test the carrying power of his gun. In an effort to spy into Boonesborough, and watch the movements of the whites, a large Indian climbed into a tree about six hundred yards distant, but in plain view. Cooper declared he could kill that Indian with his rifle. To enable him to have the most accurate shot possible, a chair was brought out on which Cooper rested his gun, at the same time steadying his back against a stump. The Indian, observing these operations, came down out of the tree, and believing himself to be at a perfectly safe distance, straightened himself up in a defiant manner, and then contemptuously made a number of insulting gestures. Cooper took very deliberate aim, and at the crack of his gun the Indian jumped into the air, gave a yell, and then fell lifeless.

Tradition further alleges substantially the following account of Samuel Porter. After a short campaign against the Indians in defense of Boonesborough and other Kentucky settlements, all of Porter's men returned to Virginia, except Samuel Porter himself, John Arter, and Stuffly Cooper. These men remained for further campaigning against the Indians. They were in the fight at Blue Licks where many of the whites were killed. John Arter was among the slain, but Porter and Cooper were unhurt and remained with Boone until the next summer when they joined the command of Colonel Bowman.

Bowman, with a small force, crossed the Ohio River, near the boundary line between Ohio and Indiana. He had not penetrated the country very far when he came upon an Indian village, which he attacked at once. In this attack, Samuel Porter stationed himself behind a hut, and, in loading his gun, he, incautiously, exposed his knee, when the excellent aim of the Indians lodged two bullets in it, completely disabling him. At this time, a negro woman who had been captured by the Indians, made her way to Bowman and advised him to fall back for Blackfish was coming with eight hundred warriors. Bowman at first was rather incredulous, but heeded the warning enough to act on it. He began to retreat. Cooper carried his friend Porter and both their guns about half a mile, when, fortunately, an Indian pony, bridled and saddled, came up with the retreating army. Just as Porter was placed upon the pony the forces of Blackfish came into sight. Porter's only hope of safety was in sticking to the pony. The Indians, however, advanced with such terrible yells that the frightened pony, becoming unmanageable, broke and ran through their line. The pony carried Porter within ten feet of Blackfish. Three fleet warriors immediately started for Porter. Having urged his pony to its highest speed he was unable, it seemed, to gain on his pursuers, when coming to a little ravine, he turned up it. At this his pursuers, who knew the country set up a fierce yell of delight. Porter, looking ahead, saw at once the cause of their exultation. Just in front a large log lay across the ravine, and there was no way to go around it. The moment was critical. The pony on reaching the log made an effort to leap over it, but fell back. Porter clung to the pony, and the Indians came rushing on with increasing yells. In the supreme moment the pony, frightened by the horrid yelling, made another effort and cleared the log, and Porter felt safe. In a moment he was on top of the ridge and the Indians gave up the chase. Turning his horse, he fired at them and then rode rapidly along the ridge for some distance.

The sun was about an hour high. He could plainly hear the roar of Bowman's guns. Just before dark he came to a beautiful, open, grassy place of some two or three acres. Here he dismounted as best he could to fix the handkerchief

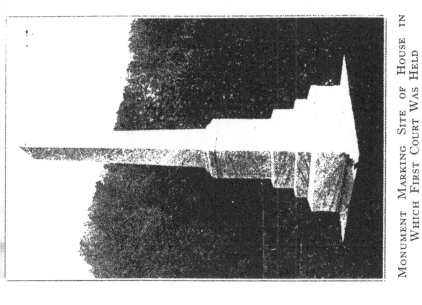

Monument Marking Site of House in Which First Court Was Held

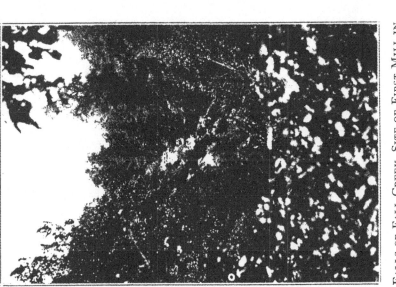

Falls of Fall Creek, Site of First Mill in the County

on his wounded knee, and let his pony graze. Holding on to
the bridle, he crawled about to allow the pony to graze on
fresh grass. When darkness came, he crawled to the root
of a tree, put the pony's bridle over his arm, and soon fell
asleep. Late in the night he awoke to find that his pony
was gone. He was then certainly in a forlorn condition.
Listening intently he heard the pony still grazing on the grass.
He waited with intense anxiety till day began to dawn, when
the pony came up and smelt his hand. Catching it, he crawled
upon it and started in the direction of where he supposed
Bowman and his men to be. He had proceeded but a short
distance when he was halted by three sentinels, one of whom
was Cooper, his friend, who stepped out and exclaimed, "My
God, Porter, are you yet alive?" They told him that he had
arrived just in time as they would cross the Ohio in only a
few minutes.

On crossing the Ohio, Porter was sent down the river to
the French trading post where the city of Louisville now
stands. Here he remained until his wounds were healed.
Late in December, he returned to Boonesborough where he
remained until the following June when he left for his home
at Porter's Fort. He was twenty-seven days on the road
but finally reached his home in safety. (Judge Wood's Letter, Draper Manuscripts, 4 C 26.)

The following incident concerning Samuel Porter's return
home has been preserved by tradition. As he passed from the
Hunter's Ford up Fall Creek to the fort, on his return from
Kentucky, he discovered a light in his father's mill house.
Approaching the mill with great caution, he was hailed with
a "Who comes there?" to which greeting he made Masonic
answer. In a few minutes he was directed into the room where
a Masonic Lodge was in session, with his father as Worshipful
Master. (T. W. Carter's Letter, Draper Manuscripts, 6 C 47.)

Patrick and Samuel Porter are represented by tradition as
having been rather intimately acquainted with the Indian
Chief Logan. The following story is related concerning this
acquaintance. Patrick Porter, while serving under General
Lewis, in some capacity or other, on the Ohio River, was approached one day by Chief Logan, who, with a smile, extended
his hand to Porter, at the same time saying, "I know you.

You are Patrick Porter. I want to be your friend. You don't know me. I am Capt. John Logan. Many time I could have killed you, but I loved you, and would not." He then made enquiry about his son, Samuel, but, at that moment, seeing Samuel coming toward them, he pointed and said, "Yonder he comes." When Samuel came up, he said to him. "I am Logan; and was your friend. Many times I could have killed you, but would not. You were too good a man. You guarded the women and children, which made me love you and your father." On being assured of their perpetual love and friendship, he then rehearsed several occurrences that had taken place in the vicinity of Porter's Fort. One of the incidents recalled was concerning a large, fine horse that was hitched to the fort gate. By some chance, the horse was left there a great while, night coming on in the meantime. Logan, who was skulking near the fort, had watched the horse with covetous eyes. Taking advantage of the darkness, he tried to steal him. Covering himself with a shock of top fodder, he began gradually to approach the horse. But just at the moment when he was nearly ready to lay hold of the horse, a child inside the fort fell out of the bed, and made such a noise that Logan, fearing discovery, dropped the fodder, and left. "Did you ever notice that shock of fodder?" asked Logan. "Yes," replied Samuel Porter. "The breaking of that child's arm saved your life, Logan; I was on guard at the fort gate that night, and observing the fodder moving toward me, cocked my gun and was in the very act of firing when you dropped the fodder and ran away. I was within twenty feet of you, with as good a gun as was ever fired." Logan replied that the Great Spirit did not let one friend kill another.

Just before Patrick Porter took his departure from the Ohio to his home on the Clinch, Logan brought an Indian boy about fifteen years old, to him with the request that he take the boy home with him and educate him. He said the boy was an orphan, having neither father nor mother, and that he wanted to live with the white people, learn their books and wear clothes as they did. Porter refused to take the boy, fearing the Indians might take offense at his action. But the third day after they had started, the Indian boy came at night to Porter's tent with a letter from Logan which stated that the Indians thought the boy was drowned in the river while they were crossing, and there would never be any trouble about it. The name of the Indian boy was Dale to which was added Arter; hence he was known as Arter Dale. Growing to manhood among the white people, he married a white woman and raised a large and respectable family. At an early age he professed religion, attached himself to the Methodist Church, and became an able minister in that church. (T. W. Carter's Letter, Draper Manuscripts, 6 C 49.)

When the Southwest Virginia militiamen rendezvoused near Black's Fort and were organized under Campbell to drive back Ferguson, Patrick Porter raised forty-two men in the Clinch Valley, and marched at once to the place of rendezvous. Upon his arrival, however, a council of war was held in which it was decided that Porter's men should return to the Clinch Valley in order to guard the frontier against possible invasion by the Northern Indians. It was strongly suspected at this time that Ferguson intended to form a junction with the Northern Indians, and thus, as between upper and nether millstones, crush the frontier settlements. Porter, on returning to the Clinch, sent spies to keep vigilant watch for Indians on the Cumberland Mountains. Some of these spies ranged even as far as the Ohio. As soon, however, as news of Ferguson's defeat reached the Clinch, Porter disbanded his company, and they returned to their homes. (T. W. Carter's Letter, Draper Manuscripts.)

FORT HOUSTON ON BIG MOCCASIN CREEK

On December 14, 1774, three hundred acres of land were surveyed for William Houston, on Big Moccasin Creek, within the present limits of Scott County, and not very far from the present boundary line between Scott and Russell Counties. A part of this boundary, at least, was later known as the Grigsby Place. The certificate of settlement of this land as made by the commissioners who laid off the land is as follows:

"We, the Commissioners for the district of Washington and Montgomery Counties, do certify that William Houston, as-

signee of James Simmons, who was assignee of Thomas Mc-
Culloch, is entitled to three hundred acres of land lying in
Washington County on Mockison Creek, two hundred and
twenty acres of which was surveyed the 14th day of December, 1774, by virtue of an order of council dated the 16th day
of December, 1773, to include his improvement, he having
proved to the Court he was entitled to the same by actual settlement made in the year 1769. As witness our hands this
21st day of August, 1781.

Jos. Cabell,
Harry Innes,
N. Cabell,
Commissioners."

According to the above certificate, the first settlement, it
seems, was made within the present limits of Scott County by
Thomas McCulloch at Fort Houston, on Big Moccasin Creek.

Houston and his neighbors erected a fort upon his land.
This fort afforded a place of safety for the earliest settlers
in this portion of Big Moccasin Valley. Even settlers as far
away as the Rye Cove, it is alleged, fled to Fort Houston in
times of danger. (Judge Wood's Letter, Draper Manuscripts
4 C 27.) Fort Houston stood near the place where the brick
residence on the Grigsby farm now stands.

One of the earliest settlers in the neighborhood of Fort
Houston was Jonathan Wood. One hundred and eighty-five
acres of land, near the lands of William Houston were surveyed for him December 15, 1774. Jonathan Wood, with his
wife and stepson, James Osborn, emigrated from eastern Virginia to his land on Big Moccasin, in the year 1773. (Note:
Jonathan Wood was born near the Potomac River in eastern
Virginia, in the year 1745, and died at his home on Big Moccasin Creek in 1804. He married the widow of Solomon Osborn, in 1767. His wife's maiden name was Davidson. She
had one son named James, by her first husband. Her first
husband was killed by the Indians. Jonathan Wood had three
sons and one daughter, named respectively John, Henry, Jonathan, and Polly. Henry Wood, the second son of Jonathan,
Sr., was born the 18th day of May, 1773, near Fort Houston,
on Big Moccasin. This record is taken from Henry Wood's
Bible, and it fixes the fact of Jonathan Wood's residence on

The Old Kilgore Fort House

Big Moccasin in February, 1773. Judge Wood, in his *History of the Wood Family in Virginia*, gives the date of Jonathan Wood's immigration to Big Moccasin Valley as 1770. He built his residence near Fort Houston, on the site known to the present generation as the Skillern Wood farm.)

Some years after the completion of Fort Houston, a band of Shawnee Indians made their appearance in the settlement. The settlers, on learning of the enemy's approach, lost no time in fleeing to the fort. The Indians then surrounded the fort, and, to all appearances, commenced a regular siege. This they continued for three days when suddenly they disappeared, going toward the northwest. While in the neighborhood, however, they inflicted much damage by stealing whatever they could lay hands on. While this three-day siege was in progress, one of the men in the fort, whose house was in sight of it, and only a short distance away, determined to go home for some purpose. Realizing the foolhardiness of the attempt, his friends tried to dissuade him from going, but were unable to do so. He had proceeded but a short distance from the fort gate when he was fired on by the Indians and mortally wounded. Seeing this, Jonathan Wood, in great danger to his own life, rushed out to the rescue of his wounded neighbor. Several shots were fired at him but fortunately none of them took effect. He succeeded in bringing the wounded man into the fort where he died that night.

At another time the Indians made a raid into the settlement of Fort Houston. By this time, Jonathan Wood had built a very large smokehouse upon which he had placed a round roof. This roof, owing to its unusual shape, gave the building a peculiar and striking appearance which at once attracted the attention of the Indians. Observing it curiously from a distance they fired several shots into it, while one who could speak English remarked that "The big man lived in it." Fearing, it seems, that the smokehouse might conceal some danger of which they did not know, they did not approach very close to it, and soon departed without doing any damage whatever. But the round roof smokehouse seemed to have lost its novelty, and consequently its power to afford the owner protection, for the next time the Indians came into the neighborhood, they burned Jonathan Wood's dwelling and all of its contents. Wood and his family, in the meantime, had taken refuge in Fort Houston.

On still another occasion, the Indians came to the home of Jonathan Wood, and, on approaching the house, so frightened his horses and cattle that they left off grazing and ran to the house. Wood was absent from home at the time, and no one was at the house except his wife and a negro slave who had only recently been imported from Africa. The negro, although acquainted with savage life in the jungles of Africa, seemed as much frightened as the horses and cattle, and sat upon the fence, making queer gestures and jabbering his unintelligible language. Either the uncanny actions of the slave or the mystery of the round roof smokehouse must have changed their purpose for they went away without attacking the house or doing other damage. This was the last visit of the Indians to the neighborhood of Fort Houston.

Jonathan Wood was a soldier in the Revolution. He was present at, and participated in, the battle of King's Mountain. He always believed that he fired the fatal shot at Colonel Ferguson in that battle. It is said that standing by his horse, and resting his gun upon his saddle, he fired seven times, taking deliberate aim each time. He had a bearskin cover for his saddle and near the close of the battle one of the enemy's bullets, striking the bearskin close to his head, threw hair and dust into his eyes. Thus blinded, he stumbled and fell, whereupon, being observed by some of his comrades who preceded him on their return home, it was reported that he had been killed in battle.

Henry, the second son of Jonathan Wood, married Sally Lawson August 14, 1794. More than two years after his marriage he lived with his father near Fort Houston. In 1797, he purchased a large tract of land in Big Moccasin Valley, about three miles east of Gate City, and now known as the Dr. Moore farm. Soon after moving to his new home, while driving his cows, Henry Wood saw an Indian skulking among the trees. On seeing Wood, however, the Indian sprang behind a large tree and disappeared. This, according to Wood, was the last Indian ever seen in that immediate neighborhood. Wood furthermore states that it frosted throughout the summer of 1816, thereby making such an unfavorable season that the corn did not mature. The 1817 crops were produced by planting 1815 seed.

Henry Wood was twice elected a member of the legislature of Russell County, of which the section where he then lived was a part. As a member of the General Assembly, he was present at the burning of the Richmond Theater, in 1811, but escaped without injury. He was Commissioner of the Revenue of Russell County in 1811, and again in 1813; he was also a justice of the peace of Russell and of Scott County after its formation. He was sheriff of Scott County a number of years.

Jonathan Wood was the first surveyor of Scott County after its formation. The compass which he used in surveying is now in the possession of John J. Wood, one of his descendants. The land which he owned is in the possession of his direct descendants.

THE OLD KILLGORE FORT HOUSE: DORTON'S FORT

Dorton's Fort was located on the Combs farm, about one mile southeast of Nickelsville. It seems to have been built sometime about the year 1790, and therefore, was not so much exposed to the dangers of Indian attack as the forts erected at an earlier date. In fact, there is neither traditional account nor written record of any attack having been made upon it by the savages. Protected, as it was, by the forts in Castlewood, Porter's Fort, Blackmore's Fort, Rye Cove Fort, Fort Patrick Henry, and Fort Houston, not to mention other forts to the east of it, Dorton's Fort enjoyed an immunity from Indian attack seldom experienced by the more exposed places on the frontier. Although Dorton's Fort was singularly free from Indian attack, it was not entirely free from Indian visitation. More than once the settlers in its vicinity were forced to seek safety within the walls of its rude stockade. It may be said, in this connection, that as the danger of Indian attack became less, stockaded forts were less frequently and strongly built. In 1790, strongly built houses were taking the places of forts in this section. One of these fortified houses, in an excellent state of preservation, still stands at the ford of Copper Creek, about two miles west of Nickelsville. It was built by Robert Killgore about the year 1790. Its walls consist of hewn logs with the opening between chinked with limestone rock and daubed with mortar. Port holes were conveniently arranged. Both the lower and upper stories are separated into two rooms by log partitions built as strongly as the outer walls themselves. The rooms seem to have been so arranged that should the first one be forced, the possibility of retreat into the next would yet remain, and so on, until a final stand could be made in the northeast room of the upper story. The house is situated on the right bank of Copper Creek; and a rather high limestone cliff on the left bank overlooks it from the southeast. It is, no doubt, the oldest house in Scott County.

An authentic tradition preserved in the Killgore family attributes a remarkable dream to Robert Killgore, the builder and first occupant of the old fort house, described above. The essential facts of his dream are as follows: A messenger on horseback drew rein in front of his door and warned him to flee to the fort for the Indians were coming. He then awoke. Falling asleep a second time, he dreamed the same dream again. He awoke this time very much disturbed, and related the dream to his wife. On going to sleep the third time, he again dreamed the same dream, but with the additional revelation this time that, as a token that his thrice-dreamed warning would prove true, he would see, on opening his door the next morning, two head of cattle, one male, the other female, approaching Copper Creek on the opposite side from his house. Sure enough, on opening the door next morning, the first thing he saw was the token as revealed to him in the dream. Being now thoroughly aroused by the strange coincidence of his dream, he lost no time in seeking the shelter of Dorton's Fort, and the following night the Indians encamped in force on the cliff overlooking his house. The Indians did not disturb Killgore's house nor do any damage in the neighborhood.

Robert, Charles, and William Killgore, three brothers, moved to Fort Blackmore at the close of the Revolutionary War. Charles Killgore was killed by Indians near Pound Gap in Wise County, while hunting. Robert Killgore, who lived in the old fort house, was a son of Charles. He married Jane Porter Green. He died March 29, 1854, and his wife died September 25, 1842.

Copper Creek Valley

THE INDIAN ATTACK UPON THE FAMILIES OF PETER AND HENRY LIVINGSTON

One of the most beautiful farms in Scott County is the "Livingston Place," now owned by the heirs of the late Peter Jett. It is situated on the North Fork of the Holston, near the mouth of Livingston Creek. This tract of land was first occupied, it seems, by William Todd Livingston, who enjoyed the rather unique distinction of being the first, and, for some years, the only, man in Washington County to have a double Christian name. Upon the death of William Todd Livingston, his sons, Peter and Henry, inherited his estate, including a large number of negro slaves. Now for some reason, the Indians often especially sought out the negro slave for the purpose of capture. This seems to have been particularly true of Benge, who, it was thought, sometimes made trips to the settlements in order to spy out the farms upon which negro slaves were employed. The presence of negro slaves on the Livingston farm, therefore, may have caused the attack which Benge and his gang made upon it. Mrs. Elizabeth, wife of Peter Livingston, a few days after her rescue, gave the following account of the affair. This account was certified to, and forwarded to the Governor of Virginia.

"April 6, 1794, about ten o'clock in the morning, as I was sitting in my house, the fierceness of the dog's barking alarmed me. I looked out and saw seven Indians approaching the house, armed and painted in a frightful manner. No person was then within, but a child of ten years old, and another of two, and my sucking infant. My husband and his brother Henry had just walked out to a barn at some distance in the field. My sister-in-law, Susanna, was with the remaining children in an outhouse. Old Mrs. Livingston was in the garden. I immediately shut and fastened the door; they (the Indians) came furiously up, and tried to burst it open, demanding of me several times to open the door which I refused. They then fired two guns; one ball pierced through the door, but did me no damage. I then thought of my husband's rifle, took it down but it being double-triggered, I was at a loss; at length I fired through the door, but it not being well-aimed I did no execution; however, the Indians retired from that place and soon after that an old adjoining house was on fire, and I and my children suffering much from the smoke. I opened the door and an Indian immediately advanced and took me prisoner with the two children. I then discovered that they had my remaining children in their possession, my sister Sukey, a wench with her young child, a negro man of Edward Callihan's, and a negro boy of our own about eight years old. They were fearful of going into the house I had left, to plunder, supposing that it had been a man that shot at them, and was yet within. So our whole clothing and household furniture were consumed in the flames which I was then pleased to see, rather than it should be of use to the savages.

"We were all hurried a short distance, where the Indians were very busy, dividing and putting up in packs for each to carry his part of the booty taken. I observed them careless about the children, and most of the Indians being some distance off in front, I called with a low voice to my eldest daughter, gave her my youngest child, and told them all to run towards neighbor John Russell's.

"They with reluctance left me, sometimes halting, sometimes looking back. I beckoned them to go. I inwardly felt pangs not to be expressed on account of our doleful separation. The two Indians in the rear either did not notice this scene, or they were willing the children might run back.

"That evening the Indians crossed Clinch Mountain and went as far as Copper Creek, distant about eight miles.

"April 7, set out early in the morning, crossed Clinch River at McLean's fish dam about twelve o'clock, then steered northwardly towards the head of Stony Creek. There the Indians camped carelessly, had no back spy nor kept sentries out. This day's journey was about twenty miles.

"April 8, continued in camp until the sun was more than an hour high; then set out slowly and traveled five or six miles and camped near the foot of Powell's Mountain. This day Benge, the Indian chief, became more pleasant, and spoke freely to the prisoners. He told them he was about to carry them to the Cherokee towns. That in his route in the wilderness was his brother with two other Indians hunting, so that he might have provision when he returned. That at his camp were several white prisoners taken from Kentucky, with horses and saddles to carry them to the towns. He made enquiry for several persons on Holston, particularly old General Shelby, and said he would pay him a visit during the ensuing summer, and take away all his negroes. He frequently enquired who had negroes, and threatened he would have them all off the North Holston. He said all the Chickamauga towns were for war, and would soon be very troublesome to the white folks.

"This day two of the party were sent by Benge ahead to hunt.

"April 9. After traveling about five miles which was over Powell's Mountain, a party of thirteen men under command of Lieutenant Vincent Hobbs, of the militia of Lee County, met the enemy in front, attacked and killed Benge the first fire, I being at that time some distance off in the rear. The Indian who was my guard at first halted on hearing the firing. He then ordered me to run, which I performed slowly. He attempted to strike me in the head with the tomahawk, which I defended as well as I could with my arm. By this time two of our people came in view, which encouraged me to struggle all I could. The Indian making an effort at this instant pushed me backward, and I fell over a log, at the same time aiming a violent blow at my head, which in part spent its force on me and laid me for dead. The first thing I afterwards remembered was my good friends around me, giving me all the assistance in their power for my relief. They told me I was senseless for about an hour.

"Certified this 15th day of April, 1794. A. Campbell."

The Lee County Court was in session when the news came that the Indians had invaded the Holston Settlements. Court immediately adjourned, and a company of men was hastily organized, under Lieutenant Vincent Hobbs, to go in search of the enemy. Hobbses' company proceeded at once to a gap in the mountain through which, it was surmised, the Indians would be most likely to pass on the return to their towns. Hobbs, upon arriving at this gap, however, found that some Indians had already passed through before him. Pressing on in great eagerness to overtake the enemy, he soon came up with two Indians kindling a fire. These were killed, and, upon examination, it was found that they were in possession of plunder which must have been taken from the Livingstons. Hobbs concluded that these two Indians had been sent on ahead to hunt and collect provisions for the main body. "The object of Hobbs was now to make a quick retreat to cover his own sign if possible, at the gap, before the Indians should discover it, and perhaps kill the prisoners and escape. Having gained this point, he chose a place of ambuscade; but not exactly liking this position he left the men there, and taking one with him by the name of Van Bibber, he went some little distance in advance to try to find a place more suitable for his purpose. As they stood looking around for such a place, they discovered the Indians coming up with their prisoners. They cautiously concealed themselves and each singled out his man. Benge, having charge of the younger Mrs. Livingston, led the van, and the others followed in succession; but the Indian who had charge of the elder Mrs. Livingston was considerably behind, she not being able to march with the same light elastic step of her sister. When the front came directly opposite to Hobbs and Van Bibber they both fired, Hobbs killing Benge, and Van Bibber the one next behind him. At the crack of the rifle the other men rushed forward, but the Indians had escaped into a laurel thicket, taking with them a negro fellow. The Indian who had charge of the elder Mrs. Livingston tried his best to kill her, but he was so hurried that he missed his aim. Her arms were badly cut by defending her head from the blows of his tomahawk. The prisoners had scarcely time to recover from their surprise before the two Livingstons, who heard the guns and were now in close pursuit with a party of men from Washington, came running up and with a gust of joy received their wives at the hands of Hobbs. Four Indians were killed and five escaped. It appears they were separated into parties of three and two. The first had the negro fellow with them, and by his account, they lodged that night in a cave, where he escaped from them and got home.

"In the meantime a party of the hardy mountaineers of Russell collected and proceeded in haste to waylay a noted Indian crossing-place high up on the Kentucky River. When they got there they found some Indians had just passed. They immediately drew the same conclusion that Hobbs had done, and hastened back to the river for fear those behind should discover their sign. Shortly after they had stationed themselves, the other three made their appearance; the men fired upon them, two fell and the other fled, but left a trail of blood behind him, which readily conducted his pursuers to where he had taken refuge in a thick canebreak. It was thought imprudent to follow him any further, as he might be concealed and kill some of them before they could discover him. Thus eight of the party were killed and the other perhaps mortally wounded." (Manuscript letter of Benjamin Sharpe, quoted in Summers' *Annals of Southwest Virginia*.)

The following letters relating to Benge's raid on the Livingstons are to be found in the Virginia State Papers, Vol. 7.

Andrew Lewis to the Governor.
April 17, 1794.

"Sir: Since I wrote you on yesterday I have received the particulars of the mischief done at Mr. Livingston's within fifteen miles of Abingdon.

"The Indians murdered one white woman and one negro child, prisoners, two white women, one negro woman and man; they were also in possession of a number of children. After setting the houses on fire, they set the children at liberty. They were immediately pursued on their trail; two other parties pushed on to take possession of certain gaps that, in all probability they would pass. One of these parties last mentioned fell in with them and fired on them, killed the white man that conducted the Indians in, and one of the Indians. At the time fire was made, both the other parties of the whites were in hearing of the guns. By their passing through the Stone Gap, in Powell's Mountain, expect they were the Southern Indians.

"P. S. The prisoners were retaken, all but the negro man who ran off with the Indians."

Under date of April 19, 1794, Andrew Lewis again writes the Governor:

"The inhabitants in pursuit of the Indians retook the prisoners and killed two of them (Bench and Indians). The rest run off. Capt. Wm. Dorton, one of my scouts, who was with a party endeavoring to head them, fell in with them that run off, being three in number, two of which he killed on the ground; the other run off mortally wounded. One only escaped without a wound."

Col. Arthur Campbell, in a letter to the governor, dated April 29, 1794, says, "I now send the scalp of Captain Bench that noted murderer, as requested by Lieut. Hobbs, to your excellency, as a proof that he is no more, and of the activity and good conduct of Lieutenant Hobbs, in killing him and relieving the prisoners. Could it be spared from our treasury, I would beg leave to hint that a present of a neat rifle to Mr. Hobbs would be accepted as a reward for his late services, and the Executive may rest assured that it would serve as a stimulus for future exertions against the enemy." In accordance with Colonel Campbell's recommendation, the General Assembly of Virginia voted Lieutenant Hobbs a beautiful silver-mounted rifle.

At another time, Colonel Campbell, in a letter to the governor, expressed solicitude for the safety of Lieutenant Hobbs, and his men. He says, "By intelligence from Knoxville, the uncle of Capt. Bench is out with thirty warriors to take revenge in Virginia. The necessity of having some men on duty near Mockson Gap, the former place of his haunts, and now we suppose of his avengers, seems urgent. Were Captain Lewis' company so arranged as to cover that settlement, and he be active in ranging the woods, it might, in a degree, appease the fears of the inhabitants. That part of Lee County which turned out so cleverly under Lieut. Hobbs in pursuit of Bench is altogether exposed; that is they have no part of the guard on duty, nearer than forty miles. My own conjecture is, that Hobbs and his friends may be the sufferers. All late accounts say that all of the lower Cherokees are for war."

The following account of the killing of Benge, related by Dr. James Huff, the last surviving member of Vincent Hobbs' party, differs in some minor details from the account given above, though, probably, not more than a perfectly credible witness speaking forty-six years later might be expected to vary. The story was printed in the *Jacksonian,* a paper published at Abingdon, Va., in 1846:

"Mr. Editor: Having recently had an interview with the venerable Dr. James Huff of Kentucky, the last of the brave party that defeated the celebrated Indian Benge and party, who gave me the following account of that affair. That some time in the month of April 1794 just before day-light, a man by the name of John Henderson rode up to Yokum station in Powells Valley now Lee County and informed the station that the Indians had broken up some families on the North fork of Holston, and had taken the wives of Peter and Henry Livingston and two servants of the former and also a black man from Edward Callyham, and that the men of the station desired to fall in ahead of the retiring party, as they were well acquainted with their route, and as was common in those times the cry of Indians was a sufficient call to arms, they very soon mustered the following brave little band of mountain soldiers: Vincent Hobbs, John Benbever, Stephen Jones, James Huff, James Benbever, Peter Benbever, Job Hobbs, Abraham Hobbs, Adam Ely, Samuel Livingston, George Yokum and —— Dotson, who were all soon equipped and on their march to a pass in the Cumberland Mountain, where they soon arrived, but seeing no sign in the trace of the recent passage of Indians they divided their company into small parties, to examine the small streams, which were thickly lined with laurel and ivy to the Kentucky side, where a short distance from the base of the mountain, one of the party, discovered a small stream of smoke rise from the edge of the laurel, and upon nearer approach, he perceived through the dusk of the evening, that it proceeded from the camp of an Indian, who at the moment was stooped down kindling his fire, whereupon he deliberately raised his deadly rifle, at the sharp crack of which the enemy received a mortal wound, and his comrades the signal that the foe was found. They soon gathered and after examination, pronounced their victim a forerunner or hunter sent forward to prepare provisions, so they camped by the dead Indian during the night, at early dawn next morning recrossed the mountain, ascended the valley, marching rapidly to gain a position in a deep hollow in the mountain, that they supposed Benge and his party would pass, the writer has seen this spot, it is one of those dark deep mountain passes where the ridge on each side seemed to reach the clouds, and the centre of the deep gloomy valley below is covered with large masses of unshaken rocks, filled every where with laurel and ivy, with a wild furious stream, tumbling and rolling in the midst.

"In this dismal place the little band of soldiers took their stand, determined to dispute the passage of Benge to the last; and to rescue the prisoners or forfeit their lives in the attempt. For the purpose of attacking the enemy, they divided into two companies, and took their stations near each other in the edge of the laurel, adopting the following as the mode of attack. The first company was not to fire until the rear of the enemy had passed them and thus attack in front and rear, while the mountain upon either side afforded no possible passage for the coward or the conquered. Having thus secreted themselves along the gloomy gulf, which has terrors enough in itself to chill the blood of the timid, without the expectation of a deadly foe, these twelve brave backwoodsmen who were accustomed to the screams of the panther and the growls of the bear, sat but a short time calmly and unterrified in their hiding places, until two of them highest up the precipice (V. Hobbs and J. Benbever), saw an Indian and the wife of Peter Benbever (Livingston), marching down the passage, but none of the rest of the party in sight, the prisoner in front of the dark rough savage, the two soldiers' iron nerves grew stronger when they saw the fair lady driven over the logs, brush, and stones by an unfeeling savage, and each man cocked his gun and crouched behind a large rock, and waited with breathless silence the approach of the Indian, which must pass within a few yards of them, but being desirous to know whether the rest of the party was yet in sight, Benbever cautiously raised his head above the rock to make the discovery and the keen eyed savage saw him at the distance of forty yards, the rest not yet being in sight, at the sight of the white man's head he stooped forward and threw off a pack and made the dark deep hollow ring with a terrific Indian yell, at the same time making a blow with his tomahawk, struck the woman on the head and she fell dead at his feet; he wheeled and bounded off the way he had come, the two heroes seeing their plan was all frustrated, rose from their hiding place and Benbever fired at the running savage without effect; Hobbs a celebrated marksman leveled his piece and held her steadily upon a spot until the Indian passed before his sight, when with that quickness, with which the backwoods riflemen are so wonderfully gifted he fired and the Indian fell shot through the brains, and this was the celebrated Benge. All the party then left their hiding places and rushed forward to rescue the rest of the prisoners when they found the Indians striving to make their escape into the laurel, and as they rushed upon the enemy who were striving to get into the laurel with the prisoners, my informant says he ran up very near the Indian, who had the other white woman, and raised his rifle to shoot him, at that instant he raised a tomahawk to strike the woman, who caught his arm and held it until my informant made several attempts to shoot the Indian as he was dragging her by the arm, but at every attempt, one of his comrades would seize his gun telling him not to shoot he would kill the woman, he then threw down his gun, drew his butcher knife and rushed towards the Indian, at that instant the Indian having crossed a log, jerked the female against it and extricated his arm and as quick as lightning entered the thicket, but as he entered he received the contents of another man's rifle, which sent him bleeding to death in the laurel. The party then collected all their prisoners and returned to the tomahawked woman and to their great joy found she was yet alive, and was shortly afterwards with the other prisoners delivered to her friends to the great joy of all.

"I would pursue this narrative further, but fearing this un-varnished relation would not be worthy of a place in your excellent paper, I for the present say no more." (Draper Manuscript 26 CC 60.) (Note: The name Benbever is a variant spelling of Van Bibber.)

PETITION OF CITIZENS NEAR BIG MOCCASIN GAP

Eight days after the capture of the Livingstons, five citizens living near Big Moccasin Gap, and in territory now comprised within the limits of Scott County, forwarded the following petition to the Governor of Virginia.

"The memorial and petition of the subscribers, inhabitants in the western part of Washington county, and the eastern settlements of Lee, near Mockison Gap.

"Humbly sheweth, That altho' we have been considered an interior settlement, yet, from various unfortunate occurences, it must appear that we are equally exposed with the most distant frontier settlements.

"That by attending to the geography of the southwestern frontier, it will appear that from the western settlement of Russell County, on Clinch River, and the eastern of Lee in Powell's Valley, there is an uninhabited space of more than twenty miles north of your petitioners' dwellings which makes us to that extent a frontier to the state.

"That the predatory parties of the Indians always industrious in discovering the weakness of our settlements, have for years past made their inroads through this vacant or uninhabited space, and have committed several cruel murders in the neighborhood of your petitioners, as will appear by the following detail.

"August 26, 1791, a party of Indians headed by a Captain Bench of the Cherokee tribe, attacked the house of Elisha Ferris, two miles from Mockison Gap, murdered Mr. Ferris at his house, and made prisoner Mrs. Ferris, and her daughter Mrs. Livingston, and a young child together with Nancy Ferris. All but the latter were cruelly murdered the first day of their captivity.

"April 1793, the same chief with a party of Indians, attacked and murdered the family of Harper Ratcliffe, six in number, about eight miles west of the above mentioned gap.

"March 31, 1793, the enemy attacked on Powell's Mountain Moses Cockrell and two others, who had horses loaded with merchandise; killed two men, took all the goods, and pursued Mr. Cockrell nearly two miles.

"July 17, 1793, Bench with two other warriors traversed the settlement, on the north fork of Holston for upwards of twenty miles, probably with the intention of making discoveries where were negro property. In this route they fired at one Williams, and took prisoner a negro woman, the property of Paul Livingston, who after two days captivity made her escape.

"And lastly, April 6, 1794, the melancholy disaster which befell Mr. Livingston's family and property, which has urged this application for assistance to prevent the depopulation of a considerable settlement.

"From the above facts your Excellency and Council will be judge of the justice of our claim, that such protection be afforded us, as the State may be able to afford and our necessities require.

"All of which we submit with deference and your petitioners will every pray.

"A. BLEDSOE
"GEORGE WILCOX
"ABRAHAM FULKERSON
"JOHN V. COOK
"JAMES FULKERSON

"April 14, 1794."

Two of these petitioners, Abraham and James Fulkerson, lived at that time near the present village of Hiltons, Va. Abraham Fulkerson lived only a few hundred yards northeast of the present town. An old loghouse now stands on, or near the site of his former dwelling. It is said that Benge intended to attack Abraham Fulkerson's dwelling on his return from the capture of the Livingstons, but a fortunate circumstance kept him from doing so. On the day the Livingstons were captured, Fulkerson was being assisted by his neighbors at a "house-raising." This work brought so many men together that Benge dared not make an attack, or even let his presence in the neighborhood be known. After watching the operations of the men at work on the house, for a time, Benge with his prisoners effected a crossing of Clinch Mountain at what is now known as the Hamilton Gap. This course enabled him to avoid detection by the settlers in the neighborhood of Fort Houston.

No doubt some of the men present at the "house-raising" were members of the rescue party that went from the Holston Settlements under the leadership of a man named Head.

BENGE'S ATTACK UPON THE HOUSE OF JOHN WALLEN

Sometime in the year 1789, John Wallen built a small cabin at the mouth of Stock Creek where Clinchport is situated now. He located his cabin on the Kentucky Path, and, no doubt, helped to entertain some of the hundreds of settlers who were at that time emigrating to Kentucky over the Wilderness Road. Wallen was not left long in the peaceable enjoyment of his new home in the wilderness. Benge and his forest bloodhounds soon found his cabin. One morning just at daybreak, his wife, on opening the door, was shot at by an Indian and slightly wounded. Quickly closing the door, she barred it to prevent its being forced. Wallen, who was yet in bed, then hastily arose and snatching the gun from its rack, shot and killed the Indian nearest the door. The other Indians then rushed upon the house, trying to effect an entrance, nor did they retreat until Wallen had killed three of them. After driving the Indians away, Wallen and his wife went to Carter's

Fort, eight miles distant. (Carter's Letter, Draper Manuscripts.)

The petition quoted above contains an enumeration of Indian depredations committed against settlers living within easy reach of Big Moccasin Gap. Most of these raids are known to have been led by Benge, the Cherokee half-breed. It may be remarked in this connection that nearly all of the Indian raids conducted against the settlements within the present limits of Scott County were led by Benge and Logan, both half-breeds.

Charles B. Coale, in his *Life of Wilburn Waters,* tells the following story concerning Benge's attack upon Cotterell and his two companions, on the top of Powell's Mountain. He says:

"It is the purpose of the writer to speak more particularly of the incursion of 1794, and to refer, incidentally, to others of later date and of less magnitude. That of '78 was led by Benge, a half-breed Shawnee, who was remarkable for his strength, activity, endurance, and great speed as a runner. He was a man of more than savage intelligence, also, as well as of great bravery and strategy, and had more than once approached the settlements so stealthily and by a route so secret, that he fell upon the scattered settlers without an intimation of his approach, and retired to his wigwams beyond the Cumberland without leaving a trace of the route he had traveled, though rangers were constantly on the lookout for his trail. One of these rangers of the Holston Settlement was a man by the name of Cotterell, and the writer must make a digression to record an incident in his history. He was famous for his size, activity, and handsome person. Benge and himself were rivals in manhood and woodcraft, each jealous of the other's prowess and courage, and both anxious for an occasion to meet in single combat. Not many months before Benge's last incursion, they met on the top of Powell's Mountain, in what is now Lee County, each with a band of followers. The Indians were in ambush, having observed the approach of the whites, who were not aware of their proximity, and Benge instructed his companions not to kill Cotterell, so that he himself might run him down and capture him. At the crack of the Indian rifles the two or three of Cotterell's companions fell, seeing which, and at once comprehending the folly of a combat with a dozen savages, he sprang away down the mountain side like an antelope, with Benge in close pursuit. Two miles away in the valley on Walling's Creek was the cabin of a pioneer, in reaching which Cotterell knew was his only chance of escape. Having two hundred dollars in specie in a belt around him, he found he was carrying too much weight for a closely contested race, and that Benge was gaining on him. Making a desperate effort, however, he increased his speed a little, and as he leaped the fence that surrounded the cabin, Benge's tomahawk was buried in the top rail before Cotterell reached the ground. Benge seeing that he had missed his aim, and not knowing how many men and rifles might be in the cabin, fled back to his companions sadly disappointed.

"A few years after this Cotterell died on the North Fork in this county (Washington) and during the "wake," while his body lay in the cabin, an old comrade, who had been in many a hard pinch with him, thus gave utterance to his thoughts and feelings as he paced the puncheon floor in great sorrow: 'Poor Cotterell, he is gone. He was a noble fellow after Ingins and varmints, and I hope he has gone to where there is as much game and as *desperate* good range as he had on Holston.'" (Coale's *Wilburn Waters*, pp. 153–154.)

THE FIRST COURTS

THE FIRST COUNTY COURT

The first court convened at the house of Benjamin T. Hollins, in Moccasin Gap, Tuesday, February 14, 1815. Hollins' house had been designated as the meeting place of the first court in the Act which formed the county. In 1915, Dr. John P. McConnell of East Radford collected a fund with which to erect a monument marking the site of the old Hollins house. Scott County people who had gone abroad but who still cherished the old home county were the chief contributors to this fund.

With the funds so raised a monument was erected and the ceremony of unveiling it took place September 29, 1915. After an appropriate address by John H. Johnson the veil was drawn aside by John C. Anderson, a direct descendant of John Anderson of Blockhouse fame.

The court record giving an account of the organization of the first court is as follows:

"A commission of the peace for the county of Scott from under the hand of Wilson C. Nicholas, Esquire Governor of the Commonwealth, bearing date the 4th day of January, 1815 with the seal of the commonwealth thereto affixed, directed to John Anderson, Samuel Ritchie, James Gibson, John McKinney, John Montgomery, William George, Reuben McCully, James Albert, John Berry, James Moss, Jacob Seaver, Richard Fulkerson, Benjamin T. Hollins, Isaac Skillern, and James Walling was produced and read and thereupon pursuant to the said commission the said Samuel Richie took the oath of fidelity to the Commonwealth of Virginia, the several oaths of office, the oath to support the Constitution of the United States, and the oath required by the Act to suppress dueling, which was administered to him by James Gibson and John McKinney, and the said Samuel Richie administered the oath of fidelity to the Commonwealth of Virginia, the several oaths of office, the oath to support the Constitution of the United States, and the oath required by the Act to suppress dueling to the said James Gibson, John McKinney, John Montgomery, William George, Reuben McCully, James Albert, John Berry, James Moss, Jacob Seaver, Richard Fulkerson and James Walling.

"John Anderson produced a commission under the hand of Wilson C. Nicholas, Esquire Governor of this Commonwealth, bearing date the 4th day of January 1815, with the seal of the Commonwealth thereto annexed, appointing him Sheriff of the county of Scott and thereupon the said John Anderson with Jacob Seaver and John Wood, securities, entered into and acknowledged bonds according to law for the faithful discharge of the several duties of the said office, which bonds are ordered to be recorded. And thereupon the said John Anderson took the oath of fidelity to the Commonwealth, the oath of office, the oath to support the Constitution of the United States, the oath required by the Act to suppress dueling.

"The Sheriff then opened the Court of Scott County in the name of the Commonwealth of Virginia.

"The Court being thus constituted Samuel Richie, John McKinney, John Montgomery, William George, Reuben McCully, James Albert, John Berry, James Moss, Jacob Seaver, Richard Fulkerson and James Walling being present. They being a majority of the whole number in the commission of the peace for said County of Scott proceeded to the appointment of a clerk. Whereupon on taking several ballots a majority of the votes was for William H. Carter. Therefore the said William H. Carter is appointed and declared to be duly elected clerk of the Court of Scott County.

"Ordered that the Court be adjourned until tomorrow morning at 9 o'clock.

"SAMUEL RICHIE."

On Wednesday, February 15, 1815, which was the second day of Court, William H. Carter qualified as Clerk by giving James Moss, William George, Reuben McCulley, and John McKinney as securities, and by taking the oaths of office.

Benjamin T. Hollins and Isaac Skillern on producing commissions from the Governor, qualified as Justices of the Peace and were added to the Court.

Andrew McHenry was appointed "attorney to prosecute for

the Commonwealth." He took the required oaths and then
he and William Smith "Gentlemen," having been duly licensed
to practice law, were, "on their motion, permitted to practice
in this Court."

The Court then recommended to the Governor that
Jonathan Wood, Henry Wood, George Wilcox, John McHenry,
John Wolfe, William Fugate, George McConnell, Sr., William
Killgore, Thomas Waddle and William Agee be commissioned
as Justices for the county.

The first case to come before the Court was that of Richard
and Jessee Gilliam who were found guilty "of an affray with
James Dykes." They were bound to keep the peace for one
year but Richard Gilliam, refusing to give security, was committed into the custody of the Sheriff until such time as "he
shall comply with the aforesaid order of the Court." Growing out of this case was the second one. John Webb insulted
the guard which had been placed over Richard Gilliam, and
for this act he was adjudged guilty of "a contempt offered to
this Court" and fined six dollars with "a capias profine
awarded."

The Court next ordered that John Wood be recommended
to the Governor as a "fit and capable person" to be
"Lieutenant-Colonel Commandant of the Militia of Virginia
in this county" and Robert Gibson, Major for the North Battalion, and Isaac Anderson, Major for the South Battalion.

The Court then certified "to the president and professors of
William and Mary College" that Jonathan Wood was a suitable person to be commissioned "principal surveyor" of the
county.

John Webb who had offered a contempt to the Court as
mentioned above was required to give "security for his good
behavior towards all the citizens of this Commonwealth."
The amount of his bond was $25 and William Adams was his
bondsman. He was furthermore taxed with the costs. This
fine was remitted by the Court on the following day.

Isaac Anderson and Isaac Skillern qualified as "under-
sheriffs" of John Anderson.

The first deed presented to the Court and ordered to be
recorded was that of John Anderson to Isaac C. Anderson.
Before adjourning on the second day of its term, the Court

imposed a fine of "eighty-three cents on Richard Gilliam for being drunk in the presence of the Court."

On Thursday, February 16, 1815, Richard Gilliam, who, as mentioned above, had been committed to the custody of the sheriff was released from said custody by giving bond to keep the peace for one year and by paying "the costs of this motion."

On Thursday, February 16, 1815, the Court aranged for the first county election by ordering "that this county be laid off into two districts for the purpose of electing six overseers of the poor." In accordance with the order the county was divided into two districts or battalions and the first Saturday in April was named as election day. In the North district or battalion the election was to be held at the house of James Moss, with Samuel Richie to superintend the voting; in the South district, the election was to be held at the house of Benjamin T. Hollins, with said Hollins to superintend the voting.

In the North district James Gibson, John McKinney, and Samuel Richie were elected overseers of the poor; and, in the South district, Jacob Seaver, Henry Wood, and Cornelius Fugate.

The Court ordered that Hiram Killgore be appointed Commissioner of the Revenue for the North district, and Samuel Richie for the South district.

The Court furthermore appointed Isaac Low, William Robinson, Joseph Dunken, George McConnell, Jr., Thomas Slone, Nimrod Taylor, Daniel Walling, and David M. King as constables for the North battalion, and Meshack Stacey, John Darter, William Adams, Jonathan Langford, Temple Hensley, Reuben Marshall, Solomon Osborne, and Hezekiah Bruce for the South battalion.

The Court then proceeded to recommend the following militia officers:

South Battalion

Richard Fulkerson ....Captain 1st Company
John McHenry ....Captain 2nd Company
William Fugate ....Captain 3rd Company
Cornelius Fugate..............Captain 4th Company

North Battalion

George George ....Captain 1st Company
Hiram Killgore ....Captain 2nd Company
John Berry ....Captain 3rd Company
James Watson ....Captain 4th Company

On Friday, February 17, 1815, the Court ordered the Clerk to tax in the bill of costs against Richard Gilliam, "Sixty-eight cents for his diet during the time he was under guard and for the services of James Davidson, William Byrd, Fielding Hensley and David Culbertson one dollar each as guards, two days each."

Henry Wood and Jacob Seaver were recommended as persons fit and capable to be coroners, and James Gibson, to be Escheator.

Tavern rates above which charges could not be made were fixed by the Court, and, following this action, a license to keep an ordinary at his house was granted to James Davidson.

John D. Sharp was the third attorney given "leave to practice" law in this Court.

On motion of John McHenry, Clerk of the Court, Alfred McKinney was appointed Deputy Clerk.

The Court recommended the following persons to the Governor "as fit and capable" to be officers in the militia of the county:

South Battalion

Jonas Wolfe, Lieutenant ....2nd Company
John Martin, Ensign ....2nd Company
Goldman Davidson, Lieutenant ....3rd Company
Clinton Godsey, Ensign ....3rd Company
Wood Osborne, Lieutenant ....4th Company
Meshack Stacey, Ensign ....4th Company

North Battalion

Robert Spears, Lieutenant ....1st Company
Daniel Walling, Ensign ....1st Company
Elijah Carter, Lieutenant ....2nd Company
James Gibson, Jr., Ensign ....2nd Company
Isaac Low, Lieutenant ....3rd Company

George McConnell, Ensign .... 3rd Company
Jeremiah Culbertson, Lieutenant .... 4th Company
William Bickley, Ensign .... 4th Company

It will be noticed that Samuel Richie signed the court records as the Judge of the Court does now. He signed as chairman of the board of magistrates for the county. It may be stated, in this connection, that prior to 1870, the county court was constituted by the body of magistrates of the county in the manner of the Old English Quarter Session. The first court was in session four days from February 14, 1815, to February 17, inclusive.

THE FIRST SUPERIOR COURT

The first Superior Court of Law was held on the 29th day of May, 1815, at "Mocquison" Gap. The Court was presided over by the Honorable Peter Johnson, Judge. William H. Carter, already the clerk of the County Court, was appointed clerk of the Superior Court also.

Andrew McHenry Benjamin Estill and William Smith qualified to practice law before the Superior Court. Andrew McHenry was appointed to prosecute for the Commonwealth.

John McHenry, Gent., foreman, John Wood, William Lawson, William Fugate, John Montgomery, William Agee, James Albert, John Berry, George Wilcox, Joseph Hickam, Jacob Seaver, John Wolfe, Richard Fulkerson, Thomas Rogers, Samuel Magee, Jacob Cleek, Dale Carter, James Walling, James Gibson, James Moss, Elijah Carter, and Jacob Rhoton composed the first Grand Jury in this Court.

The first indictments were made against persons for "gaming," playing cards, at the tavern of Benjamin T. Hollins, the stillhouse of James Moss, and the barn of the tavern of James Davidson, places "of public resort." The persons indicted and tried were fined $20 and costs, each.

THE FIRST COURT OF ENQUIRY HELD FOR THE 124TH REGIMENT

The generation living at the time Scott County was formed had been born, and reared on the frontier. Many of them had been born and reared as subjects of King George III, of England. They were familiar with the military operations necessary to make life even tolerable on a frontier infested on all sides by enemies. It is not surprising, then, that military preparedness should have a large place in their thinking. The law of the State had provided a group of military laws as powerful in their sphere as the civil law. Petty and general regimental musters had been provided for, and the male population was required to attend and participate in military training. Muster grounds were located at convenient places in the county. Jumping, wrestling, and other manly sports were practiced as well as military maneuvers.

To enforce the code of military laws a Court of Enquiry was organized for the 124th Virginia Regiment in the county.

Its first session was held the 21st day of November, 1816. It was constituted as follows: Col. John Wood, Commanding, Isaac C. Anderson and Robert D. Gibson, commanding officers of the Battalions, John McHenry, George George, William Fugate, Hiram Kilgore, Richard Fulkerson, Cornelius Fugate and John Berry, captains. James H. Stewart was appointed Clerk of the Court. William Bird was made provost marshal of the 124th Regiment.

The Court ordered that the two Battalions should be bounded as follows: The First Battalion beginning at the Tennessee line where said line crosses Clinch Mountain, and with said mountain opposite the Head of Troublesome Creek, thence to the top of Copper Ridge, where the main road crosses said Ridge, thence with said road to the ford of Copper Creek, thence up said creek to the mouth of Valley Creek, thence up said Valley Creek to the top of Copper Ridge, thence with the said Ridge to the Russell line, and with the Russell line and Washington line to the state line, and with the state line to the beginning. The remainder of the county constituted the Second Battalion. The early records show that the work of this Court was mainly that of imposing fines for non-attendance upon the musters, and allowing the claims of those who had rendered service such as buglers, drummers, and fifers. The musters were kept up until the Civil War when their military value was shown in the first years of the War.

SCOTT COUNTY MATTERS

NORTH AND SOUTH BATTALIONS

At the September term of the County Court in 1815, the county was laid off into two divisions, or districts, for the purpose of electing six overseers of the poor. These divisions were designated the North Battalion, and the South Battalion. The first county election was held the first Saturday in April, 1815. There were only two voting places: at the house of James Moss in the North Battalion, and the house of Benjamin T. Hollins in the South Battalion. This election was held for the purpose of selecting overseers of the poor. Each district could elect three discreet resident freeholders as overseers of the poor. This first election was superintended by Samuel Ritchie for the North Battalion, and Benjamin T. Hollins for the South Battalion.

THE SELECTION OF THE COUNTY SEAT

At the May term of Court, 1815, the Commission appointed for the purpose of selecting a suitable place for holding court, and erecting the public buildings, made report that the land given by James Davidson, Sr., "is the most proper and advantageous place for erecting said public buildings."

This report was dated April 15, 1815, and signed by John McKinney, Jonathan Wood, Samuel Ritchie, James Walling, James Moss, Reubin McCulley, and Abraham Fulkerson. The Court, on accepting this report, ordered that John McKinney, James Moss, William H. Carter, James Albert, and Samuel Ritchie, Jr., or a majority of them act as trustees to lay off the town lots, and make advantageous sale of the same. In conformity with the court order, the town was laid off into thirty-four lots. Its principal street from east to west was named Jackson, for General Andrew Jackson, and the principal cross street from north to south was called Gaines

for General Edmond Pendleton Gaines. Both Jackson and
Gaines had recently achieved fame in the War of 1812, as
had General Winfield Scott, another hero of the War, who had
been signally honored in the county's name.

For a brief time, the county seat bore the name of Winfield,
in honor of General Scott. The name was later changed to
Estillville in honor of Benjamin Estill, a Revolutionary soldier, who, while a member of the General Assembly of Virginia, had sponsored, it seems, the bill providing for the
organization of the county.

THE FIRST COURTHOUSE

June 15, 1815, Henry Wood, George Wilcox, John Wolfe,
Benjamin T. Hollins, and Isaac Anderson were appointed
commissioners to superintend the building of a courthouse
and jail.

On October 14, 1817, a special term of court was held to
consider "the establishment of a ferry, and the building of a
Clerk's office for this county." At this special term it was
"Ordered that Andrew McHenry, James Fullen, Henry Wood,
James H. Stewart, Jacob Seaver and George Wilcox be, and
they are hereby appointed, commissioners to draft a plan of
a public Courthouse and Clerk's office for this county." The
records do not disclose what kind of building was used after
the sessions of court ceased to be held in the house of
Benjamin T. Hollins. It seems to have been a hastily constructed wooden building which soon became inadequate for
the needs of the court.

At the June term of 1820, the Court ordered that the jail
be provided with a dungeon, and an annexed room in front,
for the jailer. Andrew McHenry was directed to superintend
the improvements on both the jail and courthouse. In 1821
McHenry was further ordered to carry on the improvements
on the jail, and to have the lower room of the courthouse
ceiled, and the clerk's office repaired.

March, 1827, the Court took under consideration the pro-
priety of erecting a new courthouse, and Michael Cleek, John
S. Martin, Edward Campbell, Isaac C. Anderson, and Lewis
B. Dulaney were appointed a committee, "to receive plans

and propositions for building said courthouse." A number of plans seem to have been submitted. In December of the same year, George Wilcox and Thompson G. Martin were appointed to draft sundry plans for a new courthouse for this county." These plans were submitted to the Court on February 1, 1828, and while the Court was taking time to decide on a plan for the new building, the work of preparing material for its erection was begun. The Court Minute Book of June 12, 1827, shows the following entry: "On motion, and seventeen out of twenty-seven justices of Scott being present, as entered, all of whom concurring except William Kilgore, Charles Kilgore, and William Bickley, it is ordered that James H. Stewart, Andrew McHenry, and John S. Martin who agree to act without compensation for their services, be and they are hereby appointed commissioners with authority to contract for the delivery on the public square in the town of Estillville one hundred and twenty-five thousand of good, hard, well burnt brick for the purpose of building a new courthouse, provided the same are delivered at a price not exceeding three dollars and fifty cents by the thousand, the said brick to be nine inches long, four and a half wide and three thick when burnt." The contractor was permitted to make the brick on the public square, if he so desired. They were to be delivered on, or before December 15, 1827. John Dickenson was awarded the contract for making the brick, and James Toncray was awarded the contract for the erection of the Courthouse. On December 18, 1829, the new building was received by the Court.

The old courthouse was sold at auction, and James H. Stewart became the purchaser for the sum of $30.26.

VARIOUS CIVIL DISTRICTS INTO WHICH THE COUNTY HAS BEEN DIVIDED

In 1818, the court divided the county into two districts as respecting constables. In this division, Clinch Mountain was made the line of division with the proviso that the constable on the south side of said mountain should have concurrent liberty of serving processes in the town of Estillville and its adjoining houses with the constable on the north side. This order was rescinded in less than a year, and the county was regarded as but one district for constables. In 1839, however, the county was again laid off into two districts for constables, and the Court then proceeded to appoint four constables for each military district, or thirty-six in all. In 1846, the county was divided into sixteen districts for school purposes, and school commissioners were chosen for each district. A similar division was made for the same purpose until the free school system was inaugurated in Virginia.

In January, 1851, the county was again laid off into six districts, and an overseer of the poor was to be elected for each district, according to the provisions of the Code of Virginia.

On April 19, 1870, James H. Shoemaker, Isaac Osborne, Henry C. Wood, and Samuel L. Cox qualified as commissioner to divide and lay off the county into suitable and compactly located townships. The boundaries of the several townships are given below:

FLOYD. Beginning at the mouth of Guest's River, thence running with the Wise County line to a point opposite Brushy Knob, from this point running south to the top of said Knob; thence a straight line to Hagan's Sulphur Springs; then with Staunton's Creek as it meanders to Clinch River; then running a south course, passing the west end of Marion Banner's farm to the top of Copper Ridge; then with the top of said ridge as it meanders to the Russell County line, and with said line to the beginning.

JOHNSON. Beginning on the top of Clinch Mountain in the Russell County line; then running with said line to the top of Copper Ridge, to the corner of the township of Floyd; then running with the top of said ridge, and with the line of the township of Floyd to the southwest corner of said township, and from the said corner a straight line to the mouth of Valley Creek; then a straight line to the top of Clinch Mountain on the Big Knob, south of the dwelling of James S. Edwards; and with the top of said mountain as it meanders to the Russell County line, the beginning corner.

FULKERSON. Beginning at the southwest corner of the township of Johnson on the top of the Big Knob, on Clinch Mountain; thence running a south course to a branch at Isaac C. Anderson's sugar orchard, east of his dwelling; then a straight line due south to the Virginia and Tennessee state line, and with said line to the Washington County line; and with said line to the Russell County line and with said line to the southeast corner of the township of Johnson; and with the line of said township along the top of Clinch Mountain to the beginning.

ESTILLVILLE. Beginning at the south corner of the township of Fulkerson in the Virginia and Tennessee state line; thence running with said line to the top of Clinch Mountain and with the top of said mountain as it meanders to a point opposite the mouth of Troublesome Creek, near Elijah Horton's dwelling; then a straight line running south of said Horton's dwelling to the mouth of said creek; then with Clinch River as it meanders to the mouth of Copper Creek; thence running with said creek to the line of the township of Johnson; and with the line of the said township, and the line of the township of Fulkerson to the beginning.

DEKALB. Beginning in the Wise County line at the northwest corner of the township of Floyd; thence running with the Wise County line to the West (the main) Fork of Cove Creek, and with Cove Creek as it meanders to the Old Camp Ground; then a straight line to the mouth of Mill Branch at Irvin's Old Mill; then a straight line to the mouth of Flower Branch; thence with Copper Creek as it meanders to the line of the township of Johnson; thence with the line of Johnson and Floyd to the beginning.

TAYLOR. Beginning in the Wise County line at the northwest corner of the township of Dekalb; thence running with the Wise County line to the Lee County line, and with the Lee County line along the top of Powell's Mountain to Kane's Gap; thence a straight line to the mouth of Copper Creek; thence running with said creek to the line of the township of Dekalb, at the mouth of Flower Branch; then running with the line of said township to the beginning.

POWELL. Beginning on the top of Powell's Mountain, at the northwest corner of the township of Taylor; thence running with the top of said mountain and with the Lee County line, to the Virginia and Tennessee state line; thence with said line to the top of Clinch Mountain, to the corner of the township of Estillville, and with the line of said township and the top of Clinch Mountain, to the southwest corner of said township; then with the line of said township to the mouth of Troublesome Creek; then with Clinch River to the mouth of Copper Creek; then a straight line with the township of Taylor to the beginning.

The commissioners who divided the county into the districts named above, also established the following voting places in the several districts: Floyd, Osborne's Ford, at Wm. H. Robinson's Store; Johnson, at Nickelsville; Estillville, at Estillville, and at Winegar's; Dekalb, Stony Creek, Cox's Old Store House; Taylor, at Rye Cove, Pendleton's Store House; Powell, at the dwelling house of H. J. Jennings, and at Roller's.

The district lines established by this commission have never been changed. Thus the necessity for the frequent division of the county into sections of varying sizes with consequent overlapping boundary lines which formerly existed was removed.

April 16, 1875, the Court ordered the county divided into two revenue districts, designated as Numbers 1 and 2, or north side and south side. A recent enactment of the General Assembly, however, has merged the two districts into one by providing that only one commissioner of the revenue be elected for the county.

TAVERN RATES

Power to regulate the rates charged by ordinaries or taverns was formerly vested in the county court. In accordance with this power the Scott County Court in May, 1817, entered the following order, fixing the rates: Ordered that the tavern rates in this county be as follows to wit: Diet 25; Grain, per gallon 12½; Forrage 17; Whisky, half pt. 12½; Apple or Peach Brandy 12½; Wine, half pt. 25; Rum 25; French & Brandy 25; Lodging 12½; Grain & Hay for two or three horses 18½; Gin, per half pint 25, which the different tavern keepers in this county are authorized to take and no more. (1–192.)

ROADS

The topography of Scott County made the task of road building very difficult. In its very early sessions, the County Court addressed itself to the construction of roads throughout the county. A large per cent of the courts' early orders from 1815 to 1870 had to do with matters pertaining to roads. In these early days, there were dreams of good roads which would give to the people of the county access to their distant markets. One of the most pretentious of these was the completion of a road from Price's Turnpike to Cumberland Gap. This road was to pass through the counties of Botetourt, Tazewell, Giles, Russell, Scott and Lee. At the September term of court 1834, Thompson G. Martin was appointed director upon the part of the Court.

June 11, 1839, the Justices of the county were called together for the purpose of laying a levy for this road; but the Court refused to lay the levy for the reason that James H. Piper had changed its location on the south side of Powell's Mountain. At the August term, however, the location was made satisfactory to the Court, and it proceeded to lay the levy and appointed Henry S. Kane, Zachariah Fugate, and Thompson G. Martin to borrow $3,000 on the credit of the county to be expended on the road.

COUNTY EXPENSES (1820)

An account of all expenses chargeable to the county since the 9th day of June, 1819, to this time (June 13, 1820).

To Solomon Osborne for killing 2 old wolves.........$	6.00
To Thomas Carter for killing 1 old wolf............	3.00
To Tiarae Culbertson for killing 3 young wolves.....	4.50
To Thomas McConnell for killing 1 young wolf......	1.50
To George Stacey for killing 5 young wolves........	7.50
To Samuel Buster for killing 1 young wolf.........	1.50
To John Boggs for killing 1 old wolf..............	3.00
To John Culbertson for killing 3 young wolves......	4.50
To Abraham Kumpton for killing 2 young wolves...	3.00
To Tiarae & John Culbertson for killing 3 young wolves	4.50
To Joel Ramey for killing 1 old wolf.............	3.00

To the Clerk for Ex-officio services............... 50.00
To the Sheriff for Ex-officio services.............. 30.00
To Andrew McHenry, Attorney for Commonwealth.. 90.00
To the Clerk for stationery....................... 3.00
To the Jailor for ex-officio services................ 25.00
To the Sheriff for keeping courthouse clean......... 10.00
To William Riggs 5 days on road as overseer........ 1.25
To John Peters 3 days on road as overseer......... .75
To John Darter 5 days on road as overseer......... 1.25
To Dale Carter 3 days last year.................. 2.25
To Cornelius Fugate 1 day for 1819............... .75
To Reuben Hale 3 days.......................... .75
To William Lane 4 days......................... 1.00
To Isom Childress 5 days........................ 1.25
To Fielding Hensley 4 days...................... 1.00
To Gideon Ison 4 days last year @ .75........... 3.00
To Gideon Ison 1 day this year.................. .25
To Andrew McHenry for wheeled carriage and draft
  horses to assist in making causeways on public road. 12.50
To his services for 16 days as overseer in working on
  public road................................... 2.00
To Hiram Kilgore for furnishing iron to mend the pub-
  lic jail and blacksmith's bill for same............ 4.90
To Nathan Richardson for procuring pipe and setting
  up stove in Courthouse........................ 4.60

(2–73)   Total $289.40

FERRIES

Before the era of bridge building, deep and swollen streams were crossed by means of ferries. Permission to establish a ferry was granted by the county court. One of the first applications to establish a ferry was made by Thomas Beard. The court permitted him to operate a ferry across the North Fork of the Holston on the road between Big Moccasin Gap and the Blockhouse. May 13, 1818, the court authorized Mr. Beard to charge the following rates for ferriage: For man 6¼, same for a horse; for every wheel of carriage, the same as for a man and horse, each head of cattle the same;

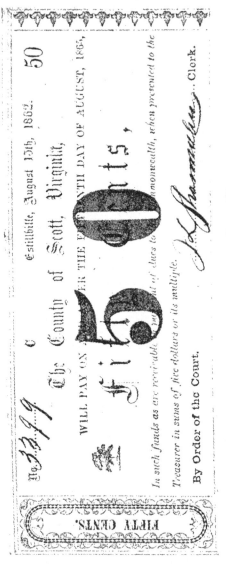

County Money in the Civil War

for hog, sheep, or goat ⅕ as much as for a man. (1–292.)

At the March term, 1819, John McKean was given leave to conduct an ordinary and operate a ferry across Clinch River. (1–396.)

On March 16, 1820, George George was keeper of a ferry across Clinch River and license was also granted to him to keep an ordinary at his ferry. This ferry was near the crossing of the Clinch by the Great Western Road to Cumberland Gap. (2–55.)

On April 15, 1832, Daniel Ramey was authorized by the court to establish a ferry at Osborn's Ford, with permission to charge 6¼ for man; 6¼ for a horse; 6¼ for neat cattle; 1¼ for lamb, sheep, hog or goat; 8 cents per wheel for carryall; 12½ for all other wheeled carriages. (4–480.)

On April 10, 1833, Joshua Speer, by order of court, established a ferry across Clinch River at a point which still bears the name Speer's Ferry. (5–62.)

Fayette McMullen, who later became congressman, kept a ferry across the North Fork of Holston on the Blockhouse Road. (6–2.)

THE COUNTY COURT AND BANK NOTES

In 1816, the county court ordered that bank notes on the regular chartered banks of the states of Virginia, and of North Carolina should be received at par value; bank notes on chartered banks of Tennessee and Kentucky should be received at two per cent under par; bank notes on banks of other states and the District of Columbia should be taken at five per cent under par. (1–135.) By Act of General Assembly of Virginia passed January 16, 1817, a list of bank notes was given together with the value that should be given to each. At the March term of the county court, 1817, it was declared that this list should pass current in Scott County. (1–185.)

By Act of the General Assembly March 29, 1862, the county court was permitted to issue county notes of less denomination than five dollars. August 12, 1862, the court authorized the issuance of such notes to the amount of twelve thousand dollars, to be redeemed in 1865. These notes were to be signed by James L. Shoemaker, Clerk. (13-281.)

WAR OF 1812

William Rhoten, who married Jaalia Templeton, was a soldier in the War of 1812. He was attached to a company of militia commanded by Capt. John Hammons. He was at first a member of the 6th, later the 5th, regiment of the United States Army. While awaiting to embark from Norfolk, Va., to whatever point he might be needed, he died in a hospital there.

Isaac Derham was also a member of the 5th regiment and a member of Captain Hammon's company.

James Rhoten was a member of Captain Hammon's company. He died in Norfolk, Va., while in service there. (1-159-160.)

Jessee Elliott, who married Catherine Lawson, was a private in Captain Hammon's company. On reaching Norfolk, Va., he was attached to the command of Col. Henry E. Coleman and later was honorably discharged on account of ill health.

Ambrose Bledsoe was a private in Capt. Abram Fulkerson's company who also rendered service at Norfolk, Va. (1-240.)

John Cole enlisted as a private in the company of Capt. George W. Camps in the regiment commanded by Colonel Coonts. Cole's service is further attested by Hiram Kilgore, a lieutenant in the same company. Sergt. James Fullen also bear's testimony as to Cole's services in the U. S. Army at Norfolk, Va. (1-366.)

William Benham served in the war of 1812, under Captain Turner. He saw service in the United States and Canada in 1814. (11-360.)

John Dixon, a private in Capt. John Hammon's company saw service at Norfolk in 1814. (11-361.)

SCOTT COUNTY IN THE CIVIL WAR AS SHOWN BY THE COURT RECORDS

On May 14, 1861, the county court ordered that Henry S. Kane, Henry A. Morison, and James L. Shoemaker be ap-

pointed commissioners to furnish the Volunteers of the county
with necessary provisions, house room, and music, during the
time they might be engaged in training; and, also, to procure
the services of a suitable person to train them and make out
and return to the court, an account of the expenses heretofore and hereafter incurred by the Volunteers up to the next
term of the court. The commissioners were further ordered to
report the probable cost of uniforming the Volunteers in a
plain and suitable manner. (13-144-145.)

At the June term, 1861, $1,500 was appropriated for the
equipment of Volunteers, and a special levy was made for
the purpose. Persons who furnished Volunteers money or
other articles of value presented their bills to the county court.
Z. W. Davidson and E. K. Herron were authorized to borrow $500 for the equipment of Volunteers. Volunteers were
exempted from the payment of county levies. (13-154.)
Michael Calopy, a non-resident, was arrested and placed in
jail for lurking about for purposes unknown. On the following day, however, he was released from custody. (13-154.)

The court, deeming it necessary for the interest and welfare
of the county that some police plan for home protection and
safety should be adopted, unanimously ordered that:

1st. The Justices of the county shall constitute a general
vigilance committee who shall always be on the alert, and, at
all times more prompt and active than ever in the performance of their duties, under the laws, for the protection of
the rights and interests of the citizens.

2nd. The court shall have control over the measures of
home protection and defense.

3rd. There shall be a control vigilance committee in each
district composed of the four Justices, and two other persons to be appointed by the court in the bounds of the district. This committee shall have power to direct and
supervise all measures of protection and defense in their respective districts, and shall report in writing to the court at
every term of all matters worthy of note.

4th. There shall be one or more Volunteer companies of
not less than forty men in each captain district, two lieutenants
and four sergeants respectively, which officers shall be elected
by the men of the companies, and confirmed by the court.

Each man shall be armed with his own rifle, musket, or shot gun, or with arms of like character loaned or furnished him by the citizens of each district from the home stock on hand or otherwise. In like manner he is to furnish, have procured for him, a sufficiency of ammunition. The companies shall be divided into platoons extending from the center to the extremities of the district, and shall act as a general patrol within their proper bounds, and under their proper officers, at least once a month, or oftener if necessary. A report shall be made of the operations of the company and of the order and security of the citizens to the central committee by the captain in writing.

5th. The needy families of all Volunteers absent in the service of the state, shall be provided for, and for this purpose the Justices of each district are appointed by the court a committee whose duty it shall be to enquire into the condition and necessities of said families, and provide at once for the same if necessary, and report in writing to the next, and every succeeding term of the court, and thereupon the proper allowances shall be made by the court.

6th. In the event of invasion, insurrection, or rebellion within the county, this court will now proceed to appoint two field officers, who shall be empowered to call out and command the voluntary forces of the county or so much thereof as may, in their opinion, be necessary for the purpose of repelling such invasion, or suppressing such insurrection or rebellion. Whereupon the court appointed Col. H. P. Neil commandant within the bounds of the 124th Regiment and Maj. John Hickam, commandant of the forces within the bounds of the 185th Regiment.

The court then proceeded to the appointment of the additional committee under the 3rd clause of the proceedings; and thereupon unanimously appointed:

Richard I. Shelton & Wm. H. Hensley.........Dist. No. 1
John Jett & James Fleenor..................Dist. No. 2
William Broadwater & Harvey P. Gibson.......Dist. No. 3
Chas. W. Bickley & Simon Stair..............Dist. No. 4
Wm. B. Cocke & Thompson Greear...........Dist. No. 5

Wm. Horton & Hiram Kilgore & Wm. Ervin.... Dist. No. 6
Isaac W. Wolfe & David McKinney........... Dist. No. 7

as vigilance committeemen in their district to act in conjunction with the Justices in their respective districts. The Home Guards already organized in the county for home protection are recognized by the court, and are directed to perform service in their proper spheres respectively for the protection of the interest and welfare of the county. (13–155–156–157.)
At the same term the court appointed Emory M. Cox and Clinton Godsey to act as a picket guard in the direction of the Big Sandy River with a view of ascertaining whether any forces were making preparations or were coming in this direction with a view to invading this county or state. (13–157.) This order was rescinded about a month later. (13–170.)
May 11, 1862, the court proceeded to enroll all the able-bodied male free negroes between the ages of eighteen and fifty years, and certified the same to the Adjutant General of the State. (13–239.)
The court having ascertained, from reliable information, that since the departure of the Southern Cavalry from Lee County, Virginia, the enemy have advanced into that county with considerable forces, both infantry and cavalry, and are now near the line of this county, moving in the direction of Bristol killing one citizen, and laying waste the country, and there being no forces in Scott or Lee counties to check the progress of the enemy: It is therefore ordered that Capts. Wm. J. Smith and S. P. McConnell be and they are hereby appointed commissioner, the said Captain Smith to proceed immediately to the authorities having command of the forces at the Salt Works and in Russell and Tazewell counties, and the said Captain McConnell proceed immediately to the proper authorities having command of the forces at Rogersville and Knoxville, Tennessee, to obtain sufficient forces from the said authorities to repel the invaders who are desolating our country and threatening the occupation of our railroad and Salt Works. (13–276) July 15, 1862.
On the same day the above order was entered, the court appointed Charles B. Smith and Charles Ison as a picket guard in the direction of Jonesville, in the county of Lee, to ascer-

tain whether the enemy were advancing in the direction of Scott County. (13–276.)

On September 14, 1864, S. P. McConnell was directed by the court to prepare a roll of honor of all the soldiers from this county entering the service of the Confederate States in her present struggle with the United States for independence. It was further ordered by the court that all the Justices of the county should assist S. P. McConnell, Clerk, in the preparation of this roll of honor by furnishing with lists from their respective communities. Major McConnell was to prepare the roll and transmit the same to Joseph Jackson, Jr., recorder for the Virginia forces. This author has searched in vain for this roll of honor. He feels quite sure that Major McConnell prepared it. (13–481.)

On September 14, 1864, when Federal forces began to come into this section, the court, out of an abundance of precaution, ordered S. P. McConnell, clerk, to remove all the Deed Books, Will Books, Minute Books, Execution Books, Judgment Dockets, Records of Births and Deaths and Bond Books from the Clerk's office to a place of safety. They were to remain in hiding until further order of the court. (13–481.)

On September 13, 1865, the court requested S. P. McConnell to return the Record Books of the Clerk's office from their hiding place to the courthouse. Major McConnell was thus the custodian of the records in their secret hiding place for the space of a year. (13–516.)

The court having understood that the county had credit for only 350 volunteers at the War Department, and believing that the Governor of the Commonwealth had acted under the impression that such was the fact when he made his late call upon the county for 120 men which is probably more than the county's due proportion as compared with other counties, and being desirous of laying before His Excellency a correct statement of facts as they exist so far as this court can gather them, beg leave to submit the following statement showing the number of Volunteers already sent into service from this county, the name of the captain of each company, the number of men in each company, and the number of recruits sent to each company to wit: Capt. Henry C. Wood, 96 in his company, 30 recruits; Henry W. Osborne, 96 men, no recruits; Henry M. McConnell, 78 men, no recruits; John W. Vermillion, 70 men, 30 recruits; William J. Smith, 88 men, 22 recruits; William S. Webb, 100 men, no recruits; James S. Haynes, 78 men, 28 recruits; Harvey Gray, 79 men, 22 recruits; Alexander Maness, 105 men, no recruits; S. P. McConnell, company of rangers, 240 men; William Baldwin, 100 men, no recruits. To the number mentioned above add 75 volunteers who have companies in the state of Tennessee, and other counties in this state which makes an aggregate of 1,349 volunteers actually in the service from this county; in addition to this all the conscripts between the ages of 18 and 35 years who have not already volunteered and entered the service, are being enrolled by the enrolling officers and sent into the service, leaving as represented by Maj. John D. Templeton, 120 men in the 124th Regiment and 140 in the 185th Regiment between the ages of 35 and 45 years of whom about 100 are unfit for duty, which will only leave 160 men able to perform military duty of the remaining conscripts in this county between the ages of 35 and 45 years. If the call for 150 men be filled, then only about ten men of that class of conscripts will be left in the county. The court submitted the above facts in the hope that the call on this county under the existing circumstances might be changed and especially as marauding crowds of the enemy are endangering the safety of life and property constantly in this portion of the state which imperiously demands that as many men as can be spared from the service, should be left for the protection of this county. (13–281-282.)

On February 11, 1862, the court ordered Thomas M. Quillin, a Justice of the Peace to furnish, or cause to be furnished, Matilda Southern, the wife of T. C. Southern, who as a volunteer had entered the service of the Confederate States, with such food and clothing as the actual necessities of the family required. (13–227.) As the war progressed the number of needy families increased, and the problem of caring for them became more difficult. On September 9, 1862, the court appointed a committee consisting of E. K. Herron in Dist. No. 1, John Jett in No. 2, Charles Quillin in No. 3, William K. Porter in No. 4, William C. Brickey in No. 5, John Duncan in No. 6, and C. C. Fugate in No. 7. The duty of this committee was to inquire into the condition and needs of the families of volunteers absent in the army, and to supply those needs in the most economical way and report to the court.

Opportunity was also given to the public to make donations of money or clothing for the use of the volunteers in the army, November 11, 1862, the court appointed Will Jones and Z. W. Davidson in Dist. No. 1, John Jett and James Bays in No. 2, Charles Quillin and James M. Quillin in No. 3, Henry R. Cox and Charles W. Bickley in No. 4, Wm. C. Brickey and F. K. Elliott in No. 5, John Duncan and Thomas W. Carter in No. 6, and C. C. Fugate and Henry J. Jennings in No. 7, to receive donations in their respective districts, and E. K. Herron was appointed to receive such donations as might be gathered by the parties named above. (13–302.) On November 10, 1863, the court directed Col. Joel H. Fleenor to convey the clothing donated by the people to General Lee's Army. (13–389.)

On April 12, 1864, Henry A. Morison was appointed by the court an agent to purchase and distribute through the county, cotton, cotton yarns, cotton cloths, and cards. As agent he was authorized to borrow the sum of ten thousand dollars from the county treasury to be repaid in New Issue Confederate Treasury Notes. (13–435–436.)

May 11, 1864, the court petitioned Gen. W. E. Jones to send a company to protect the county from the depredations of the home guards (?) as there were considerable quantities of government stores such as wool, wheat, etc., which were liable to fall into the hands of the enemy. (13–442.)

Two men, one named Cates and the other, Brown, had been placed in the Scott County jail. Both were charged with felony and were being held for the circuit court. July 2, 1864, two armed men came to Estillville, bearing a letter purporting to have been written by W. M. Bradford, a colonel of cavalry. This letter asked the release of Brown that he might be turned over to the military authorities. H. W. Holdway, Commonwealth Attorney, promptly refused to grant the request Whereupon, five days later, a band of armed men, claiming to be soldiers, and alleging that they were acting under the verbal order of Colonel Bradford, made their appearance in the town of Estillville and, by force of arms, released the two imprisoned men. The county court strongly protested against such interference with the civil authority and directed that all the evidence in the case be given to the judge of the circuit court. (13–462.)

At the October term of court it was asked that the order for conscription which had recently been issued, be suspended in reference to Scott County, at least for the time being. The reasons given for the request were that parts of the county were infested with deserters and bushwhackers, some of them resident of this county, and some of them from other counties, and East Tennessee, and many of them disposed to rob and murder, a condition requiring the effort of the whole population in favor of law and order to keep them down. If said conscript orders be now enforced, and county drained of its better population, it will give those characters full control of the community, and enable them to rob and plunder the better citizens and to heap insult and abuses upon their wives, children, mothers, and sisters. The court therefore upon the behalf of the people, humbly request the Hon. James A. Sedden, Secretary of War, to suspend said orders in this county until the authorities can arrest or drive from our midst those characters. (13–482.)

On the motion of H. W. Holdway, Attorney for the Commonwealth, William H. Epperson was made captain of the patrol. He was empowered to enroll such persons as were not already in the service of the Confederate States. He was directed to arrest deserters from the army, outlaws and marauders and conduct them at once before the proper authorities. (13–486.)

On December 24, 1864, United States troops under the command of Major General Stoneman in passing up Poor Valley, took a horse belonging to E. B. Hilton and left two other horses in the neighborhood. The court, in accordance with the regulations of the Confederacy in such cases provided, permitted Hilton to retain the discarded horses as part payment for his own.

On the same day, in the same neighborhood, United States troops took a horse from Sherwood M. Barker leaving two discarded ones in his vicinity. These the court permitted him to keep in part payment for his loss. (13–497.)

In accordance with an act passed by the General Assembly of Virginia March 4, 1865, and the instructions from the governor, the court proceeded to ascertain the number of male slaves within the county liable to draft. The number was ascertained to be twenty-eight. Out of this number the requisition stood at three slaves. Two groups of slave owners agreed among themselves to furnish two of the number required. The third were unable to agree among themselves and the matter determined by lot. The lot fell upon Elijah E. Carter. It later developed that Carter had no slave of the required age. Upon the court's balloting a second time to find who should furnish the third slave, the lot fell upon the estate of Alexander Gray. This requisition of slaves, however, never reached the Confederate fortifications as it was completed on April 3, 1865, only six days before the surrender of General Lee at Appomattox Courthouse.

March 14, 1865, the court entered the following order: In view of the great danger of fire by the public enemy to which the courthouse of this county is exposed if the same should be used for an enrolling office and quarters for an enrolling guard; and in view of the great amount of damage that is wantonly being done to the courthouse by said guard; and the great annoyance of the guard to the business of the clerk of the court; the court, as custodian of the house, doth request Lieut. W. T. Fentress, enrolling officer for this county, to remove his office and guard from said courthouse that the preservation and safety of the same be more fully insured. (13–500.)

On April 3, 1865, the court entered the following record: The court being of opinion that this county should be exempted by the governor from any further requisition according to the provisions of the first section of said act, do order that the following facts be certified to the governor for the attainment of that object, to wit: That the northern boundary of the county is quite accessible to the enemy from Kentucky; that the courthouse of the county is situated within three miles of the Tennessee line, and eight miles from Kingsport, Tenn., where a considerable force of the enemy are frequently accumulated; that the southern border of said county adjoins the said state of Tennessee which is now declared to be a free state, the action of the Lincoln Government which is seriously affecting the institution of slavery in the county, and causing the slaves to escape to the enemy upon any pretext whatever; that the enemy have made repeated raids through said county, and to the county seat, a portion of which they have burned; and that from the personal knowledge of the court and from the best evidence they have been able to obtain about two-thirds of the slaves of this county between the ages of eighteen and fifty-five have been removed from the county by escape to the enemy or other cause; and that it has been very difficult for some of the slave holders to retain their slaves of the ages specified in the requisition since it became public here, and that many of said slaves have escaped to the enemy under the influence of said requisition by reason of the unavoidable facilities that the slaves have for escaping to the enemy from this county; and it is moreover believed by the court from what has recently transpired that another requisition would have the effect of transferring into the hands and use of the enemy most, if not all, of the slaves of the ages specified in the requisition, the court further certifies that the labourers are few now remaining in the county for making subsistence for the use of the army and citizens and families of the soldiers now in the service of the Confederacy. In view of the facts submitted, the court respectfully but earnestly urges the propriety and great necessity of the exemption of this county by Your Excellency from any other or further requisition upon the small slave population remaining in the county. (13–507–508–509–510.)

October 11, 1865, the county court entered the following order: "It appearing to the court that the person and property of the law-abiding citizens of this county bordering on Tennessee are in great danger of being depredated on by marauding bands of thieves, robbers, and marauders (called bushwhackers) that still remain organized along and near the Tennessee line for carrying out their felonious purposes, aforesaid, whenever they find the citizens in a defenseless and unprotected condition. Therefore, the court, pursuant to law, doth appoint the police force of Capt. Cornelius W. White, also the police force of Capt. James Wilhelm, also the police force of Capt. William H. Montgomery, also the police force of Capt. Robert Smith, also the police force of Capt. Thomas Quillin, also the police force of Capt. William Harris, also the police force of Capt. William F. Templeton, also the police force of Thomas Herald, also the police force of Joseph Hickam, also the police force of Capt. James A. Harris, also the police force of Capt. Polk Benham to act as special police forces in this county, pursuant to the provisions of the 201st chapter of the Code of Virginia to preserve order, suppress the commission of crimes and all lawless conduct and for that purpose to arrest and have tried and punished all offenders enumerated in said law, and perform as special police forces all other acts authorized by said law.   (13–523–524.)

This court having organized pursuant to law, and civil authority being restored in this county for the trial and punishment of violations of law, therefore, it becomes necessary that the jailer, Mr. William W. Bell, be placed in possession of the jail of this county and its appurtenances for the reception and imprisonment of offenders, committed to jail by the legal authorities of this county; and that the clerk of the circuit court be placed in possession of the circuit court office which is now occupied by the provost marshal, Lieutenant Morse, and as the jail needs considerable repairs as well as the courthouse which must be done immediately pursuant to the order of court entered at this term, and as the jailer needs and his official duties require that he shall occupy the said jail, and moreover as the guard of the provost marshal, Lieut. Morse, are at the present occupying the said jail and tenements, the court doth therefore respectfully request the said provost marshal and the military authorities under whom he is acting to deliver to the said Clerk Cornelius W. White the said office, and to the said Jailor Wm. W. Bell the said jail and tenements at their earliest convenience.   (13–524.)

THE OLD-TIME SCHOOL IN SCOTT COUNTY

FOREWORD

"The Old-time School in Scott County" is a real contribution to the educational history of the Appalachian region. The conditions existing in that county are typical of those in most of the counties of the upland region of Virginia thirty-five or forty years ago. In spite of slender equipment, poor support, short session of school, and meager training of the teachers, the old-time school served its day and generation well. Most of the essentials of a primary and secondary education were effectively given in those old schools. The attention given to moral instruction was probably superior in actual effectiveness to that given in most public schools of today.

"No man better equipped for the portrayal of the old-time school could be found than Prof. Robert M. Addington. He was a student and for many years a teacher in the old-time schools, and appreciates their strength and weakness. I personally have studied and taught in the old-time school and wish here to express my indebtedness to the old-time school and the old-time school-teachers for a large part of the best that I have received in life from school.

"I personally have seen instances and practices parallel with everything mentioned in Professor Addington's sympathetic and comprehensive review of the old-time school. I recently read this article to some children of grammar school and high school age. They listened with interest, but could not realize that the account of the old-time school could be accepted as serious history of the educational conditions existing a third of a century ago. I wish to add my testimony to the literal truth and accuracy of the facts in this portrayal of the old-time school in my native county, which I know was typical of all surrounding purely rural counties in the western part of the state.

Very respectfully,

JOHN PRESTON McCONNELL,

President."

For a period of more than one hundred years rather primitive types of "old field" schools were the only schools in Scott County. These schools accumulated traditions and customs which they bequeathed to the public free schools upon their advent into the county. Owing to the fact that the public free schools owe many of their faults and a few of their virtues to this heritage, some account of the "old field" school may be given here.

They were taught either in meeting houses, or in unoccupied dwelling houses. The latter, more often than otherwise, had dirt or puncheon floors, wind doors, with shutters but no glass, and stick and clay chimneys with fireplaces wide and deep enough to accommodate logs of almost any size.

Some of these schools had as many classes as they had pupils. (This was the Batavian system with a vengeance!) There seems to have been little attempt at classification. Each pupil was called to recitation, throughout the day, in the order of his arrival in the morning—"First come, first called." There was rivalry, too, for first place; the pupils often reached the schoolhouse by daybreak, in order to be first in the circle of recitations throughout the day. Each pupil knew the order in which he arrived, and on the completion of a recitation, the teacher only had to call out, "Next."

Some of these schools were called "blab" schools, because the pupils studied aloud. The writer first attended a "blab" school taught by an elderly spinster whose husband-to-be was killed in the Civil War, perhaps, or, refusing to accept the allotment of fate, he might have suicided. Certain it is that the writer well remembers the difficulties with which he was initiated into the mysteries of the English alphabet, surrounded, as he was, by such a babel of voices as the "blab" school afforded. The schoolmistress, armed with a huge switch, would call, "Spell out," at the same time emphasizing her command with a thwack of the switch against any resonant surface that happened to be near at hand. Then would follow a great outburst of childish voices, some spelling, some reading, and some repeating impromptu verses so constructed as to fit in with the general uproar. The writer, fearing to do otherwise, would add his own voice to the confusion, by trying to say his A B C's; but, alas! he always found himself repeating the things which had been said in the loudest voice, instead of his own lesson. When the noise began to subside, both the stern command and the threatening stroke were repeated with the same results as before. The schoolmistress had neither watch nor clock. On fair days the noon hour was determined by the shade of a tree; on cloudy days, it was guessed at. The pupils were called to books by three strokes with a board on the walls of the house. This act was supplemented by the teacher calling, "Come to books!" So far as the author of this article knows, this was the last "blab" school taught in his county, and he congratulates himself upon having been able to say farewell to it as it took its departure down the stream of time.

THE FREE SCHOOLHOUSE

The "individualistic tendencies," so characteristic of Scotch-Irish stock, often asserted themselves in the location of the early schoolhouses. Every man wanted one at his own door. Thus locations were frequently the result of compromises; and the compromises placed them by the bleak roadside, on the slaty point, on the forest edge, and sometimes deep within the forest. The landowner who donated the scant quarter or half acre for its site made small sacrifice, because the land given was generally too poor to produce anything but a schoolhouse. Furthermore, in the minds of many patrons, the childish desire to play was regarded as a thing to be rather sternly repressed, consequently, it was not thought necessary to provide adequate playgrounds. At very many schoolhouses, the only ground on which the children could play was the public road, and it was not kept in very good repair!

The schoolhouses were built of either round or hewn logs, chinked and daubed with mud or moss. The labor of chinking and daubing was performed, periodically, by the teacher and the pupils.

The first public schoolhouses were equipped with split log benches with huge pegs for legs. These peg legs have been known to serve as weapons of offense and defense in altercations between teacher and pupil. Whenever it was possible to obtain lumber from a "whip saw," or an old "up and down" sawmill, the schoolhouses were seated with long and clumsy, straight-backed benches, without desks. Since neither desks nor cloakrooms were provided, the pupil, solicitous for the safety of his hat and books, often sat upon them all day long. Lunch baskets were placed sometimes on a shelf; sometimes in a corner, and sometimes at the pupil's side where he sat. And in this connection it may be remarked that, in the minds of the pupils, social and financial standing was not shown, as might have been expected, by the clothing worn, but by the school lunch. A lunch of corn bread was taken to signify poverty, and was clandestinely eaten under the hill or anywhere out of sight. The lunch of wheat bread was eaten openly in the presence of the school.

FUEL AND HEATING

The schoolrooms were heated by fireplace or wood stove. The teacher and the pupils prepared the fuel in the nearby forest and carried it on their shoulders to the schoolhouse. At noon, each boy was required to bring a load of wood to the schoolhouse yard. The teacher often inspected these loads, and if by chance any of them lacked either in quantity or quality, the boy was sent for another load, and he whose wood failed to "pass muster," dreaded the taunts and gibes of his fellows far more than the labor of procuring another load. Whole trees were often transported in this way, with a boy or two sitting on top merely to show that the tree itself did not make a load.

LENGTH OF TERM

The school terms were usually from three and a half to five months in length. They were liable to interruption by "foddering," "molasses making," and other work peculiar to the fall season. Teachers often dismissed their schools to do the work of their vocations, such as farming, preaching, surveying, etc. Instances can be cited wherein eight or nine months were required in which to close a four or five months' term of school.

THE OLD-TIME SCHOOL-TEACHER

Sometimes the old-time school-teacher was a farmer who wanted employment during the winter months; sometimes he was a preacher whose churches did not support him; oftentimes he was a cripple who was physically unable to earn a livelihood in any other way. His scholastic preparation usually consisted of such attainments as could be had in the local schools, supplemented, perhaps, by a few months' study in some "academy" or "seminary." He was well qualified if he could work the problems in an arithmetic of the practical grade. His scholarship, however, was questioned seriously if he failed to solve a problem immediately upon its presentation. Pupils and patrons easily could see when he failed to get the answer to a problem. His ignorance of the other branches was more difficult of detection. He was usually accredited with knowing more than he really did, and occasionally he was quite willing to encourage the deception.

Those teachers who believed in corporal punishment and were rough in its administration were most in demand. The average patron believed that everybody else's children needed whipping, and he wanted a teacher who would attend to that need. The deep-seated and widespread opposition to women as teachers was due, perhaps, to the general belief that a woman was unable, physically, to lay on the switch as powerfully as it ought to be laid on.

The standard unit of corporal punishment was the "lash"; penalties were measured in "lashes." In cases of disorder, arising within the school room, the offenders were designated by the teacher "pitching the switch" at them. Frequently the first intimation of impending punishment the erring pupil received would be the crash of a switch falling uncomfortably near him, and followed by the stern command to pick it up and bring it to the teacher. If there were a group of offenders, each must help to carry up the switch. It was sometimes borne by as many as six boys, amidst an expectant silence that was palpable. Before the whipping the pupil was soothed with the assurance that the teacher would rather take it himself, if it would do "the same amount of good." After the whipping, while the pupil was still wrestling with the convul-

sive sobs that shook his frame, he was further comforted by
the statement that he would remember the teacher and thank
him for it "the longest day he had to live." Now and then,
severe punishments would call forth indignant protests on the
part of angry parents. At rare intervals they became militant
and would "go upon" the teacher. An instance can be cited
in which a challenge to a duel was evoked by a school punishment. But there came a time when public opinion began
to disapprove so much whipping. Teachers then had re-
course to what they called "moral suasion," which consisted
in imposing punishments presumably less severe than whipping. Not a few teachers taxed their ingenuity in devising
unusual, if not cruel, punishments. Pupils were required to
stand on one foot, on both feet, on the floor, on a bench, and
on the stove. They were made to keep their feet within circles,
their toes upon marks, "toeing the mark," their fingers upon
a nail in the floor, "bearing down," etc., etc.

CERTIFICATION OF TEACHERS

The certification of teachers was based on neither uniform
nor severe examinations. The examinations were mostly oral.
Applicants for certificates were often examined riding along
the road in company with the county superintendent.

THE TEACHER'S TITLE

Although the old-time school-teacher was an important personage in the community, yet no distinctive title was applied
to him. He was spoken of in such terms as "Charles W.,"
"Old Uncle Bob Whitely," etc. The title of professor was
applied only to the principals of the so-called "institutes,"
"academies," and "seminaries." It had not then been cheap-
ened by its application to singing masters, dancing masters,
sleight-of-hand performers, lion tamers, and snake charmers.

AIMS OF THE OLD-TIME SCHOOL

That the old-time school would prepare its pupils for success in industrial achievement, in the professions, or even in

business, was not generally expected. It is true that the ability to spell and read well, and such a knowledge of arithmetic as would insure against being "cheated" in ordinary business transactions, was considered valuable. Yet nobody, it seems, thought the training of the schools would be of much real help in the practical concerns of life. In the inspirational talks, occasionally made by teachers and others, it was pointed out that the reward of hard work in school would be the possibility of going to Congress, or becoming President of the United States. The failure of these speakers to stress the practical value of an education may be taken to indicate that they thought an education worth while only to those who had high political aspirations.

CURRICULUM

The curriculum of the old-time school consisted of spelling, reading, and arithmetic, as studies required by public opinion, with grammar and geography as electives. In the selection of studies, both parents and pupils sometimes participated. Sometimes parents would limit the number of studies as a matter of economy in books. Sometimes pupils, pursuing the line of least resistance, would eliminate the hard studies from their lists. At all times there was no uniformity in the course, since a pupil's studies might range over five or six grades.

"THE WRITING SCHOOL"

The old-time school did not concern itself with teaching its pupils to write. That valuable accomplishment was to be acquired in the "writing schools," taught by itinerant teachers, in ten-day sessions, "at a dollar per scholar." The information thought necessary to enable the pupil to write well was set to music and sung in a song, called "Chirography." When sung, each line was repeated. The words of this song are as follows:

"Chirography is the art of writing.
Principles of writing are three in number:
The angle, curve and proportion.
The principal hand writings are four in number:

Round, oval, mercantile, and running.

Rules for writing are seven in number:

Fine, smooth, one size, one distance, one slant, on the line, and joined.

Classes of letters are four in number:

The dotted stem, the shaded stem, the direct *O*, the inverted *O*.

The dotted stem has four letters: *I, B, P,* and *R*.

The shaded stem has nine letters:

A, F, H, J, K, N, S, and *T*.

The direct *O* has six letters: *C, D, E, G, L,* and *O*.

The inverted *O* has seven letters: *Q, U, V, W, H, Y,* and *Z*.

Spaces of letters are five in number: Short letter, the middle space.

Square top letters, two spaces.

Single loop letters, three spaces.

Double loop letters, four spaces.

Spaces between letters, the space of an *O*. Space between words, the space of an *M*. Space between sentences, three *M's*. Dot your *i's* as high as a *t*. Cross your *t* three fourths of its height.

Italics, one dash below.

Small capitals, two dashes.

Large capitals, three dashes."

The written exercise had small place in the work of the old-time school. Sometimes, however, pupils were required to write and "hand in" compositions on abstract and high-sounding subjects about which they knew little or nothing.

METHODS OF TRAINING

As a prerequisite to the study of spelling, the pupil was required to learn the alphabet from "A to Izzard." When the alphabet was thought to be thoroughly mastered, the pupil was then permitted to spell "on the book." Spelling "on the book" was followed by spelling "off the book," or spelling "by heart." This was continued until the pupil was often able to spell every word in Holmes' Speller. (Holmes' Speller, it may be remarked, had a blue back, and was the successor, in this section at least, of Webster's "old blue-back" speller.)

"THE HEART LESSON," OR "NIGHT LESSON"

Every pupil able to spell orally was expected to recite a "heart lesson" sometime during the school day, usually the last thing in the evening. "Heart lessons" were studied aloud, a custom of the old-time school, which had been brought down from the more ancient "blab" school. "Head-marks" were given, and often there was much rivalry in contesting for the "premeem." The pupil who missed a "heart lesson" forfeited his place in class and had to go "foot." In addition to the large place given to spelling, the old-time school was one-tenth "spelling match."

READING

As a considerable knowledge of spelling was thought necessary before taking up reading, children did not begin to read at very tender ages. Grown men were often members of first reader classes. The test of good reading was ability to pronounce the words. Little attention was given to anything else. In some of the schools, after McGuffey's series of readers had been completed, "New Testament" classes were organized and pupils required to read "verse about."

GEOGRAPHY

The old textbooks in geography were usually arranged in catechistic order, and the teacher gave the set questions of the book and insisted upon the set answers.

ARITHMETIC

Arithmetic, of all the subjects in the curriculum, was the best taught. The old-time teacher was partial to it. His enthusiasm for it was infectious and was communicated to his pupils. Individual, not class, instruction was very largely given. Any kind of school work could be interrupted by a problem. The pupil, asking aid in the solution of a problem, had access to the teacher at all times. When the teacher had solved a problem, he passed it to the pupil, usually without comment or explanation. If the pupil failed to understand it, or any part of it, he would return with the laconic question, "Where'd you get this?" This question would call forth whatever explanation the teacher saw fit to give.

Excellent work in arithmetic was rewarded by permitting the pupils to go outside to study under the trees—a privilege much coveted and seldom abused.

GAMES OF THE OLD-TIME SCHOOL

What fifty-year-old boy does not recall, with a thrill of joy, the games of "Dare Base," "Stink Base," "King Base," "Round Town," and "Straight Town," which he played while a pupil of the old-time school? These games have made school life more tolerable for many a boy. Pupils not much inclined to books often, for the sake of its seductive games, endured the irksome duties of the school long enough to get the rudiments of an education.

"TREATING"

A curious custom prevailed among the pupils of the old-time school—the custom of "turning the teacher out," in order to force him to "treat." On the near approach of the Christmas holiday, the older pupils would begin to devise plans for barricading the schoolhouse so as to fasten out the teacher. Often they would go before daylight, bar the door, fasten down the windows, and await the teacher's coming. By the time of his arrival, the schoolhouse had been converted into such a fortress that entrance could not be effected except by bursting the doors or breaking the windows. Then would follow a parley. The pupils inside would demand that he treat, at the same time stipulating in what the treat should consist, and the amount, as a condition of his admission. Sometimes the teacher would accede at once to the demands. Sometimes he would offer to treat, if they could catch him. Sometimes he would batter down the door and enter. And sometimes he would dismiss school until after Christmas. A persistent refusal to treat was punishable by ducking in the nearest stream or pond. Extreme measures, however, were seldom resorted to, as the teacher generally yielded.

"SCHOOL BUTTER"

It was the custom also to duck any person who passed a school and "hollered" "school butter." ("Butter" is, probably, a mispronunciation of the word better, in the sentence, "Our school is better.") The writer recalls an instance which occurred many years ago, near the Virginia state line. A horseman, passing a certain school, called out, "School butter," and immediately set spurs to his horse. The teacher permitted all the larger boys of the school to join in the chase. Whatever advantage the culprit, being mounted, may have had over his pursuers was more than offset by the opportunity of the boys to take "near cuts." After an exciting race of several miles across the state line into Tennessee, the offender was overtaken and brought back, in free and easy defiance of requisition or extradition papers. He was ducked, in the presence of the school, in water too shallow for immersion, by being rolled over and side ducked at a time.

"BOARDING AMONG THE SCHOLARS"

The small salary of the old-time teacher seldom suffered diminution on account of board bills; for, among a people from whose firesides even the wandering beggar was rarely spurned, the school-teacher was a welcome guest. Thus, in addition to his regular salary, it was understood that he should "board among the scholars." So, burdened with a "hand-satchel," he went from house to house, usually, staying "week about" with the various patrons of his school. In the words of an old teacher, "He went from Dan to Beersheba, warming the spare beds of the neighborhood and feasting on the fat of the land!"

Although the teacher was a welcome guest in the homes of his patrons, yet he often further ingratiated himself into favor with his hosts by doing chores about the house; by assisting the children with their lessons; by solving problems in partial payments for his hosts; and by lending the charms of his superior learning and culture to the fireside conversation. Indeed, "boarding among the scholars" brought teacher and patron into a close acquaintanceship, thereby laying the foundation for effective co-operation. Likewise, it afforded the teacher an opportunity to study his pupils at close range, and to gauge fully the bias given the pupils' lives by the home training and the home influences. Notwithstanding all this, there yet remained, even in the days of "free board among the scholars," enough of cross purpose and censure to exempt the teacher from the woe pronounced against those of whom all men speak well.

"SPEAKING"

The old-time school gave some attention to the elocutionary training of its pupils. "The Friday evening exercise" became a close rival of "the spelling match" in popularity with the teachers. They were never quite so popular with the pupils. The rule governing these exercises generally required each pupil either "to speak" or "to make a bow." On the whole, this rule was rigidly enforced and many were the subterfuges resorted to in order to avoid its penalties. When no other escape was possible, there yet remained "Twinkle, Twinkle, Little Star," and "Mary Had a Little Lamb," old standbys which would bear repetition, and the speaking of which would procure immunity from punishment. Thus it sometimes happened that almost the entire exercise would consist of the repetition of these two poems, the variations being in the amount each pupil remembered, and in the mood, whether grave or gay, in which the pupil chanced to be.

Usually, however, the declamations and recitation presented a literary medley, ranging in variety from the nonsensical couplet, "I had a little pig and fed him on clover; when he died, he died all over," as one extreme, to "The Supposed Speech of John Adams," as the other.

And the bow, also, about which both teacher and parent seemed always anxious that it be done decently and in good order, had a wide range of curvature, veering from the slightest inclination of the head to a salaam that would do credit to an Oriental.

There was little training in modulation or gesture. Frequently, while on his way to the stage, the pupil was admonished to "let his hands hang down and look natural." Accordingly, the hands hung limp at the side, except as they were cared for by reflex action.

Young ladies, especially in public exercises, read long "compositions," whose many leaves were tied together with yards of either pink or blue ribbon.

In this connection it may be stated that rather peculiar ideas concerning oratory prevailed, and these ideas manifested themselves in the school exercise. Nearly all kinds of oratory were characterized by a singsong, locally known as "the whine" or "the tone"—a kind of hereditary recollection, perhaps, of primeval ancestral chants in the forest of Germany or elsewhere! The day of impersonation had not yet arrived. Naturalness in oratory was discounted as "just talkin'." The ideal orator must affect a deep, rotund voice with more or less of singsong, and "beat the air" with such improvised gestures as seemed to suit the occasion. Yet despite these popular misconceptions of public speaking, the Friday evening exercise furnished a training which made students from the county formidable antagonists in contests for medals abroad.

THE OLD SCHOOLHOUSE AS CENTER OF COMMUNITY LIFE

The old schoolhouses touched community life at many points. They were often the only buildings in which public meetings of any kind could be held. Their doors were open even to the little shows which occasionally furnished a pretext for the people of the community to meet at the schoolhouse. Debating clubs held their weekly or fortnightly meetings in them. They were sometimes voting places, the elections being held in them. There, too, at times, the taxgatherer sat and received payment of taxes. Political meetings, such as campaign speaking and district primary conventions, were almost invariably held in the schoolhouses. "Spelling matches," having no connection with the school, were held in them at night. Magisterial courts held their sessions within them. Very commonly, too, the various religious denominations held services as often as two or three times per month.

In addition to the regular services, one or more "protracted meetings," from one to three weeks in duration, occurred as annual events in almost every schoolhouse in the land. It was not uncommon for such a degree of enthusiasm to develop in these meetings that all school interest would be scattered to the four winds and the school itself completely "broken up," perhaps. In such an event, there was no complaint. It would have been little short of heresy to complain. Probably the nearest approach to complaint would be the cautious remark, "Somehow protracted meetings and schools don't go together very well." In summing up, it may be stated that the schoolhouses of the old time served as places of instruction; as places of amusement; as temples of justice; as customhouses; as forums of political discussion; as voting places; as lyceums; as churches.

THE "MAN-TEACHER" *vs.* THE "WOMAN-TEACHER"

Such prejudice against "women-teachers" existed that they had difficulty in obtaining positions in the old schools. A very common request made of the trustees was, "Give us a man-teacher. A woman-teacher can't manage our school." Therefore, in the old-time schools in Scott County, the teacher pronoun certainly was *he*, with its declined forms *his* and *him*. But these conditions have greatly changed and are still changing. The number of patrons who "like a woman-teacher best for little fellows" is increasing as the years go by.

"RUNNING THE TEACHER OFF"

A teacher was characterized as "tight" or "loose," according as his discipline was firm or lax. The criticism, "He's too loose on his scholars," was very damaging. Yet it sometimes happened that the continued misrule of a succession of "loose" teachers would bring about such a state of anarchy in the little kingdom of the school that insurrections and rebellions against the teacher's authority would result. A teacher, unable to govern the school in such a situation, would resign, or "just quit" without the formality of a resignation. This was called "running the teacher off."

"THE COURTIN' SCHOOL"

Many patrons as well as many teachers of the olden time had rather pronounced views respecting the relations which should exist between school boys and girls. (They were called "boys" and "girls" without regard to age.) "Sparking," "courting," "going together," note and letter writing, were placed under a ban as being incompatible with school work. In some of the best governed schools a rule forbidding these things was enforced, not only during the five school days of the week, but also during Saturday and Sunday. On the other hand, the teacher who either "courted" one of his pupils, or permitted his pupils to "court" one another, was said to have "a courtin' school." And it is so even unto this day.

"GOING TO SCHOOL"

Unfortunately many patrons of the old-time school left the question of attendance to the desires of the child. There seems to have been a widespread belief that the child should not be forced to attend school against his will. Generally speaking, only the volunteers went to school. It would never do to drive Johnny off to school. "He don't want to go, and I hate to make him. I never thought it did any good to make 'em go." Words similar to these were often heard as excuse for the child's nonattendance. Yet the same parents who seemed most fearful to coerce the child's will in the matter of school did not scruple "to drive" him to the cornfield or to the mill or elsewhere, Johnny's wish to the contrary notwithstanding. Furthermore, there was a belief that an education was not for everybody—that only a select few would ever be educated. This they expressed in the oft repeated words, "Everybody was not cut out for a scholar." These and similar considerations furnished pretexts to indifferent parents for not sending their children to school. It is no exaggeration to say that nonattendance and irregular attendance were the greatest waste of the old-time school.

"GOOD MORALS"

John Doe as teacher and John Doe as common citizen were judged by two different moral standards. It was a high compliment to John Doe, the teacher, that the more exalted standard was applied to him. Thus "good morals" was the ethical ideal which the old-school master strove to hold up before his pupils. Although his was a rather stern morality, it was none the less vigorous and vital. The evildoer usually had something more than gentle preachments to teach him that the way of the transgressor is hard. Swearing, fighting, stealing, and lying were vigorously prosecuted and sternly punished. Sometimes a list of rules, forbidding the ordinary school wrongs, was posted up in the schoolroom to be read and known of all. Very frequently, however, all the rules were condensed into the one comprehensive rule, "All do right." In addition to his legislation against evil doing, the teacher "drew morals" from the stories in McGuffey's Readers, and he had, indeed, rich source from which to draw. Use was made of the incidents having moral quality, which naturally arose out of school life. Furthermore, a small number of the schools were opened with singing, Scriptural readings, and prayer, and a much larger number were opened with Scriptural reading only. The New Testament was sometimes used as a reader. So that, on the whole, the comparison of the old-time school with the schools of today on the question of morals is not altogether unfavorable to the former.

"GENTLE MANNERS"

"Mind your manners" was an admonition frequently on the lips of the old-time teacher. The children were taught to keep their fingers from the mouth when they were addressed; to say "Yes, sir," and "No, sir," properly; to say "Good morning," or "Good evening," on meeting any one; to respect the aged; neither to mock unfortunates nor make fun of them; to "mind teachers and parents"; to remove the hat on entering the house; to wash face and hands, and comb the hair; neither to whistle in the house nor be noisy in company; to say "Thank you" as occasion required; and not to "tattle or tell tales out of school," etc., etc.

In fact, the old-time teacher had the instinctive impulses of an old Virginia gentleman, and although he was kind and courteous to his pupils, yet he was far from encouraging that familiarity that breeds contempt. He rightfully insisted upon the respect due him. The writer was once a student under a teacher who required each of his pupils to make a bow to him on entering the schoolroom in the morning and another on leaving the room in evening. A certain boy, either in a spirit of mischief or rebellion, decided to omit the required bow one evening. The teacher noticed the omission and started for the boy. After a race that was both to the swift as well as to the strong, the boy was returned to the schoolroom. It is needless to say that his second departure was satisfactory to the teacher in every respect.

THE SELECTION OF A TEACHER

In the early days of the public schools, the trustees rarely used the power to select teachers which was legally vested in them. They delegated this power to the people, who used it in various ways. The most common way, however, was by petition. The applicants circulated petitions among the patrons. It sometimes happened that these petitions were signed, and adversely signed, and signed again, with the result, perhaps, that after all the signing the patrons would appear before the trustees in person, or would write letters to them on "bonding day," expressing preferences diametrically opposite to those shown in the petitions. To straighten out such hopeless entanglements, a school election would be ordered. Then would follow a short, swift campaign, in which the characteristics of the people whose ancient forays upon the English lowlands are still commemorated in the use of the word "plunder" to designate household furnishing, would be strikingly exhibited. The school district would be rent into an "upper end" and a "lower end," or a "northside" and a "southside," according to the direction taken by the line of cleavage. In rare instances these contests resulted in the boycotting of the school by the adherents of the defeated applicants. Unfortunately, in such proceedings as have just been mentioned, the factional lines established were very slow in disappearing.

TEACHERS' SALARIES

Teachers were paid salaries according to the grade of certificate which they held. In the early days, there were three grades, third, second, and first, with the later addition of the professional grade, based on successful experience in teaching. These grades were paid monthly salaries of $15, $20, $25, and $30, respectively. It may be remarked in passing that the difference between salaries then and now was more seeming than real, because the dollar had greater purchasing power then than now.

All of a salary was rarely collected in the same school year in which it was earned. In most cases, immediate collections could be made only from "claim scalpers" at "a shave" of from five to twenty-five per cent. To John E. Smith, a former teacher, who was elected treasurer of the county, is due the credit of changing this deplorable condition of affairs.

SLATES AND BLACKBOARDS

Those were days of large slates and small blackboards. The cheap tablet had not then ushered the Paper Age into the schools. All the "ciphering" was done on slates with rude pencils, "whittled" from pieces taken from "slate rock" quarries by the roadside. The fortunate possessor of a "store pencil" was envied indeed! The "worked," or the "missed sum," was "rubbed out" in order to have "a clean slate" on which to begin anew. As the stillness of the forest is sometimes broken by the falling tree, so the stillness of the school room was often broken by the falling slate.

The blackboard, as before intimated, was a small and rudely contrived affair. It was from eight to ten feet in length, and from three to four feet in width. It was cocked up on two legs in such way as to need the support of a wall to enable it to stand up. It was too small to enter largely into school work. Even a problem in long division often taxed its capacity to the uttermost. In fact, it was used more at recess, perhaps, than "in time of books," since the pupils were not sent to the board by the teacher often enough to remove the novelty of its use.

THE OLD-TIME SCHOOLBOOKS

Most of the textbooks were hauled in wagons from Bristol, then the nearest railway station. Consequently, they were scarce and high priced. They were bought sparingly and, on the whole, used carefully. The alphabet was occasionally pasted on a paddle, similar to the New England paddle, except it had no covering of transparent horn. The letters on these paddles, being gathered from various prints, often differed so much in size as to suggest an eye test. The books were nearly always covered with strong cloth in order to prevent wear; and this covering furnished a receptacle for the safe-keeping of "thumb papers" and other trifles dear to the childish heart.

Both teachers and pupils leaned heavily upon "the school book"; the teacher, because his knowledge of the subjects he was expected to teach was limited; the pupil, because he was forced to obtain most of his knowledge from the book unassisted. The almost servile dependence upon the book, therefore, invested it with an individuality—nay, almost a personality—to its devotees. How carefully was it followed! How implicitly was it believed! How confidently was it quoted! But alack! the day when a chance misprint, or a manifest error was discovered! "The book's wrong! The book's wrong! Teacher says the book's wrong!" Thus the news would spread throughout the school. And the teacher, perchance, would assume an air of wisdom on account of the detection. But in some instances, no doubt, the claim of error was made in order to free the teacher from an embarrassing situation.

The textbooks, in most common use, were Webster's and Holmes' Spellers; McGuffey's Readers; Fowler's, Davies', and Ray's Arithmetics; Harvey's Grammars; and Maury's Geographies. This list presents an array of names under whose magic spell nearly any pupil of the old-time school can conjure up a fuller and better history than is here written.

"MAKING AN AVERAGE"

An average daily attendance of twenty or more pupils was required before the payment of the teacher's full salary. An average of a smaller number, with ten as a minimum, was paid for per capita, which sometimes greatly reduced the teacher's monthly wage. Young teachers, especially, were tormented with the fear of "falling below the average." Both old and young teachers avoided, if possible, the schools of small enrollment because they disliked the conditions indicated by the following remarks: "Hasn't the school fell off mightily? They said he had only three yesterday, and five the day before!" As a precaution against such a condition, teachers resorted to many expedients, the chief among which were diplomatic praise of the pupils and the generous offer of prizes for the best attendance.

THE OLD-TIME HIGH SCHOOL

Hitherto, in the preparation of this article, only the common school has been kept in mind, but the fact that the county had many excellent high schools, taught at various times and in various places, should not be overlooked. They were taught at Greenwood, Rye Cove, Estillville, Nickelsville, Pattonsville, Saratoga, Fincastle, Riverview, Fairview, Purchase, Cowan's Branch, Prospect, Darthula, Laurel Hill, Sugar Tree, and Glade Hollow. Many of these schools were graded according to the ideas of the time; that is, they were taught by two teachers, or principal and an assistant. The principal taught the higher branches; the assistant, the elementary branches. The principals were often either college graduates, or men of some college training. Consequently, the course of study was frequently comprehensive and generally well taught. These high schools rendered great service to the public schools because they supplied the latter with teachers who had taken more extensive courses than they were required to teach.

In the popular mind, however, the supreme event of these schools was the "exhibition" with which most of them closed. If a school closed without an exhibition, it was not adjudged successful, unless it was kept from doing so by an epidemic of measles or other like calamity. Great preparations were made for "the close." The fat ox was slain. The pupils were "practiced" on their pieces until they could "say them without a bawble." The stage was profusely decorated with evergreens and flowers. The most skillful "fiddlers" and "banjo-pickers" were employed to entertain the audience during the intervals of waiting. The pupils usually "had on store clothes." A speaker, as he retired from the stage, was the target for a volley of bouquets, hurled at him from various parts of the audience, and not infrequently these flowery missiles, being loosely tied, would wreck in mid-air and fall short of the mark. "People from all arts and parts" attended these exercises. Either an "exhibition" alone, or a "basket dinner" alone, was an attraction sufficient to draw a crowd. But a union of the two furnished such an irresistible combination that a multitude would come to hear and remain to be fed. The neighboring farmhouses usually had such an over-flow of "company" that the housewives were forced "to make down beds" in order "to sleep them." These large crowds were usually well-behaved. Only in rare instances was there "bad order" on account of drinking. The writer recalls an instance in which some drunken persons created a disturbance by loud talking and a display of pistols. Many persons in the audience, frantic with fear, sought safety wherever they could. One lady, being unable to reach the door, crawled under a bench. When the constable had restored order by making the necessary arrests, this lady came forth from her hiding place under the bench and, calling to her son, she said: "George-ah! O George-ah! Where are you, George-ah? Here's your mammah! She's not scared!"

THE OLD COUNTY NORMAL

The establishment of the county normal as an institution was almost contemporary with the inauguration of the system of public schools in the county. The early educational authorities are to be commended on account of their efforts to provide means whereby a more efficient corps of teachers could be trained for service in the public schools. This they accomplished by means of institutes at first, and later by the normal and institute combined. Thus early in the history of her public schools did "the kingdom of Scott" show that spirit of progressiveness which becometh a province of the great "Upland Empire."

From the best information, it seems that "institutes," of less than a week's duration, preceded the normals in point of time. They were held at different places in the county. Later they were made a part of the normal and were held at its close, while the examination of teachers was being conducted and teachers' certificates were being made out. The normal had a peculiarly successful development in the county and became one of the most powerful agencies for the uplift and betterment of the schools. Its sessions were held either "in the Cove" or at Greenwood. They generally continued four weeks plus the time required for the examination and institute. The work of the normal was devoted principally to the review of the common school branches; only incidental attention was given to methods of teaching and educational principles. It may be remarked, however, that the chief motive which prompted many of the teacher-pupils to attend the normal was the expectation, perhaps, that it would help them in the examination—an expectation from which they were never quite able to free themselves. But whatever the initial motive, when once at the normal they came under helpful influences.

The normals were taught by two, by three, and sometimes by four instructors. These were selected with care and generally were well qualified both by education and experience to do normal work. They were also familiar with the peculiar conditions under which their teacher-pupils had to work, and were able to give them that intelligent and sympathetic aid and counsel which is born of actual experience.

Half-hour recitations were conducted from the same stage by each instructor in turn; and the method employed was a combination of lecture and quiz. Not infrequently the quizzes dealt with the more difficult parts of the texts and often provoked interesting and instructive discussions of subjects upon which the young teacher needed information. All errors were challenged promptly.

There was no attempt to grade the work; both the prospective teacher-pupil and the professional teacher were given the same instruction.

An interesting part of the program was the time allotted to "queries." These queries were written by the teacher-pupils and addressed to whomsoever they pleased. They thus furnished opportunity for the discussion of a wide range of subjects, touching almost every phase of school work. Incidentally breadth and accuracy of scholarship were sometimes severely tested. Also this query period was sometimes converted into an "experience meeting," or a free-go-as-you-please debate.

Not only was almost every teacher in the county enrolled in the normals, but also teachers from adjoining counties were occasionally matriculated in them.

Individuality was not swallowed up in number. Both instructors and teacher-pupils became personally acquainted. Everybody knew everybody else. Consequently, lasting friendships were formed, and the professional spirit was fostered. This friendly association, which enabled them not only to know each other's best methods of teaching but also to know each other's best jokes, brought about such uniformity of aim and purpose in the teaching body that the schools were greatly benefited.

The old county normal was finally superseded by the state normal, though not entirely so until the location of the State Normal at Big Stone Gap.

Through the efforts of Supt. W. D. Smith, the first state normal ever held in the extreme Southwest was held at Gate City in 1888. Through his efforts, also, the first competitive examination for scholarships in the Peabody Normal College, at Nashville, Tennessee, ever held in this section, was conducted at the close of this normal, and two young teachers of the county won scholarships.

One hundred and eight Scott County teachers enrolled in the Bristol (Virginia) State Normal in 1896, which led to its being jestingly dubbed "The Scott County Normal." Since the location of the State Summer Normal at Big Stone Gap, Scott County has led the counties which it serves in point of attendance.

GAMES OF THE OLD-TIME SCHOOL

Elsewhere in this article mention of the influence of the old school games has been made. No phase of school life is more interesting, from a physiological, psychological, and ethical point of view, than the games. Many phases of school life are largely imposed upon the child by authority. He has no choice in the matter. In the games, however, he is left free to give vent to the major impulses of his life; he sets for himself the goal to be attained in the games; he ordains the means whereby that goal is to be reached; he surrounds his play with such rules and regulations—ethical and otherwise—as he thinks necessary, and in accordance with these he plays. Space does not permit a very extended account of the games; only the principal ones are named.

Round Town was one of the most popular games of the old school. It was so called because the corners were arranged in circular form. There were four corners, including home base. The batsman who ran the four corners made a "round" or score. The ball was delivered to the batsman by a colleague, while an opponent was stationed behind to catch the missed balls. The batsman was allowed three strikes. Merely tipping the ball was a "snib," or a "snig." To catch the ball on the fly, or on the first bounce, put the striker "out." Often he was "out" if he knocked the ball outside the "let lines." He was out if he struck at the ball and missed it, and it was caught by the "man" behind before it touched the ground or on the first bounce. It was not against the rule to catch in a hat. A base runner could not advance on "dead ball." If, while the ball was in play, he stopped on a corner and later started to run, or if he crossed the ball, he was out. If he had not crossed the ball, he could return to the corner passed, provided he was not recrossed or the corners were not "full." Usually seven rounds brought all of a side who were out back into the game again. Sometimes a round made on one lick restored all the outs; sometimes it restored only one. Paddles were used for bats. The first choice of players and the side first at the paddles were determined by "throwing up." One way of doing this was for representatives of each side in the game alternately to throw and to catch a stick. On the stick being caught, it was grasped hand over hand. The one whose hand held the top of the stick as many as two times out of three had the choice, provided his hold was firm enough to enable him to throw the stick ten feet over his head. The other way of determining choice was by throwing up a paddle, one side of which had been made wet with spittle. This was done three times, also, unless it fell favorable to the same side twice in succession. The question was put, "Which do you take, wet or dry?"

Sometimes chance was not resorted to, it being agreed that one side have first choice of players and the other the paddles. At other times a small group of the best players would propose to play against the crowd.

The chief difference between Round Town and Straight Town was in the arrangement of the corners or bases. They made a circular track in the former and a straight track in the latter.

Bull Pen had as many corners as there were players on a side. These corners were arranged in circular form so as to enclose a pen. When the corner men had taken position, the ball had to be passed to every corner man before it was "hot." The rules of the game forbade its being thrown before it was "hot." Each man was endowed with one or two "eyes" which he could save by hitting, or lose by failing to hit, his opponents in the game. Two corner men could "smuggle the ball and run corners." One corner man could throw from the center of the pen, provided he knelt on one knee to do so. An inmate of the pen, on going outside its boundaries, could be "bounced out" by a corner man, provided he did not return in a given time. The corner men, on making a hit, retreated to a safe distance, and the "penners," in making the retaliatory throw, could not pursue them farther than ten steps from the pen.

Lap Jacket was a game at which two could play, each having a switch with which he whipped the other until one of them expressed a desire to quit.

In playing Hard Knuckles, two boys would grasp each other's left hand in such a way as to present the back of a closed fist to each other's strokes, then the game would begin and would continue until one of them said, "Let's quit."

Tag was played not so often at the school as it was played at the parting of the ways, on the road to and from school.

Occasionally acting poles were erected, on which the most common feats were "prizing Isaac" and "skinning a cat."

On the marble yards of thirty or forty years ago, good usage sanctioned the following words, phrases, and clauses: Ring (although it approximated a square), taw, deadline, cornerman, middleman, tawkillance, mankillance, roundance, clearance, pickance, fudge, fat, dead, stakes, doubs, thribs, easys, hards, seven, tailor or tailer (?), dog the ring, lay up, track, man back, two best out o' three, you can't hit a buck across the river, you can't shoot a duck in muddy water, will you take a dare to shoot to here, hold a steady hand there and you'll never touch a hair.

Knucks, or Rollee Hole, was a game played with marbles. Three small depressions (holes) were made in the ground in straight line and about ten feet apart. The player was advanced by either rolling his marble into one of these holes or by hitting the marble of his antagonist. A player could take a "span" in rolling for the hole or in shooting at his opponent. If his opponent's marble lay within the circle of a span, he could turn it and take it in whatever direction he wished. The hindmost man in the game was required to hold a marble between two knuckles of his closed fist while all of his opponents took a shot at it. Therefore the game was called "knucks."

Dare Base, Stink Base, Dead Base, and King Base were often played. In Dare Base dares were given and those who were caught were added to the side that captured them. Games were won by catching all of an opposing side, or by going around the opposing side, provided there was anyone at home at the time the circuit was made. Sometimes going around could be stealthily done and sometimes the one who went around must proclaim his intention at the time of starting before it would count. In Stink Base, those who were caught were placed on the Stink and closely guarded there until rescued by their colleagues, which could be done, provided their colleagues eluded the vigilance of the guards and touched the prisoners without being caught. In Dead Base, those who were caught were "out" of the game until "a side was broken up." In King Base, the bases were arranged in circular form with one in the center. Each base was occupied by a petty king, who might add to his subjects by capturing whomsoever he could. When a king was captured, he and his subjects, too, transferred their allegiance to the king who effected the capture. The king whose domain had absorbed all the petty kingdoms won the game.

Black Man was played by having a boy act as Black Man. When the game was ready to begin, he would call out, "What would ye do to see the Old Black Man a-coming?" The general response was "Try to get home." Then the race began and each one touched by the Black Man became, in turn, a black man and aided in catching "the whites." There was an exchange of bases after each call.

Both boys and girls played Antne Over. The ball was passed to and fro, between opposing sides, over the school house roof. The side in possession of the ball would shout, "Antne!" The other side would reply, "Over!" Then the former side would say, "Over she comes!" The failure of the ball to pass over was announced by saying, "Not quite!" The side catching the ball could capture members of the other side by hitting them with the ball before an exchange of "homes" took place.

Hot Pepper or War Ball was played by throwing a ball back and forth between opposing sides. The one hit was captured for the side that threw the ball, unless some member of the side he was leaving retained him by hitting him a second time.

The girls sometimes played Town Ball, Cat Ball, Base, and Antne Over. More often, however, they played Switch or Lost My Glove, London Bridge, Cross Question or Take Home What You Borrow, Thimble, the Old Witch, Molly Bright, Frog in the Meadow, Pussy Wants a Corner, Pretty Bird in My Cup, Pleased or Displeased, William-A-Trimmeetoe, and Hoop-ee Hide.

MISCELLANY

Parents who lived too far from the old-time high schools to send their children from home, often rented cheap buildings near the schools and arranged for their children to cook and to housekeep for themselves. If boys did the culinary work it was called "baching," or "keeping bachelor's hall." If the boys' sisters did the cooking it was called "shacking," or "tramp-housekeeping."

In the olden times, contagious diseases, it was thought,

were transmitted through the air in some very mysterious manner. Mumps, measles, and whooping cough rarely failed to find their way into every session of school. Little was done to prevent the spread of these diseases, as it was thought almost impossible for a child to escape them throughout life. Rank, ill-smelling odors, such as asafetida and sulphur, were believed to be about the only safeguard against contagious diseases. Children, therefore, often wore quantities of these substances about their necks in order to ward off disease.

Cheap Panama straw hats, whose broad brims, on becoming, wet, had gone to crown, were used as dunce caps.

The absence of more than one pupil from the school room at a time was evidence, in the popular mind, that the teacher was not strict enough. Consequently, various plans were devised to prevent the occurrence of such an event. Sometimes a paddle, having the word IN printed in large letters on one side, and the word OUT printed on the opposite side, was hung by the door. The would-be absentee must turn the word OUT into view on leaving the room, and the word IN into view on returning. When the paddle was not used, a forked stick, hung by the door, took its place, and those leaving the room carried it away with them and restored it to its place on returning.

Sometimes a pupil would become so wise in matters of punishment that he always stopped short of doing enough at any one time to justify a whipping. With such a pupil, the old-school master would sometimes run an account, and when the account had remained open long enough, he closed it. Offenders were not infrequently sent to bring in the switch with which they were to be punished. Sometimes, too, the switch would develop a weakness that would greatly lessen the punishment. If the punishment was known in advance, the culprits often put themselves in readiness for the ordeal by an extra coat and a pair of trousers. Instances have been known in which vulnerable parts were protected by an armor of sheepskin with the wool side turned in. In such a case, the sound of the master's strokes can well be imagined.

Sometimes, in the school room, the old-time teacher whiled away the time by eating apples or cracking walnuts; but usually he was unwilling to grant the same privilege to his pupils. Articles of food and playthings were contrabrand and temporarily taken possession of, or confiscated outright.

Once the proud possessor of a Mason's blacking box carried his treasure into the school room. The box contained two pebbles and a nail, which caused every movement of the boy to be proclaimed with a sound suggestive of a mountain cow bell. The teacher said to the boy, "Drew, you must let me have the box." With a look of astonishment the boy replied, "No, no, teacher, I can't let you have this one. I'll bring you one tomorrow."

Small boys were sometimes punished for minor offenses by being made to sit by a girl. There was, however, an age limit to this punishment.

The old-school boy was not averse to being "a hewer of wood and a drawer of water," provided the work could be done in book time. The spring was not always near the schoolhouse. A trip to the spring was usually full of incident and presented many attractions, of which not the least, perhaps, was the proximity of an orchard, a cave, a swimming hole, a hackberry bush, a persimmon tree, a walnut tree, or pawpaw "patch."

Remonstrances about being gone too long were generally answered by saying, "The spring was muddy," or, "I fell down and spilt the water and had to go back for more."

When the schoolhouse was finally reached, an analysis of the contents of the bucket would probably show H_2O plus mud and sticks and leaves, with slight traces of other substances and a negligible number of drowned insects.

THE PASSING OF THE OLD-TIME SCHOOL

The first passenger train came to Bratton's Switch at Gate City on July 4, 1887. The day on which it came was significant because its coming emancipated the county from the thraldom of mountain barriers, Nature having kindly prepared Moccasin Gap for the purpose. Its coming further emancipated the people from the somewhat narrow and intense lives peculiar to isolated regions, by bringing them into direct communication with the outside world, their neighbors. Its coming so radically changed the material conditions of life that readjustments not only in material things, but also in things intellectual, were made necessary. Even the county seat threw off the diminutive name of Estillville and took on the larger name of Gate City. A new era of schoolhouse building was ushered in. Buildings once considered large and commodious were made to look pitiably small and shrunken in comparison with the more modern ones. Furthermore, under the influence of this new era, the punk and the steel and the flint for rekindling the fires; the candlesticks and the candle molds and the candle snuffers; the big and the little spinning wheels and the reels and the "warping bars" and the hand looms; the "flax-breaks" and the scutching knives and the hatchels; the hand cards and the carding machines; the threshing flails and the "ground hog" threshing machines and the "schooner" wagons; the flintlock and the "cap-and-ball" rifles; the cranes and the "pot hangers"; "drinking" gourds and the cedar pail—all—all these heard the call of the old and the discarded, and began to pass into the attic, or the "lumber-room." The old school was an institution of the same life that found the above mentioned things useful —nay, indispensable.

Is it strange then that the old school should hear the same call and follow its companions of the old life into the realm of the "has-beens"? Was not the prolonged whistle of the first railway engine, as it made its way through Moccasin Gap, a forecast of the passing of the old-time school in Scott County?

AN AFTERWORD

The influence of the old-time school seems to be out of proportion to its meager resources and scant equipment. It gave such service to its days and generation as its patrons expected of it. It was an indispensable link in the evolutionary development of the more excellent schools of today. Its product has been a citizenship which has measured up fairly well to the standards of modern life—a citizenship which is addressing itself earnestly to the educational problems and needs of the present. Many of the conditions described in this article have passed away; many statements of fact would sound like ancient history to the students of the schools of today. The schoolhouses are better; the equipment is better; the county received a prize for greatest improvement in school buildings at the Jamestown Exposition. A graded course of study has, some years since, been prepared for the schools of the county and they are being graded in conformity with it. Each of the seven magisterial districts of the county has a state high school. The maximum levy for school purposes has been made. In fact, tried by every test, evidences of progress along all education lines are abundant.

FREE EDUCATION AS ADMINISTERED BY THE OLD-TIME SCHOOL COMMISSIONERS

On the 21st day of February, 1818, the General Assembly of Virginia passed an Act, providing for the appointment annually, by the Court of every county and corporation, of commissioners of schools, at which poor children were to be educated. This act appropriated for each county and corporation, annually, such proportion of $45,000 as its free white population bore to the whole free white population of the State.

Annually in October, the county court was to divide the county into school districts of convenient size, having due regard to population, territory, and the number of indigent children.

The court at the same time appointed one school commissioner in each district. These commissioners constituted a board which met annually at the courthouse and elected a superintendent who was by virtue of his office, clerk and treasurer of the board. The board was given general control over the school funds of its county; it apportioned the school funds among the several school districts, according to the number of indigent children; it selected teachers, and established schoolhouses.

The commissioner's duties were (1) to register and report the number, ages, and sexes of indigent children in his district, between the ages of eight and eighteen, (2) to arrange with the local schools in his district for the tuition of children in his charge, (3) to select and enter, with the consent of fathers or guardians, so many indigent children in his district as the proportion of school funds for his district will permit, (4) to visit schools, inquire into the character and qualifications of teachers, and note the conduct and learning of the pupils, (5) to examine and certify the accounts of teachers. The superintendent's duties were: (1) to attend every meeting of the board of school commissioners, (2) to receive, disburse, and keep account of all money belonging to the school fund of his county, (3) to certify vacancies in the county school board to the county court. Henry A. Morison was superintendent of schools for a number of years under this system.

The principle of local option was applied to the free school system in Virginia at this time. Free schools could be adopted in any county by a two-thirds vote of the electorate. Free schools were never adopted in Scott County, so far as available records show. Under Article Eight of the Underwood Constitution, a uniform system of public free schools was to be maintained at public expense in the State.

THE FIRST FREE SCHOOLS IN THE COUNTY

Prior to 1870, schools were not free except to those who were too poor to pay tuition. This fact caused much prejudice against them when they were first organized in the State. People thought to accept free tuition was tantamount to putting themselves on the pauper list.

Below are given some accounts of the first free schools in Scott in 1870 and 1871.

Estillville District had 6 schools; Fulkerson, 5; Johnson, 8; Floyd, 4; DeKalb, 6; Taylor, 6; Powell, 9. Total for the county, 44.

Number of female teachers: Estillville, 1; Johnson, 2; DeKalb, 1; Powell, 2. Total female teachers for the county, 6. Total male teachers, 38.

Average salaries for male teachers, $23.83; female, $20.50.

Pupils enrolled in Estillville District, 326; Fulkerson, 289; Johnson, 367; Floyd, 238; DeKalb, 284; Taylor, 246; Powell, 400. Total for the county, 2150.

Average daily attendance: Estillville, 182; Fulkerson, 170;

Johnson, 221; Floyd, 106; DeKalb, 145; Taylor, 132; Powell, 219. Total, 1175.

Per cent of school population enrolled: Estillville, 39; Fulkerson, 48; Johnson, 49; Floyd, 51; DeKalb, 38; Taylor, 35; Powell, 47. Total, 43.

Per cent of school population in average attendance: Estillville, 20; Fulkerson, 28; Johnson, 29; Floyd, 23; DeKalb, 19; Taylor, 11; Powell, 26. Total, 24.

Per cent of those enrolled in average attendance: Estillville, 56; Fulkerson, 59; Johnson, 60; Floyd, 45; DeKalb, 51; Taylor, 53; Powell, 55. Total, 55.

Average number of pupils per teacher in the county, enrolled, 49; in average attendance, 27.

Average cost per pupil enrolled, 47¢; average cost per pupil per month in average attendance, 87¢.

Value of school property owned by district: Estillville, $50; Fulkerson, $200; Johnson, ——; Floyd, ——; DeKalb, $250; Taylor, ——; Powell, $300. Total, $800.

Number of students enrolled, 2150. Studying spelling, 2089; studying reading, 967; writing, 390; arithmetic, 418; grammar, 308; geography, 110; other branches, 17.

Estimated number of days superintendent was officially employed, 100; number of miles traveled, 110; incidental expenses incurred in discharge of official duties, $5; number of official letters written, 10; number of teachers examined, 55; number of teachers licensed, 45; number of public addresses made, 2; number of county meetings of trustees held, during year, 2; number of visits to schools by superintendent, 9; number of visits by trustees, 103; number of visits by other persons, 191.

Number of white private schools, 18; colored, 1; white teachers, 18; colored, 1.

Number of white pupils enrolled, 555; colored, 20; average attendance, white, 329; colored, 15; monthly cost of tuition per pupil, $1.05; average number of months taught, 3.75.

The books first adopted in Scott were Holmes' Spellers, McGuffey's Readers, Davies' Arithmetics, Harvey's Grammars, and Maury's Geographies.

Population of Scott County in 1870, white, 12,512; colored, 524; registered voters, white, 2083; colored, 120.

The bill authorizing public free schools in Virginia became a law July 11, 1870. The first schools were opened in November of the same year. The first superintendent of the public free schools in Scott was George H. Kendrick.

Superintendent Kendrick's first report to Mr. W. H. Ruffner, State Superintendent, stated: "Hostility to the free school system has greatly subsided, and many who were heretofore bitterly opposed are now warm and zealous supporters of the system."

In May of the year 1871, a referendum was submitted to the people as to whether they favored the levying of a school tax. It was defeated.

In 1875, the number of teachers examined was 64, and their salaries aggregated $5,238.65.

R. E. Wolfe, of Rye Cove, Virginia, succeeded George H. Kendrick in 1875. His report on the public sentiment concerning public free schools was, "All opposition has entirely ceased."

The total enrollment in the schools for the year 1875 was 3578; average daily attendance, 2243.

In 1876, R. E. Wolfe, County Superintendent of Schools, reported, "One of the most encouraging signs of the success of our schools is the growing interest manifested by the people in securing a better class of teachers. On the whole the people endorse public education."

Late in the year 1878, Dr. J. B. Wolfe was appointed to succeed R. E. Wolfe as Superintendent of Schools. Dr. Wolfe served two terms from 1878 to 1886 as Superintendent. His report to the State Superintendent of Public Instruction stated that, "Public sentiment decidedly favors the public free school system."

BOATING ON THE CLINCH AND HOLSTON

Before the construction of railways in the County, the Clinch and Holston rivers were highways of commerce. They furnished an outlet to the growing town of Chattanooga as well as to other points along the Clinch and Holston. They were navigated by various kinds of river craft, ranging in size from a log canoe or dugout to the flat-bottomed boat of large dimensions. The canoe was hewn or "dug out" of the yellow poplar tree. Its size was determined by the size of the tree from which it was hewn. It was propelled by "poles" placed against the bottom of the stream, or by "paddles" in the hands of an occupant. The "poles" or "paddles" were sometimes difficult to manipulate in swollen and swift flowing streams. If not well-managed the canoe often capsized or went downstream to the great discomfiture of the occupants. The chief use of canoes was in crossing streams in the absence of "walk logs." They were less often used in transporting goods or making journeys, yet there is some evidence of the presence of canoes in Donaldson's fleet which made the remarkable trip by water from Kingsport and Fort Blackmore to Nashboro, Tennessee.

Flat-bottomed boats varied in size from 6 feet in width and 24 feet in length, to 18 feet in width and 75 feet in length. The important thing in their construction was the gunwale, suitable timber for which was sometimes difficult to find, and when found, was manufactured by primitive methods with great difficulty. Large boats were constructed, bottom side up, at improvised docks, on the river bank. On the completion of large boat, it became necessary to have "a boat turning which consisted in turning it over in such way as to permit the 'bottom side' to be down and, at the same time, permit the boat to pass from its temporary dry dock into the river." "A boat launching" was, usually, an important event in the neighborhood because it furnished an occasion for the meeting of the neighbors to assist in the launching. If a small cabin or "shanty" was to be placed on the boat, as was often done on those of the larger type, it was built after the launching.

The timbers of the boat were put together with wooden pegs because nails "would draw out" when it took the rapids or passed over an occasional mill dam. Boat cargoes on the Clinch consisted of wheat, corn, and bacon. On the Holston, in addition to the above named articles, the cargo consisted of salt from the "Salt Works" on Holston. Large quantities of salt were transported in this way during the Civil War.

Boats of the larger class would transport a cargo of from one thousand to sixteen hundred bushels of wheat or corn at one time. It has been estimated that from ten to fifteen boats, carrying in the aggregate from fifteen to twenty thousand bushels of grain, passed down the Clinch from Scott County to Chattanooga every year. Corn in this market brought from 65 to 85 cents per bushel and wheat $1.50 per bushel. Wheat has been known, however, to bring as much as $2.31 per bushel.

No flat-bottomed boat, after having reached its destination, could "stem the tide" and make a return trip. The boat itself was disposed of in whatever way seemed best to the owner. Sometimes they were sold for a small sum, and sometimes they were given away or just abandoned.

A large boat crew consisted of about five men. These "old river dogs," as they styled themselves, after having disposed of cargo and boat, made their way back home as best they could—usually by walking. A trip to Chattanooga and return usually consumed from ten to fifteen days. River traffic in grain ceased on the coming of the railroad into the county. But old boatmen still continued to take rafts of logs to Chattanooga and other points on the Tennessee River. The timber was "logged" from the dense forests in the stream valley and adjacent hills to the river banks and there formed into rafts to await a "tide." It may be remarked that rafting was more extensively engaged in than boating had ever been. In some years, more than a hundred double rafts, containing from 50,000 to 75,000 feet of lumber, would be transported from the county down the rivers. A double raft, composed of two "strands" of logs, was from 24 to 32 feet wide, and from 160 to 220 feet long. Seven men were usually employed to take a double raft to Bumboo Shoals. At that point, two men would turn back. On arrival at Clinton, another man would turn back; four men being able to take it from that point to Chattanooga. A double raft has been known to make the run to Chattanooga in 135 hours of constant running.

On emerging into the Tennessee River, four "strands" of logs were sometimes lashed together, and, on rare occasions as many as eight "strands" were united. This latter constituted what the river men called a "fleet of logs." This consolidation enabled the crews "to divide up into shifts," some to steer while others slept.

"A fleet of logs" was about 200 feet wide and acquired almost irresistible momentum in rapid currents, in so much so that steamboats would sometimes back out of narrow channels to avoid collision.

The labor of boating and rafting was very difficult and dangerous, often requiring quick decision, unerring judgment, and great physical exertion to avoid loss of life and boat or raft. Yet the old river men cheerfully braved the dangers, and many of them acquired great skill in the management of river craft.

In 1914, C. C. Palmer wrote for *The Gate City Herald* a series of articles entitled "Running the Clinch and Holston Rivers," in which he gives a vivid description of the "run" from Fort Blackmore to Chattanooga. I here quote from these articles at some length:

"It had rained hard for nearly two days and nights. Old Clinch was sweeping the top of its banks. The tide was on. But it is snowing now, and the wind blowing fierce and cold. The river is strung for miles and miles with boats and rafts. Can they get hands enough to run all of these boats and logs? Yes, the hands. Men line the banks of the river singing, laughing, and talking, all anxious for a trip. The cold and snow do not check them. They had logged and rafted all summer and fall at a great expense. Boats had been built. The corn and wheat and bacon were piled up on the banks of the river, and packed in storehouses awaiting the first tide. They must go, or go broke.

"I will not take the time to describe a flatboat, or a raft

of logs, as most people know how they were made. However, I will tell you a few things about them. A big boat would carry from 1200 to 1600 bushels of wheat and corn. A double raft (two strands lashed, or tied together) was about 30 feet wide, 200 to 225 feet long and had 4 oars, which were pushed by 8 strong men.

"The river has been falling for some time. Old 'Boatin' Bill' Ramey and his men have come down to turn out. Cox and Pendleton and the other boys are not quite ready.

"But 'Boatin' Bill' unties his boat, pulls in the rope and sails off with Tandy Baker and 'Horse Head' Jim Brickey on the bow. It usually took 6 men to run a big boat. I don't remember all his hands, but I think some of the Pendletons and Donaldsons were on. Perhaps some of the Cox and Flanary boys were on board. Also Jim Gray (the colored fiddler). Down by Pendleton's Island they go—a little bit nervous for that is a close rub. They now have time to 'blow' a little, pass a few jokes, maybe use a few cuss words and pass the bottle but they must be careful about the booze. Starnes' bend, Crafts' mill dam and the Tim bend are not far ahead.

"At the mouth of Cover Creek Milo Taylor is turning out. On down farther Mel Starnes with Big Bill Starnes, Monroe Edwards, Tim Dingus, and Noah Hobbs were about ready to pull out. Over the mill dam and around Tim bend they go all right, Bill Ramey in the lead. You may talk about 'Steamboat Bill,' 'Buffalo Bill,' 'Big Bill' Taft and all the other big Bills but 'Boatin' Bill' Ramey was as well on to his job as any of them. It is said when he made his first trip to Chattanooga, he walked the banks of the river all the way back home and studied every island, every dangerous rock and every bad bend in the river, back to Stoney Creek, Virginia. This story may not be quite true but he knew the river perfectly.

"We are getting down near the Neal bottoms (Clinchport now). Soon we will pass the Thomas Island—on down to Speer's Ferry. All along the way the boats and rafts are turning out after 'Boatin' Bill.'

"At Speer's Ferry there is a big crowd of men standing around a camp fire wanting a trip. Worley Belt, Rod Thomas, Jim Falin, Jack Horton, and other good steersmen were hanging oars, putting up bunks and getting in 'grub' ready to go. Amongst the hands I see 'Scorp,' 'Pooge,' 'Tot,' 'Pad,' Hiram, and the Richmond and Venable boys all ready to start. 'Pomeroy' and 'Little' Bill had gone up to Clinchport after a raft. They started from Frog level usually. But here they all go singing, laughing, and working. It is snowing. But on they go. The banks lined with men and women, boys and girls to see the rafts and boats go down. Near Wolfe's ford is one boat and several rafts to go. There are the Morell boys, the Palmer boys, the Wolfes, and a host of others ready to start. There is where the writer got his first trip. He sidled up to 'Big Ike,' the steersman, and told him he wanted to go. Ike said in a loud, rough voice, 'All right, young man, but you will have a h—l of a trip.' It was awful cold and we had no bunk when we started. Abner put up the bunk and then helped push the oar with me.

"'Big Ike' was a great character. He had been logging and running the river a long time. He used to go on the boats with his father. He was an old ox driver and ox rider, a great fox hunter, and fisherman. He was good judge of corn 'licker' and usually knew where to find it. He was brave and daring. 'Boys, let's turn out. Hold out the bow, e-a-s-e,' rang out the loud, harsh words of 'Big Ike.' And we were floating down the Clinch towards Chattanooga. On we go through the narrows down to Flat Rock schoolhouse. There we see Wilburn Neeley and 'Big' Irish, 'Little' Kire, Nigger Hen, and others turning out. Pert and Siota and old 'Jimmy' are just ahead of us. F. M. Powers and 'Jim Tom' have gone on. We are now at Hiram Church's. We got over Neeley's dam all o. k., but some others were not so lucky. Ves Gillenwater, 'Coon' Carter, Fred Hill, and 'Tap' Carter stove their boat on the dam. The boat struck a rock, turned, and sank. Ask Uncle 'Coon' to tell you all about it. The Church boys, Henderson Heron and 'Curly' Tom Horton turned out just behind us." (C. C. Palmer in *Gate City Herald*.)

VIRGINIA & SOUTHWESTERN RAILWAY COMPANY

The Virginia & Tennessee Railroad Company was chartered by the legislature of Virginia on March 3, 1852, to construct a railroad from Bristol, Va., to Cumberland Gap, Tenn., and the same Act provided for the formation of the Virginia & Kentucky Railroad Company to accept the provision of the Act in case the Virginia & Tennessee Railroad Company did not do so.

The Virginia & Kentucky Railroad Company was organized and proceeded with the work of construction, which was abandoned on account of financial conditions after the war between the States. By an Act of June 17, 1870, the Atlantic, Mississippi & Ohio Railroad Company was chartered to complete the work commenced by the Virginia & Kentucky Railroad Company. The Atlantic, Mississippi & Ohio Railroad Company, having failed to carry on the work, was, by Act of April 9, 1874, released from further responsibility. On March 27, 1876, the Bristol Coal & Iron Narrowgauge Railroad Company was chartered to take over the franchises, rights, privileges, and property of the Virginia & Kentucky Railroad Company and construction was again taken up. On May 17, 1877, the charter of the latter company was amended and its name changed to the South Atlantic & Ohio Railroad Company. The construction of the road from Bristol, Tenn.-Va., to Big Stone Gap was completed about May 1, 1890.

The South Atlantic & Ohio Railroad Company went into the hands of a receiver in 1892, and on April 16, 1898, the property was sold under foreclosure and bought in by the bondholders.

The Bristol, Elizabethton & North Carolina Railroad Company was incorporated June 10, 1889, under the general law of the State of Tennessee to construct a line from Bristol to Elizabethton, Tenn., a distance of 22.4 miles.

The Virginia & Southwestern Railway Company was chartered in Virginia on February 18, 1899, and bought from a syndicate the property of the South Atlantic & Ohio Railroad Company. At the same time it bought the property of the Bristol, Elizabethton & North Carolina Railroad Company, these properties thereafter being operated as the Virginia & Southwestern Railway between Elizabethton, Tenn., and Big Stone Gap, Va. Between June, 1899, and September, 1900, the main line was extended from Elizabethton, Tenn., to Mountain City, Tenn., a distance of 35.7 miles, and a spur line from Rexford, Tenn., to Buladeen, Tenn., a distance of 11.3 miles, was built. A connecting line of two miles, between Imboden, Va., and Intermount, Va. (now Appalachia), was bought from the Imboden Coal & Coke Company January 1, 1906. On April 29, 1908, the Black Mountain Railway from Appalachia, Va., to St. Charles, Va., a distance of approximately 22 miles, was bought from the Black Mountain Coal Land Company.

The Holston River Railroad Company was incorporated December 28, 1905, under the general law of Tennessee and undertook the building of a line from Moccasin Gap, Va., on the Virginia & Southwestern Railway, to Persia Junction, Tenn., on the Rogersville Branch of the Southern Railway. This property was bought by the Virginia & Southwestern Railway Company on April 29, 1908, and construction of the line was completed, and on July 1, 1909, the Rogersville Branch of the Southern Railway from Bull's Gap, Tenn., to Rogersville, Tenn., a distance of 14 miles, was leased by the Virginia & Southwestern Railway Company and operated in connection with the Holston River Line as a part of that Railway.

The Virginia & Southwestern Railway Company, under agreements with the Louisville & Nashville Railroad Company dated February 22, 1900, and with the Norfolk & Western Railway Company dated April 4, 1905, acquired trackage rights between Appalachia, Va., and Tom's Creek, Va., a distance of 22.08 miles, making the operated mileage 189.06 miles owned, 14.00 miles leased, and 22.08 miles operated under trackage agreements.

Control of the Virginia & Southwestern Railway Company passed to Southern Railway Company May 1, 1906, by a contract under which Southern Railway Company agreed to buy a large majority of the capital stock of the Virginia & Southwestern Railway Company. Soon after this was extended to cover all of the stock. This transaction was completed on June 29, 1908, when the final payment on the purchase of this stock by Southern Railway Company was made. The Virginia & Southwestern Railway Company continued in existence and continued to operate the property until July 1, 1916, when the property was leased by the Virginia & Southwestern Railway Company to Southern Railway Company and the property is now operated as the Appalachia Division of the Southern Railway System.

SCOTT COUNTY NEWSPAPERS

The first newspaper published in Scott County was the *Scott Banner,* the publication of which began in 1873. Samuel Haynes, for many years prominently connected with newspaper enterprises here, was of opinion that there was a newspaper published in the county earlier than the *Scott Banner.* He failed, however, to remember its name and characterized it as "a small affair."

The *Scott Banner* was edited by Charles A. Heermans, of Tazewell County, Va. The printer was George B. Terrell. The office equipment consisted of an old Washington hand press, and a small quantity of type. S. P. McConnell, then county clerk, owned a small job printing outfit with which he printed such forms as were needed in the clerk's office. This job outfit was purchased and added to the *Banner* equipment.

In a short time Heermans sold his interest to Rufus A. Ayers and George B. Terrell. Terrell soon sold his interest to Ayers, who thus became the sole owner and editor. In taking charge of the paper, April 27, 1876, Mr. Ayers wrote as follows:

"After an absence from the editorial and business departments of this paper for nearly six months it has fallen to the lot of the writer to become its sole editor and proprietor and as it is customary on such occasion to say something by the way of introduction to the public, the writer has to say that the paper will continue as heretofore to support the State Conservative and National Democratic parties, but whilst the paper will be as loyal to the reasonable demand of party leaders and representatives as any in the district—yet we will not blindly follow the dictation of the representatives of any party further than their views and actions consist with right and the interest of the great body of the people, who create them, and to whom they are justly responsible for an abuse of their trust.

"It will be the aim of the paper to discuss the questions of the day fairly, fully, and independently. We claim the right to legitimately criticize the views of other journals, and recognize their right to criticize ours.

"We deprecate and will studiously endeavor to avoid the personal and individual attacks upon each other which some of our neighbors of the quill have been wont to indulge.

"The writer will always endeavor to treat his brother journalists with courtesy and respect which he hopes to receive at their hands. We will endeavor to faithfully and impartially represent all classes and all the varied interests of this section and make the paper interesting to all as a prompt, full exposition of the news of the day. To that end we desire the influence and support of all the good citizens within the range of its circulation."

Some time subsequent to the presidential election of 1876 the *Scott Banner* seems to have suspended publication. In the meantime, however, a paper supporting the candidacy of Col. J. B. Richmond for Congress was published during the congressional campaign.

On August 3, 1881, the *Scott Banner* was again published. It was sponsored this time by Smith H. Morison, Walker Morison, and R. A. Ayers, with John A. Mahoney and Samuel A. Smythe as printers. It then changed hands several times, passing under the control, in the order named, of Samuel Haynes, Robert L. Smythe, Thomas B. Garner, and, at last an old man from Washington whose name the author could not obtain. Its publication was discontinued in the year 1892 or 1893.

In 1883, a stock company of which Judge M. B. Wood was president, purchased a newspaper outfit, and began the publication of the *Progressive Age* with J. B. Adams, editor, and George B. Terrell, printer. The *Age* was published three or four years, and then suspended publication. The outfit was later moved to Big Stone Gap, Va.

John A. Mahoney conducted a paper called the *Gate City Gazette* about the year 1890. The *Gazette* was succeeded by the *Scott County Journal* which was published for a number of years. It was succeeded by C. C. Bausell's *Scott County Leader* which was discontinued in 1903 or 1904.

In the late nineties, H. A. W. Darter began the publication of a paper called *The Messenger*, the control of which soon passed to a man named Brown, who continued its publication for a short time.

The Sentinel was founded by Gus Vicars, but it had a brief existence owing to the plant's being consumed by fire.

In 1903, the *Gate City Herald* was founded by C. C. and J. C. Boatright, who were later succeeded in the ownership of the paper by L. B. Boatright. The *Herald's* successful publication continues to this day. It has recently been purchased by J. M. and C. H. Rollins.

SCOTT COUNTY IN WAR TIMES

A Community History

By ROBERT MILFORD ADDINGTON

PRE-WAR CONDITIONS

Scott County is one of the extreme southwest counties of Virginia. It is traversed by a number of narrow, trough-like valleys extending northeast and southwest. These valleys are separated by Little Pine, Clinch, Stone, and Powell's Mountains, and by Copper and Moccasin Ridges.

The valleys are drained by the North Fork of Holston and Clinch Rivers, and by Moccasin and Copper Creeks and their tributaries. The county area of about 528 square miles is divided into thousands of small farms upon which are located most of the homes of its 24,826 people. These people, for the most part, earn their living in agricultural pursuits, and were thus engaged when the war of 1917 came on to disturb "the even tenor of their way" by upsetting many of the old economic and social usages to which they had been long accustomed.

The people of Scott County, who, in August, 1914, read the news items from overseas, stating that Germany had declared war against France, and had violated the neutrality of Belgium, little thought that the war thus begun would ever assume such proportions as to have any direct personal interest to them. The probability of the United States becoming involved in a war so far away seemed too remote to be considered. Some sympathy was felt for Belgium because her rights had been so ruthlessly trampled upon, and some admiration was felt also for the plucky little nation that so bravely fought to protect her sovereignty and turn back her brutal despoiler. Aside from these feelings of sympathy and admiration, the average Scott Countian had little or no interest in the war at this time. By and by, as the war dragged on

200

year after year, and nation after nation became involved in it, as Germany's submarine policy like a giant octopus, reached out to destroy the commerce and lives of neutral and enemy nations alike, the sense of justice and fair play, characteristic of Scott County people, was powerfully appealed to. The apathetic interest in matters pertaining to the war, which had prevailed in its earlier stages, at length began to quicken. This increased interest was to be measured in part by the avidity with which all classes of the people now began to read newspapers and periodicals. Those who were not already subscribers to some newspaper subscribed, and many of those who were already receiving papers, subscribed for others. In this way, the county, to an extent never before known, was transformed into a newspaper-reading public. This ever-increasing newspaper audience was daily becoming more and more responsive to the teachings and leadership of the press. Pathetic incidents, such as the execution of Edith Cavell, the drowning of Leon C. Thrasher, the first American to fall victim to Germany's submarines, and especially the sinking of the *Lusitania* with its precious cargo of more than a thousand human lives, including one hundred Americans, were placed upon the throbbing heart of the county. Yet in spite of these incidents and the sympathy which their recital called forth, there was a deep-seated aversion on the part of the majority of Scott County people to entering this war. However, it was not possible to behold such a struggle as that daily being presented to them in the public press without taking sides. Public opinion was divided, but divided into very unequal parts. The majority sympathized with the Allies. A few— a very few—sympathized with Germany, and this number was mostly made up of those who were unable to forget the circumstances of our Revolutionary War with England.

Such editorial utterances as the following appeared in the *Gate City Herald:*

"Gentlemen, you may take sides with Germany if it gives you pleasure to do so. As for us, we are Americans and stand for America. Long live the Stars and Stripes."

"Talk for Germany and abuse the French all you please,

then tell us, please, how it is that German spies are prowling through this country and French spies have never done so."

The recital of the cruel incidents of the war—and the newspapers were rather full of such things—instead of provoking belligerent thoughts in the minds of the people, tended to increase the aversion to war already existing. Many thought, or at least hoped, that the necessity for war could be removed by diplomatic agencies; that all differences could be composed by some favorable agreement, peaceably arrived at.

On account of our relations with Mexico, the newspapers, in the early days of the war, had much to say about preparedness, but the people of the county manifested little interest in the subject. For the most part they regarded the agitation for preparedness as propaganda disseminated by the manufacturers of munitions of war and by military men.

On April 6, 1917, Congress voted to declare war against Germany. This declaration was followed closely by the announcement that the military forces of the United States would be composed of men chosen by selective draft, and June 5, 1917, was named as the day on which the drafting would begin. The tone of the newspapers changed almost overnight. They now set for themselves the task of changing and shaping public opinion in conformity with the course determined upon by the President and Congress. However, in the short space of sixty days Scott County public opinion was changed from strong opposition to the war to active and hearty co-operation in carrying it on.

CHURCHES AND SCHOOLS

The Christian people of the county, without regard to denominational preferences, sincerely believed that the United States had entered the war for just, unselfish, and humanitarian reasons. Hence the churches, without hesitation, assisted in the various drives made in the interest of Belgian relief, the Red Cross, the Y. M. C. A., and the W. C. T. U. Special services for soldiers were held in the churches. In the newspaper accounts of church services during the war period such texts as these are found: "The War at the End of Three Years," "Bolsheviki," and "Our Daily Bread" (a sermon on the conservation of food).

The schools and churches of the county actively participated in the various campaigns or drives launched in the interest of war work. School children gave to Belgian Relief and Junior Red Cross funds. All public exercises, even school commencements, were decidedly patriotic in tone. "Duty and Patriotism" was the subject of the literary address in one of the high schools. The subject, "Resolved, That selective conscription is the most effective and the most satisfactory means of raising an army to satisfy any demands of our country during the present war," was publicly debated at the commencement exercises of Shoemaker High School, 1917.

The Scott County Teachers' Association, at its annual meeting in 1917, discussed military training, Red Cross work and food conservation.

School children constituted no small part of the audiences in the various war work's campaigns. Shoemaker High School students often came in a body to the courthouse on occasions of public speaking.

DRAFT LAW AND MILITARY MATTERS

The first draft day passed without an unfavorable incident anywhere, and Scott County, together with the rest of the country, was in the World War.

Under date of May 19, 1917, C. W. Dougherty, sheriff, was notified by Governor Stuart that he had been appointed a member of the Board of Registration for Scott County. He was directed to appoint registrars at each voting precinct in the county, and to wire the names of the persons so appointed on May 25.

The registrars at the various voting precincts of the county were as follows: France, J. A. Ford; Rye Cove, J. H. Johnson; Duffield, M. S. Jennings; Clinchport, W. A. Pierson; Pattonsville, Charlie H. Neely; Rollers, T. M. Darnell; Jennings, H. H. Reynolds; Powers, T. J. Freeman; Estillville, Robert Benton; Winingers, W. T. Shelton; Big Cut, J. E. Metcalfe; Smiths, F. G. Pannell; Stony Point, U. S. McMurray; Hiltons, C. J. Hilton; Nickelsville, N. T. Moore; Addington, J. H. Redwine; Stony Creek, J. M. Harris; Peters, W. H. Nash; Osborn's Ford, Esau Huneycutt; Hoge's Store, F. B. Horne.

At the same time the notice of registration was given, a call was made for a meeting of all patriotic citizens of the county. This meeting was to be held at the courthouse on June 2, 1917, just two days prior to the draft. The call was signed by J. F. Sergent, J. H. Johnson, Samuel Haynes, J. H. Paters and A. W. Stair, committee.

"Saturday (June 2) patriotism rode on the crest of the wave in Gate City. The people came out from all sections of the county and demonstrated that mountaineers are still lovers of liberty and of their country."

Patriotic addresses were delivered by Rev. C. R. Cruikshank and Rev. G. A. Crowder, E. T. Carter, J. H. Peters, and Prof. P. T. Fugate. Patriotic airs were rendered by the Kingsport Band. This meeting was considered a success because it augured well for the draft.

There were 1,756 white men in the county who registered for the first draft and 41 colored men, making a total of 1,797. The number of white registrants by precincts was as follows: Stony Creek, 192; Peters, 79; Estillville, 221; Big Cut, 88; Winingers, 61; Hoge's Store, 42; Osborn's Ford, 109; Hiltons, 43; Smiths, 60; Stony Point, 67; Addington, 68; Nickelsville, 157; Jennings, 60; Pattonsville, 77; Powers, 57; Rollers, 73; Clinchport, 81; Duffield, 51; Frances, 59; Rye Cove, 94; registered by the board, 17. Colored registrants by precincts were: Stony Creek, 9; Estillville, 18; Big Cut, 4; Osborn's Ford, 7; Pattonsville, 1; Powers, 1; Rollers, 1.

The draft was the chief topic of interest to the people of the county during the summer of 1917. Few, indeed, were the families that were not affected by it. Like the Destroying Angel that passed over Egypt, it came into the homes of the county and set apart the strongest and most promising for the god of war. Many were the speculations as to the kind of offering fate or chance would bring to the young man of military age. Both the draftees and their anxious friends tried to remove the uncertainty and solve the mystery that hung over it all. Anything was better than suspense. To the un-traveled drafted man a trip overseas was an adventure that admitted of many dangers. Therefore, service in this country was sought in preference to service in the trenches. Most of the volunteering was done in the hope that a choice might be had as to the kind of service.

All persons drawn in the first draft were called by the local board for physical examination on August 6, 7, and 8, 1917. The order numbers of those included in this call ran from 1 to 365, inclusive. Emmett McClellan, of Wayland, Virginia, held order number 1.

On August 21, 1917, the second contingent of drafted men was called to appear before the local board for physical examination. The order numbers of these men ran from 366 to 764, inclusive.

The local examining board was composed of Dr. C. R. Fugate, physician; C. W. Dougherty, sheriff; and J. F. Richmond, county clerk.

Of the 400 young men first called before the board 57 failed to pass and 343 were pronounced sufficiently robust to endure the hardships and fatigues of army life. Of the number that passed, 268 claimed exemption, the greater part of them doing so because of the fact that they had families dependent upon them. A few made the plea of dependent parents; 75 did not apply for exemption. Those claiming exemption were given ten days in which to file certificates supporting their claims.

"Whatever some may think about it, the *Herald* is convinced that our Local Exemption Board has striven to discharge its duty with the utmost fairness to all. It has had a big task, one that would sorely test the patience of any group of men. Besides, the board had specific instructions by which to be guided and little was left optional with it. Our country had to meet grave conditions and the board was appointed to meet these conditions here. If you have been disposed to criticize any act of the board, pause and reflect, put yourself in the place of the men who have gone so patiently through the stupendous task, then we think you will be less critical. The board deserves our gratitude for the manner in which it has discharged its duty, and is discharging it."—*Gate City Herald.*

The first contingent of soldiers sent from Scott County to Camp Lee were as follows: Daniel Rhoton, Clinchport; Hugh Summers, Bellamy; Benjamin Rhoton, Clinchport; Amos Ervin, Clinchport; Preston Wm. Elliot, Mack; Wm. Pressley Elliott, Nickelsville; Ballard Chandler, Fairview; Hubert Adolphus Quillin, Gate City; John Henry Berry, Riggs; Lucian Horton Wininger, Yuma; Joe Wolfe Jessee, Nickelsville.

The local board placed Hubert A. Quillin in charge of this group. The day of entraining was made an occasion for a patriotic celebration. Stores, offices and business houses were closed, court adjourned, and a great crowd assembled at the station to bid the boys good-bye.

The ladies of the W. C. T. U. presented each of the young men with a bouquet of flowers and a khaki bag or comfort kit, each containing a New Testament, a pair of scissors and other articles useful in camp life.

On Sunday, September 16, 1917, all the churches of Gate City united in services held for the benefit of the young men who were to go to Camp Lee on the 19th of September. The sermon was preached by the Rev. Samuel Wolfe, of Knoxville, Tenn., from the text, "Greater love hath no man than this, that a man lay down his life for his friends."

On Wednesday, September 19, 1917, the local board sent a second contingent of 72 men to Camp Lee. Hundreds of friends and relatives of the men gathered at the station. The local band rendered patriotic airs. The people, though serious, restrained their emotions that the young soldiers might take their departure in a cheerful frame of mind. Charles Clinton Pendleton was put in charge of the soldiers, with J. D. Carter, Jr., and Robert McConnell as assistants. Two extra passenger coaches in which the young soldiers were to be carried to Bristol were brought to Gate City on the day preceding. Little schoolgirls from the Shoemaker High School presented each young man with a beautiful bunch of flowers. The W. C. T. U. of Gate City and Nickelsville presented each of the soldiers with comfort kits.

"Last Tuesday the following men went to Camp Lee, having by some means been prevented from going with the others on Saturday before: Conley Arwood, Isaac Gilliam, Patton Peters, Conley Wise. Scott now has 157 men in Camp Lee. The remaining men who should have gone with the last contingent were prevented from doing so by illness. They have all made satisfactory explanations to the Exemption Board and expressed a willingness to go as soon as they are able. This makes a fine showing for Scott County."

On October 29 the first contingent of colored soldiers was sent to Camp Lee. On the Friday night preceding a banquet and rally for the colored people were held at the Prospect colored schoolhouse. Patriotic addresses were made by E. T. Carter and others. On the day of entrainment the W. C. T. U. presented each colored soldier with a comfort kit similar to those presented to the white soldiers.

On Saturday, November 3, 1917, nine more men were sent to the training camp at Petersburg. This made a total of 178 men from the county, and was only two short of the county's quota. A few days later two more men were sent to camp, thus completing quota up to date.

On December 15, 1917, the Local Exemption Board began to make preparation for the second draft of soldiers from the county. A number of questionnaires were mailed out daily, and the registrants were warned of the penalty attached to a failure to fill them out. About 1,250 questionnaires were sent out. The board was assisted in this work by E. L. Taylor, Roie M. Dougherty, Richmond Bond and Edgar Counts.

All drafted men who were in need of dental work and unable to pay for it could get a certain class of work done by applying in writing to any of the following dentists of Gate City: Drs. James Semones, W. H. Perry, E. A. Hoge.

The 1918 January term of court convened only one day. It was adjourned "till court in course" on account of drafting soldiers.

Under date of March 21, 1918, the Local Exemption Board issued warning to those who had been given deferred classification on account of dependents, that unless they actually supported their dependents, recommendation to change them to Class One would be made to the District Board.

The second installment of colored soldiers was sent to Camp Lee on April 26, 1918.

On June 5, 1918, 174 white men and one colored man registered as having become 21 years of age since the first registration. On June 20, 1918, six white and two colored registrants were added to the above number. Thirty-three young men were registered on August 24, 1918.

The following citizens volunteered to act as registrars and assistants in enrolling the names of those required to register under the new draft law. The first named at each precinct was the chief registrar: Addington, John Henry Redwine and Frank Hilton; Nickelsville, R. M. Dougherty, S. E. Wampler, James A. Bond and Ernest C. Grigsby; Osborne's Ford, Dr. N. W. Stallard, W. H. Loudy and Hobart Stallard; Hoge's Store, H. B. Blackwell, A. W. Peters and Charles K. Fraley; Big Cut, J. E. Metcalf and A. T. Peters; Winingers, J. C. Rogers and T. P. Shelton; Estillville, C. W. Dougherty, F. E. Stewart, I. P. Kane and J. H. Peters; Peters, R. L. Webb and Roy Gillenwater; Stony Creek, J. M. Harris and W. B. Sanders; Frances, John L. Pendleton and J. A. Ford; Clinchport, H. C. Kidd and J. A. L. Perkins; Rye Cove, J. H. Johnson and C. D. Stone; Duffield, W. B. Horton and J. C. Parrish; Pattonsville, J. D. Carter and Charles Neeley; Jennings, H. H. Reynolds and E. L. Taylor; Flat Rock, A. J. Wolfe and Farley Palmer; Fairview, T. M. Darnell and Eugene Darnell; Hiltons, D. B. S. Stone and Bryan Hilton; Stony Point, U. S. McMurray and I. W. Larkey; Smiths, C. L. Miller and Garnet Shelley.

This registration enrolled 2,532 men for military service in the county. Nearly one-third of this number were between the ages of 18 and 21.

According to the muster roll in the clerk's office, Scott County had 693 men in the various branches of the service.

In the reports of the local board, the words "delinquent" and "deserter" were written after less than a dozen names, and most of these persons later placed themselves in charge of the board and were sent to camp without arrest.

The call for the county's quota of men to entrain October 7, 1918, to October 11, 1918, was cancelled until a later date because an epidemic of influenza was raging in the camps.

This call was renewed for November 15, but before that time arrived the Armistice had been signed, thus cancelling the call for a second time.

Company H, Second Virginia Infantry, was stationed at Clinchport for a few months following the outbreak of the war. Nineteen Scott County soldiers were members of this company. The company entrained for Roanoke for mobilization in the army on August 16, 1917.

The following list of soldiers wounded in the World War was compiled from the *Gate City Herald:* John Wolfe, Mace's Springs; Samuel Falin, Gate City; Stephen J. Dougherty, Nickelsville; Charles Preston Fleenor, Benhams; Craig Dixon, Hiltons; Garland Whited, Gate City; Alfred L. Chapman, Snowflake; Charles H. Greear, Wood; Charles W. Harris, Nickelsville; Grover L. Carter, Duffield; Thomas E. Starnes, Hill; Oscar Lee Fleenor, Gate City; Kelly Fugate, shell shocked, Nickelsville; Horton Winegar, Yuma; Corporal Samuel Thomas Haynes, Yuma; William E. Hillman, Nickelsville; Willie Powers, Clinchport; Conley B. Ringley, Hiltons; Samuel P. Castle, Nickelsville.

The following is Scott County's gold star list:

Stanley McMurray, pneumonia, camp in Colorado.
Charles Sanders, pneumonia, Camp Upton, Georgia.
Arthur Price, influenza, Camp Gordon, Georgia.
Samuel D. Lane, pneumonia, Springfield, Mass.
Wilburn P. Neeley, pneumonia, Camp Humphries, Va.
Joe Wolfe Jessee, killed in action, August 8, 1918.
Malcolm Palmer, died of disease, French hospital.
Elbert Maddux, accidentally killed, Camp McClellan.
William T. Coley, died of disease, October 9, 1918.
Ernest A. Fletcher, died of wound, October 18, 1918.
Isaac Gilliam, accident, January 31, 1919.
Connie Lambert, killed in action, October 20, 1918.
Hiram Lane, killed in action, October 2, 1918.
John W. Meade, died of disease, October 18, 1919.
Conley Wise, died of disease, January 26, 1918.
Clarence Sherman, died of disease, October 6, 1918.
George Dewey Artrip, September 30, 1918.
Charles Claren Fletcher, October 7, 1918, navy.
Joseph Stephen Taylor, killed in action, July 19, 1918.

Clayton Hammonds, killed in action, July 15, 1918.

Clayton Hammonds was the first Scott County soldier to be killed in the war with Germany. It is an interesting fact that his great-grandfather, John Wolfe, was a German, born and reared to young manhood in the valley of the Rhine. The names of two Scott County soldiers appear on the Distinguished Service list of Virginia. They are Isaac Estep, of Clinchport, and John Samuel Hartsock, of Nickelsville. Isaac Estep was awarded a Distinguished Service Cross and John Samuel Hartsock received the French Croix de Guerre. The citations accompanying these awards may be found in *Virginians of Distinguished Service in the World War,* source Volume I of the Virginia War History Commission's publications.

ECONOMIC CONDITIONS

Liberty Loans and War Savings Stamps

On May 31, 1917, J. H. Peters, cashier of the People's National Bank, was appointed sub-chairman for Scott County, "to perfect a plan of campaign for the sale of Liberty Bonds." Mr. Peters named N. M. Horton, of the First National Bank; J. L. Q. Moore, of the Farmers' and Merchants' Bank; W. F. C. Blackwell, of the Bank of Dungannon; R. L. McConnell, of the Farmers' Exchange Bank; and J. H. Peters, to receive subscriptions for Liberty Bonds. D. C. Sloan made the largest subscription, $10,000, and Mrs. J. B. Craft was the first lady of the county to buy a Liberty Bond.

The Liberty Loan campaigns did not meet with generous response in Scott County. The total quota assigned was $953,200, and the amount subscribed in all drives totaled only $323,750. Lack of interest is the reason assigned for this half-hearted response.

A Victory Loan rally day was arranged for May 7, 1918. There was a parade, including old Confederate soldiers and veterans of the World War, at eleven o'clock in the morning, followed by an automobile parade, including a Red Cross float. Hon. Preston W. Campbell addressed the soldiers at the courthouse, and after dinner an address was made by Chaplain

John L. Weber, of Camp Jackson, S. C., followed by a moving picture, "The Price of Peace," and music by a band.

Below is given the amount of Liberty Loan subscriptions handled by the banks in the county: Bank of Dungannon, $10,900; First National Bank, $45,000; Farmers' and Merchants' Bank, $15,450; the People's National Bank, $70,000; total, including items not here given, $118,150.

The amounts of allotments and sales by districts in the county in the drive of June, 1918, are as follows: DeKalb District was allotted $12,000 and paid $13,120; Estillville District was allotted $25,000 and paid $28,000; Floyd District was allotted $10,000 and paid $10,000; Powell District was allotted $12,000 and paid $13,700; Fulkerson District was allotted $10,000 and paid $8,800; Johnson District was allotted $14,000 and paid $11,450; and Taylor District was allotted $17,000 and paid $11,225.

The most intensive of all the drives was made for the sale of War Savings Stamps during the Fourth Liberty Loan Campaign. Rev. J. B. Craft was director and Professor A. W. Stair was his assistant. The following men had charge in the various magisterial districts: DeKalb District, W. S. Cox and H. C. L. Richmond; Estillville District, S. W. Coleman and Prof. A. W. Stair; Floyd District, L. P. Fraley and J. F. Sergent; Fulkerson District, J. P. Corns and W. H. Nickels; Powell District, J. H. Catron and J. D. Carter; Taylor District, E. T. Carter and G. Claude Bond.

Hon. L. P. Summers and Judges W. E. Burns, of Russell County, and Preston W. Campbell, of Washington County, made speeches in the county in this campaign.

The county's quota was $500,000.

The committee in charge made a list of about two hundred citizens who seemed to be able to invest as much as $1,000 in War Savings Stamps. A letter, signed by the committee, was sent to each person on the list. The letter read, in part, as follows:

"To purchase War Savings Stamps is no sacrifice on your part, but it shows your manhood, your patriotism and your willingness to help. Do not hesitate. For the sake of all we hold dear, for the sake of our county, which is yet far behind most of the counties in our section, respond at once. Sign your pledge card for the sum you have been assessed. Should you not have the money at the time your card is due, borrow it. Thousands are doing this everywhere. Let us have your help and encouragement and we will remain in the field with you until the last dollar has been raised."

This letter was signed by W. D. Smith, chairman; W. J. Rollins, M. B. Compton, W. F. C. Blackwell, E. T. Sproles, W. W. Ramey, secretary. The committee was designated as "The Committee of One-Thousand-Dollar Subscriptions."

At the first public meeting in this campaign held at the courthouse, $40,000 was pledged. Twenty-six one-thousand-dollar men were in the meeting. Floyd District was the first to "go over the top" with its quota of $40,000. The total amount of subscriptions in this drive was about $550,000.

FOOD AND FUEL CONSERVATION

On May 3, 1917, a company of "voluntary and disinterested citizens" issued a proclamation setting forth the importance of "increasing and conserving the food supplies," and calling upon the "people of this county to meet us at the courthouse in Gate City next Saturday, May 5, at 1 o'clock P.M. to effect a county organization." The proclamation urged all farmers and farmers' wives, all school-teachers, school boards, all county and other officers, and all citizens interested in helping Scott County feed itself, to be present. The proclamation was signed by A. W. Hedrick, county agent; J. H. McConnell, mayor; J. W. Carter, N. M. Horton, W. S. Pendleton, J. H. Peters, John H. Johnson, C. M. Quillin, I. P. Kane, W. D. Smith, B. M. Francisco, T. R. Wolfe.

In response to the above call the farmers of the county met and effected an organization by electing Rev. T. R. Wolfe, chairman, and J. W. Carter, secretary. Meetings for the purpose of organizing local clubs were arranged throughout the county. Pledge cards were distributed for the signatures of those who handled food in the homes.

Mr. A. W. Johnson was appointed Food Administrator for the county and enforced the regulations concerning flour substitutes, conservation of sugar, etc. On and after March 11, 1918, merchants were required to sell an equal amount of flour substitutes with each pound of flour. In September, 1918, the fifty-fifty rule as to flour was abrogated and "Victory mixed flour," a combination of eighty-twenty, was used instead. The millers' certificates were rescinded and the new regulations permitted families to have sixty days' rations instead of thirty.

On September 12, 1918, the Food Administrator addressed an open letter to the merchants of the county asking them to send in the twenty-five-pound certificates for sugar. He also stated in this letter that he often had letters of four to six pages, adding, "ten words gets as much sugar as ten pages."

A joint meeting of the threshers and threshing committee of Scott County, held at Gate City on Wednesday, July 3, 1918, adopted the following resolutions:

"1. Be it resolved, That we, the owners and operators of threshing machines in Scott County, realizing the great demand for wheat at this time, will use the utmost care for its conservation.

"2. Resolved, That there be no threshing done in this county before the 15th day of July, 1918, and then only when the wheat is thoroughly dry.

"3. Resolved, That every owner and operator of threshing machines have his machine in good repair before starting to thresh, and that it be kept in good repair.

"4. Resolved, That in view of the fact that we agree to thresh only when the wheat or other grain is thoroughly dry, we, the threshing committee, do insist that the farmers take every precaution in stacking and saving their grain.

"5. Resolved, That the price for threshing shall be seven bushels.

"6. Resolved, That any violator of the above resolutions will not be considered a member of the Scott County Threshing Committee."

The resolutions were signed by A. W. Johnson, Food Administrator; A. C. Starnes, R. A. Smith, William Spivey, J. A. Hurt, J. F. Meade, Clint Robertson, C. L. Wade, R. Moscow Addington, W. T. Larkin, W. L. Osborne, J. W. Horne, J. S. Culbertson, S. C. Dougherty, J. W. Frazier, N. C. Davidson, Judge Mullins, R. V. Trent, C. C. Carter, Will Taylor, W. H. Mitchell. The names of five additional men who left before the meeting adjourned should have appeared in the above list.

The Fuel Administrators for the county were John H. Johnson, chairman; J. W. Carter, secretary, and R. R. Kane.

It is remarkable how uncomplainingly the people suffered the restriction to be thrown about them by the government as to the use of flour, sugar, coal, wood, gas, and even daylight.

Farm products brought very high prices and this fact greatly increased the price of real estate during the war and immediately following its close. There was often an increase of more than 100 per cent over the former prices of land.

The local Council of Safety sought to enroll all citizens who were capable or willing to work in the shipyards or other places where the government might need them. The council further sought to enroll all those who might have oats, corn, and potatoes to spare. The members of the council were A. J. Wolfe, W. J. Rollins, and J. F. Sutton.

The local paper on May 3, 1917, had the following to say:

"You do not see many farmers idling about town these days. The farmers are discharging their duties like the truest and best of soldiers. They realize that they have to feed themselves and their families and the rest of the world and are buckling like horses to the task. Don't waste your time urging farmers to produce big crops; get out, everybody who can, and help them. By so doing you will be wielding the most effective weapon against the high cost of living."

Strangers whose behavior was in any way unusual were apt to be looked upon as German spies. This attitude of suspicion toward those whose business was unknown almost rid the county of tramps and hoboes during the period of the war.

There was no organized labor in the county during the war except perhaps the local workers on the railways traversing the county.

THE RED CROSS

A mass meeting was called for Tuesday, June 26, 1917, at the courthouse. The object of this meeting was the inaugurating of a campaign in Gate City and Scott County in the interest of Red Cross work, and also, in the interest of "Armenian and Syrian Relief."

The Red Cross campaign was discussed at the Southern Methodist Church, Sunday, June 24, 1917, and "By a standing vote in the congregation the conviction was shown to be that the people of Gate City and Scott County should get busy at once and do their part along with the rest of the country in this great humanitarian cause."

A committee composed of Ezra T. Carter, J. W. Carter, and Mrs. E. Thompson Carter was appointed to inaugurate a campaign for Red Cross Funds.

At a mass meeting held at the courthouse, June 16, 1917, the following organization was effected: Executive Committee—Ezra T. Carter, chairman; J. W. Carter, treasurer; John Henry Johnson, secretary. Ways and Means Committee—Mrs. S. H. Bond, Mrs. E. G. Quillin, and Miss Esther Kane. Publicity Committee—Mrs. E. Thompson Carter, Mrs. Ed. Whited, and Mrs. J. F. Richmond.

Through the Gate City post office many contributions were made to the Red Cross.

The Scott County Red Cross issued the *Scott County Cook Book,* made up of recipes for cooking, furnished by whosoever was interested enough to furnish a recipe.   The proceeds of the sale of this book were paid to the local chapter of the Red Cross.

August 3, 1917, was named as the date on which all members of the local Red Cross and all other persons interested in such work were requested to meet at the courthouse for the purpose of effecting a larger organization.   This organization immediately launched a drive for membership.   Red Cross booths were placed in Nickels' Department Store, M. J. McConnell & Son's Store, and the Gate City Pharmacy.   In addition to this, several young ladies solicited members on the streets and in the different stores.   The young ladies most active in this work were: Jane Richmond, Lillian Wood, Maxie King, Kathryn Kane, Reba Barker, Mae Boatright, Amelia Richmond, Georgia Whited, Lake Dougherty, Sudie McConnell, and Mary Davidson.

The officers and members of committees of the Scott County Chapter, American Red Cross, Potomac Division, were as follows:

Officers—T. R. Wolfe, president; Dr. J. M. Dougherty,

vice-president; John Henry Johnson, secretary; and Leona Jordan, assistant secretary.

Committee on Organization and Development—H. C. L. Richmond, chairman; E. T. Carter, I. P. Kane, W. D. Smith, Jr. Publicity and Entertainment—C. M. Herron, chairman; Fay Palmer, Emily Richmond, Anna Ward. Woman's Work —Mrs. E. T. Carter, chairman; Mrs. P. H. Nickels, Mrs. C. M. Perry. Hospital Garments—Mrs. E. Thompson Carter, chairman; Pearl Hash, Mamie Richmond, Mrs. W. M. Winegar. Surgical Dressing—Mrs. E. M. Corns, Mrs. H. S. Kane, Mrs. J. W. Carter, Mrs. Henry Jennings. Knitting— Mrs. N. M. Horton, chairman; Mrs. J. A. Counts, Mrs. W. E. Barker. Purchasing Supplies—Mrs. J. B. Gilley, chairman; Mrs. L. M. Smythe, Nell Counts. Shipping—E. G. Quillin, chairman; Mrs. A. W. Stair, Mrs. D. A. Sergent. Civilian Relief—J. H. Peters, chairman; D. C. Sloan, C. M. Quillin, Maxie King, and Grace Stair. Membership—Eliza Winegar, Maxie King, and Grace Stair. Junior Red Cross in Schools —Prof. A. W. Stair, chairman.

Growing out of and subsidiary to this county organization were the magisterial district organizations, which were as follows:

DeKalb District—J. H. Harris, chairman; Geo. E. Carter, Geo. C. Bevins, A. J. Greear, Professor A. Alley, S. P. Harris, William Franklin, W. L. Johnson, Mrs. P. E. Carter, Sadie Cox, Mary Baker, and Mrs. W. H. McConnell. Floyd District—Dr. N. W. Stallard, chairman; W. F. C. Blackwell, L. G. Osborne, B. T. Culbertson, C. K. Fraley, W. J. Jones, Mrs. A. J. Wolfe, Mrs. Barney Hagan, Mrs. W. H. Loudy, Mrs. P. M. Dingus, and Mrs. J. H. Bickley. Powell District —T. R. Hurst, chairman; Rev. C. P. Rogers, Jas. H. Ervin, T. M. Darnell, E. H. Jennings, E. N. Watson, Ira P. Robinett, J. Henderson Wolfe, Mrs. J. W. Stephenson, Fannie M. Wolfe, Mrs. E. G. Parrish, and Eugenia Darnell. Taylor District— J. L. Q. Moore, chairman; M. W. Quillin, J. C. Parrish, J. M. Tomlinson, S. P. Spangler, W. J. Rollins, H. V. Gillenwaters, B. F. Johnson, C. S. Pendleton, Professor W. P. Kennedy, Mrs. H. H. Necessary, Sadie Cox, and Mattie Taylor. Johnson District—Jas. A. Bond, chairman; J. M. Darter, Dr. J. M. Dougherty, R. L. McConnell, H. F. Addington, C. M. Perry,

Rev. C. H. Gibson, Rev. F. R. Snavely, Mrs. Alfred Dougherty, Corrie Quillin, and Cleo Wampler. Fulkerson District —Rev. J. W. Grace, chairman; John L. Darnell, H. J. Gardner, Dr. Sylvester Gardner, W. H. Hensley, Rev. J. W. Pullon, Emmett Pannell, Prof. J. H. Hilton, Prof. R. M. Addington, S. G. Owen, Effie Shelley, and Mrs. C. O. Johnson. Estillville District—C. W. Kels, chairman; W. A. Wininger, J. O. Shelton, J. W. Carter, D. C. Sloan, C. M. Herron, J. F. Sergent, John T. Carter, Mrs. W. D. Smith, A. R. Jennings, Mrs. F. E. Stewart, and Mrs. J. W. Whited.

Generous rivalry among the various districts was encouraged. An intensive speaking campaign was inaugurated, embracing speech-making in the school buildings at Fort Blackmore, Dungannon, Nickelsville, Hiltons, Speer's Ferry, Alley Valley, Clinchport, Mannville, Laurel Hill, Cowan's Branch, Flat Rock, and Pattonsville.

The Red Cross campaign was opened at Gate City by Frank Hall Ray of Boston. Clad in the garments of a comrade killed in battle, and displaying the scant remnant of a sleeve shot away when that comrade lost an arm, Mr. Ray earnestly implored his audience to "stand behind the tired man at Washington with deep lines of care in his splendid face."

The Scott County Fair Association in 1918 turned over to the county chapter of the Red Cross a building on the Fair Grounds, to be known as the Red Cross Building. This building was used as a reception room in which various articles made by the chapter and its auxiliaries were exhibited. An active canvass for membership was conducted during the fair.

Prof. A. W. Stair organized the schools of the county and the Junior Red Cross Auxiliaries for the purpose of gathering walnut and hickory nut hulls, peach and prune seeds, to be used in manufacturing antidotes for poisonous gases.

Miss Mary S. Sanders, a graduate nurse, was employed by the local Red Cross to give her time and attention to those who were sick with influenza, "while the epidemic continues."

The Red Cross prepared and sent many boxes of needed articles to the boys overseas.

Many Junior Red Cross Chapters were organized in the schools of the county. A school which raised an amount of money equal to twenty-five cents per pupil was eligible to membership in the Junior Association. Hundreds of school children contributed to Red Cross funds, but data as to how many schools qualified for membership in the Junior Association are not available.

In one report, Mrs. E. T. Carter, chairman of Woman's Work, stated that 32 sweaters, 13 pairs of socks, 1 pair of wristlets, 10 wash cloths, 31 hospital bed shirts, 20 pairs of pajamas, 7 pairs of bed socks, 35 pairs of pillows, and 150 property bags had been sent to division headquarters, Washington, D. C. In another report she stated that 310 garments for the French and Belgian Relief and 96 hospital bed shirts had been forwarded to division headquarters. These reports indicate the range and character of the work done by the women of the chapter. In addition to this work, hundreds of women also contributed in money to the Red Cross fund.

In 1917 the county's Red Cross quota was $2,190, and up until November 19, 1917, only $1,200 had been collected. At this time few Scott County boys had gone overseas, and the interest of the people in Red Cross work was not so easily appealed to. When many had gone overseas contributions were more liberal.

The Red Cross amounts, as contributed by magisterial districts, were as follows:

Estillville District	$2,278.55
Taylor District	623.25
Floyd District	606.50
Johnson District	354.30
Powell District	334.33
DeKalb District	247.90
Fulkerson District	150.25
Total	$4,605.10

WAR WORK AND RELIEF ORGANIZATIONS

The M. E. Church, South, appointed the following committee to solicit funds for the Armenian and Syrian sufferers: J. P. Corns, J. B. Quillin, Mrs. C. R. Cruikshanks, Mrs. H. S. Kane, and Mrs. C. W. Dougherty. Mr. Corns, Mrs. Quillin,

and Mrs. Cruikshanks were chosen to act as a permanent committee of relief "to the starving multitudes in the Holy Land." The *Gate City Herald* solicited contributions for a fund to be used in the relief of the suffering people abroad. Hundreds of school children contributed to the fund, mostly in pennies and nickels. The amount contributed was $155.63.

THE WOMAN'S CHRISTIAN TEMPERANCE UNION

The W. C. T. U. was an organization already functioning in the county at the time war was declared against Germany. It was thus an easy matter to direct the energies of the organization to war work. September 22, 1917, the W. C. T. U. gave an entertainment at Nickelsville, the proceeds of which were used in furnishing the Scott County soldiers with comfort bags. It became the fixed purpose of the organization to furnish each soldier with one of these bags, and on January 4, 1918, a meeting was called in order to provide money for this purpose. It may be added in this connection that the schools of the county assisted in collecting funds for the comfort kits.

The W. C. T. U. engaged in collecting old rubber, boots, shoes, auto inner tubes, jar rubbers—in fact, any material which could be salvaged and used in war work enterprises. Under the auspices of the W. C. T. U., April 24, 1918, was known as "rubber day." It was further urged that the value of all "April Sunday eggs" be contributed to the W. C. T. U. to be used in its war work funds.

YOUNG MEN'S CHRISTIAN ASSOCIATION

Late in the year 1917, a campaign was launched to arouse interest in the Young Men's Christian Association. Hon. W. C. McCarthy, on November 13, 1917, addressed an audience at the courthouse in the interests of this organization. Mr. McCarthy had been in Europe and had seen actual conditions there. Thus he was enabled to give graphic first-hand pictures of the needs of the boys in the trenches. E. T. Carter was made chairman, and Samuel Haynes, editor of the *Gate City Herald,* was made secretary of the Y. M. C. A. in Scott County. At the close of Mr. McCarthy's address more than $700 was contributed to the Y. M. C. A. fund. In the same campaign Nickelsville contributed $46.50; Rye Cove, $107; Clinchport, $136; Manville, $48; Dungannon, $160; Prospect colored school, $10.30; making a total of $1,200.

"The Red Cross Society, the Young Men's Christian Association, and the Woman's Christian Temperance Union are organizations that are doing all in their power to comfort, relieve, and help the soldiers. They are helping them at every stage, from the doors of their homes to the trenches and prisons of Europe. Let's help these organizations in every way in our power."

POST-WAR CONDITIONS

The first issue of the local paper after the Armistice carried the following headlines: "PEACE TERMS SIGNED; HOSTILITIES CEASE MONDAY, NOVEMBER 11, AT 6 A.M.; THE GREAT WORLD WAR COMES TO A CLOSE."

In another column the following news item appeared:

"The first intimation we had here that peace had been made came from the Kingsport whistles at daylight Monday. Soon our church bells were imitating old Liberty bell, guns were being fired, children were marching the streets waving flags, and everybody was wildly rejoicing. It was a great day in America."

The signing of the Armistice put an end to the drafting. In a short time the Local Exemption Board received the following telegram from Adjutant General Stern:

"Do not entrain any more men or call any more for entrainment on any call already issued. Men already on the way to camps will be returned to local board."

The soldiers of the county, on being discharged, returned to their homes one by one or in small groups. Mention of their return was seldom made in the local paper.

The names of two Scott County soldiers appear on the Distinguished Service List of Virginia; they are Isaac Estep, of Clinchport, and John Samuel Hartsock, of Nickelsville. Isaac Estep was awarded a Distinguished Service Cross, John Samuel Hartsock was awarded the French Croix de Guerre.

The citations follow: "Estep, Isaac, of Clinchport, Scott County, Virginia. Private, Company C, 9th Infantry, 2nd

Division. Son of Thomas Estep. Distinguished Service Cross; La Fontaine au Croncq Farm.

"Citation: 'For extraordinary heroism in action near La Fontaine au Croncq Farm, France, November 4, 1918. Being on duty as a stretcher bearer, he displayed exceptional daring, gallantry and disregard of danger to self in removing wounded from a field so swept by machine gun fire that the ordinary man would have felt justified in leaving them there until the storm had abated. Of the five men engaged in this work one was killed, and Private Estep and one other wounded, while the clothing and equipment of all were riddled by bullets.' " (Virginia War History Commission, Source Volume I, p. 50.)

"Hartsock, John S., of Nickelsville, Scott County, Virginia.

"Private, Company A, 7th Machine-Gun Battalion, 3rd Division. French Croix de Guerre with Silver Star; Château-Thierry, May, 1918.

"Citation: 'He distinguished himself by his great coolness on the night of May 31 at Chateau-Thierry. Isolated with French and American comrades in the midst of the enemy, he succeeded in extricating himself and in regaining our lines.' " (Virginia War History Commission, Source Volume I, p. 69.)

OLD HOME MANUFACTURES

The old "house site" was selected with reference to convenience to water. This custom placed most of the houses on low land. Nearly all dwelling houses had a doorway facing toward the south. In the very early days they had one small window somewhere near the fireplace. It was always securely closed at night by means of a strong shutter. Later on, when glass could be obtained, the windows were somewhat enlarged in size, but seldom increased in number.

The home of the prosperous pioneer consisted of a "big house" and "kitchen." They were sometimes built end to end with only a large rock chimney between; sometimes the kitchen was built at one side of the "big house," the space between being covered by an extension of the kitchen roof and called an "entry," and sometimes the kitchen was located some distance from the "big house." Both "big house" and kitchen had large rock chimneys with great, wide fireplaces. If there was no fireplace in the second story, "the shoulder" of the chimney began to slope at the height of the first story. These shoulders were often so large and sloped so gently that weeds and "prickly pears" (cactus) grew upon them. The stones were placed in the chimney as they were "bedded" in the quarry.

The poor settler's cabin was built of round logs and had only one room, with, perhaps, a "lean-to" or shed-like addition to one side. The chimneys were built of "sticks and clay." From the ground up to the shoulders these chimneys consisted of an outside wall of split timbers and an inside lining of rough stones and clay mortar, held in place by the outside wooden walls. From the shoulders up the stem of these chimneys was built of sticks thickly covered over with clay to prevent fires.

WOODEN PUMPS

The old-time farmhouse was often supplied with water which was conveyed by pump logs. A hole was bored through a section of log six or eight feet long, with an auger made specially for the purpose. These logs were placed end to end from the spring to a wooden upright. In 1832 the Estillville Water Company supplied the town with water through a system of wooden pumps. The difficulty of pump making induced men such as Samuel T. Francis, George and James Proffitt, and James Nickels to follow pump making as an occupation.

NAILS

Nails were not often used in the construction of buildings in the very early days of the county's history. Even the roofs of the humbler dwellings were held in place by the weight of heavy timbers or rocks. Heavy timbers were joined by mortising and further fastened with wooden pegs. The wooden peg was always used in the construction of flat-bottomed boats. It was also much used in cabinet making.

Such nails as the pioneer made use of were fashioned in the blacksmith shop. The "shop nail" was succeeded by the "cut nail," and after the "cut nail" came the "wire nail," with which the present generation is familiar.

MAPLE SUGAR

In the early days, large forests of sugar maple trees covered many sections of Scott County. But most of these forests have long since been cut away, and the land upon which they grew has been converted into rich grain fields and meadows. Before they were cut away, however, the making of maple sugar was an important industry. Most of the sugar then used was manufactured at home. In 1840 the output of the "sugar camps" of the county amounted to 60,000 pounds. (Howe's *History of Virginia*.)

The best sugar was made in the months of January and February, before "the sap ran too high." "A good sugar spell" often came in January. Then all hands went to the sugar camp, which for convenience was usually built near the center of the "sugar orchard." The camp consisted of three walls, covered like a shed, the cover extending in front over the furnace or "bank" of kettles. The side toward the furnace was always left open. The openings in the walls were "chinked" with moss, or closed by nailing boards over them. Thus the heat of the furnace fire made the camp a very comfortable place on chilly nights.

When the kettles were filled with "sugar water," fires were lighted in the furnace and kept steadily burning until the contents of the kettles had been boiled down to a sweet syrup. Not much attention was given to the kettles until their contents had reached the syrup stage. It then became necessary to see to it that they did not "boil over." This was accomplished by lifting some of the syrup into the air and letting it fall into the kettle, thus cooling it, or else by throwing a small piece of fat meat into the kettle, thus pouring oil on the troubled waters.

Sugar trees were "tapped" either by cutting a sloping "notch" in the tree or by boring a hole with an auger. A "spile" made of elder or some other kind of wood, usually cedar, was then inserted in such way as to receive the sap as it flowed from the tree and convey it into the trough. When the wound in the tree had become dry by exposure to the air, thereby retarding the flow of the sap, it was "freshened" by cutting the notch larger or boring the hole deeper.

The sap was caught in small troughs, usually made of poplar timber. Care was exercised in selecting such timber as would impart neither undesirable color nor taste to the sugar. The sap was carried in pails and buckets, gourds being used for the purpose of dipping it from the troughs. In some of the larger orchards it was hauled to the camp with oxteams.

The climax in the manufacture of maple sugar was "the stir off." This consisted in boiling the thick syrup until it became sugar. The sugar was then molded into cakes by being placed in vessels and allowed to cool. The teacup was very frequently used for this purpose, forming what was called "the teacup cake." Egg shells were used in forming toy cakes for the children.

SOAP MAKING

The old-time housewife manufactured the soap used by her family. Such a thing as "store soap" was unknown in this section for many years after its first settlement. Preparation for the manufacture of "homemade soap" usually began by selecting for firewood some variety of timber whose ashes yielded a large percentage of potash, such as hickory. An ash hopper was then constructed by first erecting a frame within which boards were placed in such fashion that the upper ends were held in position by the frame while the lower ends fitted into a narrow V-shaped trough. When completed the hopper itself was V-shaped.

The narrow trough was covered with straw to prevent its being filled with ashes in such manner that the lye could not flow out freely. When the hopper was filled with ashes, the process of leaching out the lye began. This was accomplished by pouring water upon the ashes and allowing it to filtrate through them. This was called "running off lye." The lye, on being boiled down, was thickened into soap by the addition of "soap grease." The soap was stored away in troughs prepared for the purpose. Gourds and terrapin shells were used as receptacles for small quantities of soap.

LIGHTING

Primitive methods of lighting were employed by the early settlers. Torches, pine knots, grease burners and candles were used, according as the settler could afford them. Candles were molded from tallow in molds prepared especially for the purpose. These molds had capacity for molding four, six, or twelve candles at a time. The candles were burned in candlesticks and snuffed with candle snuffers. Beeves were killed not only with a view to supply meat for the table, but also to furnish tallow for candle making. The year's supply of candles was molded in the fall and winter.

COMPASS MARK

In order to determine when twelve o'clock came, "a compass mark" was placed in the doorways that opened toward the south. The housewife noted with care the near approach of the sunshine to this mark, for when the two had nearly coincided it was time to blow the horn or tin trumpet for dinner.

DRIED FRUITS

The winter's supply of fruits and berries was either "sun-dried" or "kiln-dried." The glass fruit jar did not come into general use in this section until about fifty years ago. The "fruit scaffold" and the "dry kiln" were, therefore, a necessary part of the equipment in the preparation of fruits and berries "so they would keep." Owners of large orchards sometimes built "dry houses" and dried the fruit on a large scale. There was considerable trade in dried fruits and berries. The price paid was low—just a few cents per pound.

MOLASSES MAKING

Nearly every farm had its "cane patch." In the very early days, the cane stalks were bruised or mashed with a hammer or an ax, and then pressed to extract the juice. Sometimes the bruised stalks were boiled in order to remove the juice from the stalk. A little later the wooden cane mill came into use. It was thought to be a wonderful invention. By its use the juice could be crushed out of two or three stalks at a time. The crushed stalks were often gathered up and on being twisted like a rope were "run" through the mill a second time. The wooden mill did not run smoothly by any means; it protested against every movement by a screaking that could be heard a long distance. A liberal use of soft soap was required to lessen the friction and reduce the noise. The juice was boiled in kettles arranged in furnaces The wooden cane mill and kettles were followed by the cast iron mill and molasses pan or evaporator, which are still in use.

The owners of sugar orchards seldom grew cane, because when the "sap ran too high" to make good, firm sugar, maple syrup was made. The resourceful housewife often made a substitute for molasses out of ripe persimmons. The persimmons were cooked in an oven until the juice could be easily pressed out. The juice was then boiled down to the thickness desired.

COOKING

Cooking was done on the fire in bakers, pots, and ovens. The heated bakers and ovens were placed over beds of live coals on the hearth. They were furnished with lids upon which live coals could be heaped, thus adding heat to their contents. Bakers and ovens remained where they were placed on the hearth. It was the pot about which the cook had the greatest solicitude. The wood might "roll down"; the dog irons might turn over; the fore stick might "burn in two." There was always the possibility that something might happen to upset the pot and spill its contents in the ashes. To guard against such mishap, the "potrack" and the crane were used. The "potrack," or "pothanger," was attached to a piece of wood called "the lubber pole," which was firmly placed up in the great throat of the kitchen chimney. The "potrack" consisted of a bar of iron perforated with holes at short intervals from each other. A rod of iron bent in the shape of a slender S was then hung in one of these holes. A pot was hung on the other end of the bent rod, which served as a hook. The pot could be raised or lowered at will, thereby adjusting its position with reference to the fire. The crane was a kind of derrick placed firmly at one side of the fireplace. It consisted of an upright bar of iron to which at proper height was fastened a horizontal bar. One end of the horizontal bar could be raised or lowered at will. The pot was suspended to this bar and then could be turned on or off the fire easily. Bakers, pots, and their lids were lifted with "pothooks." In many old kitchens there was an assortment of pothooks. Tiny hooks for tiny pots, middle-sized hooks for middle-sized pots, and great, huge hooks for great, huge pots. A fire shovel, a poker, "a pair of tongs," a pair of dogirons, and sometimes "a pair of bellows" helped to complete the equipment of a kitchen well furnished in respect to cooking utensils.

Bread trays and wooden bowls were made from blocks of wood, usually buckeye. Churns were made of red cedar, with red and white staves alternating. The "churn dasher" was either a short cross or a circular piece of wood, filled with auger holes, in the center of which a handle was inserted. Buckets, pails, piggins, keelers, tubs, barrels, and hogsheads were all made of wood by coopers, some of whom turned out beautiful handiwork. One of the best known coopers in the county was Jeter Frazier. John Breckenridge formed water kegs from a section of a sassafras tree without reducing it to staves. These kegs were widely used.

The pioneer often found it necessary to economize the space inside his cabin. The falling leaf table was well suited to small space; by a sliding contrivance, the leaves could be lifted up or lowered to the side of the table at will. A close rival to the falling leaf table, in the matter of economizing space, was the "trundle bed." It was pushed under a "big bed" by day and drawn forth into the open floor for the young pioneers at night.

BUTTER AND CHEESE MAKING

Pasturage on the wild peavine and the grasses of the range was so good that relatively large numbers of cattle were kept. The more prosperous farmers usually had an ample supply of milk for all domestic uses. There was a better market for cheese than butter; consequently, cheese was manufactured for the local trade. It was pressed in strong boxes, so placed that pressure could be brought to bear upon it by means of levers. Beef rennets were carefully preserved because the milk could not be curdled for cheese making without them.

BASKET MAKING

The art of basket making was known to many of the early settlers, some of whom acquired much skill in various kinds of wicker work.

The basket oak and the willow were rather widely distributed, thus affording plenty of material upon which the basket maker could practice his art. Nearly every farmer had a number of "feed" baskets of various sizes which he had either made himself or had purchased from a basket maker. Closely related to basket making was the manufacture of "scrub brooms." These were generally made of hickory wood and were peddled about the country by the maker. The price of a scrub broom was a hog's jowl, or twenty-five cents.

SHOES AND BOOTS

The early settlers, adopting an Indian fashion, wore moccasins. These they either made themselves or had the Indians make for them. Then came the "shoe pack," which was only a slight improvement upon the moccasin. The last on which the shoe pack was made bore striking resemblance to a glut. Boots and shoes made of home-tanned hides would often "draw up" on becoming wet. In such a case, the labor of pulling them on and off was difficult. Although, unfortunately, no good device had been found for pulling them on, a "bootjack" could be used in pulling them off. Soles were put on with pegs made of walnut or maple. Shoes were laced with strings of leather cut from ground hog or other tough hide. They were polished by greasing or by blacking with pot black or charred locust bark. Women and children were barefoot in warm weather. People often carried their shoes until they were within sight of the church, when they would stop and put them on. After church they would take them off again and make most of the return trip home barefoot.

The leather was home-tanned. Troughs were prepared for the purpose. Hair was removed from the hides by soaking them in strong wet ashes. No bark was used in this home-tanning process. Later on, however, bark tanneries were established in different parts of the county. These tanneries were well patronized and did a thriving business. The tanner usually kept one half of the hide for tanning the other half. The process was very slow and required about a year for completion. Some of the old tanneries were Hickam's, at Estillville; Nottingham's, at Nottingham; George Bond's, in Moccasin Ridge, near Snowflake, Virginia; George and C. W. Bond's, at Nickelsville; Jackson and Sutton's, at Nickelsville; and Christopher Dean's, above Nickelsville. Nottingham's and Bond's tanneries were discontinued only a few years since.

THRESHING

In the very early days, grain was trodden out of the sheaf by horses or cattle. A large shed was built for this purpose. The "small grain" being spread down on the floor of the shed, horses or cattle were driven over it. Barns with grain-tight threshing floors were built later. The grain was placed on the threshing floor and beaten out with a flail. The flail was made of a hickory sapling about an inch in diameter at the larger end. About two and a half feet from the larger end the sapling was beaten with the back of an ax until a hinge-like movement could be secured. The small end of the sapling constituted the handle of the flail.

Grain was winnowed by a sheet or other cloth held in the hands of two persons, while a third let fall the chaffy grain. As the grain fell, the two persons manipulated the sheet in such manner as to blow the chaff from among the grain. Careful co-operation and co-ordination were required on the part of those who manipulated the sheet in order to produce the best results. Fan mills for separating the wheat from the chaff were introduced into the county between 1830 and 1840, judging from appraise bills.

BEDSTEADS

There were a great variety of bedsteads, ranging in size from the huge poster, which required a stepladder to climb on it, to the small bunk-like bed built like a shelf against the wall of a log cabin. Springs were unknown and consequently not missed. The old-time bed was not lacking in resiliency. This was imparted to it by its being "corded" with flaxen ropes. Auger holes were bored in both the side and the end railings. Ropes were pased through these holes from side to side and from end to end. They were then drawn taut and a peg driven in to keep the "cords" from becoming slack. After a period of use, however, they would again become slack, requiring that they be "re-corded."

WAGONS AND SLEDS

Many of the early settlers came to this section from North Carolina in North Carolina schooner wagons. The part that gave this particular kind of wagon distinction and no doubt suggested the term "schooner" was the bed. It differed from the ordinary bed in being built very high both fore and aft. Since this same type of wagon has been used by the western pioneers, the peculiar shape of its bed, no doubt, afforded protection from enemy attack. Wagons are not well suited to steep land where there are no roads. Therefore, most of the hauling on the farm of the pioneers was done on the sled. There were two kinds of sleds, the "whole" and the "half" sled. The "whole sled" consisted of two runners held together by three crosspieces, the main one of which was in front and to which the horse was hitched. The other two rested upon standards inserted into the runners by mortising. Upon the crosspieces which rested on the standards a floor was laid; deep notches were then sawed in boards or planks of proper length in such way that they could be built, pen-like, upon this floor, thus forming a "bed."

Corn, potatoes, and other farm products were hauled to market in such sleds. Their capacity was designated as a "one-horse" or "two-horse" sled, as the case might be.

The "half sled" differed from the "whole sled" in that it had no standards and only two crosspieces to bind the runners together. Instead of standards, a block of wood was pinned to each of the runners to give the rear crosspiece proper height above the ground. The "half sled" was used in hauling wood, the load being "locked on" with a log chain. One end of the wood always rested upon the ground.

FLAX

Almost every family grew flax for the purpose of obtaining supplies of flax linen for towels, sheets, "straw ticks," shirts, pants, thread, and ropes. The flax was harvested by hand, the plants being pulled up by the roots. It was spread upon the ground until the stalk had "rotted" enough to be easily broken. It was then bound into bundles and stored away. The next step in its manufacture was the process of "breaking." This was done in a machine called "flax break." In this machine, the brittle stalks were broken so that they could be separated from the fiber. The separation of stalk and fiber was largely brought about by "scutching." Scutching was done with a large, two-edged, wooden blade with a handle called "scutching knife." A board of the desired length was driven into the ground and a wisp of the broken flax, held over the top of this board with one hand, was stroked with the "scutching knife" in the other. Some of the coarse fiber or "tow" was removed from the wisp in this operation. The fiber was next heckled to still further remove the broken stalks and coarse fiber, and to straighten the fiber. The heckle consisted of an oblong piece of wood filled with sharp wooden or metal spikes four or five inches long. The wisp of flaxen fiber was drawn through this machine in a manner very much like combing. After heckling, the wisp was twisted into form similar to a twist of tobacco, and was then ready to be spread upon the distaff for spinning.

Flax was always spun upon the little wheel because it permitted the spinner, while sitting, to gather deftly the fiber from the distaff and pay it uniformly to the spindle as it was being twisted into thread. Wool was usually spun upon the big wheel, so called because of its size, the spinner walking to and fro between the spindle and the rear of the wheel. The little wheel was turned by a treadle upon which both feet could be placed. The big wheel was turned by "a spinning stick" held in the right hand while the "roll" of wool was held in the left.

The little wheel received the thread on a spool, which could be removed easily and another put in place. The big wheel received the thread upon the spindle, which had been encased with paper or a piece of corn shuck, so that it could be removed from the spindle. The space occupied by the spindle was left open on removal, thereby permitting a stick to be passed through the "brooch," as it was called.

On being spun, the thread was then transferred from the brooch or spool to a machine called a "reel." This machine stood upon a low tripod base. The upright body contained a wooden mechanism which clicked the number of "cuts" which had been wound. The thread was wound upon the spoke-like arms of the reel, which all radiated from a common center or hub. The arm bore striking resemblance to the croquet mallet. To one of the arms was fastened a handle which enabled them to be turned as if by a crank. A "cut" consisted of thirty-six threads. Four "cuts" made a yard. On being removed from the reel, the yarn was usually spoken of as a "hank."

The labor of making wool ready for weaving was about as difficult as that of preparing the flax. The wool on being removed from the sheep was usually dirty, oily, and full of burrs. It must be washed clean and the burrs picked out by hand with much labor. It was then "carded" with "hand cards" into "rolls" for spinning. Many years subsequent to the pioneer days a few carding machines were built in the county. Those who had large clips of wool patronized the carding machine. As indicated above, the "rolls" of wool were spun upon the big wheel and made ready for weaving. The thread, on being reduced to hanks, was usually put on spools or "quills" preparatory to weaving; that is to say, thread intended for the warp or "chain" was "spooled"; that intended for the woof or "filling" was "quilled." Spooling and quilling were done by means of the little wheel and a "pair of winding blades." The "winding blades" were used to hold the hanks of thread and consisted of an upright piece of wood, on the top of which were placed the "blades," crossed at right angles and so arranged that they rotated upon a pivot as the thread passed from the hank to the spool or "quill."

WARPING BARS

On being spooled, the warp was then ready to be placed upon the "warping bars." These consisted of two upright bars held together by crossbars. The bars had wooden pegs inserted at definite intervals and so arranged that a definite length could be given to the "chain." From the starting point by way of the various pegs to the peg that marked the required length of the warp and back again was called "a bout." The removal of this warp from the bars required care that it might not be tangled. On its removal from the bars, the warp was then ready to be put on the hand loom. This was a rather complex process, comprising a number of things. The chain was sized before beaming.

First, the warp was "beamed"; that is, the warp was slowly and carefully turned on the beam, the threads being passed through the "rake" to prevent tangling. The beam was turned by a bow stick, which was inserted in large auger holes bored in the end of the beam. The bow stick was kept in the beam all the time, and when not in use, was tied to keep it securely in place. The cross in the chain was pressed by two "rods," one inserted before the cross and one after. In cool weather an oven filled with live coals was placed beneath to render the chain more flexible.

Second, the chain was carefully passed through "gear," which consisted of thread tied in loops and attached to treadles and pulley-like contrivances so that they would be raised or lowered at the will of the weaver. Half the chain was carried by one gear and half by the other. Half the chain could be lifted and the other half lowered, alternately. This opening of chain furnished space through which the shuttle with its quill of filling could be passed.

Third, the chain or warp was passed through the sley. Two or more threads of the chain were drawn through each open space of the sley by means of a reed hook, locally called "hook-um-a-davy." The sley was made of splints of reed placed vertically and held in position by being firmly wrapped with waxed thread. The warp passed through the interspaces formed by the splints. The capacity of a sley was stated in terms of so many hundreds, as four hundred, five hundred, etc. The ends of the chain were then firmly tied together and a stick inserted. This stick was fastened to the "cloth beam" by means of ropes. The cloth beam was kept in proper place by ratchets. The weaving began against this stick and as soon as a piece of cloth sufficiently long had been woven, the "temples" were inserted. The temples were used in holding the cloth to the desired width. They could be opened and closed like a hinge and had sharp teeth-like projections to insert into the cloth.

The weaver sat on a seat provided for the purpose just in front of the breast beam. She "tramped" the treadles with her feet and worked the batten and shuttle with her hands. She watched the rods to see that they did not approach too

near the gears. She released warp from the "chain beam" and
rolled the cloth on to the cloth beam. The cloth beam was
held in proper place by ratchets. She watched for broken
or tangled threads. She often filled the quills that supplied
her shuttle. Two or three yards per day was considered a
fair day's weaving.

The cloths woven in the old hand loom were jeans, linsey,
flannel, blankets, flax, tow linen, counterpanes, coverlets, and
rag carpet. They were colored to suit the taste of the one
who planned the cloth. Jeans was usually gray or brown.
Linsey was usually striped, a preference being shown for the
warm, red colors. The carpet was also striped. Sometimes
the striped effect was produced not only by the filling but
also by the chain. Blankets were not often colored. Counterpanes and coverlets were the greatest triumphs of the hand-
loom weaver's art. They were often artistically designed and
beautifully woven. The filling of a counterpane was cotton
and not often colored; the filling of the coverlet was yarn
and always colored. Beautiful designs were produced by
clever manipulation of the treadles. The weaver was guided
in this manipulation by a diagram called a "draft."

Barks, roots, and berries furnished most of the coloring
materials. Sumac berries, madder, and aniline furnished the
reds. Oak bark and log wood furnished black. Cedar berries
furnished a dove color. Colors were extracted by boiling, and
the colors were set by using mordants, such as vitriol, etc.

The hand loom was a very ancient machine. The Bible
speaks of Goliath's spear as being as large as a weaver's beam.
When handed down to our first settlers, the loom was already
venerable with age. The pioneer settlers lost no time in setting them up. They found space for them in some part of
their dwellings, or under a shed, or, sometimes, a building
called "the loom house" was erected for the purpose of hous-
ing them. When the old historic Blockhouse ceased to be
used as a dwelling by the Anderson family, it was converted
into a loom house and resounded to the peaceful strokes of
the batten instead of the warlike discharges of the rifle as an
Indian enemy was being driven away. Any ordinary carpenter could construct a loom, for which service he usually

received from eight to ten dollars. The labor of weaving was usually performed by women. Occasionally, however, a man, Silas Marner like, became a weaver.

Most of the old hand looms have become silent. They are decaying in outhouses or under old sheds. Occasionally, however, one is requisitioned for a web of rag carpet. Hand weaving is rapidly becoming a lost art. Many housewives did not cease with the production of cloth enough to clothe the family, but continued to weave and carefully store away the surplus. It was the ambition of every mother to give each son and daughter at least a coverlet and a blanket upon their marriage. Unmarried women often wove and stored away the products of their loom against the time of need. This evidence of thrift and industry was spoken of and highly commended in the pioneer neighborhoods.

The cloth was cut and made into clothing by hand. This work was usually done by the mother and her daughters. Later on the services of a seamstress or tailor were brought into use to fashion the finer garments. The housewife wove or sewed by day and knit by night. Stockings for the family were homeknit. The yarn was often specially prepared for this purpose by being "doubled and twisted." Hostesses often entertained visitors, knitting all the while, and her visitors, if housewives, often knit, too. An invitation for a neighborly visit was often extended in the form of: "Come over and bring your knitting." In addition to the family supply of stockings, shawls, suspenders ("galluses"), comforters, cuffs, and other articles were also knit. Men often wore very large knit shawls, after the Scotch Highland fashion, instead of overcoats. These shawls were fastened with knitting needles, one end of which was firmly inserted into a bullet for a "head." When a metal pin was not available, a sharp wooden peg or a large thorn was substituted.

Clothing not in use was hung on the wall or kept in chests or leather covered trunks. In the homes of the more prosperous, bureaus or "clothes presses" were found. Clothing for a journey was packed into a satchel made of thick heavy cloth or "store" carpet, or saddlebags made of leather. The women of the household did the washing and ironing. The nearest approach to a washing machine was the "beetling stick." This was a stout stick with which the wet clothes were beaten, the clothes having first been placed upon a bench or a short section of a large tree called a "beetling board."

FARMING MACHINERY

Farming machinery was made at home. The coulters, bull tongue, single- and double-shovel plows, iron teeth for harrows, the "weeding hoes," the "sprouting hoes," "sang hoes," and the mattocks were produced in the blacksmith shop. The wooden parts of these implements were fashioned by the farmer himself. The first harrows had wooden teeth. The prototype of the big plow made its appearance in these early days, though most of its parts were made of wood. Harvesting machinery consisted of sickles, scythes, and cradles, the woodwork of which was formed by the farmer. The snathe with its curves was hard to fashion, so that the farmer who was less skilled in woodwork often searched the forest for saplings having the requisite curves. Instead of being harrowed in, seed was generally "brushed in," that is to say, the seed having been sown, a cedar brush to which a horse had been hitched was dragged over the plowed ground, in this way covering the seed.

Horse collars were made of platted corn shucks. Ox yokes were made of ash and the bows of hickory. Axes were often "upset" and plows "laid," which meant in either case the remaking of an old ax or plow. The fields, or "clearings," were fenced with rails made of timber that grew upon the land cleared. The timber was cut into sections ten feet in length, called a "rail cut." "Rail cuts" were split with mauls, iron wedges, and wooden wedges, called "gluts." Putting the first rails in place was called "laying the fence worm." It was laid in zigzag form to give greater stability to the fence. A fence ten rails high and well propped was considered a good one. Gardens and yards were usually enclosed with palings about five feet in length and having the upper end sharpened to a point.

THE "SANG DIGGER"

The north hill sides of Scott County, with their deep, rich, leaf mold soils, produced an abundant crop of ginseng and other herbs of real or supposed medicinal value. "Sang," however, had the greatest commercial value. The author has heard his great-grandfather say that the first tax he ever paid was to help build the old courthouse in Russell County, and that he dug "sang" in order to get the money to pay it. The "sang digger," equipped with a "sang hoe," an implement very much like a mattock with the blade left off, would enter the dense forest in midsummer in search of the ginseng, so highly prized by the Chinese as a medicine.

MEDICINES

The medicines used in treating diseases were homemade. They consisted of teas and poultices made of many different substances. For instance, in the treatment of measles, a tea of "sheep nanny" was administered. The mysterious character of disease brought more or less superstition into its treatment. The remedy for shingles was thought to be an encircling of the affected part with blood from a black cat's tail. A buckeye or some other talismanic object was thought to keep off attacks of rheumatism. Burns, cancers, tumors, growth, or knots of various kinds, and warts were charmed by a "charm doctor." The charm usually consisted of a whispered incantation, composed of the names of the Trinity repeated in a certain order. "Stump water" would remove the freckles from the faces of the homely girls, and "love powders" would bring their beaus abjectly to their feet. There were many "herb doctors," who placed both field and forest under contribution to furnish the medicines which they prescribed to their patients. One of the most unique of these was Anthony Kane, an ex-slave. Many people now living remember what a striking figure he presented as he made the rounds to visit his patients or came to visit the county seat. Teeth were pulled with pincers. If they were hollow and ached, the remedy was usually burnt alum or a strong "ooze" of oak bark.

HATS

Wool hats were sometimes made by local hatters. Two of the best known of these were James Dougherty and Stephen Paxson. Dougherty lived on Valley Creek, near Sugar Tree. He was born in Ireland and died near Sugar Tree. Paxson lived in the town of Estillville and conducted an extensive hat factory there.

FIRES

Fires were kindled by means of flint and tow or punk. Sometimes "seed fire" was brought from a neighbor's hearthstone in the form of live coals or chunks.

MISCELLANY

Up until a recent date, coffins were made of black walnut or wild cherry by local carpenters.

Floors were made by hewing the logs with a broadax. A log when hewn and ready to be placed in the floor was called a "puncheon." Plank was first sawed with a "whipsaw." The log was rolled upon a frame constructed for the purpose. This frame was high enough to permit the saw to be drawn up and down through the log. The old "up and down" saw mill, run by water power, succeeded the "whipsaw."

Various devices were used to reduce the grain to meal or flour. One of the simplest was that of beating the grain in a mortar with a pestle. This mode of crushing the grain was especially employed when the settlers were compelled to keep closely "forted in" on account of the Indians. The grater was employed when the corn had passed the roasting ear stage but was yet too soft to grind.

Two types of water grist mills were built, "the overshot" and "the undershot." The distinction between the two types was in the method of applying water power. The "overshot" mill was equipped with a large wheel to which the water was conducted by means of a mill race and forebay, and allowed to fall upon the wheel and fill its large wooden cups. The weight of the water in the cups put it in rotation and kept it turning. The "undershot" mill had a wheel enclosed in a tublike arrangement to which the water was conducted by a flume, and the wooden cups of the wheel were filled in such way as to put it in motion and keep it turning. Both meal and flour were "sifted" in sieves whose leather bottoms had been punctured full of holes by means of a hot wire. The old county court must grant license before a mill could be built in the early days.

Wild animals were caught in very primitive traps. The type in most common use was called a "deadfall." It consisted of a heavy weight of some kind, supported by "triggers" to which the bait was attached. The animal, on touching the bait, "throwed the trap" and was caught beneath its weight. A bird trap consisted of a pen supported on one side by triggers to which the bait was attached. When the trap fell, it rested upon the ground, thus imprisoning the birds within the pen.

Most of the musical instruments were homemade, such as the fiddle and banjo. In the very early days, however, the musical instrument in most common use was the dulcimer. It was peculiarly a product of pioneer handiwork. It was a stringed instrument and was played similarly to the banjo, except the strings were "picked" with a goose quill instead of the fingers.

The pioneer serenader made the charivari memorable by the use of a "dumb bull." The "dumb bull" was made by stretching rawhide over one end of a bee gum. To the center of the rawhide a waxed thread was fastened. Hideous noises were produced by slipping the thumb and fingers along the waxed thread.

Toys, such as the modern child uses, were unknown to the pioneer children and, being unknown, they were not missed. The pioneer child devised his own, very simple, toys. By the magic of his imagination, the "bean pole" was transformed into a gun, or a tomahawk, or a horse, whichever best suited his childish fancy. Girls played with rag dolls to whose faces features had been given by the use of charcoal markings. The bark whistle and the "cornstalk fiddle" gratified the childish desire for noisy toys. The grapevine swing, with its harmless accidents, gratified the childish desire for risk.

Wax and tar were obtained from pine by very primitive

methods. Wax was extracted by boiling the rich pine and skimming off the wax. Tar was extracted by placing the rich pine under an old inverted kettle and then building a fire upon the same, thus heating the kettle and its contents until the tar flowed out in a thick, viscid stream. Wax was applied to the thread used in sewing leather, and tar was used as a lubricant for wagons, etc.

Beeswax was applied to the thread used in sewing garments.

The "waxed end" was inserted by means of hog bristles into holes made in the leather with a "sewing awl."

Writing pens and toothpicks were manufactured of goose quills. Bunches of quill feathers might often be seen hanging on the kitchen walls, awaiting manufacture into these articles. A penknife was used for the purpose.

Elisha Wallen built a powder mill on Powder Mill Branch, near Duffield, and attempted the manufacture of powder on a large scale. He used a sweep or "slow John" operated by water power with which to pulverize the charcoal. To one end of the sweep a large pestle was attached. As the sweep was lifted up and then let fall suddenly by means of a crank-like arrangement run by water power, the heavy pestle dropped into a mortar filled with charcoal. Near the powder mill was a large cave, called Powder Mill Cave. It passed deep into Pine Hill in the direction of Horton's Summit. This cave, no doubt, together with Petre Cave, near Ward's Mill, furnished saltpetre, a necessary constituent in the manufacture of gunpowder. The dirt bearing saltpetre was placed in hoppers similar to an ash hopper, and the saltpetre was leached out with water which was then "boiled down."

Persons who committed minor offenses against the peace and dignity of the Commonwealth were sometimes punished in Scott County, as they were in New England, by being placed in stocks and pillory, and exposed to the jeers and taunts of the passerby, or else being tied to a whipping post and given a certain number of lashes on the bare back. Even as late as 1835, William Morison was commissioned by the County Court to erect stocks and pillory and whipping post as convenient to the courthouse as might be and report the same to the Court. (Court Minute Book, 1835.)

The care of very young children was entrusted to the "womenfolk," usually the mother. The white mother, like the squaw, carried her baby in her arms when she walked, or when she rode. Sometimes she pacified her child with a "sugar teat" and rocked it to sleep in a sugar trough. At other times she frightened it into obedience by the dreadful prediction, "Hush, or the Indians will get you."

The pelts of wild animals supplemented the products of the old hand looms in supplying wearing apparel to the early settlers. Bearskin and deerskin were much used for clothing, and the coonskin for caps.

Hunting shirts made of linsey were almost universally worn by the men. They served the purpose of both a shirt and a coat. The "tail" of the garment could be snugly tucked beneath a girdle or allowed to hang loose. When tucked beneath a girdle, the "bosom" of the shirt could be made to blouse, thus furnishing a capacious receptacle for whatever the wearer chose to place therein.

Children, in warm weather, were sometimes clothed in "tow shirts" made long enough to reach the ankles.

Farming, gardening, and many household operations were thought to be influenced by the phases of the moon and the signs of the zodiac. Those who did things "when the signs were not right" were thought to be inviting failure and loss. Almanacs were carefully scrutinized in order to know when the potatoes should be planted, the hogs killed, the fenceworm laid, the boards nailed on the roof, etc.

Many superstitions and folklore sayings passed current among the people, tending to influence their actions in certain contingencies. It was considered bad luck to burn sassafras, to break a looking glass, to return again to the house after having started on a journey, to set out an evergreen which died within the year, to have a ringing in the ears called "death bells," to turn a chair with one post for a pivot, to hear a rooster crow in the doorway of the dwelling house, to possess a crowing hen, to hear a raven croak, to dream of muddy water, to bring a hoe, mattock, or other farming implement into the house, and on the other hand, it was considered good luck to find a horseshoe, to find a pin with the point toward you, to be the first wrapped in a new quilt, etc.

Children were often told that the tangles in their hair were witch stirrups, "caused by witches having ridden them."

Nearly every neighborhood had within its borders some locality about which superstitious stories grouped themselves with more or less persistency. This locality might be an old deserted cabin, a dense laurel thicket, or a deep hollow with a lonely stretch of road. In the very early days before the land was cleared and the swamps drained the jack-o'-lantern or will-o'-the-wisp furnished the basis for many weird stories. It was alleged that the jack-o'-lantern with its seductive light would lure the benighted traveler far away from the course he should take, into some deep, dense thicket, and then mysteriously disappear, leaving him to find the way out as best he could. It was also asserted that the only way the unfortunate traveler could break the spell that was leading him so far afield was to turn his clothes and wear them "wrong side out."

Unusual appearances in the sky, such as comets, "shooting stars," "northern lights," etc., made deep impressions upon the minds of the people. These disturbances "in the elements" were usually regarded as harbingers of calamity, such as war, pestilence, and famine. Many old people vividly remember the great meteoric shower of November 12, 1833. They alleged that the stars fell as thick and fast as snowflakes in a snowstorm. The uneducated thought "the end of time had come" and acted accordingly. The superstitions about the thunderbolt at the root of the tree stricken by lightning, and the "bag of gold" at the end of the rainbow, were oft repeated and generally believed, especially by the children.

Hogs were fattened on the "sweet mast," which consisted of white oak acorns, chestnuts, and beechnuts. They were allowed "to run on the mast" until about two weeks prior to killing time, when they were put in pens and fed on corn to remove "the wild taste from the meat." In the later winter they ate "bitter mast," which consisted of black and chestnut oak acorns. They were of the "razorback, chiselnose" variety, and oftentimes "ran wild." There were wild hogs on Moccasin Ridge as late as 1880.

Milch cows were fed on shucks and nubbins; neat cattle were fed on shucks or other "roughness." The supply of "roughness" was usually exhausted by the first of March and then resort was had to the buds on the trees. Beech and other trees were felled to furnish the buds. This was called "budding the cows."

One Swift, whose Christian name has not been given, is reputed to have come to Bean's Station, in East Tennessee, in the year 1790 or 1791. He had with him a journal which seemed to show that he had a silver furnace somewhere about the Red Bird Fork of the Kentucky River and that he knew the location of a silver mine. The output of this furnace was fabulously rich. The ores which were fed into it were clandestinely gathered from the deep recesses of the mountains by Swift and his companions. No one outside was permitted to know the secret of its location. It was alleged that the Cherokee Indians knew of its existence in a very ancient time and had procured ores from it. The Indians' connection with it added an air of mystery to the legend. Story after story grew up about it as a central theme. Many a futile search was made to locate it, but it was as elusive as the will-o'-the-wisp.

Knox, Josh Bell, Wolfe, and Estill counties, Kentucky, laid claim to its location, but the story was too fanciful to settle down in any one place, so it drifted into Scott County, Virginia, where people of a former generation have talked about it, believed in it, and many even have made diligent search to find it.

THE MANUFACTURE OF IRON IN THE COUNTY

The transportation of heavy, or bulky material was a problem difficult for the people of the county to solve prior to the days of railroads. The nearest markets were Bristol, Abingdon, and earlier still, Lynchburg and Richmond. The difficulty of distant transportation was overcome, in part, by the establishment of small local manufacturing plants. Consequently many sections had iron furnaces, the output of which supplied the people with iron enough for the manufacture of "bull tongue," and "double shovel" plows, coulters, horseshoes, hoes, nails, shovels, tongs, "dog irons," etc.

The first attempt, it seems, to establish an iron furnace within the present limits of Scott County was made by a man

named Miliham on the North Fork of Clinch. This furnace
is designated in the Court records as Miliham's Iron Works.
I have been unable to find out how long it was operated. The
next furnace was erected at Whitesforge on Big Moccasin
Creek about five miles east of Gate City. It was built in
1849. On May 15, 1849, William B. White, an old Ironmaster, who had learned his trade at the Bushong Furnace,
on Beaver Creek, Tennessee, moved the Court for permission
to erect Iron Works on the lands of Ruhama and Almira
Bevins, non-residents of the State. The order of publication
was printed in the *Southwest Virginian,* a paper published at
Abingdon, Va. The Court granted permission to erect the
dam across Big Moccasin Creek provided Ruhama and Almira
Bevins were paid the valuation of one acre of land, March
14, 1850. William White made prospecting tours through
Moccasin Ridge and Copper Ridge at the time above mentioned, with the view to locating an iron furnace. His purpose was to determine in which of the two sections the best
grade of iron ores was to be found. After some discussion of
the qualities of the iron found in each of the two ridges, with
William Dougherty, another ironmaster, Mr. White decided
to locate his furnace and forge on Big Moccasin as before
stated, a short distance from the former post office of Whitesforge.

The ore which was smelted at this forge was, in the main,
picked up from the surface of the ground, in various sections
of Moccasin Ridge. Many old workers in iron attest the
superior quality of the output of this forge. It is said that
William Millard, an excellent blacksmith in his day, could
fashion a horseshoe nail from a cold rod of this iron.

Before "stone coal" came into general use in this section
the services of the charcoal burner were indispensable to the
ironmaster and blacksmith, consequently the burning of
"coal pits" was an auxiliary occupation to both trades. Jeter
Frazier was put in charge of the large "coal pits" required to
furnish Whitesforge with "coal" in its early days.

Prior to his establishment of Whitesforge, William White
had operated a forge on the Holston River. "Nat" Hicks was
also associated with him in the operation of the forge on Big
Moccasin. (Data furnished by Capt. D. S. Hale.)

SOCIAL LIFE, GAMES, CUSTOMS, AND SUPERSTITIONS

The isolation of the pioneer made him long for social relationships. Opportunities affording promise of social intercourse were seldom missed. The frontiersman would travel many miles to attend "meeting," being prompted to do so almost as much on account of his desire to talk with someone as to worship. Even his daily labors were made to furnish occasions for neighborly gatherings of various kinds. "Workings" usually consisted of logrolling, grubbing, house-raising, rail-making, and fence-building for the men, quilting and wool-picking for the women, and apple-peeling and bean-stringing for both men and women. The working was often followed by a "party" or "play" at night. Both the old and the young, the married and the unmarried, participated in these merry-makings. Taffy pullings and weddings nearly always furnished occasions for "a play."

Below is given a brief account of some of the games played at these parties: "Skip-tum-a-loo" was played as the players sang the words:

> "My sweetheart's gone, what shall I do?
> My sweetheart's gone, what shall I do?
> Steal me another one, skip-tum-a-loo,
> Steal me another one, skip-tum-a-loo."

The game was one of stealing partners, the skipping being done as the thief with his stolen partner returned to position in the circle of players. Each theft created a vacancy that could only be filled by another theft.

"Skate Around the Ocean" was played as the following words, which gave direction to the players, were sung:

> "Skate around the ocean in a long summer day,
> Skate around the ocean in a long summer day;
> Come into the ocean in a long summer day,
> Come into the ocean in a long summer day;

246

Back your beauty in a long summer day,
Back your beauty in a long summer day;
Face your beauty in a long summer day,
Face your beauty in a long summer day;
Kiss your sweetie in a long summer day,
Kiss your sweetie in a long summer day."

The "ocean" was enclosed by the circle of players.
"Weevelly Wheat" was played to the music of a song of
which the following is the first stanza:

"It's over the river to feed the sheep,
It's over the river to Charlie,
It's over the river to feed the sheep
On rye, buckwheat, and barley."

"Weevelly Wheat" was considered a dancing game and consequently was condemned by those opposed to dancing. It
was sometimes given, however, the more harmless name of
"Boston," and played in homes that would not have tolerated
it for a moment, if its true name had been known.

The most popular of all the old-time games was "Snap."
The opportunity it afforded of selecting a partner and of being
selected as one, the exciting race that followed the "snap,"
and, especially the reward that came at the end of the race,
commended it most highly to the favor of the old-time
merrymakers generally. Other games played at the old-time
parties were "Twistification," "The Three Suitors," "Pleased,
or Displeased," "Cross Question."

The play songs were frequently sung by the whole party
joining in lustily. Sometimes, the services of a fiddler were
engaged and the games enlivened by strains of music from
such tunes as "Black Eyed Susan," "The Soldier's Dream,"
"Shady Grove," "Leather Britches," "Sourwood Mountain,"
and other fiddle classics known to the people of this section.

Courting was generally called "sparking." The pioneer's
parlor was at the same time his living room, and bedroom,
so most sparking was done by "sitting up" at night. The
extreme limit for sitting up was "chicken crow." The girl
who spurned the attentions of a suitor was said to "slight"
or "kick" him. Marriage occasions were made happy and
festive events. Great preparations were made for them. Bid-

den guests were "asked to the wedding." Those who were not "asked" sometimes showed their resentment by cutting off the horses' tails and mutilating the saddles of the bidden guests, or by joining in a more or less boisterous charivari. The prospective bride and groom usually selected a certain number of young men and ladies from among their acquaintances to act as "attendants." These attendants followed close upon the movements of the bride and groom, appearing upon the "floor" with them while the marriage ceremony was being performed, etc. The day following the marriage, the newly wed "couple" with their attendants started for the home of the groom on horseback. The festivities at his home were spoken of as the "infair." They were largely a repetition of the things which occurred at the wedding. The guests played all night. Sometimes the bottle or "Black Betty" was passed around freely until most of those who drank at all had become more or less intoxicated. "To get tight," that is, slightly intoxicated, was excused and not condemned outright; "to get down drunk" was more or less condemned. The young couple were liable to be "charivaried" both on the night of their marriage, and of their "infair." It was the custom for the bride's parents to furnish her, at least, a cow, a horse, bridle, and side saddle, a feather bed with "cover enough to keep a bed warm," including a blanket and coverlet. It may be remarked, in this connection, that fathers usually gave their sons their land on condition that the sons pay the daughters a specified sum of money at some future date. The law of primogeniture was hard to forget.

The ownership of land added greatly to a young man's eligibility in the estimations of mothers having marriageable daughters. Such a young man was considered "a good chance."

Skill in the use of a rifle was esteemed a very desirable accomplishment. In the very early days, almost every man possessed a rifle and carried it with him everywhere he went. Boys at tender age became the proud possessors of guns and joined their fathers on hunting and military expeditions. When not engaged in hunting wild game or fighting Indians, the early settlers often indulged in shooting matches. These matches furnished excellent opportunity to display marksmanship. A spot was located at a distance agreed upon by the participants. A prize to be given the best, and second best marksman was arranged for. This prize might be a sheep, a turkey, or a beef. Whatever the article, it was valued and each participant paid so much for the chance of a shot until the amount paid equaled the value set upon the article. The one who "drove center" or "knocked the black out" won the prize. Many of the old marksmen personified their guns by calling them some familiar name, such as "Old Nancy," "the Slim Witch," etc. A farm was sometimes offered in exchange for a rifle gun.

Horse racing was often indulged in as a sport. Large crowds sometimes witnessed these races. Long stretches of level land were selected for the purpose of carrying on the sport. One of these pieces of level land near Nickelsville is still locally known as "the Race Path." Horse racing was one of the leading amusements at the old musters.

In case of sickness and death, the whole "settlement" came to the aid of those in distress. When the illness was very severe, the patient was "set up with," and ministered to during the night. If the man of the house was unable on account of ill health to tend his crop, or harvest the same, or to prepare his winter's wood, kind and sympathetic neighbors gathered in and did the work for him. When death occurred, the whole neighborhood came "to set up at the wake," and otherwise assist and comfort the bereaved. The night of the wake was spent in singing hymns. Relatives of the deceased did not fear lest there would not be "hands enough to dig the grave." Nearly every homestead had its own private burial ground. There was, it seems, a widespread aversion to being buried in a public graveyard. When possible, a sunny knoll facing the east was selected for the location. Oftentimes rather short burial services were held at the time of interment, and more elaborate funeral sermons were preached later on. Graves were marked by uncarved stone. For evidence, one may see the old pioneer graveyard at Fort Blackmore.

HUNTING

It is not possible to measure the influence of wild game upon the early history of this section. Next, perhaps, to its rich virgin soils, wild game was the greatest inducement to the hunter-pioneer to brave the dangers of the vast wilderness, infested, as it often was, by hostile savages. Many of these men, although imbued with the hunter's spirit, had never known the pleasure of unrestricted hunting. In the countries from which they came, hunting was a privilege open only to those who were permitted to hunt in the royal game preserves of the Old World. In the great forests of this country, these untitled men had access to an abundance of game unknown even to the largest game preserves of the Old Countries. It can well be imagined, then, with what zest they entered upon these newly found privileges. Some of these men as long hunters, and fur traders, explored the country, sought out, and marked traces which were followed later by the adventurous home-seekers and their families.

The early exploration and settlement of the Appalachian, and Trans-Appalachian region would have been hardly possible without the food which the abundance of game supplied.

In Scott County, the presence of these hunters is indicated by such names as Hunters' Valley, Hunters' Branch, and Hunters' Ford, the old name for Osborn's Ford. Travelers through the wilderness often waited at the Blockhouse on the Holston until a number, sufficiently large to travel in safety to Kentucky, had gathered there. They would spend the interval of waiting in hunting on Clinch Mountain, passing to and from said mountain along Hunters' Branch; hence, the name.

For many years subsequent to the formation of the county, its mountain forests were infested with wolves. Their presence was a great menace to young live stock of all kinds. As late as 1835, the county court authorized the payment of seven dollars for killing an old wolf.

Foxes, squirrels, opossums, and raccoons have been rather abundant throughout the years. Only those who have hunted these animals in the old southern style know the thrill of such sport. A good "coon dog," or a good "fox hound," was considered a very valuable possession. The marksmanship, which the old squirrel rifle developed, has been used with telling effect on more than one battle field.

Before the advent of the pointer dog and the shotgun, the

wild turkey, the partridge, and the pheasant were plentiful. Now the wild turkey and pheasant are almost extinct, and the partridge is fast becoming so.

The streams of the county formerly abounded with many varieties of edible fish. In the very early days of the county, fish were taken, for the most part, in fish traps. Fish traps were often bought and sold, and thus became matters of record. One of the most famous of these was "McLean's fish dam" on which Benge and his captives crossed Clinch River after his capture of the Livingston family.

AN OLD COUNTY COURT DAY

The first day of the old county court drew large crowds of people in every condition of life, from all parts of the county. Every means of conveyance known at the time was used to convey those who had business, as well as those who had no business, to the county seat. Those who lived at a distance often started the day before, and spent the night with a friend on the way, so as to reach the courthouse by nine o'clock court day.

The large crowds afforded an excellent opportunity for buying and selling all kinds of merchandise. "Cheap John" vendors of such articles as soap, razors, and handkerchiefs were nearly always present. The patent medicine man with his Punch and Judy skits sold medicines which, if his language had been literally true, would cure all the ills human flesh was heir to. He often resorted to the trick of connecting his medicine with some long-haired, long-bearded hermit, or with the Indians, thereby investing it with an air of mystery which increased the sale.

Gingerbread, molasses cakes, pies, apples, chestnuts, chinquapins, and papaws were offered for sale on the streets. Mrs. Linda Lark was one of the best known of these gingerbread vendors in her day. She was usually seated somewhere near the entrance to the courthouse with her wares temptingly displayed on a small table. With her, it took no noisy calling to effect a sale. Mrs. Lark was succeeded by Russell Peters. For many years he attended every court and other public gatherings as a seller of fruits in their season. He was a past master in so crying his wares as to create an appetite for them. All kinds of business were transacted on the first day of court. Business engagements were often made by the statement, "I'll see you at court"—a promise that was not always kept. The political speaker often took advantage of a court-day crowd to make campaign speeches. Sometimes representatives of rival parties would have engagements on the same court day, one holding forth in the courthouse, and the other somewhere else in the town. In the absence of newspapers, these political discussions had an educative value. Sometimes "old scores," and political arguments were settled by an appeal to a "fist and skull" encounter.

The alley just back of the public square was called, "Jockey Street." Here were long lines of hitch racks, placed there by an order of court. Here the horses were hitched; here the horse "swapping" took place; here old, broken-down horses were put through paces to which they were not accustomed; here dim and sightless eyes, by the use of various devices known only to the jockeys, were made to have a brilliant luster; here spavins and fistulas, knots and blemishes were minimized by such an ingenious use of the King's English as almost to escape the trader's notice.

In front of nearly every store there were "style blocks" for the purpose of assisting ladies to mount and dismount horses. The ladies used side saddles in riding horseback. A rather small percentage of the court-day crowd consisted of ladies.

Often the owner of a "good traveling" horse would ride to and fro in front of the courthouse in order to display the gaits of his horse. If the rider should happen to be under the influence of a stimulant, as he sometimes was, he would ride through the streets all day long. And on rainy occasions, the unpaved streets would be converted into a veritable "loblolly" of mud by the travel of hundreds of horses.

One of the institutions of the old-time court day was the "Claim Shaver." He went about through the crowds seeking those who had jury claims, witness claims, and "county paper" of all kinds, which he would offer to purchase, at the same time hinting how difficult it would be to collect such claims. These were often shaved as much as fifty per cent.

Major S. P. McConnell once told the author that the first court in Moccasin Gap was convened with some difficulty and delay because many of its commissioned officers were engaged in a game of ball called "Longballet" which they were reluctant to quit until the game had been finished.

THE SCOTT COUNTY CENTENNIAL IN 1915

Suggestions that the one hundredth anniversary of the organization of county government should be fittingly observed were made in 1914. At the request of Supt. W. D. Smith, R. M. Addington prepared a brief sketch of the county history for use in the schools. This sketch was published in pamphlet form and distributed to the teachers; it was also published in the *Gate City Herald* in the issue of February 18, 1915. There was some discussion as to the most suitable date on which to hold the celebration. It was finally decided to hold it in connection with the county fair for that year, and September 29, 1915 was fixed as the date.

The *Gate City Herald,* under date of September 23, 1915, carried the following paragraphs:

"The County School Board and many of the teachers of the county were in session here Saturday, considering the part the schools will take in the Centennial Celebration on the 29th. The schools will bring their students in large number to join in the march to Moccasin Gap. Each student will wear a white ribbon tied in a bow, and it is probable that this feature of the procession will be most inspiring."

An invitation to the school children of the county was issued by the committee on arrangements as follows:

"The school children of the county are requested to assemble at the Courthouse next Wednesday forenoon at 11:30 in order to march to Moccasin Gap where the unveiling will take place. Those in charge of the children will please instruct them to promptly meet this request."

The following general invitation was issued by the committee:

"All citizens of the county are urged to attend the Centennial Celebration to be held September 29. This will be the only opportunity you will ever have of attending a celebration of this kind in Scott County. Let every family come and bring dinner so you can have old friends and acquaintances join you at the dinner hour and once more enjoy Scott County's hospitality. Let's make it a day of happy associations to be cherished by parent and child far into the future."

Wednesday forenoon, the day set for the celebration, the rain poured down, at times falling in torrents. For this reason the program could not be fully carried out. The march to the monument and dinner at the Gap were abandoned and the exercises transferred to the courthouse.

At 11:30 the bell rang and the large courtroom quickly filled to its capacity. The Roda band, directed by S. T. Witt, made music for the occasion and put the audience in a spirit to enjoy the exercises.

Seated on the stage were S. H. Bond, chairman, C. T. Duncan, orator of the day, John P. McConnell, R. A. Ayers, Isaac S. Anderson, and I. P. Kane.

Prayer was offered by Isaac S. Anderson, after which S. H. Bond introduced C. T. Duncan who spoke in part as follows:

"Ladies and Gentlemen:

"It affords me great pleasure to be with you today, and to participate with you in the celebration of this the one hundredth anniversary of the formation of this great county of ours. I say ours because it is my native county. It was within its borders more than seventy-five years ago that my eyes were opened to its beautiful sunlight. Here I was raised to manhood's estate. My father and mother are buried here. This is the nativity of my kinspeople and friends for the last one hundred and fifty years, and today like the great Mac-Gregor upon his return to Scotland after his long exile, I can stand in this vast audience and exclaim, 'My foot is on my native heath.' Therefore, I cannot let you claim all the glory and greatness of this grand old county, grand in its mountains and hills, grand in its beautiful valleys and fertile fields, grand in its magnificent manhood, but grander still in its beautiful daughters and magnificent mothers. I rejoice with you in your possession of all these things, but at the same time I claim them as partly my own.

"The county of Scott has produced many great and good men who have aided in its development in every department of human interest and industry. To undertake to enumerate and pay tribute to each of those would be a task too Herculean to be attempted on an occasion of this kind. It is sufficient to say that in agriculture and stock-raising, in all its branches, our people have even been among the foremost; in education and the promotion of that which is best and highest our people have never lagged behind. In morals and religion Scott County and its people have always stood firm and fast for the best, firmly relying upon, and following the teaching of the humble Nazarine who spoke and taught as none ever taught before. In that time of dark and deep distress when the dark and somber clouds of war enveloping the whole of our beautiful Southland, enveloping Virginia in blacker and more sombre shadows than any other part of our overshadowed land, the boys from Scott County were always at the forefront of the fiercest fighting on the many battle fields of Virginia and elsewhere, wherever their services were demanded. It is sufficient to say that many of them were the followers of Lee and Jackson and that they never 'lagged behind.' (Here the speaker gave reminiscences of 'Judges and Lawyers Whom I Have Known,' which constituted the greater part of his address.) He closed with the following peroration: 'A word more in reference to your magnificent citizenry, both past and present. You have a splendid county inhabited by a noble people, a history of which you should all be proud. It would be too big a task to mention the names of the great and good people who have passed away leaving their works and examples for your guidance. I commend to you the history of your county and its people and I pray you may do your full duty as men and women. I thank you for the kind attention you have given to the broken and scattered talk I have compelled you to listen to. I now bid you good-bye until tomorrow when I hope to see you at your county fair.' "

Mr. Duncan was followed by John Preston McConnell in an address in which he discussed various phases and problems pertaining to life in the county.

A sandwich dinner, superintended by James T. McConnell, was served in front of the Courthouse at the close of the speaking.

In the afternoon the sun shone out, and at four o'clock many persons had gathered at the monument in Moccasin Gap where the ceremony of unveiling was performed. John H. Johnson made an address at the conclusion of which Master John C. Anderson, a direct descendant of John Anderson, the first sheriff of Scott County, pulled the cord which unveiled the monument.

W. S. Cox was chief marshal of the day. George B. Darter prepared the foundation, and put the monument in place. It was paid for by donations made by Scott County people who lived elsewhere. It bears the following inscription:

This monument
Marks the spot where
The First Court of
Scott County Was Held
February 14, 1815
Erected to
Commemorate One
Hundredth Anniversary
of Scott County, Virginia
1815–1915

The night following the delivery of the Centennial Address, C. T. Duncan died very suddenly at the home of his friend and host, John M. Johnson. The hope expressed in the closing sentence of his speech was not to be realized.

SOME OLD CHURCHES

THE NICKELSVILLE BAPTIST CHURCH

A futile search has been made for the first church organized in Scott County; for the first minister who preached to a congregation within its borders; for the denomination that was first to have a group of worshipers within its territory. The history of these first religious organizations would make interesting reading but available records do not disclose them. The pioneer, seemingly unconscious of the fact that he was making history in which his posterity would be greatly interested, signally failed to write it down, and make it available for the future historian. He was so busy in the conquest of difficulties and enemies that he did not take time to chronicle the details of the struggles incident to that conquest.

The pioneer was not irreligious; he brought into the wilderness such ideas of religion as were prevalent in his home country. His religious opinions were subject, however, to the reaction brought about by an entirely new environment. Religious leaders, such as Bishop Asbury and Squire Boone, followed hard upon the frontier as it traveled west. Stories of the good bishop, the great Methodist organizer, and Lorenzo Dow, an early evangelist, were repeated by the grandchildren of the pioneers to whom they ministered.

The author will endeavor to give some account of those old churches concerning which he has been able to gather data, beginning with the old Baptist church at Nickelsville, Va. This church was organized some time prior to February 21, 1807, the date of the first entry in the old church book, some of the leaves of which are missing. The entry is as follows: "Choose Brother Robert Kilgore Moderator. Rec'd by letter Br. James Ramey. Rc'd by letter Br. Thomas Esterling. Names of the members of the arm on Copper Creek, Robert Kilgore, James Ramey, Thomas Easterling, Thomas Burton, Israel Davis, John Buster, Elizabeth Sallards, Martha Gray, Jane Kilgore, Jane Buster, Nancy Burton."

On April 16, 1808, the following entry was made: "David Jessee, Wm. Wells, Edward Kelly choose as a Presbytery to constitute a Church and to look in the ordination of Br. Robert Kilgore. Br. Kilgore given up to said brethren to come under a regular examination adjourned till next day met according to adjournment. Report made by the Presbytery that Br. Kilgore answered all questions to our satisfaction."

The following is a list of the questions and answers of Robert Kilgore's examination as they are recorded in the old church book:

"What view have you of God?

Answer—I view Him as a Spirit Almighty, Eternal, Immortal, invisible, without body, parts or passions.

What view have you of the Trinity?

Answer—I believe in the Father, Son, and Holy Spirit, Equal in power and glory.

What think you of the Holy Scriptures of the Old and New Testament?

Answer—I believe the Scriptures to be the history of God's will and the only rule for faith and practice.

What think you of man in his first erectitude?

Answer—I believe he was created in God's image in innocence and happiness.

What think you of man in his present state?

Answer—I believe man fallen and depraved through every power of body and soul.

How can a God of infinite power and purity be just and yet the Justifier of the ungodly?

Answer—Through the atonement made by Christ and no other way.

How is the sinner justified before God from the guilt of sin?

Answer—By faith in Jesus Christ.

Is the act of faith what justifies from the guilt of sin?

Answer—It is the righteousness of Christ and rec'd by faith as the instrument that justifies from the guilt of sin and man is planted in the grace that sanctifies.

What views have you about the intermediate state of the soul and the body?

Answer—I believe immediately death passes (?) it passes at once into happiness or misery there to remain during the separate state these mortal bodies of saints and sinners will be raised Spiritual ones and capable of utmost happiness or misery."

Robin Kilgore, as he was affectionately called, was pastor of his home church for a period of more than forty years. In 1820, on the petition of the Stony Creek Baptist Church, he was permitted to use part of his time to attend that church "with the ministry of the word on the 4th Saturday in each month."

At the September meeting, 1847, the first mention is made of the controversy between the mission and anti-mission members of the church. This controversy resulted in the withdrawal and exclusion of a number of the members of the church, February 19, 1848. The members who were excluded on account of their anti-mission belief formed themselves into a church which more nearly represented their belief on missions. June 19, 1852, the church passed the following resolutions: "Resolved, That Bro. John R. Gray give notice to each member of this church supposed to have attached themselves to the anti-mission Baptist that the church desires them to attend her next conference and make known their intentions on that subject so that the church may know what disposition to make of their names as it is contrary to our policy to unfellowship, or exclude a member simply for holding anti-mission sentiments."

In July following, the church entered another resolution: "Resolved, That the church examine herself and book to know whether she had done wrong with the Antis, or not, at her next conference."

The early church meetings were held in a building which stood on the lands of Samuel Hartsock, and known as the Copper Creek Meetinghouse until 1855. Samuel Hartsock was under contract to permit the Baptist Church to use this house as a place of worship. The church register first mentions Nickelsville in the minutes of March 15, 1850. Minutes of the church often mention the fact that meetings were held in private dwellings, especially in the winter season. On

November 20, 1852, the church resolved to hold its meetings in the Good Intent Schoolhouse. For some reason a number of church meetings were held in this building.

At a meeting held in January, 1854, the church resolved "to build a plain, comfortable, neat brick house of worship in the town of Nickelsville; said house to be built 35 by 47 feet, 13 feet high, of solid wall, such other finish of windows, doors, seats, stoves, pulpits, Baptistry, steeple, bells, etc., as a committee appointed for the purpose may from time to time deem within reach of our means."

On December 15, 1855, W. M. Baldwin, chairman of the building committee, reported as ready for use, "a plain, though very neat, fashionable, and comfortable brick house, on a lot of one acre of land obtained of Bro. I. Fuller, Esq., a few hundred yards west of Nickelsville. The house is 33 by 45 feet, 16 feet story." The chairman's report was accepted, and December 29, 1855 was named as the date on which dedicatory services would be held. The sermon of dedication was preached by Eld. W. M. Baldwin, and Eld. David Jessee "closed with a lively exhortation."

The buiding cost about twenty-five hundred dollars.

On the completion of the new church building, the church had a dream of education that it was never quite able to make come true. Among a number of resolutions relating to schools, one to establish an institution of higher learning to be known as the Nickelsville Baptist Male and Female Academy was passed; it was to be built "on the lot of land now owned or occupied by this church." Eld. W. M. Baldwin, G. W. Hartsock, Dr. Thomas Cook, W. G. Baldwin, J. R. Gray, and Walter Gray were appointed a Board of Trustees "for the better regulation of the schools among us." Money enough, however, to erect a school building was never collected.

The old church building continued in use until the year 1919 when it was considered unsafe. It was then decided to erect a new building which was begun in 1920. August 10, 1921, the ceremony of laying the corner stone was conducted by Rev. J. B. Craft who placed a New Testament under the southwest corner of the building. Rev. L. C. Wolfe preached the dedicatory sermon September 3, 1922.

A. R. Kilgore had charge of the construction of the building, and much of the success of the undertaking was due to his faithful services.

THE COPPER CREEK OR "ADDINGTON FRAME" CHURCH

In the Minute Book of the church September 1847, mention is made of the controversy that had arisen in the church on the question of missions: Under date of January 15, 1848, the Minute Book of the Copper Creek (Nickelsville) Baptist Church has the following entry: "The church being greaved with Charles Addington, Sr., Charles Culbertson, Sr., Elizabeth Culbertson, Edward Harris, Nancy Addington, Winney Whitley, Nancy Gilam, Sary Easterling, Margret Easterling, Thomas Vicars, and wife, Hanner Dean for disclaiming a felowship with the church and separating themselves in a separate body from the church, apoint brethering Charles Kilgore, Sr., Robert Kilgore, Elias Marshall and James Easterling to sight said brethering to attend our next meeting in course. Done by order of the church."

Sarah Easterling, Margaret Easterling, Nancy Gilliam, and Edward Harris made due acknowledgments and were restored to fellowship. Most of the others were excluded as being anti-mission in belief. These excluded members furnished the nucleus for the Regular Primitive Baptist Church at what was later known as the "Frame." Soon after the division of the church the question of the use of the old Copper Creek Meetinghouse arose. This dispute resulted in a resolution made by the missionaries directing Robert Kilgore and J. R. Gray as a "committee to notify the antichurch with a written notice not to interfere with the Copper Creek Meetinghouse in any way." The date of this resolution was November 20, 1852. For many years the antimission organization held its meetings in private dwellings, in the "Addington Schoolhouse," and in the Copper Creek Meetinghouse, going first to one and then to another. The antimission party of the Copper Creek Church held its first meeting October 2, 1847. The members entered into the following covenant: "We, the Regular Baptist Church at Copper Creek, being convened at James Culbertson's for the purpose of holding our church meeting do covenant, and agree to subscribe our names as Regular Baptists."

Silas Ratliff was made Moderator and James Culbertson, Clerk. Jessee Davis, Charles Culbertson, and James Culbertson were the first Trustees of the Copper Creek Church.

In 1857, Charles Addington, Sr., and Jessee Davis were sent as delegates to an association held at Stony Creek for the purpose of constituting a new association out of a part of the Washington Association.

The first mention of the Big Meetinghouse ("The Frame") was made May 9, 1857. The Trustees of the new house were Stephen Kilgore, Jeptha Culbertson, Joshua Addington, Berry Compton and C. C. Addington.

In 1861, in a paragraph designated as "Item 10th," in the church record, the Stony Creek Association advised its churches "that if any of their members shall aid or assist the federal government in any way contrary to the laws of the Confederate States that they shall be dealt with for disorder, and unless full satisfaction be given, that the same be excluded from the church." To which advice, the "brethren of the Copper Creek Church" made reply in part as follows: "The advice given by the Association to the churches is contrary to the orthodox principles of the Baptists. It is unscriptural, uncharitable, and full of bigotry."

At the August meeting of the Copper Creek Church, in 1866, a number of its members petitioned that a new church be constituted at Point Truth. This petition was granted and the new church was organized the 4th Saturday in August, 1866.

In June, 1882, it was decided to abandon the old Frame Meetinghouse, and build a new church house. At this same meeting a committee was appointed to procure a deed for a site. The new house was to be ready for occupancy by May, 1883.

In 1897, the Three Forks of Powell's River Association addressed a circular letter to its component churches on the doctrine of Predestination and Election. This letter contained the statement, "That Christ's death and suffering on the cross was only for the redemption of all the vessels of mercy or bodies of the chosen Saints in this time world. The Eternal Child or Spirit that is often called Eternal Life was not redeemed or atoned for, but being the product of an incorruptible seed was not lost, never fell in Adam, and consequently needs no redemption." It further asked that the churches "endorse the doctrine of eternal vital unity and absolute predestination of every event that comes to pass in this time world." The Copper Creek Church objected to the circular letter "on the grounds that the doctrine set forth is not the doctrine taught by the abstract of principles of the Stony Creek Association." In 1898, the Copper Creek Church addressed the following query to the Stony Creek Association which met that year with the Valley Church: "Must we, the Copper Creek Church as Primitive Baptists, endorse the circular letter of 1897 of the three Forks Powell River Association? In other words is that circular letter a correct exponent of the Regular Primitive Baptist Doctrine?" The delegation that bore the query to the Association was at first seated, and then later adjudged in disorder by the Association. The question that had caused a difference of opinion in the Association also divided Copper Creek Church in twain, one part accepting the doctrine set forth in the letter, the other rejecting it. This division brought up the question as to which part of the church should have control of the church building. In November, the part of the church of which William E. Addington was Moderator forbade the holding of any meeting in the church house except on its regular sessions and directed the sexton to keep the church doors locked during the intervals between its meetings. The matter was taken into court with E. W. Addington, L. J. Addington, C. C. Addington, Chas. P. Wampler and Wm. H. Blankenbeckler, Trustees and Members of the Regular Primitive Baptist Church of Copper Creek, Plaintiffs, and Jno. M. Addington, G. W. Addington, D. J. Addington, W. A. Compton, and Tyre Mead, Trustees, and J. W. N. Addington, J. C. Addington, F. G. Whited and Henry Collier, Defendants. The case lingered in court two or three years before final settlement. Under date of December 18, 1901, the court awarded title to the property, and custody of the original records to the plaintiffs. The defendants were given the use of the church as a place of worship at stated periods, with permission to make copies of such of the original records as they might desire.

The names of some of the ministers who have served the church follow: Elders David Jessee, Jr., Morgan T. Lipps, William Addington, H. Smith, Parmer Sufferage, S. Killgore, Elder Kizer, Elias Colier, William Moore, Martin Good, J. P. Peters, William E. Addington, James M. Quillin, Miligan Killgore, T. R. Carter.

The names of some of the old churches of the same faith mentioned in the records of the Copper Creek Church follow: Livingston Meetinghouse, Obey's Creek Church, Tom's Creek Church, Three Forks of Powell's River Church, Addington Schoolhouse, Meetinghouse on Clinch River near Buster's Shoals, Mill River Church, Grayson County, Virginia, Dougherty Schoolhouse, Big Glade Church, Big Meetinghouse, Sugar Grove, Stony Creek Church, Little Stone Gap Church, Blue Spring Church, Bold Camp Church, Valley Church, Dump's Creek, Fairview Schoolhouse.

Following the minutes of the church meeting held in November 1886, the church clerk entered the following note: "On Sunday night of this church meeting, Our Pastor and beloved Father in Christ, Elder David Jessee, departed this life. He had served this church as their Pastor and Moderator for many years and was greatly beloved by his brethren and sisters of the church.

"C. C. Addington, Clerk."

At the June meeting, 1901, the Church unanimously passed resolutions expressing appreciation of the long and efficient services of C. C. Addington who had served as its clerk for more than thirty years, and, at the same time, expressing deep regret that "from frailty of age," he had found it necessary to resign.

THE STONY CREEK BAPTIST CHURCH

As this is written the Minute Book of the Stony Creek Baptist Church lies on the desk before the writer. It is faded on account of age and much use. Some of its pages are missing, and some of those yet remaining are scarcely legible. The earliest legible date is August 26, 1815, but the church was organized in 1801. This date is shown in biographical sketches of two of its first members, William Brickey, Sr., and David L. Cocke. These sketches are to be found in the Minute Book of the Stony Creek Regular Baptist Association. According to this record William Brickey, Sr., was born in Botetourt County, Virginia, December 29, 1779, and became a member of this church at its organization in 1801. He was its first clerk, and one of its first deacons. He married Elizabeth Cox, a daughter of David Cox.

David L. Cocke, another of its first members, was born at Castle's Woods, Russell County, June 12, 1785. At the tender age of fifteen or sixteen, he made public profession, and joined an arm of the Reed's Valley Church which held their sessions at his father's house, which arm was organized into a church the same meeting that he was baptized. The date of the meeting was August 22, 1801.

Many of the church minutes began with the terse, but significant statement: "Church sat, and found in love." An entry of August 26, 1816, states, "Then came forward Brother Gnash, and made his excuse for neglecting his church meeting; they (the church) forgive him also." The last legible date in this old church minute book is August 24, 1819.

The list of church members prior to 1819 are: David Cox, John Buster, Elizabeth Carter, Shade Estep, Samuel Estep, Mary Estep, Elizabeth Wallice, William Wells, Thomas Owins, Jeams, a black man, Hannah Riggs, Salley Mullets, Sarah Buster, David Buster, William Buster, Bates Buster, Margaret Hammon, John Buster, Samuel Buster, James Cocks, Caty McConnell, Black Sarah, Black Sook, Charley Buster, Simon Stacey, Nansey Cox, Nathan Swinney, Wynoah Carter, Sherod Kid, James Brickey, William Brickey, John McKinsey, David Cox, Sr., Thomas Lander, Pattie Tailer, Chloe France, William Steward, James Albert, Charles Buster, John Fraisure, Nimrod Tailer, Pattie Kinsey, John Sturgin, Sam Pitman, James Gibson, and Ruth Gibson.

THE SULPHUR SPRING BAPTIST CHURCH, LATER CALLED
DARTHULA

The date of organization of this church could not be ascertained. Much of the old church minute book is missing. The first legible church order reads as follows: "Appointed committee to examine and correct church book list of members. Left unchanged by the committee." This list contained the following names: Elizabeth Hobbs, Mary Darter, Martha Hilton, Matilda Ryan, Mary Agee, Catherine Hilton, Margaret Vineyard, Nancy Hart, Francis A. Claman, Kesire Hobbs, Mary A. Coley, Jane Denison, R. M. Denison, W. H. Bevins, Martha Cleek, Rachel B. Bevins, Margaret Cleek, Sopha Ann Cleek, Mary Wadkins, Martha E. Cleek, Sarah A. Cleek, Mary J. Barker, Sara E. Price, John H. Hilton, James Ramey,

Josiah McClellan, Rebecca Ramey, Robert McNutt, Wm. H. Agee, E. H. Quillin, David M. Jayne, James M. Hilton, W. L. Hilton, Samuel Hilton, Austin Brown, E. B. Hilton, Sarah J. Vineyard, Rebecca Murphy, Catherine Collins, Anna McClellan, Harriett Hilton, A. J. Hobbs, Elizabeth Q. Hilton, John Wallace, Fanna Browder, Michiel Darter, W. L. Coley, Mary J. Ramey, Elinor Ramey, Wm. Ramey, Polly Ramey, David Taylor, Malinda Taylor, Elizabeth Johnson, Watson Whitiker, Elizabeth Bounds, Mary E. Darter, James K. P. Darter, Mary Parmer,

Aga Ramey, G. B. Quillin, Nansy S. Quillin, James A. Hilton, Rebecca Peters, Mary E. Taylor, Nancy S. Ramey, George Coley, Jeremiah Marion, Abel McNutt, Robert Blalock, Almira Darter, Mary C. Hilton, Eliza Strong, Eliza Hart, Vaughan Hilton, Wm. Blalock, Elizabeth L. Hilton, Rebecca Darter, Noah Hobbs, Nansy S. Hilton, David Hobbs, Polly Ann Coley, Melvina Quillin, William Coley, Lucinda Carrow, Martha Johnson, Annas Pratt, Margaret Blalock, Susan Martin, Sarah Ann Smith, Susan McNutt, Rachiel Cleek, Florence Cleek, Elizabeth Lawson, Anna Blalock, M. L. Ingram, Emaline Ingram, Peter Johnson, Eliza Cleek, Thomas Cleek, Philip McNutt, David Epperson, Mary Wallace.

Felix Syms, Washington Ramey, William H. Ramey, Henry Syms, Henderson Hobbs, Mary V. Walker, John Taylor,

Nancy Smith, Polly Quillin, Mary Ramey, James H. Denison, William H. Ellis, Mary Cleek, Martha Kilgore, Henry Darter, Judith A. Graham, David Hilton, Margaret Claman, John Hilton, Polly Denison, Anny Fields, Jeremiah Fields, Emly Payne, E. J. Blessing, Nancy Seaver.

HUNTER'S BRANCH M. E. CHURCH, SOUTH

The exact date of the organization of this church could not be ascertained. Tradition fixes the date at about the year 1800. The families of William Agee who married a Miss Childress, and David Freeman formed the nucleus of the early church, it is said. A list of its early members follows: Isaac Cookenour, Hesikiah Crumly, David Freeman, Lavina Cookenour, Isaac Agee, J. B. Agee, Malikiah Crumley, Charity Crumley, J. S. Agee, Rachel Agee, Mary Ann Cookenour, L. C. Freeman, D. T. Freeman, R. Y. Reynolds, James I. Agee, Mary J. Agee, Elizabeth Agee, Sarah Freeman, Elen Reynolds, Mary K. Hickam, Nancy S. Agee, Susan M. Agee, Mary Freeman, Elizabeth Darter, Anna Freeman, Polly Agee, Mary A. Freeman, G. H. Nottingham, Martha Nottingham, Jemima Davidson, Nancy E. Agee, Amelia Nottingham, Eva Freeman, M. L. Agee, Kate Agee, Rachel Agee, Nelie Reynolds, Kate Freeman, Susie Horn, Lilla Freeman, Bertha Horn, Flora Horn.

The following is a list of ministers whose names appear on the church minute book, as having served the church in some capacity: Samuel Patton, George Eakin, T. K. Catlett, Samuel D. Gaines, J. T. Smith, H. L. Wood, F. A. Farley, J. T. Frazier, D. R. Smith, G. W. Renfro, John S. Bowine (?), J. A. Mahoney, S. S. Weatherly, R. M. Hickey, J. C. Runyon, J. W. Hillman, F. H. Farley, J. L. Weber, J. E. Fogleman, S. W. McConnell, W. C. Carden, J. W. Smith, C. H. Fogleman, S. T. McPherson, J. F. Jones, J. I. Cash, E. L. McConnell, J. S. Hensley, A. B. Moore, W. T. Evans, F. Snavely, J. T. Houts, Barney Thompson, K. W. Cox, G. W. Fox, J. W. Stewart, J. B. Simpson, K. G. Munsey, T. H. Francisco, Reubin Steele, John B. Corns, J. H. Torbit, John Craig, L. C. Delashment, F. D. Crumley, W. L. Richardson, J. W. Belt, Eli K. Hutsell, John Baringer, J. E. Neff, E. H. Casady,

E. A. Shugart, E. E. Gillenwaters, W. M. Bellamy, James Edwards, Washington Boling, John M. Crismond, John H. Kenady, I. P. Martin, G. S. Wood.

THE CAMP MEETING

The camp meeting seems to have had its origin in the religious needs of the people living in sparsely settled communities on the frontiers in the South. In the absence of suitable houses in which to worship, religious meetings were often held in groves. Inclement weather, however, frequently made some kind of shelter necessary. At first, brush arbors and tents furnished this shelter. Later on many of the "camp grounds," more substantial buildings of logs or plank, were erected.

The main auditorium consisted of a large brush arbor or tent. The more substantial ones were covered with clapboards. "The camps" were located with more or less regularity about the central building. The camp meeting was a very effective evangelizing agency, and it was peculiarly a Methodist institution.

Scott County seems to have had two camp grounds in the early days: one about two miles southwest of Pattonsville, called the Forkner Camp Ground, named for the Rev. Isaac Forkner; the other was Rye Cove Camp Ground on Cove Creek, near the dwelling of Isaac Carter. Meetings at these places have long since been discontinued.

One of the oldest, if not the oldest, camp ground now in use in this part of Virginia is that at Jonesville. Miss Katherine Spencer has furnished the author with a description of it which conforms so nearly to the type of such meetings that it is here quoted:

"The Jonesville Camp Ground is situated in a grove of fine trees. It has stood for more than one hundred years. (Since 1810.) The first buildings were burned during the Civil War but were later restored. The large tent was at one time surrounded by weatherboarded tents, having three or more rooms. Most of them have been torn away.

"The large auditorium or tent is seated with wooden benches, most of them without backs. The shed is supported by huge wooden pillars with stone foundations. On both sides of the tent are wings on hinges which can be raised or let down. The tent has a dirt floor covered with straw. A platform has been raised back of the pulpit for the choir.

"The shed was at one time lighted with gasoline lamps, and, perhaps, before that, with candles, and now by electricity.

"The camp ground is surrounded by a stone wall with three gates. Just outside the main entrance stood an old wooden church which has lately been replaced by a new brick one. A few hundred yards down the hill is a pump, and just outside the stone wall there used to be a cave where the people kept their meat fresh, but the cave is now filled up.

"The camp meeting convenes about the last week in August. The tent holders move in on Friday and stay until Monday. In the days gone by, the tent holder would be aroused in the early morning by a trumpet call which was the signal to get up and prepare for the devotional exercises, the time for which being later announced by a second trumpet call.

"The ministers had a special tent, and often after prayers they would be invited to the different places for breakfast.

"The campers came in wagons, bringing their bedding, and food to last throughout the meeting. They came from different parts of the country.

"Camp meeting is the great homecoming for Lee County. It is a great social event, the people coming from all over the county and some of the nearby cities.

"We have some of the finest talent of the Methodist Church to preach and lecture. People of other churches come and take great interest. We are hoping to make the old Jonesville Camp Ground a great religious center for the young people."

SHOEMAKER COLLEGE

The General Assembly of Virginia by an act approved March 1, 1894, granted a charter to Shoemaker College. By virtue of this act it was empowered "to confer and bestow upon its pupils or graduates such diplomas or certificates or other evidences of graduation, distinction, or proficiency, as said pupils may acquire in their various studies or employments, according to regulations of said college and the determination of its teachers, instructors, trustees, or other officers."

With the money obtained from James L. Shoemaker's estate, supplemented by private subscriptions, a building was erected on an eminence just east of Gate City. It was ready for occupancy October 22, 1897, at which time its first session began.

The first Board of Trustees consisted of Supt. W. D. Smith, chairman, I. P. Kane, secretary, John M. Johnson, M. T. Hash, and W. M. Jennings.

The first faculty consisted of A. L. G. Stephenson, president, Mathematics and Natural Science; R. M. Addington, English and History; L. R. Warren, Languages; Miss Effie Bean, Music; Miss Virginia Matheson, Art; Miss Kate Starnes, Primary Department.

Courses leading to the degrees of Licentiate of Instruction, Bachelor of Arts, and Master of Arts, were offered.

Stephenson was succeeded by Prof. F. B. Fitzpatrick, as president, with Miss Cornelia Poindexter, teacher of Latin, German, French and Pedagogy; R. M. Dougherty, History and Mathematics; Dr. W. H. Saunders, Physiology; Miss Flora Kate Carter, Primary Department; Miss Mollie Starnes, assistant Primary Department; Miss Mamie E. Porter, Vocal and Instrumental Music.

The institution was continued as a college until 1906, when it was changed into a high school, and it so continues.

SCOTT COUNTY IN 1830

"Scott was established by Act of Assembly in 1814, and formed from portions of Lee, Washington, and Russell. It is bound N. and N.E. by Russell—E. by Washington—S. by Sullivan and Hawkins Counties of Tennessee—W. by Lee. Its mean latitude is about 46° 47' N., its longitude 5° 40' west of Washington City—its mean length 26 miles—its mean breadth 24 miles, and area 624 square miles.

"The face of the country is mountainous and uneven. Clinch Mountain passes through the county from N.E. to S.W. —all the principal ridges and streams take the same direction. The county is exceedingly well watered by good springs, creeks, and rivers, and possesses water power in abundance.

"The soil is generally good, some of superior quality, the poorest well suited to small grains,—good meadows can be made almost anywhere. The county is well suited to rearing stock.

"The principal growth consists of poplar, hickory, beech, sugar maple, white and black oak, lynn, buckeye, black walnut; chestnut on the mountains and ridges, and wild cherry is found in many places.

"The chief productions are Indian corn, wheat, rye, oats, hemp, flax, etc., and apples and peaches in abundance. Many horses, horned cattle, and hogs are reared in, and driven out of the county.

"*Rivers, etc.* The North Fork of Holston and Clinch rivers run through the county—each affords the facilities of boat navigation down them in times of freshets; and with some improvement would add greatly to the convenience of the country for the purposes of trade; they both afford fine fish. Clinch River, for a river of its size, is remarkable for its fish. Some of the largest taken in it are of the following weights: blue cats, 30 to 40 lbs.—salmon, 15 lbs.—carp, 15 lbs.—red horse, 7 lbs., etc.

"Big Moccasin Creek rises in Russell County at the foot of Clinch Mountain—winds along the north side of the mountain a distance of about 30 miles to Big Moccasin Gap. Little Moccasin Creek rises at the foot of said mountain in a differ-

ent direction, runs along the mountain a distance of about
seven miles to said Gap where the two streams form a junction,
flow through the Gap on nearly level ground, and pass on to
the North Fork of Holston. Clinch Mountain here is large
and the Gap, although formed abruptly, is so level that the
main western road in passing through it, does not ascend more
than in passing up a gently flowing stream. Big Moccasin
Gap is situated about one mile east of Estillville.

"Sinking Creek empties into Clinch River about 22 miles
north of Estillville, is 6 or 7 miles long, and large for its length.
It rises on the south side of said river, in Copper Ridge, and
when it approaches within three-fourths of a mile of the river,
sinks, passes under the bed of the river and rises about one
hundred feet from the river on the north side, and runs back
into the river—the stream rising has often been proved to be
the same that sinks. Fish from the river pass into the mouth
of the creek in the fall of the year in large numbers, winter
underground, and return to the river in the spring, when many
are caught in a trap fixed between the creek water and the
river.

"*Minerals, etc.* Iron ore abounds in every part of the
county. Coal of good quality is found in many places.
Marble, considered good, abounds about Estillville—lime and
free stone quarries are abundant—salt water has lately been
discovered by boring at the distance of upwards 300 feet below
the surface, in the Poor Valley, near the North Fork of Holston, and about 8 miles east of Estillville. The proprietor,
Col. James White of Abingdon, is now letting down pipes and
making preparations to work the well. The quality and quantity of the water is not yet fully ascertained in consequence
of the interference of fresh water, which was struck first near
the surface; there, however, appears to be no doubt among
those employed at the well but that it may be profitably
worked.

"The Holston Springs situated on the North Fork of Holston, south of Estillville 2 miles, or 4 miles as the road runs,
is considered by many to be not inferior to any springs in the
State for medicinal virtues of the water, but as yet has gained
no great celebrity in consequence of the accommodations being
inferior to those of most other watering places.

"The White Sulphur Springs (Hagan's), near the Rye Cove
north west of Estillville 8 miles, is considered equal to the

Catawba Springs in Washington county. There are many other Sulphur Springs in the county of less note.

"There are in the county, exclusive of the town of Estillville, 9 meetinghouses, 6 of which belong to the Methodists and 3 to the Baptists; the Methodists also have 18 or 20 other preaching places in the county, where they have societies formed and preach every other week; 6 stores, 4 tanyards, 10 licensed houses of private entertainment, 4 hatter shops, 33 mills, some of which are very ordinary, others make good flour, but none are entitled to the appellation of merchant mill. To 10 or 15 of these mills, saw mills are attached, and to two, carding machines.

"The climate is somewhat milder than that of Washington or Russell counties—vegetation commencing at Estillville one or two weeks sooner than at Abingdon or Lebanon. There is but one practicing attorney besides those residing at Estillville, and no regular physician.

"The population in 1820 was 4,263, in 1830, 5,724. It belongs to the 15th Judicial Circuit and the 8th District. Tax paid in 1833, $646.73; in 1834, on lots $25.76; land, $273.95; 180 slaves, $45.00; 2032 horses, $121.92; 13 studs, $55.00; 3 carryalls, $3.00; Total, $524.63. Expended in educating poor children, in 1832, $242.61; in 1833, $361.56.

"*Towns, Villages, Post Offices, etc.* Estillville post village and seat of justice 357 miles south west of Richmond and 433 south west of Washington. It contains besides the county buildings, 61 dwellings houses, 2 houses of public worship, 1 Methodist and 1 Presbyterian, 1 academy, 1 common school, 1 female do., 4 mercantile stores, 2 tanyards, 2 saddlers, 3 blacksmiths, 1 extensive hat manufactory (this was Stephen Paxson's), 2 cabinetmakers, several house carpenters, and various other mechanics. It is situated on Moccasin Creek, between North Fork of Holston and Clinch rivers, and 4 miles from Holston Springs, which are now visited by much company and said to be equalled by none except the Sweet Springs, to which they have considerable resemblance. This place is supplied with water by means of pipes, through which it is brought 800 yards and is conveyed to every dwelling. The water is of the purest and best quality. This place possesses some of the best water falls and sites for manufacturing establishments in Western Virginia, and other advantages not to be surpassed by any village in the State. The country around abounds with stone, coal, and iron ore, and salt water has lately been obtained in great quantity within 6 miles of the courthouse. A northern, southern, eastern, and western mail arrives in this village once a week. Population, 200 persons, of whom three are resident attorneys, and two regular physicians.

"County Courts are held on the 1st Wednesday after the 2nd Monday in every month—quarterly in March, June, August, and November.

"Circuit Superior Courts of Law and Chancery are held on the 2nd Monday in April and September by Judge Estill.

Osborn Ford P.O., 20 miles north of Estillville

Pendleton P.O., situated 12 miles north of Estillville

Stock Creek P.O., situated 11 miles west of Estillville, near the Natural Tunnel." (Martin's *Gazetteer of Virginia,* published in 1835.)

THE SYCAMORE CAMP

About one mile above the Natural Tunnel on the banks of Stock Creek, then sometimes called "Buckeye Creek," there once stood a giant, hollow sycamore. It was of such enormous size that fifteen persons, it is said, could easily find shelter within it at the same time, hence the name "Sycamore Camp." The remains of the tree could still be seen in 1831. (Martin's *Gazetteer of Virginia.*)

SCOTT COUNTY IN 1840

(Extracts taken from Howe's *Historical Collections.*)

"Scott was formed in 1814, from Lee, Washington, and Russell, and named for General Scott: Its mean length is 24 miles; mean breadth 23 miles. It is drained by the North Fork of Holston and Clinch Rivers, each of which affords the facilities of boat navigation in time of freshets. Big and Little Moccasin and Sinking Creeks also water the county. The face of the country is mountainous and uneven, and much of the soil is good. Iron, coal, marble, limestone, and freestone are found within its limits. About 60,000 pounds of maple sugar are annually produced. The population in 1840, was 6,911 whites, 344 slaves, 48 free colored making a total of 7,303.

"Estillville, the county seat, is 344 miles southwest of Rich-

mond, and 40 miles from Abingdon. It contains 3 stores, a
Methodist Church, and about 60 dwellings. The Holston
Springs are on the North Fork of Holston, 4 miles from the
Courthouse. The medicinal qualities of the water are excellent, and its growing reputation, together with the improvements lately made, draw a large number of visitors. The
water contains all the ingredients of the White Sulphur
Springs, the principal difference is the existence in the later,
of sulphuretted hydrogen. The uniform temperature of the
water is 68½°, which renders it a natural medicated bath of
the most agreeable heat."

DESCRIPTION OF THE NATURAL TUNNEL

(From Howe's *Historical Collections.*)

"The Natural Tunnel is situated upon Stock Creek about
12 miles from Estillville (now Gate City). The description
is extracted from the communication of Lieutenant Colonel
Long, of the United States Army, and published in the monthly
American Journal of Geology for February, 1832: To form
an adequate idea of this remarkable, and truly sublime object,
we have only to imagine the creek to which it gives passage,
meandering through a deep, narrow valley, here and there
bounded on both sides by walls, rising to the height of two or
three hundred feet above the stream; and that a portion of
one of these chasms, instead of presenting an opening cut from
the summit to the base of the high grounds, is intercepted by
a continuous unbroken ridge more than three hundred feet
high, extending entirely across the valley, and perforated
transversely at its base, after the manner of an artificial tunnel,
and thus affording a spacious subterranean channel for the
passage of the stream.

"The entrance to the Natural Tunnel, on the upper side of
the ridge, is imposing and picturesque, in a high degree; but
on the lower side, the grandeur of the scene is greatly height-
ened by the superior magnitude of the cliffs, which exceed in
loftiness, and which rise perpendicularly—and in some instances in an impending manner—more than 300 feet; and
by which the entrance on this side is almost environed, as it
were, by an amphitheater of rude and frightful precipices.

"The observer, standing on the brink of the stream, at the
distance of about one hundred yards below the outward opening of the Natural Tunnel, has in front, a view of its arched

entrance, rising seventy or eighty feet above water, and sur-mounted by horizontal stratifications of yellowish, white, gray rocks, in depth nearly twice the height of the arch. On his left, a view of the same mural precipice, deflected from the springing of the arch in a manner to pass thence in a continu-ous curve quite to his rear, and towering, in a very impressive manner about his head. On his right, a sapling growth of buckeye, poplar, lindens, etc., skirting the margin of the creek, and extending obliquely to the right, and upwards through a narrow, abrupt ravine, to the summit of the ridge, which here and elsewhere is crowned with a timber-growth of pines, cedar, oaks, and shrubbery of various kinds. On his extreme right, is a gigantic cliff lifting itself up perpendicularly from the water's edge, to the height of about 300 feet, and accom-panied by an insulated cliff, called the chimney, of about the same altitude, rising in the form of a turret, at least sixty feet above its basement, which is a portion of the imposing cliff just before mentioned."

AN OLD SETTLERS' STORY ABOUT THE NATURAL TUNNEL

"A gentleman informed us that the time he first visited the Tunnel, some persons were inside extracting saltpetre, and that the smoke belching forth from its mouth and curling up the gorge, enhanced the natural gloom and hideousness of the scene. In the late war, when saltpetre was very scarce, the small fissure in the wall of rock—at that place over 300 feet high—attracted attention, and it was determined to explore it. An adventurous individual, by the name of George Dot-son, was accordingly lowered from the top by a rope running over a log, and held by several men. The rope not being suf-ficiently long, the last length, which was tied around his waist, was made of bark of leather wood. When down to the level of the fissure, he was still 12 or 14 feet from it horizontally, being thrown so by the overhanging of the wall of rock. With a long pole, to which was attached a hook, he attempted to pull himself to the fissure. He had nearly succeeded, when the hook slipped and he swung out into the middle of the ravine, pendulum-like, on a rope of perhaps 150 feet in length. Re-turning on his fearful vibration, he but managed to ward him-self off with his pole from being dashed against the rock. When away, he swung again. One of his companions, sta-tioned on the opposite side of the ravine to give directions, in-stinctively drew back for it appeared to him that he was slung

at him across the abyss. At length the vibrations ceased. At
that juncture Dotson heard something crack above his head;
he looked and saw that a strand of his bark rope had parted.
Grasping with both hands the rope immediately above the spot,
he cried out hastily, 'Pull, for —— sake, pull.' On reaching
the top, he fainted. On another occasion, the bark rope being
replaced by a hempen one, he went down again and explored
the cave. His only reward was the satisfaction of his curios-
ity. The hole extended only a few feet." (Howe's *Historical Collections*.)

"A PERILOUS MOMENT"

(A story of the Natural Tunnel.)

"Soon after the close of the Civil War, the Rev. H. C. Neal
was sent to travel a circuit in Scott County that included the
Natural Tunnel within its bounds. Returning one Monday
morning from a charge where he had preached the day before,
his route led him over the Tunnel, and he stopped to take the
view from its summit.

"Now, the surface of the Tunnel on each side of the highway, is covered with a low growth of bushes, and on its southern side, from which the view is the more remarkable, it is
comparatively level to within a short distance of the edge when
it begins a gradual but constantly increasing slope downward.

"Turning from the highway, the preacher rode through the
bushes, intending to hitch his horse and then proceed on foot.
But in winding about he had gone further than he suspected,
and feeling the animal sink in front, he checked him, and
looking forward, beheld the yawning chasm only a short distance away.

"He was now on the edge of the downward slope with only
some small bushes between him and the abyss. Apprehending
no danger, however, he was quietly gazing into the immense
void, when his horse suddenly slipped forward. Rain had
fallen the night before and the thin coating of dirt was soft
and yielding. The rider now perceived his danger and attempted to turn his horse's head, when the animal again slipped
forward.

"The danger was now real—the slope was becoming steeper
—the edge of the chasm nearer. The rider drew hard on the
reins, and soothed his horse with soft, encouraging words.
Intending to throw himself from the saddle, he relaxed

slightly his hold on the reins; but at once the animal again began slipping.

"Tightening his hold on the reins, he checked the slipping for the instant; then, almost imperceptibly, it continued.

"The danger was now imminent—the preacher realized it, the horse did also, and trembled in fear. The draw of the chasm—that reaching up of invisible hands to pull them down —could be felt. Momentarily they neared the edge.

"It was at this terrible instant that the sliding forward suddenly ceased, and the horse sank to his haunches.

Carefully, cautiously, and soothingly, the rider slipped from the saddle and seized a low, stout shrub with one hand while he held the reins with the other. Crawling upward the length of the reins he caught another shrub, and then pulling gently he turned the horse's head, when the animal struggled to his feet, and followed the rider to the summit.

"Here the trembling horse stood panting, and the rider lay on the ground so overcome with weakness that it was some time before he was able to walk.

"Returning to the scene of the narrowly escaped tragedy— this time on foot—he saw that a ridge of flint protruding above the limestone had caught the animal's feet and held the weight of the horse and rider in that perilous moment." (Prof. H. W. Fugate in *The Youth's Companion.*)

SCOTT COUNTY IN 1930

Southwestern Virginia, Incorporated, an organization that is doing much for the industrial development of this section of Virginia, arranged with the Engineering Extension Division, Virginia Polytechnic Institute to make an industrial survey of Scott County. The survey was prepared by R. L. Humbert, director of surveys, and is replete with facts and figures of interest to citizens of the county. I quote the chapter on the *Present Industrial Development,* given in the above mentioned survey.

"At the present time there is a limited amount of industry in Scott County. The list herewith given in connection with this discussion shows that but four of the sixteen groups listed in the Census of Manufactures, published by the United States Department of Commerce, are represented in the county.

"The greater part of the industry in Scott County is located at Gate City, the county seat and largest community. Two of the four 'lumber and allied products' plants, the largest printing establishment, and the largest quarrying operation in the county are located here. The towns of Dungannon, Cassard, Hilton, and Clinchport all have very limited industry at this time. The quarrying operations lead the local industrial field in so far as capital invested, volume of production, and number employed are concerned. These are the only large-scale operations in the county.

"The above discussion does not include the mining operations, which are taken up separately. Mining, however, is not carried on as extensively in Scott as it is in Lee County, so that business conditions in Scott are not so much a reflection of conditions in the coal fields.

"*Source of Raw Materials.*—Most of the raw materials now used in Scott County are secured at home. The lumbering operations obtain wood from the local forests; the mills utilize homegrown grains; the concerns in the 'stone, clay, and glass products' group obtain almost their entire supply of raw materials locally. Scott County is rich in natural resources and many have merely been touched. The study of the county's natural resources shows that Scott is in many respects a frontier county now awaiting development."

CLASSIFICATION OF INDUSTRIES

Food and Kindred Products

Elmore Darnell's Cannery (Hill)
Bond's Mill (Nickelsville)
Gillenwater's Mill (Hill)
Jayne's Mill (Gate City)
Lunsford's Mill (Hilton)
W. P. McConnell's Mill (Snowflake)
Neeley's Mill (Clinchport)
Peter's Mill (Fort Blackmore)
W. E. Price's Mill (Speer's Ferry)
Ramey's Mill (Speer's Ferry)
Bellamy's Mill (Gate City)
Darnell's Mill (Gate City)
Williams's Mill (Gate City)

Lumber and Allied Products

Gate City Planing Mill (Gate City)
Tate Planing Mill (Yuma)
Wing Planing Mill (Dungannon)
H. P. Grogan Handle Company (Gate City)

Paper and Printing

Service Printery (Nickelsville)
Gate City Printing Company (Gate City)

Miscellaneous Industries

Marcem Quarries Corporation (Gate City)
Pennsylvania Glass Sand Company (Cassard)
Silica Sand Corporation (Hilton)
Simpson and Crawford (Clinchport)

AGRICULTURE IN SCOTT COUNTY

"Scott County Farms.—According to the United States Census of Agriculture, 1925, there were 3,696 farms in Scott County, the same number recorded in 1920, but 302 less than the number for 1910. Most of the farms range in size from 3 to 260 acres and almost one-third are from 20 to 50 acres in size. The consolidation of some of the smaller farms has increased and should continue to increase gross receipts to Scott County farmers. Contrary to the usual situation in southwestern Virginia, the number of farms has materially decreased since 1910.

Farms of Scott County According to Size in 1925

Size	Number
3 to 6 acres	343
10 to 19 acres	506
20 to 49 acres	1,047
50 to 99 acres	949
100 to 174 acres	554
175 to 259 acres	182
260 to 499 acres	89
500 to 999 acres	25
1,000 to 4,999 acres	1
Total	3,696

"Farm Population and Wealth.—The total farm population
in 1925 was 17,907. This figure indicates that approximately
72 per cent of the total population of Scott County live on
farms.
"The total gross income for the county in 1928 was $2,-
395,300—an average of $648 per farm. Among the 100
counties of Virginia, Scott ranked 22nd in amount of gross
farm income. This income was realized from an investment
in land and buildings of $11,978,674, according to the 1925
Census of Agriculture."

The Population of Scott County by Magisterial Districts 1930

Floyd District 1,934
Dungannon Town 282
Fulkerson District 2,693
Johnson District 3 247
Nickelsville Town 263
Powell District 3,564
Clinchport Town 338
Duffield Town 170

HIGHWAYS

There are 702.5 miles of public highways in Scott County.
According to the records of the State Department of Highways, 70.72 miles of these roads belong to the state system.
There are 28.25 miles of hard-surfaced construction and 42.47
miles of conditioned highway. The remaining 631.78 miles
are included in the county and district roads.
Federal highway No. 411 enters the county about nine miles
northwest of Bristol, Washington County, and follows a general northwesterly course into Lee County, passing through
Gate City and Clinchport. State highway No. 108 runs from
north to south, beginning at federal route No. 411, about two
miles east of Gate City and extending to the Tennessee border.
The highway is all hard-surfaced within the county. State
route No. 107 branches off from federal highway No. 411 at
Gate City and follows a northerly course across the eastern
portion of the county. State highway No. 106, now under
construction, leaves federal route No. 411 at Clinchport and

follows a northwesterly direction, passing over the famous Natural Tunnel and going into Lee County. The entire length of this highway is to be improved by hard-surface construction. State route No. 122 from Coeburn, Wise County, enters the county, passes through Dungannon, and intersects route No. 107 northeast of Nickelsville.

COURTHOUSE, GATE CITY

WRECK OF RYE COVE SCHOOLHOUSE

THE RYE COVE TORNADO

On Thursday, May 2, 1929, one of the most destructive storms ever known in this county, swept over Rye Cove, leaving a track of damage and death in its wake. It came up suddenly out of the Southwest, and struck the Rye Cove School building at 12:55 P.M., just as the pupils were beginning to assemble for the afternoon session of school. In a moment the building began to collapse, and the air became filled with flying timbers, and the bodies of pupils. When the storm had subsided, it was found that one teacher and twelve pupils had lost their lives, that scores of other pupils had suffered injuries of greater or less severity, and that the school house had been lifted from its foundations and completely wrecked.

The injured ones were rushed to the King's Mountain Memorial Hospital at Bristol, and the hospitals at Kingsport. The Red Cross organization came at once to the aid of the suffering. Generous and sympathetic people in Gate City, Kingsport, Bristol, and elsewhere responded nobly to the needs of the injured and the bereft.

A beautiful memorial school building has been erected on the site of the one demolished by the storm. It is called the Rye Cove Memorial High School. At the suggestion of Mrs. W. D. Smith, a bronze tablet, suitably inscribed, and bearing the names of the teacher and pupils who were killed in the storm, has been placed on the school building. The inscription on the tablet follows:

Rye Cove Memorial High School is erected to the memory of the children who lost their lives when the school house was destroyed by a tornado, May 2, 1929.

LIST OF THE DEAD

AVA CARTER (Teacher)	POLLY CARTER
MILLIE STONE	BRUCE COX

283

BERTHA DARNELL	LILLIE CARTER
JAMES CARTER	MONNIE CARTER
BERNICE FLETCHER	GUY DAVIDSON
CALLIE BISHOP	MONNIE BISHOP
EMMA LANE	

PLACED BY MRS. W. D. SMITH

Farm houses and farm property in the path of the storm were greatly damaged. Its path may be roughly described by saying that it extended from Carter Town in Rye Cove to the head of Stony Creek, where it seems to have lost its fury.

THE INDIAN CAVE

Scott County has a number of interesting caverns within its territory. In Powers Hill, near Dungannon, overlooking Clinch River, and in line with the subterranean passageway of Sinking Creek through Powers Hill, there is the "Sounding Cave," so called because it seems to be the home of the Cave-dwelling Echoes, and the "Petre Cave," so named because it furnished saltpetre during the Civil War. Then, too, near the Natural Tunnel, there is a cave into which the daring Capt. Joseph Martin entered and killed an armed Indian. But the cavern that seems to be most nearly connected with prehistoric times, and well known to the aboriginal inhabitants of our territory, is located in the Purchase Ridge in sight of Duffield, Va.

This cave measures from 8 to 10 feet in diameter and from 25 to 30 feet in depth. It seems to have been used by the Indians as a burial place. Some years ago, the late Col. A. L. Pridemore had a thorough investigation made of its contents and found that it contained a large quantity of human bones, long, black human hair, teeth, skulls, Indian pipes, shells, beads, fragments of deer horns, and small pieces of mulberry wood. It is said that medical students were able from this collection of bones, to fit out complete skeleton with few misfits as to size of bones.

Colonel Pridemore obtained an excellent collection of Indian relics from this cavern, which he later donated to the College of William and Mary. (Data furnished by J. D. Carter, Sr.)

"FORTY-NINERS" FROM SCOTT COUNTY

February 2, 1848, James Marshall, superintendent of a saw mill belonging to Captain John A. Sutter, rode into Sacramento, carrying a small quantity of shining particles of gold which he had picked up in a mill race where he worked. Gold had been discovered in California. Sutter tried to keep it secret, but all to no avail. When the news of the discovery reached the old settlements in the east, men took the "gold fever," rushed to California by every means of travel that would bring them to this land of fabulous wealth. Of the number who went from Scott County were the following: Ewell Gardner, William Gardner, J. C. Larkey, Sr., John H. Hilton, E. B. Hilton, W. O. Hilton, Elijah Hart, Henry Hicks, John Larkey, and Samuel Steele. Most of these men lived to return home, rich in experience, and with varying quantities of the shining metal that had induced them to make a transcontinental journey in search of it.

INTERESTING COURT ORDERS

Ordered that hitch racks sufficient to hitch 150 horses be erected along the back street of Estillville and that Ephraim Hickam superintend the construction to be made of locust timber. (14–97.)

May 17, 1867, ordered that in future all persons are prohibited from using the courthouse of Scott County for any purpose except for the purpose of Religious Worship, Sabbath School, and Prayer Meeting, and the meetings of the Masonic Fraternity of Catlett Lodge, and if the officer registering the voters of this county shall require it they may use the courthouse or any of its rooms except the county and circuit court clerk's office. (14–214.)

John D. Templeton, Sheriff of this county, came into court and with the assent of the court resigned his office as Sheriff. Whereupon in pursuance to general order No. 48 this court would respectfully recommend to General J. M. Schofield, commanding the 1st military district, William C. Fugate, as a suitable person to execute the duties of Sheriff in this county, August 16, 1867. (14–266.)

In accordance with the above recommendation, William C. Fugate was appointed Sheriff, September, 13, 1867. (14–275.)

Ordered that James M. Hickey be and is hereby appointed a commissioner for the purpose of examining the courthouse to see how much the said house is damaged by holding concerts therein and report to court. (14–276.)

On motion permission is granted Prof. Gale and students to use the courthouse for necessary time for the purpose of holding their Exhibition therein at the close of the present session of the school. (14–420.)

Ordered that Henry S. K. Morison be and is hereby appointed a commissioner to purchase a suitable carpet for the courthouse and make such improvement about the courthouse door as in his judgment will be most conducive to comfort also to have two good iron scrapers placed upon the steps of the courthouse. (15–402.)

The court taking into consideration the improvement necessary to be made on the public jail do hereby appoint Andrew McHenry to repair the same so as to make a dungeon of the present jail, the debtor room to be ovei it, and an entry south in front of the doors with annexed room for the jailor and family to be built, the whole of brick or wood with grates, locks, and doors, etc. The said McHenry to be and remain under the direction of this court, and to perform the same with the public money, and for his attention to have one hundred dollars, and said McHenry is also to cause in like manner such repairs to be made to the courthouse as this court may direct. (2–78.)

Ordered that the clerk of this county be permitted to keep his office at the Holston Springs. (M 1–236. October 14, 1817.)

On the motion of John Dickinson, who produced the Sheriff's receipt for the tax imposed by law, a license is granted him to keep an ordinary at the house called the Estillville Hotel in Estillville in this county until the next May term of court on his entering into bond in the penalty of $150, with good security conditioned as the law directs; the court being satisfied that the said John Dickinson is a man of good character, and not addicted to drunkenness. (4–19. May 13, 1828.)

A writing executed by John Dickinson emancipating his negro slave Clara and her infant child Mariah from and after the 1st day of October, 1829, was acknowledged in court and ordered to be recorded. (4–70. October 15, 1828.)

The court taking into consideration the necessity of a good road from Abingdon to Estillville, Scott County, and being fully convinced that to come down what is called the lawyer's path crossing the North Fork of Holston to Little Mocksin Gap and thence down the river and Poor Valley to Big Mocasin Gap, so as not to cross the river between the two Gaps, would be much the best and nearest way; and do respectfully request the court of Washington County, to have the said way opened so far as it passes through their county; and do hereby assure the court of Washington County, that nothing shall be wanting on the part of the court of Scott County, to complete the said road, so far as it passes through the county of Scott. (February 10, 1839. 4–97.)

On the motion of Charles C. Johnson who has been returned to represent this district, including this county, in Congress and whose election is contested by Joseph Draper, it is ordered that Lewis B. Dulaney and John S. Martin be appointed commissioners on behalf of said Johnson to take the depositions of witnesses in said contest, they being first duly sworn for that purpose. (4–415 October 11, 1831.)

Ordered that on tomorrow be let to the lowest bidder the building of a stock and pillory to be done and finished in six months from this date, and to be done and completed in workman-like order, June 11, 1816. (CM 1–99.)

Ordered that Stephen Wallen be overseer of the road from the center of Clinch Mountain in Big Mocqueson Gap to the Flat Lick, October 17, 1787. (Court Minute Book, Russell, 1–80.)

Ordered that William Huston view the best way for a road from the Kentucky Road in Big Mocqueson Gap to Huston's Mill, October 17, 1787. (Court Minute Book, 1–80.)

Ordered that John Watts Crunk be overseer of the road from John Blackmore's Old Fort to the Flat Lick. (Court Minute Book, Russell, 1–246.)

The Court having received a communication from the Board of Commissioners for the purpose of carrying into effect the provisions of an Act passed 4th March last entitled, "An Act Making Provisions for the Removal of Free Persons of Color," which has been duly considered, and it appearing to the Court that there are no free persons of color in this county who are willing to emigrate to the western coast of Africa. It is therefore ordered that it be accordingly certified to the Board aforesaid. (5–116.)

The Court deeming it expedient to have a pillory, whipping post, and stocks erected on the public square of this county, do hereby appoint William H. Morison a commissioner who is requested to have the same built out of proper materials on the best terms he can, to be paid for out of the next county levy, and that he make report thereof to this Court. (6–70.)

Tobacco was a medium of exchange when the territory of Scott County was first settled. Court witnesses and court officers were often paid in tobacco.

Ordered that Andrew McHenry be appointed as commissioner to superintend the making af a ducking stool, and to be erected as near the courthouse as possible.   (June 11, 1816 CM 1–99.)

William Agee came into court and moved the court to have it entered of record that the earmark of his stock is a swallow fork in the left ear and under-kut in the right which is accordingly done.

BIOGRAPHICAL SKETCHES

JAMES L. SHOEMAKER

JAMES L. SHOEMAKER was born near Lebanon, Russell County, Virginia, December 7, 1807. He was descended from an honorable ancestry. James Shoemaker, his grandfather, was a member of an old English family and immigrated to America in the year 1749. When the Revolutionary struggle with the mother country came on, he espoused the cause of independence, enlisted in the American Army, and fought under Col. William Campbell, of Washington County, at the battle of King's Mountain. His maternal grandfather, Solomon Litton, was born December 24, 1751, in Washington County, Virginia. Solomon Litton and his family were among the early immigrants into the State of Kentucky. In 1778, while the Revolutionary War was raging and the American patriots were being assailed by the British soldiers on the one hand and the Indians on the other, Litton, his wife, and two daughters were captured by the Indians and carried to Quebec, at which place they were held until the close of the war, when they were exchanged. Elizabeth, one of the captured girls, became the wife of Joseph Shoemaker, the father of James L.

Following out the pioneer impulses which took him to Kentucky, James L.'s father continued to go west—this time to Lafayette County, Missouri. Here James L.'s father died, and his mother survived her husband three years.

James L. Shoemaker's opportunities for acquiring an education were very meager. Like many young men of his time, his chance to prepare for the duties and responsibilities of life was simply to assume them and learn by experience. How well he did this is shown by his success in business and the philanthropic disposal of a lifetime's savings.

He began business in Estillville (now Gate City) as a member of the firm of Alderson and Shoemaker. Later he bought Alderson's interest and continued a successful business in his own name. He was not an ambitious man, seeking high positions and political preferment; he chose instead to serve the people of his county in less remunerative, though probably more important, trusts. He was enumerator of the federal census of 1840 and 1850, land assessor several times, and county court clerk. In all these positions his integrity and accurate business methods made him a trusted official. The papers submitted by him as land assessor were declared by the officials at Richmond to be the best in the state.

This quiet, businesslike, patriotic citizen, remembering his own difficulties in obtaining a limited education, and seeing the great need for increased educational facilities in Scott County, had for some time prior to his death cherished the idea of giving a large part of his wealth to found an institution of higher learning, to be called "Shoemaker." He often expressed the purpose of giving

$5,555 for the erection of a building and the remainder of his estate for an endowment fund, the proceeds of which were to be expended in paying the expenses of deserving students, financially unable to help themselves. It was his desire that the institution be located in Scott County, where, as he said, "I have made my money here in Scott County, and I want these people to be the beneficiaries of it when I am gone."

After his death, which occurred January 9, 1894, it was found from his will that he had given the principal part of his estate to the cause of education. Scott County realized $7,500 from his estate. This sum was used in founding Shoemaker College.

Two daughters were born to James L. and Aurelia Paxton Shoemaker; Elizabeth, born January 10, 1844, and died September 9, 1845; Mary A. W., born June 8, 1846, and died September 1, 1852.

His wife was a daughter of Henry and Rachel Ritchie Salling. They were married July 5, 1842. His family and he are buried in Estill Cemetery, Gate City, Virginia.

JONATHAN WOOD II

JONATHAN WOOD, JR., was a son of Jonathan Wood, Sr. He was born near Fort Houston, on Big Moccasin Creek, April 23, 1778, and died April 2, 1848. He took prominent part in the early history of the county. He was recommended to His Excellency the Governor of Virginia by the first court as a suitable person to be added to the list of magistrates for the county. Acting on this recommendation, the Governor appointed him as magistrate, and he qualified at the June term of court, 1816. At the May term of 1819, he qualified as a constable of the county. On February 13, 1821, he became sheriff of the county, a position which he again held in 1822. He served as commissioner of the revenue for the South Side; he was also county surveyor for many years.

JONATHAN WOOD

JONATHAN WOOD, the subject of this sketch, was descended from a long line of Johns and Jonathans, these being, it seems, favorite family names in the Wood family. Many of his descendants have borne and continue to bear the names John and Jonathan to this day. John Wood, the father of Jonathan, was born in Westmoreland County, Virginia, about the year 1708. Soon after his marriage he settled in Loudon County, near where Leesburg now stands. Here he accumulated a large estate for that day.

John Wood had three sons, Isaac, John, and Jonathan, the last named being the subject of this sketch.

Jonathan Wood was born in the year 1745. He married the widow Osborne, whose maiden name was Nancy Davidson, in the year 1767. In about the year 1770, he immigrated to Southwest Virginia and located on Big Moccasin Creek, within the present limits of Scott County. His home was situated near Fort Houston, to which place he went for safety in time of threatened Indian attack. For an account of his experiences as a pioneer in Big Moccasin Valley see the history of Fort Houston, given elsewhere in this work.

Jonathan Wood had three sons and one daughter, named respectively, John, born March 25, 1771; Henry, born May 18, 1773; Jonathan, born April 23, 1778; Polly, born February 19, 1799.

Jonathan Wood, Sr., died November 13, 1804. His wife Nancy survived him more than twenty years. She died April 17, 1827.

JAMES P. CURTIS

AMONG the skillful workers in wood and metal which old home manu-
facturing produced, none, perhaps, outranked James P. Curtis. He
was the son of Claiborne Curtis and was born near Norfolk, Virginia,
October 28, 1824. In 1844, he was married to Lucinda Meredeth, of Pulaski
County, Virginia. In 1881, he came to Scott County and located near Hiltons,
Virginia.

As a cabinet maker, Mr. Curtis' handiwork was much sought after. He
manufactured a turn plow that had a wide sale. He invented a churn that
could be run by the motion of a rocking chair. He was also a millwright
and wagon maker. But he was best known in this section as a gunsmith.
During the Civil War he manufactured sabers for the Confederate Army. It
is estimated that as many as a thousand guns were the output of his shop.

He was the father of sixteen children, of whom five are yet living, Hugh C.,
Robert L., Thomas P., Mollie, and Edna.

James P. Curtis died July 30, 1908, and Lucinda, his wife, died March 4,
1908.

GEORGE McCONNELL, SR.

A T THE close of the War of the Revolution, George McConnell, Sr., accompanied by a brother and a sister, came from Ireland to this country. They landed at the Port of Philadelphia and located in the State of Pennsylvania. Soon after his arrival, George entered the employ of a German gentleman named Snavely, who was engaged in a wholesale mercantile business in Philadelphia. Snavely had one child, a daughter, named Susana, whom George married. His father-in-law then gave him an interest in the mercantile business. On the death of Susana's parents the entire business passed to George and his wife. In the course of time, however, George McConnell had large sums of security money to pay, which so crippled his business that he determined to seek a new country in which business could be done on less capital than in Philadelphia. With the remnant of his fortune, he set out to find a new country and settled within the present limits of Russell County, Virginia. Here he again engaged in the mercantile business. Failing to profit by his Philadelphia experience, he again became involved in security debts, with the result that he closed out his business and moved within the present limits of Scott County, where he bought a farm and became a farmer. Here he was pursued by debt and forced to sell his farm. It was purchased by his son, George McConnell, Jr., who permitted his parents to remain in their old home until so enfeebled by age it was thought unsafe for them to be left alone.

George McConnell, Sr., was commissioned a justice of the peace for Scott by the Governor of Virginia, upon the recommendation of the court that he was a suitable person to hold such office. The oldest justice in a county became sheriff, according to statutory provisions. George McConnell held the office until he became the oldest justice and therefore became sheriff of the county. In the performance of his duties as sheriff, he hanged John Tumns, the first man executed for murder in Scott County.

The children of George, Sr., and Susana McConnell were: George, Jr., Kate, Thomas, Price, Elizabeth, Henry S., Joab Watson, Priscilla, William G., Samuel R. and Susan.

FAYETTE McMULLEN

FAYETTE McMULLEN was born and reared in Scott County, Virginia. He was fortunate enough to secure a good common school education for his day. He earned a livelihood by driving a stage coach. Entering the field of politics early in life, political honors came to him in rapid succession until his later days, when his political good fortune seemed to desert him. In September, 1826, he was appointed commissioner of the revenue for the South Side of Scott County, and he qualified for the office at the next term of court. He was also made captain of the One Hundred Twenty-fourth Militia Regiment in the same year. In February, 1832, he became a member of the county court. He discharged the duties of these smaller offices in such way as to attain a large measure of local popularity.

In 1838, he was elected to the Senate of Virginia, an office to which he was re-elected each succeeding term until 1849. In 1849, he was elected to Congress, in which body he served four consecutive terms, from 1849 to 1857. In 1857, he was appointed Governor of Washington Territory for a term of four years. He was also a member of the Confederate Congress and served in that body from February 22, 1864, until the capture of Richmond.

After the Civil War, he sought re-election to Congress, but was defeated each time.

He met death in a railroad accident near Marion, Virginia, in 1881.

DR. J. B. WOLFE

J. B. WOLFE was born at Charlottesville, Virginia, February 18, 1833, and died at Joplin, Missouri, June 19, 1906. He was educated at the University of Virginia, receiving both his academic and medical training in that institution.

In the late fifties, he came to Scott County and not long thereafter married a Miss Wilson, of Russell County. Some years later he purchased the Robin Kilgore farm, at the Old Fort House, near Nickelsville, and lived there many years.

Late in the year 1878, he became superintendent of schools of Scott County, succeeding R. E. Wolfe in that office. He held the office for two consecutive terms. Under his administration the schools of the county prospered and greatly increased in number. His scholarly attainments fitted him to administer the free school system in its infancy and do pioneer educational work in the county.

Dr. Wolfe was one of the leading physicians in the county, as well as one of its most polished scholars. He was member of the Baptist Church and a minister of the gospel. He is buried in the cemetery at Nickelsville, Virginia.

JOHN McKINNEY

JOHN McKINNEY emigrated from the neighborhood of Mt. Airy, North Carolina, into this section, while it was yet a part of Washington County, some time between the years 1785 and 1800. He settled on what is now known as Red Hill, near the village of Pattonsville, Virginia. He acquired a large landed estate and undertook the growth of cotton on a large scale with the many slaves he had brought with him from North Carolina. The climate of this section, however, not being suited to the successful growth of cotton, he directed his attention to the cultivation of tobacco. He grew tobacco on a large scale and manufactured it into cigars and plug tobacco. He also planted large apple and peach orchards on different parts of his large plantation.

It is thought that he sustained a close and familiar relationship with Daniel Boone, if not a kinsman, as the following letter found among his papers seems to disclose:

"Tuscaloosa County, Allabama.

"Dear Brother Sister I onc mor Right you a few Lines to inform you that wee ar all well at this time only muself I have ben Down about tow month and am very sik at this time wee have Received a letter from our Dauter at Brother James they are all well at that time you have Rot to mee concerning my part of that land I dont know hardly what to Right. I am willing to take Sixty Dollars for my part but I Dont how I am to get from here to their after it I am in great need of it but propety wont sute mee If you have a mind to giv mee that and can send it to me by the mail it will obled mee very much.

So nothing more only Remains

Your Friend
Daniel Boone.

It is thought that reports of the country made by Boone, who came from an adjoining county in North Carolina, influenced McKinney to settle in this section.

In 1804, he was appointed captain of militia for Lee County by the Governor of Virginia. He represented the County of Lee in the General Assembly of Virginia from 1906 to 1809. When Scott County was organized, he was a member of the first court, and in September, 1815, he was the ruling magistrate or chairman of the county court. In 1815, and again in 1816, he was appointed commissioner of the revenue for the North Side. In 1816, he qualified to celebrate the rites of matrimony. In 1818, and again in 1824, he was made school commissioner for the school district in which he lived.

In 1819 and in 1820, he qualified as sheriff of the county. It is said that while living in the same house, he was sheriff of Lee County, and then later sheriff of Scott County when it was formed.

In partnership with W. H. Carter and a Mr. Osborne he discovered and made salt at what is now known as Blackwater, Virginia. Many of John McKinney's papers, in an excellent state of preservation, are in possession of his descendants. Some of them date back to the year 1775 and show a wide range of business transactions.

He leaves no descendants in this section bearing his name; branches of the Morison, Harris, Young, and Carter families are descended from him.

He died about 1824 or 1825, and his wife died in 1840.

He is buried in an unmarked grave on Red Hill, about one mile south of Pattonsville, Virginia.

JOHN ANDERSON

JOHN ANDERSON was born in Augusta County, May 6, 1750. He married Rebecca Maxwell, daughter of George Maxwell, who was a soldier at the Battle of King's Mountain. The time of his coming to the Blockhouse on the Holston is not certainly known—some time prior to 1782. On August 24, 1781, the commissioners of Washington and Montgomery counties granted him title to 200 acres of land, lying on south side of Clinch River, in Elk's Garden, since he had proved to the court that it was settled and improved by him in the year 1775. (*Bristol Herald Courier*, Boone Trail Edition.) This fact would place him among the first settlers in this section. He was the owner and builder of one of the most widely known stopping places on the Wilderness Road to Kentucky. In fact, the Blockhouse may be regarded as the starting place for that road for a number of years. During the ten or fifteen years period of greatest travel into Kentucky, many thousands of people passed his door into the Wilderness. Hundreds of these travelers, no doubt, stopped at the Blockhouse for some sort of entertainment—to rest awhile, for a meal, for a night's lodging, or, perhaps, to spend several days in awaiting the gathering of a company sufficiently large to travel through the wilderness in safety.

William Brown, who traveled over the Kentucky Trace in 1782, thus records his stay at the Blockhouse: "We waited hereabouts near two weeks for company and then set out for the wilderness with twelve men and ten guns, this being Thursday, July 18." (1782.) Such companies as are here mentioned, no doubt, were often entertained by John Anderson and his family. It sometimes happened that his guests could make no other return for their entertainment than to furnish him with wild game during the period of their stay. Hunter's Branch was so called because the Blockhouse hunting parties passed up and down its course in going to Clinch Mountain to hunt. John Anderson and the few keepers of ordinaries, thinly scattered along the Wilderness Way, made large contribution to the early settlement of Kentucky and the Middle West.

The Blockhouse was not immune from Indian attack; twice Anderson and his family had to flee to Fort Clapp, near Abingdon, to avoid being massacred by the Indians. (*Bristol Herald Courier*, Boone Trail Edition.)

On February 14, 1815, the first day of the first term of court held in Scott County, John Anderson produced a commission from Wilson C. Nicholas, then Governor of Virginia, appointing him sheriff, the most important office in the county at that time. John Wood and Jacob Seaver were his sureties. Isaac Anderson and Isaac Skillern were his deputies.

John Anderson was recommissioned sheriff of the county at the February term of court, 1816. On June 11, 1817, he was authorized to celebrate the rites of matrimony according to the rules of the Presbyterian Church, of which he was a member. The records of the clerk's office fail to show that he ever exercised the authority thus vested in him.

His children were: William, born October 31, 1776; John, born October 5, 1778; Mary, born February 15, 1781; Elizabeth, born March 6, 1783; Audley, born March 11, 1785; Sarah, born February 7, 1787; Isaac C., born May 3, 1789; Jane, born January 30, 1791.

John Anderson died at the Blockhouse, October 13, 1817, at 12:30 P.M. and Rebecca, his wife, died February 21, 1824, at 2:30 P.M.

REV. ROBERT KILGORE

CHARLES KILGORE, the father of Robert Kilgore, was born in Ireland, about the year 1744. He, with four brothers, immigrated to America about the year 1763. After the Revolutionary War, he and two of his brothers, William and Robert, Sr., came to Fort Blackmore, in Scott County. In March, 1783, Charles Kilgore, James Green, and a man by the name of McKinney left Fort Blackmore and went to the Pound River in Wise County to hunt, and while there they were surprised by Indians, and Charles Kilgore and James Green were killed. McKinney made his escape and returned to the fort. A searching party led by McKinney found the bodies of Kilgore and Green, and buried them in the hollow of a large chestnut tree on the north bank of the Pound River, a short distance above the mouth of Indian Creek. Charles Kilgore left one child, a son named Robert, then about eighteen years of age. James Green left a young widow and a baby boy one or two months old. About two years subsequent to the death of his father and Green, young Robert Kilgore married Jean Porter Green, the widow, who was a daughter of the pioneer, Patrick Porter. To this union were born the following children: Charles, born December 1, 1785; Susana, born June 2, 1788; Robert, born February 12, 1791; Jean, born July 20, 1793; Winney, born April 10, 1796; Nancy, born July 15, 1799; Ann, born, June 15, 1801; Mary, born December 21, 1807.

Robert Kilgore is now best known by a piece of his handiwork, which still survives in fair condition. He was the owner and builder of the Kilgore Fort House, situated at the ford of Copper Creek, about two miles southwest of Nickelsville. He seems to have erected the building sometime between his marriage in 1785 and the year 1790. He occupied the old fort house until his death in 1854. More than once he and his family were threatened with Indian attack in the early days of his occupancy of it.

He was one of the pioneer Baptist ministers in this section.

He died March 29, 1854, and his wife, Jean Porter Green Kilgore, died September 25, 1842. Both are buried in the cemetery at Nickelsville, Virginia.

REV. REUBIN STEELE

ALTHOUGH the gospel ministry of the Rev. Reubin Steele ceased more than fifty years ago, yet he is affectionately and reverently remembered by those who knew him unto this day. He was a tower of strength to the church of his choice in this section, and left the savor of a good name wherever he went.

He was born September 29, 1802, in Wythe County, Virginia. When he was three or four years of age his father moved to Whitley County, Kentucky, where Reubin grew to manhood. On reaching manhood's estate, he returned to Virginia and spent most of his life in the counties of Russell, Lee, and Scott. His conversion grew out of a promise made to his dying father, that he would try to meet his father in heaven. He was first given license to exhort, in which capacity he served for five or six years.

On June 7, 1827, he was married to Miss Elizabeth Newberry, daughter of Samuel and Jerusha Newberry.

He was licensed to preach in 1836 by the quarterly conference of Clinch River Mission or Jonesville Circuit, over which Samuel Patton presided.

His first wife died in 1837, leaving him with five small children.

His second marriage was to Miss Elizabeth Forkner, daughter of Rev. Isaac and Sarah Forkner, September 9, 1841. The fruit of this marriage was ten children.

His first ministerial work was done in the mountains of Southwest Virginia, close along the Kentucky border, in 1837. He was truly a pioneer in this field where he formed a number of societies which he later organized into a mission that was served by him in 1838, under the direction of Thomas K. Catlett, his presiding elder. In 1839, he traveled the Clinch River Mission, and in 1840 he was junior preacher upon the Greeneville Circuit under G. F. Page. He was admitted into the Holston Conference in 1841. After traveling circuits for a period of three years, he located, the condition of his family being such that he could not go far away. He was ordained deacon in Knoxville, Tennessee, October 9, 1842, by Bishop Waugh. During this time he was directly instrumental under God in the conversion of seven thousand souls and eight thousand accessions to the church. He was chaplain of the Sixty-fourth Virginia Regiment during the Civil War.

He was familiarly and affectionately called "Reubin Steele," "Brother Steele," and "Father Steele" by the people to whom he had ministered so long.

He died August 20, 1876, and his funeral sermon was preached by the Rev. John Boring to a large concourse of people at Pattonsville in October of that year.

AUBURN LORENZO PRIDEMORE

A L. PRIDEMORE was born near Purchase, Scott County, Virginia, June 27, 1837. He received a limited education, owing to poor educational opportunities in his neighborhood during his boyhood days. He managed, however, to complete preparatory studies, which constituted his educational equipment for his life work. He graduated in the school of experience—a school which developed many strong men in his day. During the Civil War he raised a company of volunteer infantry for the Confederate Army and served as its captain until June, 1862. Military promotions came to him rapidly. He was promoted to major, then lieutenant colonel of infantry, and to colonel of cavalry. He commanded the Sixty-fourth Virginia Cavalry until the close of the War. In 1865, he was elected a member of the Virginia House of Delegates, but the War prevented him from taking his seat in that body.

On returning to civil life, he decided to study law and was admitted to the bar in 1867. He commenced the practice of law in Jonesville, Virginia.

He was elected to the State Senate in 1871–1875. Two years later, he was elected as a Democrat to the Forty-fifth Congress. On the expiration of his congressional term, he resumed the practice of law in Jonesville, which he continued until the time of his death, May 17, 1900.

THOMAS, JOSEPH, AND NORRIS CARTER

THOMAS, JOSEPH, AND NORRIS CARTER, three brothers, sons of Peter and Judith Norris Carter, of Fauquier County, Virginia, were among the earliest settlers in the Rye Cove. Thomas was born April 24, 1731. He removed his family to the Cove in 1773, where in March, 1774, he obtained a grant of 197 acres of land. In 1783, he acquired an additional grant of 1,420 acres, to include his improvements.

When Fincastle County was abolished, he then became a citizen of the new County of Washington. Some years later, without having moved his domicile, he became a citizen of Russell County.

Thomas Carter administered the estate of Dale Carter, who was murdered by the Indians. He qualified March 18, 1778, with Richard Stanley and William Houston as his sureties. He was an overseer of roads in Washington County from 1776 to 1784. He was a justice in the first court of Russell County and also a lieutenant of the militia. In 1788, he represented Russell County in the General Assembly of Virginia. His will was probated in Russell County, October 25, 1803. His son, Charles, was clerk of the County of Lee for many years.

Norris Carter, a brother of Thomas, lived on Cove Creek and was the father of six sons, from whom a large number of the Carters of the present day are descended. His will, probated August 13, 1816, was the first probated in Scott County. Judge C. T. Duncan, a great-grandson of his, made the principal address at the centennial celebration of the organization of the county in 1915.

Joseph Carter, the other brother, settled in what is now called Cartertown and built the house now owned by J. Mosby Carter, a great-great-grandson. The house is built of logs and at first had only small portholes for windows. These portholes in later years were enlarged to the size of modern windows. (Data furnished by Prof. I. C. Coley.)

ELDER DAVID JESSEE

DAVID JESSEE was born in Russell County, Virginia, March 20, 1805, and departed this life November 13, 1886, aged 81 years. His first marriage was to Martha Stinson, of Russell County; his second marriage was to Mary J. Elam, in September, 1869. By his two marriages, he reared a large and respectable family of eighteen children.

His conversion to Christ resulted from his hearing a sermon preached from the text: "Set thy house in order, for thou must die and not live." For almost fifty years, David Jessee was the faithful and beloved minister of many churches of his faith and order. With the exception of two years, he was chosen moderator of the Stony Creek Association from the time of its organization until his death. He preached his last sermon in Russell County, October 13, 1886.

At the fireside, he was a pleasant voiced and interesting talker. In the pulpit, he was neither brilliant nor eloquent as such things are ordinarily judged, but his excellent Christian character and his burning zeal for his Master gave to his sermons great weight. He was greatly beloved by the people to whom he ministered.

DAVID COX

I T HAS been stated elsewhere in this book that tradition represented David Cox as being one of the very early settlers at Fort Blackmore. Thomas W. Carter, in a letter to Dr. Lyman C. Draper, states that "David Cox died at his home on Stony Creek, one half mile north of Fort Blackmore, about 80 years of age. He came from North Carolina. He came to this county about 1791 and died about the year 1820." W. S. Cox, in a statement dictated a few hours before he died, says that the old Cox family Bible failed to give the date of his birth, but gave the date of his death as being February 28, 1828. If Carter was correct in giving his age as being about 80 years, then he must have been born about 1748.

Tradition represents David Cox as having been at one time a companion of Daniel Boone; that he was captured in the neighborhood of Stony Creek by the Indians; that he was carried as a captive into the North; that, after a period of from two to four years in captivity, he returned to his home on the Yadkin River, where he interested a number of persons in an attempt to make a settlement at the mouth of Stony Creek.

In the spring of 1777, when Benge is represented as having made a visit to Fort Blackmore, it was David Cox who, it was alleged, furnished Matthew Gray with an extra rifle, with which to shoot the gobbling Indian.

April 3, 1793, David Cox purchased 180 acres of land from Samuel Auxe. In 1817, David Cox, James Albert, and John Duncan, by paying the delinquent tax on the John Blackmore tract of land, became owners of a tax claim against it. As an outcome of this transaction, James Albert became the owner of "Blackmore's Old Fort," consisting of 300 acres. This same tract was then sold under a deed of trust to Goldman Davidson, who in turn sold it to James S. Cox.

JUDGE MARTIN BYRD WOOD

M. B. WOOD was born at Pleasant Hill, Scott County, Virginia. He was the son of J. O. Wood and Ann Godsey Wood. From a very early age he was a good student and developed a brilliant mind. Books of history and travel gave him great pleasure. He also read all the books of fiction obtainable. In those days they had high bedsteads, with curtains all around them, and as his father required all to work in the field, he often would hide under the bed and read. In March, 1862, he joined Stonewall Jackson's company in the Valley of Virginia and was wounded at the battle of Sharpsburg, September 17, 1862. It was a long time before he could walk. He then attended school at Virginia Military Institute, where he remained until it was burned in 1864 by the Federal General Hunter.

In 1867, the Wood family removed to Estillville, Virginia (now Gate City), and his father, James O. Wood, was elected clerk of the county court of Scott County, and M. B. Wood was made his deputy. He studied law and in 1870 was elected clerk of the county and circuit courts of Scott County. He was later elected judge of the court. In 1872 he was married to Miss Kate Mildred Dinwiddie. He later wrote a book of high literary merit, entitled *The Wood Family in Virginia,* and much other valuable history relating to the early settlement of Southwest Virginia. He moved his family to Bristol, Virginia, in 1888, where he lived until his death, November 17, 1908.

EMMETT W. McCONNELL

EMMETT W. McCONNELL was born in Scott County, Virginia, near Nickelsville, March 17, 1868. His parents were George W. McConnell and Nancy Berilla Greear. He is descended from George McConnell, Sr., the progenitor of the McConnell family in this section. In his boyhood, he attended the public schools at Glade Hollow schoolhouse, near his home. In 1886, his father sold his farm on Valley Creek and removed with his family to the State of Kansas, where young McConnell spent a portion of his young manhood.

Young McConnell chose for his life work a rather unique field in which to operate—that of originator, producer, and builder of scenographic spectacles and extravaganzas—a field in which he has achieved great success. Through his connection with world fairs and expositions, he has become an international figure, holding important concessions at expositions both in the United States and Europe. He is the creator and owner of many widely known scenographic spectacles. He began his career with the historical cyclorama of the Battle of Missionary Ridge, exhibited at the Spring Palace, Fort Worth, Texas, in 1890–91. He next produced the volcano of Kilauea of Hawaii for the World's Fair at Chicago, in 1893. The realistic reproduction of this volcano gave him an international reputation and his spectacles became an almost indispensable part of an exposition, no matter where held.

His spectacle of the battle between the Merrimac and Monitor, exhibited at the Jamestown Exposition, was invented and made at the request of Gen. Fitzhugh Lee. The British naval review spectacle, shown at the Shakespearian Exposition in London in 1910, was produced for Lady Randolph Churchill, wife of Lord Churchill and mother of Winston Churchill, the lord high admiral of the British Navy, at the time of the coronation of George V. Mr. McConnell was awarded a gold medal for this spectacle. At the Hunting Exposition in Vienna, Austria, under the auspices of Franz Joseph, Emperor of Austria, and under the personal direction of the Duke of Fürstenberg, he produced the Battle of Lissa, the first naval engagement between ironclad ships in Europe. He was awarded a gold medal of the first order for this achievement.

Mr. McConnell, in building Philippine, Hawaiian, and Samoan villages, imported great cargos of natives, their beasts of burden, their wares, and implements of their daily toil.

He is now (1932) making preparations to reproduce King Solomon's Temple and the Battle of Château Thierry for the Century of Progress Exposition, to be held in Chicago in 1933.

He has had part in the following expositions:

Spring Palace, Fort Worth, Texas, 1890–91.
Chicago World's Fair, 1893.

Midwinter Fair, San Francisco, 1894.

Tri-State Exposition, Tacoma, Washington, 1894.

Cotton States Exposition, Atlanta, Georgia, 1895.

Tennessee Centennial Exposition, Nashville, Tennessee, 1897.

Trans-Mississippi Exposition, Omaha, Nebraska, 1897–98.

Pan-American Exposition, Buffalo, New York, 1901.

South Carolina and West Indian Exposition, Charleston, South Carolina, 1902.

Louisiana Purchase Exposition, St. Louis, Missouri, 1904.

Jamestown Exposition, Norfolk, Virginia, 1907.

Seattle Exposition, Seattle, Washington, 1909.

British-Japanese Exposition, London, 1910.

Hunting Exposition, Vienna, Austria, 1910.

Panama-Pacific International Exposition, San Francisco, 1915.

Bronx International Exposition, 1918.

Sesqui-Centennial Exposition, Philadelphia, Pennsylvania, 1926.

Century of Progress, Chicago, Illinois, (in preparation), 1933.

The following is a list of some of the scenographic spectacles he has exhibited at various expositions:

Historical cyclorama of the Battle of Missionary Ridge; volcano of Kilauea; Hawaiian, Samoan, Fijian, Tahitian, and Solomon Islands villages; historical cyclorama; palace of illusions; Battle of Gettysburg; chute the chutes; old plantation; Hobson sinking the Merrimac; the Moorish palace; Philippine villages; the Johnstown flood; Jerusalem on the day of the crucifixion; Second Battle of Manassas; spectatorium, New York to the North Pole; the Galveston flood; Battle Abbey; marine "Shouspiel"; creation of the world; Battle of Lissa; mountain scenic railway; fighting the flames spectacle; Congress of the American Indians; King Solomon's Temple; the Battle of Château Thierry.

SUPT. W. D. SMITH

W. D. SMITH was born in Mecklenberg County, Virginia, June 1, 1861. His father, William A. Smith, enlisted in the Confederate Army as a member of the 59th Regiment of Virginia Volunteers, in May, 1861. His father was killed at the Battle of Petersburg, Virginia, July 10, 1864, after having seen more than three years of active service in the Confederate Army.

His mother having married a second time, the family came to Southwest Virginia, and located in the Clinch River Valley in Scott County, near the Hagan Springs. Here young Smith lived until he was about 14 years old.

His opportunities for an education were limited. The public free schools had not yet gotten well under way, and the private schools within his reach were not good. His attendance upon school was often interrupted by the necessity of turning aside to earn a livelihood. The family's removal to the vicinity of Estillville brought him within reach of Estillville Academy, then conducted by Prof. John B. Harr, an efficient and successful teacher. He entered the academy and at once took high rank as a pupil.

Unfortunately another removal of the family took him out of school for a time, but Professor Harr, by this time greatly interested in him, sought him out and generously provided the means for him to re-enter school. While in

312

school he was employed as a guard of the county jail by night, thus earning enough to defray his expenses in school.

He went from Estillville Academy to the Hamilton Institute, at Mendota, Virginia, a school then conducted by H. H. Hamilton and H. W. Bellamy. He was a pupil of this school for the period of three years.

On the completion of his course in Hamilton Institute, he became a teacher in the public free schools of his county under the supervision of Dr. J. B. Wolfe, then county superintendent.

In 1886, W. D. Smith was appointed county superintendent of schools, an office for which his experience as a teacher was an excellent preparation. He has held this office continuously from 1886 to the present time (1932). Superintendent Smith has been closely identified with whatever educational progress the county has made during the more than forty-five years of his incumbency in office.

When he came into office, he found the public schools poorly housed in log buildings, without equipment of any kind. He at once set for himself the task of providing better school buildings. The old buildings were discarded as rapidly as possible, and more commodious frame or brick structures erected. Through his efforts, his county was awarded the distinction for the best improvement in school buildings at the Jamestown Tercentennial Exposition in 1907.

As a benefactor to worthy and aspiring young men and women, struggling for an education, no one who has lived in the county has equaled him. Many who have now reached mature life can attest the truth of the preceding statement. In fact, helpful sympathy for young people which often took the form of financial aid to them is an outstanding characteristic of him.

Superintendent Smith has never sought high political office though more than once such preferment could have been his for the asking.

At various times, he has served as a member of the board of trustees for William and Mary College, for the State Teachers' College, East Radford, Virginia, and for the Virginia Intermont College, Bristol, Virginia. His long experience as a successful educator, taken with a very high order of executive ability, rendered his services valuable on any board of trustees.

W. D. Smith, I. P. Kane, and N. M. Horton organized the First National Bank of Gate City.

November 14, 1895, he married Miss Sallie Lou Minnich, a lady of rare beauty, ability, and culture, who was a great inspiration, and help to him in his various fields of labor. Their children are W. D., Jr., Rhea E., Howard C., and Sallie Lou.

LEONIDAS REUBEN DINGUS

L EE" R. DINGUS was born near Wood, Scott County, Virginia, January 4, 1873. His parents were Philip M. and Martha Banner Dingus. His early educational training was obtained, for the most part, in the public free schools of his native county. Outstanding among his early teachers, he is pleased to recall the names of Prof. Joe C. Vicars, and Prof. Wm. Floyd Ramey as being particularly helpful to him in the character of their instruction. He mentions Bickley's Schoolhouse, "Sugar Tree," and Riverview Seminary as places where he attended school in his boyhood.

Dr. Dingus is an alumnus of Milligan College, A.B., 1894; the University of Virginia, M.A., 1907; and Ph.D., University of Virginia, 1914; Graduate Student University of Chicago, summers of 1908, 1910, 1911, 1920; University of Berlin 1912–14; he also spent the summer of 1907, studying in France and Germany.

He has held professorships in the following institutions of learning: Professor of English and History, South Kentucky College, 1903–05; Professor of German, Richmond College, 1914–1920; Professor of Romance Languages, Transylvania College, 1920–25; Professor of Modern Languages, Transylvania College, since 1925.

314

Dr. Dingus' literary work embraces a wide range of subjects. His contributions to literature are as follows: "Study of Literary Tendencies in the Novellen of Theodore Storm"; "Chaucer's Verb" (based on a study of the "Knightes Tale" and the "Nonne Priestes Tale"); "The Indo-European Root 'Dha' as it Appears in Modern English"; "Beowulf Translated into Alliterative Verse—Selections"; "Max and Thekla in Schiller's 'Wallenstein' "; "Heinrich Heine's Attitude toward Religion"; "Southern Lyric Poetry"; "A Brief on Schiller's Esthetic Philosophy"; "New Europe and the Language Complex"; "The Virginia Contribution to Kentucky and Transylvania"; "Transylvania, the Pioneer College of the West"; "Founding of Transylvania College"; "Rivers as National Boundaries"; "A Word-List from Virginia" (being localisms and dialect words used in Scott County); "Lavan, a Short Story"; "The Abode of True Ideals, a Sketch"; "George and Polly, a Story of the Civil War."

Dr. Dingus did war work with the Food Administration at Richmond, Virginia, from the early summer of 1918 until the close of the War with Germany.

September 14, 1907, he married Miss Elizabeth Kilbourn, of Lancaster, Massachusetts, and has one daughter, Elizabeth.

Dr. Dingus is one of the ripest scholars the county has produced.

REV. FRANK Y. JACKSON

FRANK Y. JACKSON was born in Goodson, now Bristol, Virginia, and was brought to Scott County, a babe in his mother's arms. He grew to young manhood in the town of Nickelsville. He received his early training in the public free schools and the "subscription" schools of his home town. He regards himself fortunate to have been a pupil under the following teachers: Wm. Floyd Ramey, Joseph H. Ketron of Kingsley Seminary, T. W. Jordan, and E. E. Wiley.

In his young manhood, Mr. Jackson worked in the office of the *Scott Banner,* the county's earliest newspaper. While in the *Banner* office, he set the type for, and printed the first issue of bonds of the South Atlantic & Ohio Railroad.

Mr. Jackson attended Emory and Henry College in preparation for the ministry. He joined the Holston Conference in the year 1890, and has served the conference continuously since that time.

His first conference assignment was to the Bland Street Church, Bluefield, West Virginia. During the period of his ministry, he has served the following Churches in the order named: Mary Street, Bristol, Va.; Athens, Tenn.; Ducktown, Tenn.; Athens, W. Va.; Highland Avenue, Knoxville, Tenn.; Dayton, Tenn.; Centenary, Knoxville, Tenn.; Bland Street, W. Va.; Marion, Va.; Sweetwater, Tenn.; Grace Street, Bluefield, W. Va., Magnolia Avenue, Knoxville, Tenn.; Broad Street, Kingsport, Tenn. Mr. Jackson has always been an evangelistic pastor. He has conducted many successful evangelistic campaigns in various parts of the Holston Conference.

He married Miss May Carter, of Sweetwater, Tenn.

COM. RILEY F. McCONNELL, U. S. NAVY

R ILEY F. McCONNELL was born at the homestead of his grandfather,
Dr. A. B. McConnell, on Copper Creek, near Wayland, Virginia, July
22, 1884. His parents were J. H. ("Hop"), and Polly Alley Mc-
Connell. His early school days were spent in the public free schools of his
neighborhood, and at Shoemaker College at Gate City, Virginia.

In 1903, he was appointed to the U. S. Naval Academy by Congressman
William F. Rhea, from which institution he graduated June 6, 1907. While
at the academy, he took an active part in athletics, making the varsity foot-
ball, track, and gymnasium teams, and was selected as one of ten mid-
shipmen to take a special course in jiudo (Japanese wrestling).

Upon graduation, he was ordered to the U.S.S. *Vermont,* one of the battle-
ships of the Atlantic Fleet then commanded by Rear Admiral Robley D. Evans.
He served on the *Vermont* for five years, during which time he performed
the usual and routine duties assigned to a junior officer on capital ships.
For three years he was the ship's fire control officer and spotter. The ship
won the Gunnery Trophy for two years, and McConnell was commended
by his superior officers for the part he had in the contest. While on the
Vermont he made his first cruise around the world.

On July 8, 1912, he was ordered to temporary duty at the receiving ship,

Norfolk, in command of the Training Station at St. Helena. On August 12, 1912, he became Chief Engineer of the U.S.S. *Des Moines.* While he was serving on the *Des Moines,* she sailed for Mexico, and was present at Vera Cruz when that city was first taken by Felix Diaz.

On June 25, 1913, he was ordered to the Navy Yard, Mare Island, California, as Radio Officer of the Pacific Coast. In that capacity, he had charge of all the government radio stations on the West Coast, including those in Alaska. In the fall of 1913, he made an expedition to Alaska to repair and recondition the radio stations as far north as Sitka, Alaska. On July 10, 1915, he took command of the U.S.S. *Fortune,* and made a survey of the Samoan Islands for the purpose of locating a site for a radio station.

In 1917, he was transferred to the U.S.S. *Arkansas* as Navigator. The *Arkansas* joined the British Grand Fleet, thus becoming part of the Sixth Battle Squadron. After the surrender of the German Fleet, the *Arkansas* escorted the *George Washington* to Brest as it bore President Wilson to the Versailles Peace Conference. He was placed in charge of the radio activities of the Third Naval District. He received a letter of commendation from the Navy Department for the manner in which this duty was performed.

November 6, 1920, he was transferred to the U.S.S. *Ohio* as Executive Officer, and as officer in charge of the radio research laboratory which was maintained on this vessel. While in charge of this laboratory, the U.S.S. *Iowa* was placed under radio control, it being the first vessel ever to be so maneuvered.

He graduated from the War College in 1924, and was immediately assigned to duty at the Naval Torpedo Station, Newport, Rhode Island. In 1925, he went to Shanghai, China, and reported to Admiral C. S. Williams as his assistant Chief of Staff.

Upon the completion of his duty with the Asiatic Fleet, he was assigned to duty in the Bureau of Navigation. His duties in the Bureau of Navigation were to organize the Merchant Marine Reserve. His next service was on board the U.S.S. *Chicago* as Executive Officer.

His decorations: Victory Medal (Grand Fleet), Haitian Campaign Medal, Yantze Service Medal, Expert Rifleman Medal.

His promotions are: June 29, 1903, Appointed Midshipman; June 7, 1907, Past Midshipman; June 7, 1909, Ensign; June 7, 1912, Lieutenant (Junior grade); August 21, 1916, Lieutenant; October 15, 1917, Lieutenant. Commander; Sept. 21, 1918, Commander (Temporary); July 1, 1919, Lieut. Commander (permanent); November 1, 1923, Commander (Permanent).

On September 26, 1911, he married Miss Grace Otteson, Smith College graduate in Class of 1911, at Plainfield, New Jersey.

SYLVESTER P. McCONNELL

S YLVESTER P. McCONNELL was born March 16, 1829, and died
April 23, 1918. He was the son of George and Polly Compton Mc-
Connell, and the grandson of George, Sr., and Susanna Snavely Mc-
Connell. His ancestors had large part in the public affairs of Scott County
in its early days.

S. P. McConnell had long service in the public affairs of his county. Perhaps, no man of his time was better versed in county matters than he. In
1860, he qualified as Notary Public which was the beginning of his career as a
public officer.

At the county election held in May, 1864, he was elected clerk of the county
court for a term of six years. His term of service was interrupted, however,
by the close of the Civil War. While clerk, he secreted the court records,
for the period of a year, to keep them from being destroyed by Federal
forces. This act, no doubt, kept the records from being destroyed.

He was elected treasurer of the county, November 8, 1870. On January
1, 1874, he qualified as deputy treasurer for J. M. Harris. On May 27, 1875,
he was elected county clerk and circuit court clerk for a term of six years.
He served as deputy clerk under both John M. Johnson and Charles M.
Carter. On the death of J. H. Taylor, circuit court clerk, Major McConnell

was appointed to serve in that office until a successor of Taylor could be elected.

Through his long association with the courts, he had acquired a very extensive and trustworthy knowledge of law and the practical workings of county government. Thus he was freely consulted by his fellow citizens on matters of law, a service he was delighted to render.

He was deeply interested in the Confederate Reunions, and was chiefly instrumental in organizing the Capt. W. S. McConnell Camp of Confederate Veterans for Scott County. He prepared himself both in spirit and costume to celebrate these occasions.

In 1859, he was married to Miss Emeline Tolbert.

He is buried in Estill Cemetery, Gate City, Virginia.

GEORGE TALMAGE STARNES

GEORGE T. STARNES was born May 31, 1895, in Hunters' Valley, Scott County, Virginia. His parents were Peter J. and Martha Jane Starnes. His early educational training was received in the local public free school in his community. He was a student in the Rye Cove High School from 1910 to 1914; he entered Emory and Henry College, June, 1914, and was graduated from that institution with the degree of Bachelor of Arts; he entered the United States Army and served one year in France. On being discharged from the Army, he taught two years in the high schools of the state. He entered the Graduate Department of the University of Virginia, in June, 1921, and received the degree of Master of Arts, in June, 1922. He was Instructor in Economics, University of Virginia, 1922–24. He was a student at Harvard University, 1924–25, and received the M.A. degree there and the Ph.D. from the University of Virginia, in June, 1925. He was Assistant Professor of Commerce and Business Administration, University of Virginia, 1925–29, Associate Professor, 1929——.

Dr. Starnes has made substantial contribution to the literature of his chosen field of work—that of Economics. He is the author of "Sixty Years of Branch Banking in Virginia." He is also author of "Labor in the Industrial South," in collaboration with F. de Uyver and A. Berglund. He has contributed many articles on scientific and historical subjects to some of the leading magazines of the country.

He is a member of the Phi Beta Kappa, and Beta Gamma Sigma fraternities. He is also member of a number of scientific and learned societies. His name has appeared in "Who's Who in America."

He mentions J. Mitchell Taylor and Will Bond as teachers to whom he owes "a lasting debt of gratitude."

He, furthermore, mentions Walter J. Rollins and family as having rendered invaluable aid to him during the period of his struggle for an education.

He married Miss Miriam Thurman of Floyd County, Virginia, September 14, 1923. He has one son, William Thurman Starnes. He makes his home at Montibello Circle, University, Virginia.

DR. BAYARD T. HORTON

BAYARD T. HORTON, B.S., M.D., M.S. in Medicine, F.A.C.P., was born on the old Watkins' farm on Opossum Creek, Scott County, Virginia, December 6, 1895. His parents were Thomas F., and Ellen Watkins Horton. In 1898 they moved to Gate City, Virginia. He received his early training in Shoemaker College, which was later converted into Shoemaker High School, from which he graduated in 1914.

He entered the Academic Department of the University of Virginia in September, 1914, and continued his academic studies until December, 1917, at which time he entered the United States Navy and served during the World War. In the fall of 1918 he returned to his Alma Mater and entered the Department of Medicine. During the summers of 1919 and 1920, he completed his academic work for the B.S. degree, which had been interrupted by the World War. He received the degree of Bachelor of Science in 1921, and Doctor of Medicine in 1922 from the University of Virginia.

He was an intern in the University of Virginia Hospital from July, 1922, to July, 1923.

On leaving the University of Virginia he accepted the Professorship of Biology at Emory and Henry College, Emory, Virginia. He was also the college physician while at Emory. He entered The Mayo Foundation as a

Fellow in Medicine July 1, 1925. His services included general diagnosis, twelve months; pathologic anatomy, eighteen months, and medical hospital, two years. Following these services, the University of Minnesota bestowed the degree of Master of Science in Medicine, in 1928. He was appointed a first assistant in medicine, October 1, 1927; instructor in medicine, The Mayo Foundation, in July, 1929; and associate in medicine, The Mayo Clinic, in July, 1930. In June, 1929, he was awarded the John Horsley Memorial Prize of $1,000 from the University of Virginia for fundamental research in the field of surgery. His subject was, "Pyloric Block, with Special Reference to the Musculature, Myenteric Plexus, and Lymphatic Vessels." The American Medical Association had previously awarded him a certificate of honor for this work which was presented before the Minneapolis Session in 1928. In 1929 The American Medical Association, at the Portland, Oregon, Session, again awarded him a certificate of honor for clinical, physiologic, and pathologic studies of diseases affecting the blood vessels of the extremities.

He is a fellow of The American Medical Association, and of the American College of Physicians, and is a member of the Minnesota State Medical Association, The Central Society of Clinical Research, the Association of Resident and Ex-Resident Physicians of The Mayo Clinic and The Mayo Foundation.

He has contributed numerous articles to many of the leading medical journals of the United States, and he has delivered addresses before many of the principal medical societies in this country.

He is a member of the Sigma Xi, and the Phi Chi fraternities.

He was married to Miss Jane Heyl, of Charlottesville, Virginia, June 14, 1922.

BIBLIOGRAPHY OF B. T. HORTON, M.D.

1. Pyloric musculature with special reference to pyloric block. *Am. Jour. Anat.*, 41:197–225, 1928.

2. Hypertension and polycythemia; the so-called Geisbock's syndrome. *Med. Clin. N. Amer.*, 11:1535–1541, 1928.

3. Unusual cases of thrombo-angiitis obliterans: their association with polycythemia vera and traumatic myelitis. *Med. Clin. N. Amer.*, 12:1617–1627, 1929. (With G. E. Brown.)

4. Systemic histamine-like reactions in allergy due to cold: report of six cases. *Am. Jour. Med. Sc.*, 127:191–202, 1929. (With G. E. Brown.)

5. Evidence shown in roentgenograms of changes in the vascular tree following experimental sympathetic ganglionectomy. *Arch. Surg.*, 21:698–701, 1930. (With W. McK. Craig.)

6. A study of vessels of extremities by the injection of mercury. *Surg. Clin. N. Amer.*, 10:159–170, 1930.

7. Pyloric block with special reference to musculature, myenteric plexus and lymphatics. *Arch. Surg.*, 22:438–462, 1931.

8. Intermittent claudication in the extremities with pulsating vessels. *Med. Clin. N. Amer.*, 14:783–797, 1930.

9. Bacteriologic studies in thrombo-angiitis obliterans. *Proc. Staff Meetings of the Mayo Clinic*, 5:337–338, 1930. (With Anna H. E. Dorsey.)

10. Intracranial arteriovenous fistula: diagnosis by discovery of arterial blood in jugular veins. *Proc. Staff Meetings of the Mayo Clinic,* 5:178–180, 1930. (With L. H. Zeigler.)

11. Primary thrombosis of the axillary vein. *Jour. A.M.A.,* 96:2194–2196, 1931.

12. Abnormal arteriovenous communications. *Med. Clin. N. Amer.,* 15: 227–232, 1931.

13. Thrombo-angiitis obliterans among persons past middle age. *Ann. Int. Med.,* 5:613–624, 1931. (With G. E. Brown.)

14. Hemihypertrophy of the extremities associated with congenital arteriovenous fistula. *Jour. A.M.A.,* 98:373–377, 1932, (Jan. 30).

15. Incidence of lead in the urine in patients with peripheral vascular disease. *Proc. Staff Meetings of the Mayo Clinic,* 4:296, 1929. (With M. H. Powelson and A. E. Osterberg.)

16. Scleroderma treated by cervicothroacic ganglionectomy. *Proc. Staff Meetings of the Mayo Clinic,* 4:241–242, 1929. (With P. A. O'Leary and A. W. Adson.)

17. Atypical syndromes in Uremia; lipodystrophy involving lower extremities. *Med. Clin. N. Amer.* (In Press.)

18. Experimental thrombo-angiitis obliterans: bacteriologic and pathologic studies. *Arch. Path.* (With Anna H. E. Dorsey.)

19. Thrombo-Angiitis Obliterans among women. *Proc. of the Staff Meetings of the Mayo Clinic,* 7:107–109, 1932 (Feb. 24). (With G. E. Brown.)

20. Duodenal Diverticula. *Proc. of the Staff Meetings of the Mayo Clinic,* 7:185–186, 1932 (March 30). (With Selma C. Mueller.)

JOHN PRESTON McCONNELL

JOHN PRESTON McCONNELL, born on Obey's Creek, February 22, 1866, son of Hiram Kilgore McConnell and Ginsey Elizabeth Brickey McConnell, has been actively identified with educational and social welfare work and the development of the resources of the state, both human and material.

Educated at Milligan College, National Normal University, and University of Virginia, he has devoted his larger efforts to education as teacher in the elementary and secondary schools, college professor, dean and president. While professor in Milligan College, Tennessee, he conducted teachers' institutes and directed teacher-training enterprises in Tennessee and Virginia. The range and variety of his interests and activities are unusual in their scope. He has actively participated in a personal and official way, in most curative, constructive, forward-looking and upward-looking movements that have engaged the attention of the people of Virginia and the South for more than a third of a century.

Early in life he became a whole-hearted prohibitionist; has been identified with various organizations, state and national, throughout his life in opposition to liquor in any form for beverage purposes. He was a delegate to various prohibition conventions and an early member of the Anti-Saloon League of Virginia, member of its board, an officer, and for eight years President of the Anti-Saloon League of Virginia.

He was one of the first of the leaders in social welfare work in Virginia to actively advocate state institutional provision for the scientific treatment, educational, and vocational training of crippled children. He was one of the early promoters of the State Conference of Charities and Corrections and was for four years state president of this conference. He has always regarded his activities and identification with this conference as one of the most effective and satisfactory achievements of his life. In his addresses in all parts of the state and in almost every conceivable way, he maintained that the real test of a civilization is the care that the state provides for those who cannot care for themselves, such as children, aged, delinquent, abnormal and subnormal, the blind, and defective members of society.

In recognition of the work of himself and his wife in this field, three successive governors of Virginia have appointed his wife, Clara Louisa Lucas McConnell, for five-year terms, a member of the State Board of Public Welfare, which position she still holds.

As an educator and official in various capacities dealing with social problems, he became conscious of the hurtful effects of tobacco, narcotics, stimulants, excitants and alcohol in all forms for beverage purposes. He has waged for a generation an unceasing campaign in the schools and through various organizations to educate the people, particularly the youth, against the use of alcohol, tobacco, opiates, and narcotics.

For exactly a quarter of a century he has been either vice-president or president of the Co-operative Education Association of Virginia which has a membership of more than eighty thousand in all parts of the state, whose platform stands for better schools, better health, more satisfactory living conditions and conveniences in the home (particularly the rural homes), libraries in every high school community, better roads, better church facilities, better means of communication and social contacts. Much of his time and energy for a quarter of a century has been devoted to the promotion of the various ideals of the Co-operative Education Association.

Throughout life he has recognized the dignity and fundamental character of rural life and its basic industries, such as: agriculture, horticulture, stock-raising, and fruit-growing, and all of their related interests and activities in the State of Virginia. Through different organizations in the state, he has striven to bring to the minds of the people the worth of rural occupations and opportunities.

In his educational program he has always stood for equality of opportunity, training, and culture, for both men and women, and has always favored co-education. Early in life he adopted a definite conviction that there was no nobler vocation open for human beings than teaching. He has gloried in the title of teacher, holding that "God never made any man too smart or any woman too pretty to be a school-teacher." The fundamental conviction of Dr. McConnell is that ignorance is a cure for nothing, and that there is no thralldom so debasing as the thralldom of ignorance. He believes in education of all of the people and education for every vocation. This has been an absolute fundamental in his educational and social welfare projects and adventures.

He early embraced the ideal of preventive medicine and has campaigned the State of Virginia repeatedly urging communities, individuals, and groups to adopt preventive and constructive policies of public health rather than to rely upon curative policies or remedies.

He received in the colleges and universities a very thorough and extensive classical or liberal arts education, receiving the Bachelor of Arts and Master of Arts degree from Milligan College, and the degree of Doctor of Philosophy from the University of Virginia. He has found this type of education very beneficial and pleasant on account of its culture and its liberalizing effect on character and human life; however, he early realized that this classical and liberal arts education was not meeting the actual needs of the great masses of the people and that the teachers in public schools were very poorly trained for their work. He early reached the conclusion that the modern education with emphasis on modern science and preparation for the daily ordinary tasks of life of the great masses of people was fundamental in a democracy and was the surest guarantee of good citizenship, self-respect, economic and social efficiency.

In Tennessee and later in Virginia he became an active propagandist for the establishment of the very best type of teacher-training institutions. Notwithstanding his classical and cultural training he resigned as Professor of History and Dean of Emory and Henry College, where life was most congenial in every respect, to develop a State Teachers' College at Radford. In the last twenty years, he has been offered the presidency of three great colleges and one university with larger salary and fewer difficulties than confronted him in the development of the State Teachers' College at Radford; nevertheless, he unhesitatingly declined to accept any of those honorable positions and adhered to his task of training women for teaching and for all of the vocations that are open to cultured college women of the twentieth century. His ambition was and has been to make this college one of the best teacher-training institutions in North America. The recognition that has been accorded this college by the Southern Association of Colleges and Secondary Schools, the American Association of Teachers' Colleges, and other state and national evaluating agencies shows that this ambition has been achieved.

About seventeen per cent of all the white public school-teachers in Virginia are trained in this college, although there are forty-four different educational institutions furnishing teachers for the state.

He has participated in the organization and promotion of practically every educational and social welfare organization in Virginia and the South for the last third of a century. Dr. McConnell was the leading spirit in the establishment of the Virginia Society for the Study of Education and was its first president. He has held practically every office in the State Teachers' Association with a membership of more than ten thousand white teachers. He was president of the Southern Education Association, covering the whole South, in 1919. He was also president of the Southern Sociological Congress for the study and promotion of social welfare movements throughout the South.

As an illustration of his wide range of interests and activities, he has for almost twenty years been a member of the State Y.M.C.A. Executive Com-

mittee, a Director of the Children's Home Society of Virginia for the same
number of years, a Director of the Virginia Tuberculosis Association, a trustee
of the Crippled Children's Hospital for the State, a member of the Educational Committee of the State Chamber of Commerce for many years, and
chairman of the Educational Committee of the State Bankers' Association.
He has been a member of the Board of Trustees of various institutions of an
educational and social welfare character.

To promote education and social uplift in the Appalachian region, he and
Prof. J. R. Hunter of Emory and Henry College founded in 1911 the Appalachian School Improvement Foundation. This organization has amazing
accomplishments to its credit in Southwestern Virginia, East Tennessee, and
Western North Carolina. He was a moving spirit in calling state conventions
and promoting state-wide campaigns in Virginia in behalf of better schools,
better roads, and the general promotion of social welfare in the early twenties.
He has been a speaker and actively identified with the program of the Good
Roads Association of Virginia.

He has never been a candidate for political office. He was nominated for
Congress on the Prohibition ticket in the First Congressional District of
Tennessee, but, removing from the district, he did not make the campaign.
For many years he has been urged to become a candidate for State Superintendent of Public Instruction and also Governor of the State of Virginia. He
has never thought favorably of such candidacy, feeling that the education of
the people of Virginia in the first third of the twentieth century is the most
important and far-reaching service that he can possibly render the state.
This has been a very definite conviction with him from his early days when
he dedicated his life to the education and the promotion of social welfare
in general.

Thirteen years ago he became president of the Farmers and Merchants'
Bank at East Radford, Virginia, reorganized, and converted it from a state
to a national bank, and made it one of the leading banks in Southwest
Virginia. Supplementary to this banking enterprise, he participated in the
organization and became a director in many financial corporations such as
Radford Finance Corporation, Radford Insurance Corporation, Baldwin Land
Company, Radford Hospital Corporation, and various other business enter-
prises which have been uniformly successful.

Seven years ago he, in co-operation with others, organized Southwestern
Virginia, Incorporated, the most successful organization of its kind in Virginia,
in the interest of the development of the resources of Southwestern Virginia,
covering about one-fifth of the state.

He has for forty years been actively identified with the state and national
enterprises of the Christian Church of which he is a member. He is a member of the Board of Directors of the National Board of Education of the
Christian Church. He has been a member of the Board of Managers of the
Christian Church throughout North America, chairman of the National Board
of Recommendations of the Church, and chairman of the Commission on
Budgets and Promotional Relationships of this Church in Virginia.

In all of these activities the secondary desire of Dr. McConnell has been to show the public that a teacher can be a man of affairs and have a wide range of interests and achievements even though he is engaged in educational work. He has written a great number of newspaper articles, published addresses, and a book entitled "Negroes and Their Treatment in Virginia in 1865–67." He was a contributor to the ten volume history entitled "The South in the Building of a Nation," dealing with a period of Virginia History at the close of the War Between the States to the beginning of the twentieth century. He was also a contributor to the Library of Southern Literature.

Notwithstanding these various activities in fields more or less closely related to education, Dr. McConnell's chief ambition and interest has always been education. He taught in the public schools of Scott County, Rawlings Institute, Charlottesville; was professor of Latin and Greek in Milligan College, Tennessee, for ten years; was Professor of History and Dean of Emory and Henry College nine years, and was elected president of the State Teachers' College at East Radford, Virginia, in 1911, which office he still holds. Under his administration this college has grown in nineteen years to be recognized as one of the leading colleges in the state of Virginia and is recognized as a standard college throughout the nation.

W. D. SMITH, JR.

FEW young men who have only reached the early thirties in age have been able to crowd so many and varied achievements into a few short years as W. D. Smith, Jr. He was born at the Smith homestead, six miles from Gate City, Virginia. His parents were W. D., and Sallie Lou Minnich Smith. His early school days were spent in the local schools. He graduated from Shoemaker High School. In January, 1915, he matriculated in the University of Virginia, where he specialized in English and Literature under the instruction of Professors Charles W. Kent and C. Alphonso Smith. Prior to his entry into the University, however, he had evinced a taste for literature, and, as a juvenile writer, had contributed poems to the *Bristol Herald Courier,* and some stories to the *Times-Dispatch,* Richmond, Virginia. He went to New York City in the spring of 1916, where he contributed articles to various newspapers, and some poems to the *Pagan,* a magazine devoted to poetry. During these early years of writing, he used the *nom de plume* of Rex Rolland, Dan Walmere, etc. He now writes under the pen name of Rex Smith.

In 1917, he entered William and Mary College in which institution, he soon became editor of the *Flat Hat,* the leading student publication of that college. Returning to his native county in 1918, he taught English and History in Shoemaker High School for a time. Sometime later, he went to Detroit, Michigan, and joined the staff of the *Detroit News*, writing on general reportorial subjects. He then joined the Reserve Officers Navy Corps at the University of Michigan in which institution he continued to specialize in Literature, English, and History.

In 1920, he entered Washington and Lee University for one term. While at Washington and Lee, he still continued his newspaper work by joining the staff of the *Washington Herald*. About this time, he was named to the United States Diplomatic Service, and sent to San Jose, and Costa Rica, where he served as Vice Consul and Acting Consul. He assisted in handling the negotiations concerning the Panama–Costa Rica boundary dispute. The United States Government awarded him a medal for his services in this matter. His next diplomatic service was that of Vice Consul General at Lima, Peru. Sometime during his diplomatic service in South America, he became a guest student in San Marcos University.

On resigning his diplomatic office, he returned to the States, and joined the staff of the *San Francisco Examiner*. During his connection with this paper, he contributed articles, essays, and poems to the *Overland Monthly*, and the *San Franciscan*. In 1928, he went to Hollywood to write stories for motion pictures, at the same time maintaining his connection with the *Overland Monthly* and the *San Franciscan*. He became nationally known by his critical studies of noted personages which were featured by the *Theatre Magazine* of New York.

In the summer of 1929, he went to Europe, and traveled through Italy, the Balearic Islands, Germany, and Bavaria, collecting material for various literary enterprises which he had in mind. He joined the staff of the *New York Herald*, covering the French Foreign Office, and the various embassies in the French Capital. He covered alone the wreck of the British Dirigible R 101, with its tragic loss of life.

Returning home on account of his mother's illness, he accepted a position with the Associated Press as editor and staff writer of Spanish and Latin-American news for papers in the United States, and international news for papers that were members of the Associated Press throughout Latin America. He now (1932) is chief of the Associated Press Bureau in Madrid, Spain.

He has a volume of poems in course of preparation, entitled, "The Moon Minstrelsy."

CHARLES CROMWELL ADDINGTON

CHARLES CROMWELL ADDINGTON, the centenarian, was born in
Culpepper County, Virginia, October 10, 1777, and died at his home
on Copper Creek, January 18, 1882, aged one hundred and four years.
His father, William Addington, was born in London, England, and grew up
to young manhood in that city. He had excellent educational opportunities,
and in consequence thereof, acquired a good education. About the time he
reached the age of twenty, a steady stream of emigrants was then flowing
from the city of London and other parts of Great Britain into the North
American Colonies. Young Addington was also seized with the desire to join
the throng and emigrate to America, much against the wish of his parents.
They tried to dissuade him from going but failed. At length his father, seeing
that he was determined on making the adventure, furnished him with money

334

BIOGRAPHICAL SKETCHES 335

to pay his passage overseas and supply his needs for some time afterward. On landing at Norfolk, he traveled widely through eastern Virginia and North Carolina, and finally located near Culpepper Courthouse, Virginia. Here he married Margaret Cromwell, about the year 1774. When the Revolutionary War began, William Addington volunteered, and was made a commissary officer in Washington's army. He served in this capacity until the Surrender of Cornwallis at Yorktown, October 19, 1781, an event which he witnessed.

Soon after the War, William Addington moved to Caswell County, North Carolina, where he remained a short time. Hearing of a rich country in southwest Virginia where the land was good, the range fine, and bear, deer, and wild turkeys in abundance, he decided to seek this wonderful country. In the summer of 1785, he, in company with twelve other families, came to Russell County, Virginia, where he located in the Valley, north of the mountain, near Hyter's Gap.

Charles Cromwell Addington was a boy about eight years old when his father located on the southwest Virginia frontier. Among the immigrant families from North Carolina which settled about Hyter's Gap, was one named Doty; Anna, a daughter of this family, became the wife of Charles Cromwell Addington on January 2, 1802, and, in April of the same year, he located on Clinch River, within the present limits of Scott County, at a place known as the William Gillenwaters farm. This farm then had about ten acres of cleared land; the river bottoms were wet and marshy. During his residence there, the family contracted fever and ague, in consequence of which the location was adjudged unhealthful, and he removed to Copper Creek in the spring of 1805, where he lived until his death in 1882.

When Charles Addington first came to Russell County, that section was often visited by hostile Indians. His home was located near a fort to which the family often had occasion to flee for safety. He frequently related, in substance, the following story as having occurred near his home:

In the year 1790, the Indians made several raids in the neighborhood of Hyter's Gap. On one of these raids the house of a neighbor, named Musick, was attacked just at the break of day. Stealthily approaching the house, the Indians shot and killed Musick through a crack in the wall. They then forced an entrance and took his wife and nine children captive. It was three or four hours before the depredation became known to the neighborhood. Musick's dead body was accidentally discovered by someone who called at his house on an errand. As soon as the murder became known, the rifle-bearing men of the neighborhood gathered at the Musick homestead, and women and children were rushed to the fort for protection. The trail of the Indians was soon found, and the riflemen went in hasty pursuit. But the enemy, by this time, were about nine hours travel ahead of their pursuers. Late the third evening the scouts came in sight of the Indians as they were kindling their first camp fire. A council of war was held to determine the best manner of attack to rout the enemy and save the lives of the prisoners. It was decided that an attack should not be made until dawn the next morning. The plan of attack was: All were to charge the camp at full speed, one-third of the company were to discharge their guns into the air over the camp to make the Indians believe they were being shot at, the remaining two-thirds were to hold their fire in reserve, and shoot to kill if necessary. It was hoped in this way to so frighten the Indians that they would break camp and run without killing any of the captives. The plan succeeded admirably; the Indians fled headlong, leaving the prisoners unharmed, and much valuable plunder behind. Thus Mrs. Musick and her children were restored to her friends.

Charles Cromwell Addington was thrice married and twice widowed. The date of his first marriage has been given. March 15, 1840, he married Sarah Butcher, who died —————. January 4, 1869, he married Susan Moore, a widow, who survived him.

On October 10, 1877, his numerous posterity, and friends, honored him with a Centennial Dinner. On a table about two hundred feet long, the best food of the neighborhood was generously spread, and more than a thousand persons partook of the dinner.

On his one hundredth birthday, it was estimated that he had reared sixteen children, and had one hundred and seven grandchildren, four hundred and forty-three great-grandchildren, and seventeen great, great-grandchildren, making five hundred and fifty-three in all.

HENRY CLINTON WOOD

HENRY CLINTON WOOD was born in Scott County at Pleasant Hill, the old Wood homestead about three miles east of Gate City. He was the son of James O. and Elizabeth Godsey Wood. He spent most of his life in his native county. He received his early elementary training in the private schools of his county and then entered Fall Branch Seminary, a school then offering a liberal course in the higher branches of learning for that day.

When the Civil War came on, H. C. Wood organized a company in the county, which became part of the 37th Virginia Infantry Regiment. Captain Wood's company participated in the battles of Cross Keys, Port Republic, Gains' Mill, and Cold Harbor. At Gains' Mill, Col. S. V. Fulkerson fell mortally wounded. His death made necessary a re-adjustment of the officers of his regiment. Capt. Henry Clinton Wood was made Major, and J. H. (Harvey) Wood, his brother, was promoted to the position of Captain. Major Wood was present at, and participated in, forty-two engagements, varying in magnitude from the battle of Cross Keys to the battle of Gettysburg. He was wounded in the battle of Chancellorsville, but lost little time from his command. His was an excellent record in the Army. In military as in civil life he was very popular, making friends wherever he went. His military service was rendered in the Stonewall Jackson division of the Confederate Army. Upon leaving for the War, the ladies of his county presented him with a silk flag. At the Battle of Gettysburg, he captured a Federal flag. These two flags were preserved, and highly prized by him.

A number of political honors came to Major Wood. He was recognized as a prominent leader in his party for many years. He served two terms in the Senate of Virginia, and was Speaker of that body for the years 1881 and 1882. In 1885, he was the Republican nominee for Lieutenant Governor on the ticket with John S. Wise, but was defeated. In 1892, he was a candidate for Congress, but was defeated.

On his return from the War, Mr. Wood engaged in a successful mercantile business. He was prominently identified with the development of southwest Virginia. He labored a number of years in the endeavor to bring a railroad through his native county. He was the first president of the South Atlantic & Ohio Railway, which now owns the Appalachian Division of the Southern Railway.

He moved from Gate City to Bristol in 1891, and spent the remainder of his life in that city. He there became connected with numerous and important business enterprises. He made large contributions to the business and industrial development of his section.

He was a Mason, an Elk, and a Steward in the State Street Methodist Church of Bristol.

He was never married.

He was born February 15, 1836, and died December 8, 1909.

He is buried in the East Hill Cemetery, Bristol, Virginia.

RUFUS ADOLPHUS AYERS

R UFUS ADOLPHUS AYERS was born in Bedford County, Virginia,
May 20, 1849. His father, M. J. Ayers, was a son of Rev. John
Ayers, of the Methodist Episcopal Church, South; his mother, Susan
Lewis Wingfield, was a descendant of John Lewis, ancestor of the distin-
guished Lewis Family of Augusta County, Virginia.

While young Ayers was still of tender age, his father died, leaving the
family in straitened circumstances. He was, by this misfortune, thrown upon
his own resources, and compelled to make a way for himself.

He was enrolled as a pupil in Goodson Academy, Bristol, Virginia, until
1861, when the War closed the school. He never again re-entered school.

He worked as a clerk in a retail store until April, 1864, when he enlisted
in the Confederate Army, and continued in the service until the close of the
War. After the close of the War, he resumed the mercantile business only to
abandon it in 1873 to gratify a cherished ambition to study law. This he did
under his uncle, Judge G. A. Wingfield, of Bedford, Virginia.

On September 12, 1871, R. A. Ayers was appointed a Justice of the Peace
of Estillville District; and on May 27, 1875, he was elected Attorney for the
Commonwealth.

At about this time he was made Reading Clerk in the House of Delegates.

On April 27, 1876, he took charge of the *Scott Banner* as editor and proprietor. In this same year Mr. Ayers prepared a charter for a railroad between Bristol and Big Stone Gap, Virginia, and organized a company for its construction. In 1881, he assisted in the organization of the Virginia Coal and Iron Company. He organized the Bank of Gate City in 1889; the Interstate Finance Company and the Wise County Bank in 1901 and 1902; the Tazewell Coal and Land Corporation in 1904.

In 1880, he was Supervisor of the Census for the Fifth District of Virginia by appointment of President Hayes. In 1885, he was elected Attorney General of Virginia. He was given a vote of thanks by the General Assembly of Virginia for the course he took while Attorney General in reference to the State debt.

He represented the counties of Buchanan, Dickenson, and Wise in the Virginia Constitutional Convention of 1901.

He was a member of the Masonic fraternity and served as the Master of a Lodge.

On June 8, 1870, he married Victoria L. Morison. Three children of this marriage survive: Kate Lewis Ayers Pettit, Harry J. Ayers, and James B. Ayers.

He is buried in Estill Cemetery, Gate City, Virginia.

H. S. K. MORISON

HENRY SOLON KANE MORISON was born in Estillville, Scott County, Virginia, June 12, 1846, and died there November 9, 1899. Two of his ancestors, Peter Morison and Jonathan Wood, fought at the battle of King's Mountain under Col. Isaac Shelby.

He was the son of Henry A. Morison and Louise Elizabeth Kane.

His early education was obtained in Estillville Academy. In 1863, he entered the Virginia Military Institute as a cadet where he continued until that institution was destroyed by fire in Hunter's raid. He was prevented by illness from participation in the battle of New Market, where the Cadet Corps so signally distinguished itself. However, he took part in all other military enterprises in which the Cadet Corps engaged.

At the close of the war, he began the study of law in the office of his uncle, Henry S. Kane. In 1866, he entered the law school of the University of Virginia, of which John B. Minor was then a distinguished instructor. He was admitted to the bar in 1867, and commenced to practice in Scott and Lee counties. Within the period of his early practice, he formed a partnership with Colonel James W. Humes, of Abingdon, then one of the leading members of the bar in southwest Virginia. At the expiration of five years, this partnership was brought to an end by the premature death of Humes.

341

In 1870 he was elected Commonwealth's Attorney for Scott County and served until 1874, when he was elected Judge of the County Court, which office he held for six years. He was elected Judge of the Seventeenth Judicial Circuit in 1885, and served until 1892, when he resigned to resume his practice. The celebrated murder case of the Commonwealth vs. Dean was tried before him. Dean was convicted upon circumstantial evidence after two mistrials, in which more than one hundred witnesses testified, and although the case was appealed to the Circuit Court, and thence to the Supreme Court, the sentence was confirmed and executed.

After resigning as Judge of the Circuit Court, he was retained in a number of important cases. One of these was Emory and Henry College vs. Shoemaker, a case which attracted much attention because of the interests involved. He prepared a brief in this case, which for deep and analytical research, elegant and illustrative amplification, has seldom been surpassed.

Death came to him suddenly at 2:07 P.M. as he sat in his library with his family. The Board of Supervisors, then in session, ceased consideration of the business in hand, and passed resolutions of respect. (Supervisor Minute Book 2, page 376.)

He married Miss Annice Kyle, daughter of Col. A. K. Kyle, of Rogersville, Tennessee.

REV. JAMES B. CRAFT

THE subject of this sketch was born near Hill Station, Scott County, Virginia, April 16, 1859. His parents were William Craft and Margaret Stewart Craft. Having been born in the country, he knew a hardy, healthy boyhood. He was first a pupil in the so-called subscription schools, under the following teachers: Miss Laura Rhoton, R. H. Darnell, John Wolfenbarger, and Capt. George R. Dove. On passing from the subscription schools into the free schools he came under the instruction of such teachers as Profs. T. H. Mason, R. E. Wolfe, M. A. Riggs and A. Alley, for all of whom he cherishes fond recollections.

He professed faith in Christ at about the age of 20, in a revival meeting held by the Rev. Moses L. Ingram, and became a member of the Cartertown Baptist Church.

On September 15, 1880, he was united in marriage to Rachel P. Gillenwater, daughter of H. S. and Phebe Pennington Gillenwater. The children of this marriage were Mary Ellen and Ryland G.

Rev. Craft was baptized in Clinch River on New Year's Day, 1883, by the Rev. W. H. Hill. He was also licensed to preach by the Cartertown Baptist Church on the same day of his baptism. Three days later, he preached his first sermon at the home of Mrs. Elizabeth Darnell, an aunt of his, whose house had been a preaching place for many years. His ordination as a minister took place in Rye Cove on the 4th Sunday in March, 1883. D. L. and Emily Horton, first cousins of his, were the first persons baptized by him. He was one of the two first state Evangelists appointed by the Baptist State Mission Board. He has been twice elected Vice-President of the Baptist General Association of Virginia. He has been one of the Trustees of the Baptist Orphanage of Virginia for a number of years, a position which he continues to hold. As a Trustee of the Virginia Intermont College, at Bristol, Virginia, he has assisted a number of young women in obtaining scholarships, and other aid, in that institution. He also served as a member of the Board of Trustees of Bluefield College during the period of its early organization.

Rev. Craft represented Scott County in the House of Delegates for the session of 1887–88, but preaching the gospel has been his life's work for more than 46 years.

It is estimated that more than 5000 persons have professed faith in Christ in meetings in which he has labored, and the baptismal ordinance has been administered to more than 1500 people by him.

In July, 188-, the County Normal School, then in session at Washington Institute, Rye Cove, Virginia, presented Rev. Craft with a Bible in token of its esteem and appreciation. The presentation was delivered by the late Mark Horton.

In February, 1896, his first wife died. Some years later he married Miss Susan Carter of Rye Cove. By his second marriage, one daughter, Rachel, now Mrs. R. V. Wolfe, was born to him. In 1914, his second wife died, and on July 27, 1918, he was united in marriage to Miss Louise Tyler Ford, daughter of Senator George Tyler Ford of Loudon County, Virginia.

PATRICK HAGAN

P ATRICK HAGAN was born in County Tyrone, Province of Ulster,
Ireland, February 2, 1828, and immigrated to America in 1847. His
father was John Hagan and his mother was Ellen Campbell Hagan,
both members of prominent families in the old country. The name carried
the characteristic Irish prefix O' across the seas, but the O' has, for the most
part, been dropped here in America.

Patrick Hagan spent his childhood and youth in a village, and attended
the local schools. He had perfect health, and was fond of outdoor sports.
Quite early in life, he developed a taste for tales of adventure, history, and
literature which had much to do in shaping his life, and arousing his youthful
ambition. His parents hoped that he would become a priest when he had
reached manhood's estate, but the priestly orders did not appeal to him.
At the age of sixteen, he left the land of his nativity and came to America,
which was then becoming known to Europeans as a land of opportunity.
At the age of seventeen he became a partner with his brother in the grocery
business in Richmond, Virginia. Soon after his mercantile venture with his
brother, he decided to study law and at once became a pupil of Joseph Stras,
of Tazewell County, Virginia, a man deeply learned in the law. Mr. Hagan
was admitted to the bar in Scott County, at the August term of Court, in
1854. At the September term of Court, 1854, he was admitted to citizenship
by order of the Superior Court of Scott County.

345

In 1860, Mr. Hagan formed a law partnership with Mr. Jonathan Richmond, a brilliant lawyer of Lee County, which partnership continued until the premature death of Mr. Richmond. The office of Commonwealth's Attorney was made vacant by the death of Mr. Richmond. Mr. Hagan then became a candidate for the office. He was opposed by Peter C. Johnson. Mr. Hagan won in the contest, and was twice re-elected to the same office.

Mr. Hagan was an energetic and persevering worker. He made substantial and steady advance in his profession. As his practice grew, he began to specialize in pleading and land titles. In this branch of the law, he achieved almost national prominence. His briefs before the Supreme Court of Virginia were characterized as models of lucidity, law, and concise argument by Professor John B. Minor.

In the financial and business world Mr. Hagan's achievements fully measure up to his success in the law. He accumulated a considerable estate through the income of a large law practice, and through wise investments in coal and other mineral lands in southwestern Virginia. Patrick Hagan's generosity was almost proverbial. Those stricken by poverty seldom appealed to him in vain. The poor were his friends.

In his extensive law practice he was often met, either as colleague or opponent, with such men as Hon. William Pinkney Whyte, Hon. John Randolph Tucker, and Gen. B. F. Butler, and in such company he took high rank.

Mr. Hagan was a lover of books, and read widely and carefully. Often in common conversation he would quote some fine passage of literature. He was an author himself, having written articles on a wide range of subjects. In religion, he was an ardent believer in the doctrines of the Roman Catholic Church.

Mr. Hagan married Mrs. Elizabeth Grubb, whose maiden name was Elizabeth Young, a daughter of Jonathan and Sallie Roberts Young. Eight children were born to this union, four of whom yet survive.

Mr. Hagan died at his beautiful country home, Sulphur Springs, Scott County, Virginia, February 23, 1917, at 7:30 A.M.

He lies buried in a private cemetery near by the home he loved so well.

JAMES BUCHANAN RICHMOND

JAMES BUCHANAN RICHMOND was born February 27, 1842, in
Turkey Cove, Lee County, Virginia. His father, Jonathan Richmond,
was a farmer, merchant, Chairman of the old Lee County Court, State
Senator, and General of Militia. His mother was Mary Dickinson before her
marriage.

In his boyhood, he worked on his father's farm. He received his early
training in the schools of his neighborhood. He was also a student in Emory
and Henry for a time. He entered the Confederate Army as a volunteer,
in June, 1861. He was made a captain of Company A, 50th Virginia Infantry, which position he held for a year. He was then promoted to the
rank of Major, and later to Lieutenant Colonel of the 64th Virginia Mounted
Infantry, in which position he served until the close of the War.

In 1865, he became a merchant at Jonesville, Virginia. He was later
associated with Wright Stickley in the mercantile business at Fort Blackmore; he then removed to Estillville, Virginia, where he continued in the
mercantile business for a short time.

About this time, he decided to study law, and entered the University of
Virginia, where he became a student under Professor John B. Minor. He
was admitted to the bar in September, 1874.

In 1873, he was elected to the Legislature of Virginia, and in 1878, he was elected to the Forty-sixth Congress of the United States. In 1885, he qualified as Judge of the County Court of Scott County. He retired from the bench to become General Counsel for the South Atlantic & Ohio Railroad, a position which he held until the company was reorganized.

He was chosen to represent Scott County in the Virginia Constitutional Convention in 1901 and 1902.

On his retirement from the bar, he became president of the Peoples National Bank, which position he held until his death.

He was twice married: first to Lizzie Duncan, 1864; second, to Kate Morison, 1870.

He died in Baltimore, Maryland, April 30, 1910, and is buried in Estill Cemetery, Gate City, Virginia.

This Page Is Dedicated to the Memory of Gus N. Addington,
County Clerk. Born June 26, 1899, Died February 29, 1932,
After Having Completed Only Four Years and Two Months
of His Term of Office

INDEX

Johnson, Peter, 133
Johnson, W. L., 216
Jones, Stephen, 121
Jones, Will, 150
Jones, W. J., 216
Jonesville Camp Ground, 268
Jordan, Leora, 216
Junior Red Cross, 203, 216, 217

K

Kanawha River, 22, 71
Kane, Anthony, ex-slave, 238
Kane, Esther, 215
Kane, Henry S., 144
Kane, I. P., 208, 212, 254, 270
Kane, Kathryn, 215
Kane, Mrs. H. S., 216
Kane, R. R., 214
Kane's Gap, 25
Kelly, Edward, 258
Kels, C. W., 217
Kendrick, George H., 188
Kendrick's Gap, 5
Kennedy, John, 23
Kennedy, W. P., 216
Kentucky, 14, 19, 20, 23, 37, 38, 41, 42, 49, 67, 74, 98, 152
Kentucky Path, 12, 17, 21, 24, 25, 26, 74, 102
Kentucky River, 22, 74
Kentucky Road, 102, 289
Kidd, H. C., 208
Kidd, Mark, 103
Kilgore, A. R., 261
Kilgore, Charles, 103
Kilgore, Charles, Sr., 261
Kilgore, Hiram, 131, 132, 147
Kilgore, Jane, 258
Kilgore, Miligan, 264
Kilgore, Robert, 114, 257, 258, 259, 303; Fort House, 113; his remarkable dream, 114
Kilgore, S., 264
Kilgore, William, 130
King, David M., 131
King George III, 134
King, Maxie, 215, 216
King's Mill, 40, 49, 54
King's Mountain Memorial Hospital, 283
Kingsport, 24, 88, 152
Kingsport Hospitals, 283
Kinkead, James, 96

Kinkead, John, 26
Kizer, Elder, 264
Knoxville, Tenn., 120

L

Lambert, Connie, 209
Lammey, Samuel: captured, 32
Lane, Hiram, 209
Lane, Samuel D., 209
Langford, Jonathan, 131
Lark, Mrs. Linda, 251
Larkey, J. C., Sr., 286
Larkey, John, 286
Larkin, W. T., 213
Laurel Hill, 174
"Lawyer's Path," 288
Lee County, 91
Length of School term, 158
Lewis, Andrew, 91
Lewis, Col., 44
Lewis, Jacob & family murdered by Indians, 82
Liberty Loan & War Saving Stamps, 210
Life of Wilburn Waters, 126
Lighting, 225
Lincoln Government, 153
Lipps, Morgan T., 264
List of soldiers wounded in World War, 209; list killed in World War, 209
List of Stations on the Clinch, 66
Little Carpenter, 53
Little Fellow, son of Nancy Ward, 96
Little Flat Lick, 12, 25, 26
Little Moccasin Creek, 24, 41
Little Moccasin Gap, 81
Little Pine Mountain, 23, 24
Little Stock Creek, 12
Little Stone Gap, 7
Livingston Creek, 12, 115
Livingston, John, 41
Livingston, Mrs. Elizabeth, 115, 116, 117
Livingston, Paul, 41
Livingston, Peter & Henry, 115
Livingston Place, 115
Livingston, Samuel, 41, 121
Livingston, Susana, 115
Livingston, William, 41, 115
Local Board (draft), 205, 207
Logan, the Mingo Chieftain, 34, 35, 52, 54, 55, 57, 72, 108

Long Hunters, 19
Long Island of Holston, 24, 39, 87, 94
Looney, James, 34, 36, 52, 53, 56, 59, 61 71
Loudy, W. H., 208
Loudy, Mrs. W. H., 216
Low, Isaac, 132
Lusitania, 201
Luttrel, W., 24

M

Maddux, Elbert, 209
Magisterial districts, 138
Mahoney, John A., 198
Making an average (school), 173, 174
Maness, Alexander, 149
Mansker, Casper, 19
Manufacture of Iron, 244, 245
"Man-Teacher," 168
Maple Gap, 103
Maple Sugar, 223, 224
Markland, Nat B., 8
Marshall, Elias, 261
Marshall, James, 285
Marshall, Reuben, 131
Martin, Brice, 8, 78
Martin, John S., 289
Martin, Joseph, 78, 87, 94, 95, 285
Martin, Thompson G., 141
Martin's Station, 22, 24, 28, 82
Masonic Lodge, 104, 107
Matheson, Virginia, 270
Maury's Geographies, 173
McCarthy, W. C., 219
McClellan, Emmett, 205
McConnell, Emmett W., 310, 311
McConnell, George, Jr., 131
McConnell, George, Sr., 130, 133, 296
McConnell, Henry M., 149
McConnell James T., 225
McConnell, John P., 46, 128, 254, 255, 327, 328, 329, 330, 331
McConnell, Mrs. W. H., 216
McConnell, R. L., 210, 216
McConnell, Riley F., 318, 319
McConnell, Robert, 206
McConnell, Sudie, 215
McConnell, Sylvester P., 148, 149, 197, 320, 321
McCulley, Reuben, 5, 128
McCullouch, Thomas, 110

McDowell, Mrs.: killed by Indians, 41
McGillvary, British Agent, 98
McGuffey's Readers, 163, 170, 173
McHenry, Andrew, 5, 130, 133, 288, 290
McHenry, John, 131, 132
McKinney, Alfred, 132
McKinney, David, 147
McKinney, John, 5, 128, 131, 143, 299, 300
McLean's fish dam, 116
McMurray, Stanley, 209
McMurray, U. S., 203, 208
Meade, J. F., 213
Meade, John W., 209
Meade, Tyre, 263
Medicines, 238
Meetinghouses 1830, 273
Mendenhall, John & Richard, 14
Messenger, The, 199
Metcalf, J. E., 213
M. E. Church, South, 12, 218
Meteoric Shower 1833, 243
Mexico, 202
Middle Fork of Holston, 33
Middle Stations on Clinch, 56
Millard, William, 245
Miller, C. L., 208
Mills, list of, 279, 280
Miscellany (school), 181, 182
Mississippi River, 4
Mitchell, W. H., 213
Moccasin Creek (Big), 13
Moccasin Gap (Big), 23, 38, 40, 41, 48, 49, 51, 54, 57, 61, 73, 74, 91, 95, 102, 120
Moccasin Ridge, 245
Molasses Making, 226
Monroe, John C., 96
Montgomery, John, 44, 95, 103, 128
Montgomery, William, 154
Mooney, James, 18
Moore, J. L. Q., 210, 216
Moore, N. T., 203
Moore, Sergent, 52
Moore, William, 264
Moore's Fort, 55, 56, 59, 61, 69
Morison, H. S. K., 287, 341, 342
Morison, Henry A., 144, 150
Morison, Smith H., 198
Morison, Walker, 198
Morison, Warwick, Sr. (Col.), 39

Made in the USA
Las Vegas, NV
08 September 2023

77258389R00223